Concert Music
of the Twentieth Century

Its Personalities, Institutions, and Techniques

Mark A. Radice

Ithaca College

Prentice
Hall

Upper Saddle River, New Jersey 07458

D0218738

Library of Congress Cataloging-in-Publication Data

Radice, Mark A.
   Concert music of the twentieth century : its personalities, institutions, and techniques/
Mark A. Radice.
      p.   cm.
   Includes index.
   ISBN 0-13-030466-2
      1. Music—20th century—History and criticism.   2. Musical analysis.   I. Title.

ML 197 .R22 2003
780'.9'04—dc21

                                                                                      2002072252

VP, Editorial Director: *Charlyce Jones Owen*
Editorial/Production Supervision and Interior Design: *Harriet Tellem*
Senior Acquisitions Editor: *Christopher T. Johnson*
Editorial Assistant: *Evette Dickerson*
Prepress and Manufacturing Buyer: *Ben Smith*
Marketing Manager: *Christopher Ruel*
Marketing Assistant: *Scott Rich*
Director of Marketing: *Beth Mejia*
Cover Design: *Kiwi Design*
Cover Art: Wassily Kandinsky (1866–1944) Russian, *Composition #8*, Summit Labs/
   Superstock/ARS (Artists Rights Society), New York.

This book was set in 10/12 Palatino by Stratford Publishing Company and was printed by
RR Donnelly and Sons. The cover was printed by Phoenix Color Corp.

© 2003 by Pearson Education, Inc.
Upper Saddle River, New Jersey 07458

All rights reserved. No part of this book may be reproduced, in any form or by any means,
without permission in writing from the publisher.

Printed in the United States of America
10 9 8 7 6 5 4 3 2 1

*For all who work for freedom,
justice, and peace.*

ISBN 0-13-030466-2

PEARSON EDUCATION LTD., *London*
PEARSON EDUCATION AUSTRALIA PTY, LIMITED, *Sydney*
PEARSON EDUCATION SINGAPORE, PTE. LTD.
PEARSON EDUCATION NORTH ASIA LTD., *Hong Kong*
PEARSON EDUCATION CANADA, LTD., *Toronto*
PEARSON EDUCACIÓN DE MEXICO, S.A. DE C.V.
PEARSON EDUCATION—JAPAN, *Tokyo*
PEARSON EDUCATION MALAYSIA, PTE. LTD.
PEARSON EDUCATION, UPPER SADDLE RIVER, *New Jersey*

Contents

Introduction

The focus of this book is "concert music." By that I mean music intended for contemplation rather than atmosphere. It must be approached thoughtfully, and it must be interpreted and evaluated in order for its significance to be appreciated. Every piece that I have discussed in these pages was written by a composer who had something important to say and at least enough skill to have been reasonably successful in that effort. Much of the repertoire ties in with a long-standing, Western European tradition of art music, but much of it reflects the cultural diversity that has been such a powerful influence during the past several decades.

Beginning around the early twentieth century, a major shift in æsthetics has been apparent in all the arts. That shift relieved art of the responsibility to be pretty. Although music and art may still be pretty in some instances, music that is not may nevertheless merit consideration; consequently, questions like "Isn't it beautiful?" or "Do you like it?" are not always the most useful questions. (I have, by the way, included many compositions that I feel are indescribably beautiful, and my selection of repertoire has not been driven by an urge to stretch the envelope of tolerance.) The more important issues are: What is the point of this piece? How does this composition affect me as an individual, and what impact might it have on society in general? What musical materials are used, and how do those materials relate to the effectiveness of the work as a totality? I have not tried to answer these questions: That will be the reader's prerogative. I have tried to provide data about the piece, the composer who wrote it, and the context in which it originated, so that the reader may judge justly.

Traditional Western European parameters for music criticism have largely presumed a Darwinian, evolutionary pattern that moves from simplicity to complexity, from the primitive to the refined; however, current trends in music-historical inquiry tend to place criticism within a broader context of cultural relativism. Consideration of music should certainly include evaluation of scores as autonomous manifestations of musical process; at the same time, "cultural values can be historically located . . . and significance [can] also be socially located. . . ."[1]

This premise has profound implications, for it overturns the notion that musical style progresses in a linear fashion. To put it simply: A composer's works do not necessarily demonstrate a consistent stylistic evolution. For any number of reasons, a composer may write a piece that is, so to speak, out of sequence.

In some cases, these stylistic aberrations are not the result of artistic choice. Contextual issues often reveal tacit requirements imposed on the composer—and thereby the music: The total playing time of a CD; the length of a film; the constitution of an ensemble; the ability of the performers; the nature of an occasion involving music; the makeup of the audience; and a host of other factors may come into play. Our understanding and evaluation of music is a dynamic process and one that is subject to change; hence, there can be no litmus test for identification of the great masterpiece. "Musical meanings are not labels arbitrarily thrust upon abstract sounds; these sounds and their meaning originate in a social process and achieve their significance within a particular social context."[2]

The "social contexts" of concert music are expanding daily—some might even say at an alarming rate. To many, these broader social contexts represent a compromise or even a decline in what has been called "Western Civilization." But such fears are unfounded. Current music-historiography is not intended to obliterate, marginalize, or dilute the Western tradition. Bach, Haydn, and Beethoven might say with Pilate: "Quod scripsi scripsi"—What I wrote, I wrote! Their works and the works of others who served the art of music are secure, but they must be made secure in a contemporary world, and that world extends beyond local, regional, or national boundaries. What surprised me in conducting the research for this book, is the extent to which non-Western nations have already embraced Western musical practices and used them in conjunction with their own distinctive idioms to produce new and exciting possibilities for music making.

Much Western European historiography seems motivated by a perspective that may stem from the dominance of monotheism in the West: Critics seem bent on identifying a messianic equivalent in the realm of music and other arts; hence, Bach is the culmination of his era; Mozart is the genius of the late eighteenth century; Beethoven is the colossus who rules the early nineteenth century; and so on. In the present age, audiences, styles, and media are increasingly diverse and specialized. The possibility of a universal synthesis is, therefore, highly unlikely, and the notion of "the great composer" may need to be revised, just as, beginning around the 1950s, house-calling general practitioners gave way to specialists.

The boundaries of this study are only those imposed by practical considerations of publication. There is a limit to the amount of material that can be covered in 300 pages; nevertheless, I have made every effort to make diversity a key element in my selection of topics for discussion, and I believe that the examples included here can serve as models for other investigations by interested readers. Because this book is a survey rather than a monograph, I have attempted to give a broad array of representative works rather than focus on an area that may be of specialized interest; hence, the names of male composers and musicians are more numerous than those of females; Americans and Europeans more numerous than Asians or Latinos. This fact notwithstanding, the book *does* contain substantial discussions of Asian and Hispanic music. It reflects, as well, the growing involvement of women in the field of composition. Some of the personalities considered are famous Americans who loved liberty, their country, and democracy; but the Communists are here, too. And so are the Fascisti, and the Nazis, and the Socialists. No repertoire has been included or excluded because of the composer's religious preferences or sexual orientation, and homosexual, bisexual, and transsexual composers are discussed side-by-side with Christians, Buddhists, Taoists, Muslims, agnostics, and atheists. This is appropriate for an era that has repeatedly seen proof that music may or may not be a humanizing force, and that good music may or may not be written by good people.

In addressing the musical cultures of non-Western nations, I have tried to provide only as much background about those cultures as may be necessary for the appreciation of their music. In the case of Western nations, I have assumed that most readers will be familiar with their recent histories, but may need some help recalling details of the more distant past. In these cases I have given a rough overview of conditions at the close of the nineteenth century, but I have generally gone no farther.

Histories of "modern music" (whatever that means) have tended to prefer works that seem to point ahead to later developments. I remain unconvinced of the validity of such evolutionary and linear paradigms. These narrow views have often resulted in the total neglect of much well crafted, thought-provoking, and useful music.

Though my title includes the words "twentieth century," I have not hesitated to reach farther back to provide essential information or significant contextual details. I should stress that this approximate chronological line of demarcation really tells us nothing about the character of the music or its structural elements. Given these rather vague guidelines, the task of organization becomes the first critical challenge that any historian must face.

Within the context of such diversity, the impossibility of providing viable coverage of all areas of musical endeavor will be readily apparent. As an alternate course, I have preferred to select key composers, performers, theorists and teachers, and institutions. The subjects that I have chosen for discussion are usually composers or performers; however, in other cases they are political figures, scientists, or even publications or organizations that have had a significant impact on music. My criteria for making such decisions are, I hope, simple: (1) Is the repertoire or the particular work performed with sufficient frequency to be considered standard? (2) Does the music embody or reflect in some special way distinctive aspects of culture or technology since around 1900? (3) Has the individual, composition, publication, or organization had a dramatic impact on the subsequent course of music history? (4) Is there a good chance that a technically accomplished performer or ensemble would include such a piece on a concert or recital program? (5) Is it reasonable to suppose that an intelligent listener would be interested in investigating this repertoire? or, (6) Does the music have the power to stir the listener to thought? If the answer to all, or even several, of these questions is "yes," then the repertoire in question falls within the domain of this text. Readers should be aware that criterion number six liberates me from any obligation to take note of music simply because of its pervasiveness or its commercial significance; hence, "Muzak" appears in the *New Harvard Dictionary of Music*, but not in this book.[3]

Even with these basic criteria, organization remains an issue. The present history is intended to examine in some detail the lives and works of those composers who have occupied positions of particular importance. The discussions contained within this text are arranged according to several considerations: national context, chronological context, and international significance. In some instances, I have consolidated my topics in a single place so that readers may locate all pertinent information conveniently. When this seemed counterproductive, I have adopted a more conversational approach and freely mixed topics. For a few figures, the context of a national overview has been impossible because they were frequently "on the move"; hence, discussion of their activities may begin at one point only to be taken up at some later point in the book.

Our pursuit of the journeys of these important musical figures disrupts our consideration of ongoing trends within a single nation; however, in most cases, these changes in locale were made because the original base of operation had become stagnant, or because the events transpiring in some other place offered brighter prospects to the key players of our discussion. These shifts therefore provide an opportunity for lateral rather than linear continuity of our history.

The chronological sequence of events has been critical in the organization of my information, but it is often more informative to trace the progress of an idea in a particular context over a period of time than to maintain a year-by-year accounting of events. This fact has led to various anachronisms—the discussion of Bartók before Debussy, for example. Recognizing this circumstance, I have begun the book with an overview of important musical trends, including Impressionism, Expressionism, Serialism, and so forth. These introductory explanations should provide sufficient information for dealing with musical styles abstracted from their historical sequence.

A further consideration relating to historical sequence has to do with dates: I have generally limited the use of parenthetical dates to the names of composers and particular pieces. In those instances where multiple dates seemed appropriate, such as for a first version and a revised edition of a composition, I have provided these. I have included dates where they seemed to me most useful: They are invariably included in the primary discussion of each composer, even if that composer has been mentioned previously; however, in cases where chronological context is important to the discussion, I have included the dates even if this resulted in a duplication.

My use of illustrative musical examples focuses on musical materials rather than their use within a particular piece. Messiaen's modes of limited transposition; pentatonic, modal, and artificial scales; tone rows; borrowed themes, and other elements can be shown in musical notation without showing their appearance in a copyrighted piece of music; hence, my examples tend to be abstract rather than specific.

References to pitch names are with capital letters. When these appear without super- or subscript numbers, the pitch is within the octave from middle C to B-natural (or, the pitch is an abstraction unaffected by its appearance in a particular register). Pitches in octaves above middle C appear with superscript numbers beside the capital letters: C^1, C^2, etc. Pitches in octaves below middle C are indicated with subscript numbers: C_1, C_2, etc.

I have included documentation of my sources throughout this book. Whenever possible, I have given preference to English-language sources; however, for those topics with limited bibliographies, I have used foreign documents. All translations of these are mine unless otherwise indicated.

Transliteration of Chinese is problematic. For the first half of the twentieth century, the most common system was that devised by the British Orientalists Sir Thomas Wade and Herbert Giles. This system, generally known as the Wade-Giles system, was superseded since 1958 by the Pinyin system, which is the official manner of romanization used by the People's Republic of China. Since 1979, Xinhua (New China News Agency), as well as the United States government, has used Pinyin for all official communications; however, blind adherence to one system or the other accomplishes little, since many names and terms first became known in the West in Wade-Giles transliterations. I have, therefore, drawn from both systems and chosen the most commonly used spellings. I have dropped all diacritics from Wade-Giles transliterations; hence, the word *ch'in* (*qin* in Pinyin transliteration) appears simply as *chin*, the word *p'i-p'a* as *pipa*, and so forth.

Publication is an essential step in establishing a composer's reputation and influence. In contemporary society, publication of commercial sound recordings may be even more significant than publication of scores. I have not hesitated to check various dot-com sites to see how widely my academic intuition departs from reality. Happily, almost all of the composers and works that I have considered are reasonably well represented by recent print and sound publications.

Since bibliographies tend to be most useful in monographs, I would refer the reader interested in further information to the notes at the end of each chapter. Ephemeral sources have been consulted, but not cited in the preparation of this text, nor have I listed them among the notes, since they tend to be no more stable than sand castles built during low tide.

Notes

1 Derek B. Scott, "Music and Sociology for the 1990s: A Changing Critical Perspective," *Musical Quarterly* 74 (1990), 399–400.
2 Scott, "Music and Sociology," 402.
3 Don M. Randel, ed., (Cambridge, Massachusetts: Belknap Press, 1986). Defined there as "A trade name for music intended solely for use as background in work or public places. . . . It is made available through both radio and closed-circuit broadcast. Such

music can be designed for specific environments and schedules so as, it is claimed, to enhance the productivity of workers, increase the receptivity of customers, etc. The name has also come to serve as the generic (and sometimes pejorative) term for any bland background music. . . ." (p. 524).

Acknowledgments

The days of the single-author history text are over. Perspectives are now so diverse that no individual can hope to achieve an all-encompassing view, especially in a discipline like music, which is intrinsically interdisciplinary. This situation is particularly acute in studies of recent repertoires, but it is no cause for alarm. In fact, I can think of no better pretext for consulting colleagues and experts than to inquire of them their views on the many topics discussed in the pages that follow. To thank every person would be impossible, but many contributed substantially by examining my texts and offering their advice. Among these, I am particularly grateful to Karel Husa, who painstakingly read the entire text, not simply for accuracy of data and interpretation, but even for typos, spacing errors, and other minutiæ that I had never intended for him to note when I gave him the typescript; but note them he did, and his meticulous attention and perceptive insights have greatly improved the final text. I am grateful as well to Dana Wilson, who helped me to formulate the scope and focus of the book through conversations and memoranda, and who assisted me in clarifying my sometimes knotty prose.

Obtaining scores, data, and recordings was difficult in some instances. Iris Koo, Gordon Stout, Yoshie Miyahara Poelvoorde, and Kimiko Shimbo, Chief Secretary of the Japan Federation of Composers, generously shared their knowledge and resources with me for the segment on "Music in Asian Countries." Information concerning the most recent works of Einojuhani Rautavaara was provided by the Philadelphia Orchestra Association Archives. I am sincerely grateful to them for their help.

Mary I. Arlin, Marjorie Porterfield, and Daniel McCarter offered many helpful suggestions after reading earlier incarnations of the text. Others have recommended refinements of my treatments of particular subjects. Among them, I am indebted especially to David Cannata ("Rachmaninoff"), Max Lifchitz, and Pablo Cohen ("Music in Latin America"), Helen Greenwald ("An Italian Interlude"), Linda Arsenault ("Three Students from Messiaen's Studio"), Daniel Pinkham and George Crumb ("New Patronage: Campus Composers"), Shin-ichiro Ikebe ("Concert Music in Asia: Japan"), Zhou Long, Su Zheng, Chen Yi, and Chou Wen-chung ("Concert Music in Asia: China"), John Adams ("John Adams"), and Timothy A. Johnson, Greg Woodward, and Dana Wilson ("Minimalism").

In some instances, I did not feel sufficiently informed to write cogently about topics that I nevertheless considered interesting and important. In those cases, I asked specialists to draft the texts included in this book. If, in putting their contributions into final form, I was compelled to condense the information provided by Peter Rothbart ("Electronic Music") and Linda Arsenault ("Xenakis"), it was because of length considerations that I had agreed upon in advance with Chris Johnson, the editor for the music division of Prentice Hall. Even in these abbreviated formats, their remarks are invaluable preparations for encounters with these specialized repertoires.

As a reader, I have always been partial to heavily illustrated books; accordingly, I tried to include a variety of images in this book. Some were in mighty sad shape when I turned them over to Fred T. Estabrook, but with his keen eye and some help from computer graphics programs, he was able to adjust contrast levels, remove scratches on negatives, and effect a host of other transformations. Some of the images are unique items in the Karel Husa Archive of the James J. Whalen Center for Music at Ithaca College. As curator of that Archive, I have had free access to its rich and varied holdings. Since the Archive was a gift from Maestro Husa, I am once again indebted to him. Two images, those of Chen Yi and Zhou Long, have graciously been provided by Jim Hair. The photos of Shin-Ichiro Ikebe, Teizo Matsumura, and Toshiro Mayuzumi are courtesy of Kimiko Shimbo, Chief Secretary of the Japan Federation of Composers. The ærial photo of Todeiji Temple was provided by the Japan Information Center. The photo of George Crumb by Sabine Matthes was provided courtesy of C. F. Peters Corporation, that of Sofia Gubaidulina by Monroe Warshaw courtesy of G. Schirmer, Inc.

My colleagues and students at the James J. Whalen Center for Music at Ithaca College have helped me to identify some of the critical trends that have taken place during the last century or so, and their insights, enthusiasm, and support have enriched the content of this book. Readers who may wish to offer further suggestions are invited to write to me at: mradice@ithaca.edu

I would also like to thank the reviewers for this book: Robert Conway, Wayne State University; Jean Boyd, Baylor University; and Ken Keaton, Florida Atlantic University.

Mark A. Radice
James J. Whalen Center for Music
Ithaca College

Chapter 1

Changing Styles of the Early Twentieth Century

Musical styles changed more rapidly in the twentieth century than in earlier historical epochs. Thomas Edison's phonograph was displayed as a curiosity during the Paris Exposition Universelle of 1889.[1] Today, hi-tech sound reproduction equipment is commonplace. Music publication and distribution, the opening of the first commercial radio station in 1920—Pittsburgh's KDKA, the development of television in 1939, and other advances in media technology have resulted in an unprecedented rapidity in the turnover of styles.

The early twentieth century witnessed a diversity of styles including Impressionism (sometimes called Symbolism), Expressionism, Futurism, Neoclassicism, and Serialism. The later part of the century saw other styles, such as Integral Serialism, Intermedia, Polystylism, Tintinnabular style, and more.

Impressionism is a term that was coined in 1874 by the French art critic Louis Leroy to describe the paintings of Claude Monet, Alfred Sisley, and Berthe Morisot, whose works represent images; however, they are presented in suffused light, amidst shadows, often appearing without clearly defined contours. When used in reference to music, the term is associated with Claude Debussy and other turn-of-the-century composers whose music plays with instrumental color, eschews clear periodic structure, and uses continuous exposition and development of musical materials rather than segregating these two processes. Debussy's *Trois esquises symphoniques: La mer* (1905) is an excellent example of this style.

As an alternative designation, some critics prefer the term "Symbolist" music. The Symbolist movement

began in the 1870s with the work of Stéphane Mallarmé and became one of the most significant in French poetry of the late nineteenth century. . . . The Symbolists intended to liberate the technique of versification in a way that would make for greater fluidity. Poetry was to evoke, not to describe. The poet should offer impressions, intuitions, sensations, not precise details or description. . . . Symbolism permeates Wagner's operas, where people, objects, sentiments, and specific acts are brought to the attention of the audience through the use of recurrent leading motives that evoke these items. . . . Symbolism coupled with the cult of Wagnerism in France produced the conception of the essential musicality of poetry. The theme of a poem could be orchestrated and expanded by the choice of words having color, harmony, and an evocative power of their own. . . . [Arthur] Rimbaud, [Paul] Verlaine, and Mallarmé are three poets whose names are generally associated with Symbolism.[2]

Debussy knew many of the leading Symbolist poets personally. His tone poem *Prélude à l'après-midi d'un faune* (prelude to the afternoon of a faun; 1894) is based on Mallarmé's poem by that title. Because of Debussy's acquaintance with the poets and his use of their texts for his vocal works, the term seems more suitable (at least for his music) than Impressionism.

In Impressionistic or Symbolistic music, the obscurity and ambiguity is a fundamental stylistic feature. Meters are often clouded by changing divisions of the beat and by ties from one pulse to the next. These manipulations of the beat appear throughout the melody of Debussy's piano piece "La Puerta del Vino" from the second book of Preludes (1913). Tonality is ambiguous too. In "Clair de lune," the best-known movement of his *Suite Bergamasque* (1890), Debussy uses enharmonic modulation in the central portion (*En animant, poco a poco più animato*) to move from the key of D-flat to C-sharp. This reinterpretation of key opens a whole new set of tonal possibilities; yet after this splash of harmonic color, Debussy reverts in an instant to the key of D-flat.

Scales also provide melodic and harmonic surprises. The old church modes and exotic scales, such as the pentatonic scale and the whole-tone scale, can either suggest or negate traditional diatonic harmony. Particular techniques, especially "chord streams" (="planing"), can be used either to support or subvert harmonic function. Passages employing this device contain familiar sonorities, but they appear without any respect for their traditional harmonic functions. The whole-tone scale, for example, contains neither fifths nor fourths, which are the two crucial intervals for root movement in cadential patterns in functional harmony; nevertheless, dominant-seventh chords, augmented triads, and major triads (abbreviated as major thirds without the fifth) can all be derived from the whole-tone scale. The implications of these dominant-seventh chords (spelled enharmonically or abbreviated) cannot be realized in the whole-tone scale since the associated tonic tones are not contained in the scale; hence, Impressionistic pieces often rely on *implication.*

Expressionism was a movement in literature and art at the turn of the century. Most of the Expressionists were German-speaking, and their æsthetic tenets reveal great concern with the subconscious mind and subjective perceptions. For the

Expressionist, "reality" was the individual's psychological response to a stimulus rather than the external details. In music, Expressionism is best represented by certain works of Schönberg, such as his monodrama *Erwartung* (1909), and Hindemith, especially his opera *Cardillac* (1926; rev. 1952); but the heritage of Expressionism can be traced to the late works of Wagner and the early operas of Richard Strauss, especially *Salome* (1905) and *Elektra* (1908).[3] These works exhibit a brutality and intensity that make the works of the Italian *verismo* composers seem tame.

The chromatic scale is the source of Expressionistic tonal materials, but the twelve chromatic tones are used as though consonant with one another. Melodies typically contain wide leaps and irregular phrases. One might argue that "phrases" do not even exist. Dissonance is often extreme, and the harmonic and melodic styles are unpredictable, fragmented, and disjunct. This style imposes severe limitations, since the instability of the music works best with sentiments of anxiety, dread, and fear.

Futurism originated in Italy during the first decade of the twentieth century.[4] Its main proponent was Filippo Tommaso Marinetti, whose essay "Le futurisme" (futurism) appeared in the Parisian journal *Le Figaro* in 1909; however, the tenets of Futurism are apparent in the writings of other Italian avant-garde artists of the time, especially Giovanni Papini's *Crepuscolo dei filosofi* (twilight of philosophy; 1905).

Like Impressionism and Expressionism, Futurism manifested itself in literature, graphic and plastic arts, and music. The paintings and sculpture of Umberto Boccioni, Carlo Carrà, Gino Severini, and Giacomo Balla, which appear in major art collections throughout the world, attempt simultaneously to depict movement, speed, time present and time past, and the dynamic impact of technology.

The Italian Futurist movement's most prominent musical figures included Francesco Balilla Pratella (1880–1955),[5] Luigi Russolo (1885–1947), his older brother, Antonio Russolo (1877–1942), Nuccio Fiorda (1897–1975), and Franco Casavola (1891–1955). Few of the Futurists' manifestos were devoted exclusively to music, but Pratella wrote the "Manifesto dei musicisti Futuristi" (manifesto of Futurist musicians; 1910). The most important composer of the group was an amateur, Luigi Russolo. Active first as a painter, he turned his attention to music in 1913. He gradually developed a concept of *intonarumori*, an "art of noises," whereby mechanical devices would provide alternatives to the conventional instruments. These devices were divided into four categories: *rombi* (rumbles), *fischi* (whistles), *bisbigli* (whispers), and *stridori* (screeches). Percussive noises and human voices were also used. Russolo's instruments have not survived, but his premise of synthetic sound has played a crucial role in contemporary music.

Russolo also devised a system of notation that accommodates quarter tones, microtones, and metamorphic sonorities. These innovations anticipate electronic music, *musique concrète*, and other sounds that are now common. Mainstream composers who knew Futurist music include Debussy, Edgar Varèse, Arthur Honegger, Darius Milhaud, Igor Stravinsky, and Sergei Prokofieff.

In the early 1920s when Futurism was on the decline, *Serialism* came onto the scene in the works of Austro-German composers, especially Schönberg, who first applied it in his Piano Suite (1923). The procedure involves a systematic rotation of all twelve chromatic tones, with no repetition of any tone until the full cycle has been stated. The composer is free to select the order of tones; hence, tonal implications may either be avoided or emphasized. The particular register of individual tones is of no consequence, and twelve-note music is often disjunct. Serialism may be viewed as an extension of late-Romantic, chromatic harmony; thus, it is by no means a radical or unprecedented idiom.

In serial works of the mid and late twentieth century, an expansion of the concept to *Integral Serialism* (sometimes called *Total Serialism*) is often encountered. Integral serialism characteristically applies serial organization to parameters such as instrumentation, duration, dynamics, register, attack, articulation, and so forth. Composers who cultivated this style include Milton Babbitt, Pierre Boulez, and Karlheinz Stockhausen.

The pervasiveness of Serialism in concert music of the mid twentieth century has been greatly exaggerated.[6] In part, this surmise owes to the fact that at the time, serial music was generally much more dissonant than other idioms employing expanded tonality. Though it may not have been more prevalent, serial music was nevertheless more conspicuous. Another factor was that responsible composers and theorists in academic situations taught Serialism as one of a number of contemporary approaches to composition. In this respect, assignments in serial composition were not that much different from those in two-part counterpoint, diatonic harmony, or chromatic harmony; however, students generally remember their forays into Serialism and set theory with some degree of remorse.

Neoclassical styles arose from the growing importance of historical musicology during the late nineteenth century. Pioneering European scholars included Eduard Hanslick, who taught music history and aesthetics at the University of Vienna beginning in the 1850s; August Wilhelm Ambros, who held a similar post at the German University of Prague beginning in 1869; Hugo Riemann (Leipzig), and Hermann Kretzschmar (Berlin). In 1904, Kretzschmar became the first person to hold a professorship of musicology. The American Musicological Society (AMS), founded in 1934, has also done much to make the musics of earlier eras accessible.

With the revival of older repertoires, a vast array of techniques and musical materials began to enter into modern scores. In some cases, composers adapt the procedures to suit their present circumstances. In other cases, we have veritable forgeries. In still other cases, we might encounter something akin to Marcel Duchamp's notorious *Mona Lisa*, which replicates da Vinci's canvas with exacting detail save for the addition of a mustache and goatee. One could, as a musical equivalent, write a stylistically pure, Baroque concerto grosso only to destroy its purity with an anachronistic instrumentation.

Retrospective scores may exhibit the resources of any period—or even multiple periods, and the term neo"classical" ought not to be taken too literally.

Important neoclassicists include Stravinsky, Ralph Vaughan Williams, and John Harbison.

The dissemination of these various musical styles took place at different rates in different contexts. Urban centers typically offered a more diverse and up-to-date selection of musical fare, whereas smaller, rural areas progressed more slowly. Not all urban centers welcomed progressive musical trends, however, and in some cases, musical organizations were decidedly proscriptive in their programming. In many cases, these attitudes were thought to be in the best interests of the general populace of a nation. Artistic organizations and the media were, after all, not only means of entertainment, but also powerful vehicles for the formation of popular tastes and attitudes. At various times and in various nations, these media were subverted for political rather than artistic agendas. We must bear in mind that patriotism and nationalism are closely related but yet distinct phenomena:

> Nationalism . . . is an expression of a shared history, ethnicity, and cultural characteristics of a nation. In times of social pressure, the ideology of nationalism often intensifies its exclusion of the foreign and focuses more and more on the homogeneity or purity of a national group. Patriotism is also politically useful for creating unity of sentiment and purpose, and like nationalism it emphasizes the shared history and cultural characteristics of a group, but it does so without regard to the ethnicity of its members.[7]

Accordingly, German music was out of favor in Paris during both the World Wars, French music was viewed with suspicion in Berlin and Vienna during those same periods, and music by Jews was excluded from concert programs in Fascist Italy and Nazi Germany. For these negative examples, however, corresponding positive ones could be cited, and national musics must be evaluated individually.

Notes

1. Concerning the musical aspects of the 1889 exposition, see Elaine Brody, *Paris: The Musical Kaleidoscope, 1870–1925* (London: Robson Books, 1988), Ch. 4, "Music at the Great Expositions," pp. 77–96.
2. Brody, *Paris: The Musical Kaleidoscope*, p. 158.
3. Concerning Expressionism, see John and Dorothy Crawford, *Expressionism in Twentieth-Century Music* (Bloomington: University of Indiana Press, 1993).
4. See Mark A. Radice, "*Futurismo:* Its Origins, Context, Repertoire, and Influence," *Musical Quarterly* 73 (1989), 1–17.
5. Regarding Pratella and Futurism, see Giuseppe Cangini, *F. B. Pratella, Il futurismo in musica* (Santa Sofia di Romagna: Tipografico dei Comuni, 1982).
6. Joseph N. Straus, "The Myth of Serial 'Tyranny' in the 1950s and 1960s," *Musical Quarterly* 83 (fall 1999), 301–343.
7. Carlo Caballero, "Patriotism or Nationalism: Fauré and the Great War," *Journal of the American Musicological Society* 52 (fall 1999), 595.

Chapter 2

National Musics

Ethnicity, religion, language, economy, and currency, for example, may unite inhabitants within a specified geographical region; on the other hand, they may also create minority groups within that region. When the sense of alienation between antithetical populations becomes intolerable, warfare often results. War commonly leads to an intensification of a national stereotyping.

Since the early twentieth century, mass media and venues that have functioned in the manner of mass media (such as opera houses, art museums, theaters, concert halls, churches) have often been subject to governmental regulation. In some countries, government agencies were either liberal or indifferent toward media, while in others, there was a deliberate and consistent effort to monitor the messages being transmitted to the public.

Monitoring of public communication was not always restricted to totalitarian regimes or undertaken with malicious intent. Agencies like the Interstate Commerce Commission (ICC) and Federal Communications Commission (FCC), for example, were established to ensure equitable and reliable access to facilities. The ICC, the first regulatory commission in the history of the United States, came into being in response to public outcry against railroads that were discriminating against certain commercial interests by imposing exorbitant rates on selected users. When the agency was formed in 1887, it had jurisdiction over rail commerce only, but its authority quickly expanded to include telegraph, telephone, wireless, and other media. Similarly, the FCC, which was established in 1934 to regulate state, national, and international communications, is primarily a protective agency rather than a vehicle for censorship. This organization, which supplanted the Federal Radio Commission that had been created in 1927, regulates standard, high-frequency, relay, television, and broadcasting stations, as well as aviational, maritime, amateur, and emergency broadcasting frequencies. Recently, the FCC has expanded its supervision of facilities to include telephone and cable companies.

The line between guardianship and censorship, however, is a fine one; and the transition from one mode to the other can be made almost imperceptibly. This is particularly the case when government regulatory agencies are already in place. In such instances, no ostensible change in governmental structure may be apparent: The issue then becomes a change of philosophical orientation or interpretation by those in control. In general, democratic nations have been comparatively liberal in dealing with the arts.[1] Dictatorial systems tend to tolerate criticism less well, and repressive tactics are more frequently encountered in these contexts.

When music is colored by nationalistic considerations, the result is usually an idiom that employs known musical conventions: tuneful melodies; consonant harmonies with dissonances used cautiously; predictable phrase structures; identifiable formal designs; familiar instrumentations; and a readily comprehensible message. When nationalistic pieces involve a dramatic scenario, they tend to use the vernacular. Stories may be familiar, or they may use familiar characters in a somewhat different context. In aggressively nationalistic compositions, a delineation of characters into protagonists and antagonists (or, to put it plainly, "good guys and bad guys") may be apparent.

Nationalistic tendencies are particularly apparent in works that emanated from nations newly formed in the late nineteenth century (e.g., Germany and Italy), and from others that came into being during the course of the twentieth century (e.g., Czechoslovakia, USSR).

Central and Eastern Europe

The nineteenth century was a period of struggle for most of the peoples in Central Europe. Though many distinct ethnic and cultural groups inhabited the area roughly between present-day Germany and Russia, most were subject to the authority of the Austro-Hungarian Empire (i.e., Dual Monarchy) between 1867 and the disintegration of the Empire in 1918 at the end of World War I. The alliance between Austria and Hungary was not a natural one; cultural and linguistic differences among the populace of the Empire precluded unification of such diverse citizenry under a single government. The union of the two nations resulted mainly from Austria's fear of Prussia.

Following Austria's defeat in the Austro-Prussian War (1866), the Emperor Franz Joseph conceded to Hungarian self-determination in exchange for the continued union of Hungary with Austria under the rule of the Hapsburgs. The Leitha river served as the dividing line between the two states. The western portion of the empire (called Cisleithania, or "this side of Leitha") included Austria, Bohemia, Moravia, portions of Selesia, Slovenia, and portions of Poland. The eastern portion (called Transleithania, or "across Leitha") consisted of Hungary, Transylvania, Croatia, and part of Dalmatia. Austrians, Slavs, Hungarians, and Italians were forced to live in this context, where they constantly struggled to maintain their personal, ethnic identities. Nationalism was rampant in most regions of the empire, particularly in the eastern and southeastern portions. Indeed, Archduke Francis Ferdinand had planned to make Croatia the center of a third monarchy consisting of the southern Slavic regions. This plan was prevented from becoming a reality by the Archduke's assassination (Sarajevo, 1914), which led in turn to the outbreak of World War I (1914–1918).

Throughout the nineteenth century, the Dual Monarchy was plagued by uprisings. Insurrections occurred in Lithuania in 1812, '31, '63, and 1905. Similar battles for independence were waged in Poland in 1846, '48, '61, and '63. In Czechoslovakia as well as Hungary, the populace attempted to throw off Hapsburg domination in 1848. In April of 1849, Lajos Kossuth, as the elected president, declared Hungary an independent republic. When Franz Joseph I arranged an alliance with the Russian Tsar, Nicholas I, and the combined Austrian and Russian armies devastated the outnumbered Hungarians, Kossuth was forced to capitulate to Russia and flee.

At the conclusion of World War I, the map of modern Europe was drawn at the Paris Peace Conference. The Treaty of Versailles was signed on 28 June 1919. For a brief time, the inhabitants of the area between Germany and Russia were organized into independent nations. Most of these young nations soon came under the sway of the Soviet Union.

Internal and international politics affect musical culture. In some cases—such as the rapid dissemination of avant-garde styles when artists like Hindemith, Krenek, Schönberg, and others fled from the Third Reich—these tumultuous political situations have ultimately yielded some positive results. Trouble-spots on the globe invariably precipitate a relocation of some portion of that area's scholarly and artistic population. Such migrations, coupled with the ever-increasing impact of media coverage of political conflicts, force multicultural interactions to take place. Music in its various manifestations is thereby spread abroad. In assessing the activities of particular artists, it is essential to keep in mind the political climates in which they lived and worked.

In many of the Eastern bloc countries, technology was accepted only gradually. Mass media of the early twentieth century was also primitive. As a consequence, regional distinctions in such matters as dialect, dress, and cuisine lingered longer in some areas than others.

For the musician of Central and Eastern Europe, the ethnic idiosyncrasies in native folk musics were not only effective avenues for the expression of patriotic sentiment, but also offered rich alternatives to the traditions of Western Europe. The synthesis of art music and folk music allowed composers to be innovative while simultaneously drawing on musical traditions of the people. Several Central European composers explored with great success the possibilities of such a synthesis. Here we shall consider the work of three such composers: Leos Janáček, Zoltán Kodály, and Béla Bartók.

Leos Janáček, 1854–1928

[handwritten: ↙ birthplace]

Janáček was born in Moravia (i.e., Eastern Czechoslovakia) as the son of a school teacher and organist. From 1865 until 1869, he studied at the Abbey of St. Augustine in Brno. Subsequent work at the Brno Teacher Training College from 1869 until 1874, and the Prague Organ School for the 1874–75 academic year, readied him for the prestigious Leipzig Conservatory, where he spent 1879–80. His training was rounded out by a stint at the Vienna Conservatory in 1880. At this point, he was poised to embark on his career in his native land. He directed the Czech Philharmonic from 1881 until 1888, founded the Brno Organ School and taught there from 1882 until 1920, and taught from 1920 to 1925 at the conservatory in Brno (which was then a part of the Conservatory of Prague).[2]

Janáček's first important compositions were choral works. For his own teaching, he wrote an instruction manual for vocal technique and a harmony text. Early works show the influence of his friend Antonin Dvořák. Janáček began to collect Moravian folk songs around 1885, and for a brief time, he edited and published a folk-music journal. Soon his music began to show the influence of Moravian folk repertoire. Like the famous Professor Higgins, Janáček noted differences in inflection and accentuation in various districts.

[handwritten margin note: Moravian influence]

The ethnographer Frantisek Bartos played an important role in Janáček's prolonged research. In 1888, Bartos needed the composer's skills to notate the folksongs he wanted to collect in the Valachian region of Eastern Moravia. With Janáček's assistance, he collected over 2,200 during the next twelve years.[3] Janáček discovered valuable materials in Moravian folk music since

[handwritten margin note: helped to collect for Bartos]

> the folk music of Moravia is rooted in diverse sources such as ancient chant, old Slavonic modes, and the rhythms of old Moravian and Slavonic dance music. . . . In addition, the hilly landscape of Moravia isolated some musical styles within regions.[4]

[handwritten margin note: sounds of Janáček's music]

Janáček appropriated the characteristic features of this music for his own compositions, such as *Jenůfa* (1904), *Kát'a Kabanová* (1921), *Příhody Lišky Bystroušky* (cunning little vixen; 1924), *Věc Makropulos* (Makropulos case; 1926), and *Z mrtvé ho domu* (From the house of the dead; never completed). The premiere of *Jenůfa* was given in Prague in 1916. Noteworthy, too, is the *Glagolska' Mse* (Glagolithic Mass; 1926), which contains a stunning solo organ part.

The great success of *Jenůfa* established Janáček's international reputation, but his *œvres* include many fascinating instrumental works, such as the symphonic poem *Taras Bulba* (1918), the First (1923) and Second (1928) String Quartets, a sextet for wind instruments entitled *Youth* (1924), the Sinfonietta (1926) for orchestra,

[handwritten margin note: piece led to success]

three volumes of national dances of Moravia for piano (four hands; 1891–1893), and two later volumes of Moravian dances (piano solo; 1912). This output is complemented by choral music and solo songs.

Both string quartets are programmatic works. The former is a musical response to Tolstoy's short story "The Kreuzer Sonata," which explores the life of a woman whose abusive husband eventually beats her to death. The Second Quartet bears the subtitle "Intimate Letters," which refers to the many letters that the composer wrote to Kamila Stösslova, a married woman much younger than Janáček, whom he met in 1917. Though programmatic, both quartets are in four movements with clear links with the traditional generic design. At the time Janáček was composing the sextet for winds entitled *Youth*, he was providing information for Max Brod, who was writing a biography of the composer. Movements in the piece recall childhood memories that Janáček shared with his biographer. The Sinfonietta is also programmatic, and the four movements following the opening Fanfare are musical postcards of scenes in the cities of Prague and Brno.

Though Janáček's melodic style is derived from folk music, he generally composed melodies in the folk manner rather than using actual quotations. Musical phrases in his works tend to be short and organized in irregular patterns. Repetition of phrases, sometimes with variants, is common. In many pieces, such as the organ solo of the Mass or the Fanfare of the Sinfonietta, he superimposes several repetitive figures. These features lead to constantly changing meters, a characteristic of Janáček's music. The composer himself stated the issue clearly: "Measure a piece in a single meter? That is a theory; measuring in various meters is more authentic."[5]

Janáček's works tend to be accessible despite their progressive idiom. This is because his works retain a strong sense of tonal focus and, though complex, his rhythms are incisive, powerful, and anchored to a unifying motivic plan. His instrumentation is also full of marvelous effects—note for example the diversity of string sonorities that he uses in the first movement of his First String Quartet.

As a young man, Janáček composed less than in his old age. Perhaps the acquisition of technique and facility is responsible for this fact, but one critic has pointed out that "the majority of his outstanding compositions were written after 1918, the year of Czech independence, an event that thrilled the sixty-four-year-old composer and revitalized his creative energies."[6] If this is the case, then we see in Janáček the positive potential of nationalism.

Zoltán Kodály, 1882–1967

As a child, Kodály played the violin and sang in choirs. His earliest compositions were choral works and chamber music for use by his immediate family. These early musical experiences had a strong influence on his later compositional activities. He entered the Budapest Academy of Music in 1900, where he was in the composition classes of Hans Kössler (1853–1926). Kössler's pupils included Béla Bartók and Ernö Dohnányi. Kodály's artistic models during his days at the Academy were Brahms and Debussy. Kodály came to know the latter composer's music in 1907 during a visit to Paris. He returned with some of these Impressionistic scores to Hungary, where he shared them with Bartók.

Kodály began collecting folk music with Bartók in 1905. They quickly realized that what had traditionally passed as Hungarian folk music was not authentic Hungarian music at all; instead, it was a nineteenth-century style that had been developed primarily by Gypsy musicians. This ersatz "folk music" is generally designated with the term *verbunkos*. Kodály completed his Ph.D. in 1906 with his dissertation on "Strophic Construction in Hungarian Folksong." That same year, he joined the faculty of the Budapest Academy, and in 1919 became its director.

Kodály attempted to synthesize art music and folk elements, and his progress is clear in the Sonata (1915) for unaccompanied cello, Op. 8. His early works in this hybrid style were often featured by the International Society for Contemporary Music, an organization formed in 1922 in Salzburg under the guidance of the musicologist Edward J. Dent. At the preliminary ISCM conference, Kodály's Serenade (1920) for two violins and viola, Op. 12, was one of the featured works. Additional new works by Kodály were heard at the first (1923) and second (1924) ISCM Festivals.

Kodály came to national attention in his homeland in 1923, when he was commissioned to compose a large work for chorus and orchestra celebrating the fiftieth anniversary of the unification of Buda and Pest; this score was the *Psalmus Hungaricus*, Op. 13, for tenor, mixed chorus, children's choir, and orchestra.

In the *Psalmus Hungaricus*, Kodály wrote a public work with a clear message and accessible musical materials. These characteristics contributed to the solidification of Kodály's mature style. Perhaps his best-known work is the folk opera, *Háry János* (1926), and the orchestral suite in six movements that the composer extracted from it. The movements in the Suite are: (1) "The Tale Begins," (2) "The Viennese Musical Clock," (3) "Song," (4) "The Battle and Defeat of Napoleon," (5) "Intermezzo," and (6) "Entrance of the Emperor and His Court." Kodály's ties with folk traditions are apparent in the first movement, which is a symphonic depiction of a sneeze: Hungarian custom has it that if a storyteller sneezes during his story, then that story is true. Much of the music has immediate appeal, especially the "Intermezzo," which is in simple song form (i.e., A-B-A) with driving rhythms in the outer sections and a contrasting, lyrical tune in the middle portion. The use of cymbalom—a nineteenth-century instrument that is a triple-strung hammered dulcimer with a cast-iron frame—is also conspicuously popular.[7]

Other important works include the First String Quartet, Op. 2 (1908; published 1910), and the Second String Quartet, Op. 10 (1917; published 1921), the *Dances of Galánta* (1933), and the *Te Deum* (1935). The *Te Deum* uses quartal harmonies and melodies, an idiom that had been used earlier by Alexander Skryabin (1872–1915), whose works Kodály doubtless knew.

Kodály's reputation rests not only upon his original compositions, but also upon his innovations in music education. Actual participation by the student is stressed in Kodály's method. Many of his pieces, such as the *Bicenia Hungarica* (begun 1937), a four-volume collection of progressive, two-part songs, were intended for this purpose. Kodály's methods have found many adherents throughout the world. One of the prime difficulties in using his methods, however, arises from the unavoidable differences between Hungarian and English accentuation.

Béla Bartók, 1881–1945

Almost invariably, the works of Béla Bartók are compelling musically, appealing intellectually, and balanced structurally. The musical style that he developed during the course of his brief career represents a high point in the synthesis of Central European folk music with Western European art music. Though he did not always use actual folk music in his compositions, many of his musical gestures suggest folk music. Other structures owe to the fact that Bartók was a pianist of the highest technical and musical accomplishment; accordingly, musical ideas that have their origin in the idiomatic movement of ten fingers frequently appear. Still other ideas are of his own invention and have no precedent in the Western European tradition. Striking, too, is Bartók's unique harmonic idiom, which often includes conventional triads. Perhaps the most personal feature, though, is his fascination with symmetry. His endless striving for balance and cohesion pervades every aspect of his art, and symmetrical designs impact melodic contours, harmonic structures, formal designs of individual movements, and even the architectural schemes of multimovement compositions. These constructive features integrate Bartók's music in an organic way that can be explained theoretically and perceived audibly.

Bartók was born in Nagyszentmiklos, now a village in Romania, but within Hungary at the time of his birth. After the death of his father in 1888, Béla, his sister Erzsebet, and Paula Bartók, their mother, moved to various towns within Transleithania. Paula Bartók (*née* Voit) was a school teacher and pianist, and she gave Béla his first instruction on the instrument.

When the time came for Bartók's advanced studies in music, he auditioned for and was accepted with scholarship to the Vienna Conservatory; but Vienna was not for him. As a nationalist, Bartók hoped for a more congenial musical environment at the Budapest Academy of Music.[8] He studied there from 1899 until 1903, mainly with István Thomán (1862–1941) for piano and Hans Kössler (1853–1926) for composition.[9] Bartók's affection for Thomán is apparent in the letter to his mother that he wrote on 21 January 1900, where he says:

> Professor Thomán has been doing his good deeds again: he told me to buy Schubert's *Impromptu* as edited by Liszt; when I told him, No, this month I really couldn't as I had no money, he bought it for me 'as a souvenir'. Then he secured free admission to the [Emil] Sauer recital for

me, and so I was able to sell the ticket I had already bought. And now he's given me a ticket for the *Valkyrie*. He has also mentioned the question of the scholarship to the Principal, who said he would very much like to award it to me because he believes that I will fulfill the hopes they place in me.[10]

Béla Bartók

As a young musician, Bartók studied the music of great composers in the Western European tradition. He was most fascinated with the music of Brahms (1833–1897), Strauss (1864–1949), and Debussy (1862–1918).[11]

Bartók's first encounter with Strauss's music was in 1902, when he heard *Also sprach Zarathustra*. Strauss's influence appeared soon after in Bartók's own tone poem *Kossuth* (1904). Kodály was responsible for introducing Bartók to the music of Debussy in 1907. As we know, Debussy spent the summer of 1879 as pianist for Nadejda von Meck, the well-known benefactor of Tschaikovsky. He acted as her resident pianist during subsequent summers as well. While in her service, he eventually traveled with her and her family to Italy, Switzerland, Austria, and Russia. For their domestic music-making, he wrote his earliest chamber works, the Piano Trio in G and a Nocturne and Scherzo for 'cello and piano; but more important, he became acquainted with the music of Russian nationalists, especially Musorgsky. The modal and pentatonic scales used in this repertoire fascinated Debussy and quickly made their way into his music. Bartók was surprised to find these familiar musical materials in the scores of a Frenchman, and he was impressed by the integration of Eastern European and Asian elements within the context of Debussy's highly personal and individual musical style.

Bartók's interest in folk music can be documented as early as the year 1903. In the letter to his mother dated 1 April of that year, he gave incipits of two folk songs, hoping that she might tell him words to the tunes.[12] Could he have been trying to use the texts to confirm his affective understanding of the melodies?

In 1905, Bartók and Kodály set out on the first of many field trips to collect folk music. In the course of his career, Bartók researched the music of the Arabs, Bulgars, Croatians, Hungarians, Romanians, Serbs, Slovakians, Turks, and Walachians. The most fruitful years for folk music collection were those from 1905 until 1914. The outbreak of World War I resulted in Bartók's being restricted to field work within Hungary.

Bartók's folk music research led to important publications throughout his career. The first of these was a Székely Folksong published in 1905. Two series of Hungarian Folksongs were compiled in 1905 and 1906 respectively. For the 1906 collection of Twenty Hungarian Folksongs, he collaborated with Kodály: Each composer contributed ten folk song settings for solo voice and piano. Sometimes Bartók's research assumed a purely academic character, and one of his final publications was an examination of Serbo-Croatian folksongs.

Among Bartók's early works, the Fourteen Bagatelles, Op. 6 (1908), stand out for their originality and diversity. In the first, Bartók combines an E-major melody with a recurring scale pattern based on the Phrygian mode on C. This experiment with bitonality was the first of many compositions in which Bartók employed a polytonal idiom.[13] Intervallic symmetry provides the compositional foundation for the second Bagatelle. Formally, the piece is in three short sections. The first and last sections are related thematically and rhythmically. A repeated major second serves as the harmonic element in these outer sections while the melody grows from a chromatic expansion of the second. The central portion contains very little chromatic motion; instead, Bartók creates contrast by using augmented intervals and whole-tone passages. This sort of symmetrical construction was explored by Bartók in later compositions like the Fourth and Fifth String Quartets, the Music for Strings, Percussion, and Celesta, and in the Third Piano Concerto. The third Bagatelle consists of a nervous, ostinato figure in the right hand and a slow, irregular melody in the left hand. The pitch content of the ostinato pattern derives from the movement of the five fingers over the chromatic tones within a major third. Each of the Bagatelles is predicated on the working out of some germinal principle, and the set presents, in miniature, the essential elements of Bartók's style.

Other important early works include the First String Quartet, Op. 7 (1909), the four-volume collection of easy piano pieces, *For Children*, which was completed in the same year, as well as the *Allegro barbaro* and *Duke Bluebeard's Castle* (both 1911). The *Allegro barbaro* has become a staple in contemporary piano repertoire and need not be discussed here. *Duke Bluebeard's Castle*, though performed from time to time, has not yet achieved the notoriety that it deserves.

Bartók wrote rather little dramatic music: the single opera just mentioned and two ballets, *The Wooden Prince* (1916) and *The Wonderful Mandarin* (1919). The intensely expressive style of *Duke Bluebeard's Castle* is amazing in light of the opera's position as the first of Bartók's stage pieces. At the opening of the fifth door, for example, we feel Bluebeard's power as the orchestra, with full organ, thunders out the main, pentatonic theme beneath his declamatory statements. (Here the melody is harmonized with chords built of thirds, but Bartók avoids their implications.) Similarly, we sense Judith's helplessness and fear in her short, unaccompanied responses.

The tale of Bluebeard originated in Charles Perrault's *Tales of Mother Goose* (1697), but the scenario worked out by Bartók and his librettist, Béla Balázs, differs from Perrault's version in that Bluebeard is present and watches as his wife,

Judith, opens each of the seven doors. The first door conceals his torture chamber, the second, his armory, the third, his treasure chamber, the fourth, a garden of bleeding plants, the fifth, the view of Bluebeard's vast and sorrowful domain, the sixth, a lake of tears. The fateful seventh and final door contains Bluebeard's previous three wives. As the door opens, they walk silently onto the stage. After a moment, they exit through the same door accompanied by Judith. As the door shuts, darkness engulfs the stage.

The orchestra used by Bartók in *Duke Bluebeard's Castle* is large and colorful, but it is never allowed to dominate the vocal lines. In setting the text, Bartók uses a declamatory style that is faithful to the Hungarian tongue. Most of the text is set syllabically, and recitational melodic figures are frequently repeated. Many of the melodic gestures are based on the traditional pentatonic or so-called "gapped" scales of folk music.

Bartók's one-act opera is devoid of dramatic action: no grand marches, no coronations, no prayer scenes or love duets! Instead, the drama is psychological; it is a character study of an introverted man with a dark past and his interaction with an extroverted woman and her desire to know him totally. In a sense, the absence of action is the key to the opera's effectiveness. The intensity that is normally made apparent through gesture and spectacle in opera is expressed here through the orchestral music, which employs a system of recurring motifs. Furthermore, in the relative absence of visual distractions, the listener is forced to focus on the pure emotion of Bartók's score.

The first performance of *Duke Bluebeard's Castle* took place 1918, seven years after its completion. In the intervening years, Bartók composed a fairy-tale ballet, *The Wooden Prince*, which was presented with acclaim in 1917. The triumph of *The Wooden Prince* led to Bartók's becoming the focus of wider interest in his homeland. The premiere performance of *Duke Bluebeard's Castle* came in the wake of that interest.

Another consequence of Bartók's recently acquired fame was an invitation by Emil Hertzka in 1919 for the composer to publish with Universal-Edition of Vienna. From that year until 1938, when the firm was compelled by Nazi authorities to drop Bartók's music, almost all of the composer's music was published by Universal. Later, Bartók published with Boosey and Hawkes.

The compositions of the 1920s are Bartók's most austere. A higher level of dissonance becomes apparent; lines are more angular and wide-ranging; and tonal focus seems lost at times. The two Sonatas (1921, 1922) for violin and piano and the First Piano Concerto (1926) are paradigms of this style period. Other important compositions of the '20s include the five-movement piano suite, *Out of Doors* (1926), and the Third and Fourth String Quartets (1927, 1928).

Out of Doors contains the first example of "Night Music" in Bartók's works. In his night music, Bartók recreates the nocturnal sound-world of nature. Chirping birds, chattering insects, and the primal sounds of woodland *fauna* contribute to this mysterious yet enticing soundscape. Night music appears intermittently in

Bartók's works; fascinating examples of this musical topic appear in the third movement of *Music for Strings, Percussion, and Celesta,* and in the central movement of the Third Piano Concerto.

In 1929, Bartók chanced to meet Paul Sacher (1906–1999), whose musical interests were vast. He was keenly interested in early music and founded the Schola Cantorum Basiliensis for the study and performance of early music. He was equally interested in contemporary music and conducted the Basler Kammerorchester, which specialized in recent repertoire. Sacher conducted premieres of works by a variety of twentieth-century luminaries including Hindemith, Honegger, Strauss, Stravinsky, and, of course, Bartók. It was for Sacher and his chamber orchestra that Bartók wrote the *Music for Strings, Percussion, and Celesta* (1936), perhaps his finest and most characteristic composition. Other scores for the musicians of Basle include the Sonata (1937) for two pianos and percussion and the Divertimento (1939) for string orchestra.

In the *Music for Strings, Percussion, and Celesta,* Bartók applies the concept of symmetrical design on a more extensive basis than he had previously. The first movement is a fugue in which the subject appears in alternating rising and falling fifths, starting on the tone A, and progressing until the tones E-flat and D-sharp are reached. These tritones are the symmetrical division of the octave. The interval of the tritone also functions as a unifying motif in each of the movements. Bartók divides the orchestra as well, into two antiphonal choirs between which entrances of the subject are symmetrically divided. Furthermore, Bartók begins in the midrange voices (i.e., viola) and progresses symmetrically to the higher and lower registers. Finally, the overall dynamic shape of the movement is an arch: Tonal motion, dynamic intensity, and orchestration all climax at the axis of symmetry. In the concluding portion of the first movement, Bartók treats the inversion of the subject in stretto, thereby mirroring in a condensed way the exposition of the movement. Listeners should note how, in the final measures of the movement, the subject and its inversion appear in counterpoint and converge on the unison tone A.

The number of movements in Bartók's compositions often relates to symmetrical planning; consequently, three- and five-movement designs are common. In the three-movement Third Piano Concerto, the central movement is itself a symmetrical form in three sections. Quite interestingly, the musical materials of the outer sections are a parody of the *Heiliger Dankgesang* movement of Beethoven's String Quartet in A minor, Op. 132. The central section of the movement is an example of Bartók's night music. The Concerto for orchestra, which was commissioned in 1943 by the Koussevitzky Foundation, is an example of a five-movement plan. The second movement of this piece is based on five musical subjects, each of which is played by a different pair of five winds: bassoons, oboes, clarinets, flutes, and trumpets.

Owing to the death of his mother and the increasingly tense political situation in Europe, Bartók decided in 1940 to emigrate to the United States with his wife, Ditta Pásztory, and his children, Béla and Péter.[14] In the five years before his

EXAMPLE 1
Bartók, Music for Strings, Percussion, Celesta

APPROXIMATE POSITION OF THE ORCHESTRA

	Double Bass I	Double Bass II	
Violoncello I	Timpani	Bass Drum	Violoncello II
Viola I	Side Drums	Cymbals	Viola II
Violin II	Celesta	Xylophone	Violin IV
Violin I	Pianoforte	Harp	Violin III

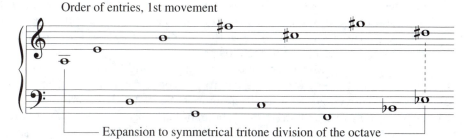

Order of entries, 1st movement

Expansion to symmetrical tritone division of the octave

Fugue subject

Expansion to symmetrical tritone division of the octave

death, Bartók devoted particular attention to the concerto as a genre. In addition to the two concertos mentioned earlier, he composed the Concerto (1945) for viola and orchestra for William Primrose; it was incomplete at the time of Bartók's death, as were the last seventeen measures of the Third Piano Concerto. Both were completed by Tibor Serly (1901–1978), a Hungarian immigrant and composer who had studied at the Budapest Academy with Kodály from 1922 until 1924.

Certain of Bartók's works are recognized monuments of their sort. In this category must be placed the six string quartets and the six volumes of progressive piano pieces collectively known as the *Mikrokosmos*.

The First String Quartet to which Bartók attached an opus number, Op. 7, was completed in 1909. Actually, he had written an earlier quartet, in 1899, but it was never published. The Op. 7 Quartet shows the influence of folk music, particularly in its use of motivic patterns and ostinato figures. The Second String Quartet, Op. 17 (1917), is a symmetrical design in three movements with the Allegro as the central movement. The Third String Quartet is a single, continuous piece whose main thematic elements are all derived from one concise motif. It is, perhaps, the most highly integrated of any of the six quartets. An important stylistic change can be seen in the Fourth Quartet, which marks the end of Bartók's austere period. Here, he seems to be cultivating a more accessible, appealing style. Particularly attractive is the fourth movement of this symmetrical, five-movement work, the Allegretto pizzicato. This movement is also noteworthy because of its close affiliation with the folk-music style from which Bartók derived so many of his ideas. Though plucked instruments, such as the lute, guitar, vihuela, pandora, chitarrone, harp, psaltery, harpsichord, and many others, were common in Western European ensembles of the Mediæval and Renaissance periods, they virtually disappeared in later music. In the instrumental music of rural Central Europe, Bartók found that plucked strings played a vital role. The Allegretto pizzicato of the Fourth Quartet approximates the sort of plucked-string sonorities that Bartók heard in the orchestras of the indigenous peasants.

The Fifth String Quartet, composed in only a month's time in 1934, is a symmetrical, five-movement work. The central movement is a three-section scherzo and trio. This movement is particularly interesting, not only because it forms the axis of symmetry in the Quartet as a whole, but also because it is one of Bartók's most elaborate essays in Bulgarian rhythm. The metrical impulses of the scherzo are grouped according to the pattern 4 + 2 + 3; those of the trio are grouped in the pattern 3 + 2 + 2 + 3.

The Sixth String Quartet (1939) is the last major work that Bartók wrote before emigrating to the United States and the last of his completed quartets. This Quartet evidences Bartók's lifelong admiration for the music of Beethoven and includes a parody of his *Grosse Fuge*, Op. 133. This is but one of numerous Beethoven parodies that can be found in Bartók's works.[15]

No study of Bartók's life and works would be complete without a discussion of his activities as a teacher. As a student at the Budapest Academy, Bartók used German editions of Bach, Haydn, Mozart, Beethoven, Schubert, and other masters since Hungarian editions were not available. Bartók saw it as his duty to provide these editions. He also went on to edit works by early keyboard masters like Domenico Scarlatti and François Couperin. All this was not enough, however. In 1926, for his son Péter, Bartók began the six volumes of progressive piano studies now known as the *Mikrokosmos.* Completed in 1939, the 153 pieces contained in the series range from works suitable for the first day at the keyboard to others that have become standard repertoire for the concert pianist. The titles of the pieces usually identify the compositional or pianistic focus of the lesson; hence, volume five contains a study in "Staccato and Legato," another called "Fourths," one called "Whole-tone Scale," and so on. A few pieces have distinctive titles, for example, the well-known "From the Diary of a Fly," which appears in volume six. The music of *Mikrokosmos* introduces the young pianist to the old church modes; whole-tone, pentatonic, and symmetrical scales; asymmetrical rhythms; and other resources of twentieth-century music. Like the two- and three-part Inventions of

Bach, the pieces do more than teach discipline to ten unruly fingers; they also give a foretaste of contemporary compositional techniques.

Russia and the Soviet Union

During the last half of the nineteenth century, Russia made great progress toward becoming an industrial nation of prominence in the European community. The Trans-Siberian railroad, begun in the closing years of the reign of Tsar Alexander III, was completed in 1916 after twenty-five years of work. Metal works and machine manufacturing made impressive strides, as did the manufacture of textiles. Communications systems were coming into existence, and by 1870, most of the cities and towns in Russia were linked by telegraph lines. Similar advances were being made in the area of education.

> Although the universities did not grow at a rapid rate, the number of students in secondary schools more than doubled between 1864 and 1875. There were more than 5,000 university students in Russia in 1875, and more than 78,000 gymnasium students, including 27,470 women students. After 1869, in both St. Petersburg and Moscow, higher courses for women were offered.[16]

Equally impressive was the strong cultural presence of specialized institutions, such as the Medico-Surgical Academy of St. Petersburg, the St. Petersburg Institute of Technology, and the Petrovskii Agricultural School of Moscow. These two cities came to be the focal points of Russian culture during the turn of the century. Two of the specialized institutions in these cities are conservatories of music: one, founded and directed by Anton Rubinstein (1829–1894), is in St. Petersburg; the other, in Moscow, was founded and directed by Anton's brother, Nikolai (1835–1881). Both Rubinsteins were concert pianists. Anton's career was brilliant. Following his Moscow debut in 1939, he concertized throughout Europe and America. He wrote instructional and historical works such as *Erinnerungen aus 50 Jahren* (reminiscences from 50 years), *Die Musik und ihre Meister* (music and its masters), as well as several studies of piano technique and literature. He was a friend of Franz Liszt's, and his reputation was immense.

In his autobiographical writings, Rubinstein recounted the following bizarre incident.

> On one occasion while I was performing my religious duties, I went to the confession in the Kazan Cathedral. After confession I proceeded to the table to have my name enrolled in the books. The deacon began his inquiries: "Your name, rank, and vocation?" "Rubinstein, artist," I said. "Are you employed in the theatre?" "No." "Then perhaps you give

lessons in some school?" "No," I replied. The deacon appeared surprised, but no more so than I. We both remained silent. "I am a musician, an artist," I replied. "Yes, I understand, but are you in the government service?" "I told you I was not!" "Well, may I ask your father's profession?" "A merchant of the second guild." "Now then, we understand! You are the son of a merchant of the second guild!"[17]

The quotation is to the point; there were very few professional musicians in Russia in the mid nineteenth century who were natives of that country. Russia trailed behind Western Europe, perhaps because of the vastness of the country, which was 8,764,586 square miles at the time World War I began. Musical culture was generally an imported item from France and Italy. Baldassare Galuppi (1706–1765), Tommaso Traetta (1727–1779), Giuseppe Sarti (1729–1802), Giovanni Paisiello (1740–1816), Antonio Salieri (1750–1825), and Hector Berlioz (1803–1869) were among the composers who spent extended periods in Russia. It is significant too, that Anton Rubinstein himself had been born to a German mother who took him to Western Europe for his early musical training—one of the reasons he was resented by some of the musicians who were Russian by both birth and training.

With foreigners occupying Russia's professional music posts, native musicians had few choices: They could find creative outlets in folk music or they could dabble in art music. Finding resources to begin the formation of a music school was also difficult; textbooks on harmony, counterpoint, orchestration, and so on, were not available in Russian. Rimsky-Korsakoff's textbooks on harmony (1884) and orchestration (1896) were among the earliest attempts to fill this need.

Rubinstein was able to secure the assistance of the Grand Duchess Elena Pavlovna, wife of the Tsar's brother, Michael; she gave Rubinstein some rooms in the Kamennoi-Ostrov palace to use for meetings and music classes. He founded the Russian Musical Society for the promotion of music education and concert-life. After having gathered a cooperative group of instructors including Theodore Leschetitzky (1830–1915) and Henryk Wieniawsky (1835–1880), Rubinstein prevailed upon the Duchess Elena to obtain a charter for the music school from Tsar Alexander II. The Tsar granted this request in 1861, and the St. Petersburg School of Music came into being in 1862.

Nikolai Rubinstein, whose official occupation until his death was "government clerk," began teaching music in Moscow. In 1860, he formed the Moscow chapter of the Russian Musical Society, acting as its director and professor of piano. Nikolai's school in Moscow was granted a charter in 1864 and opened in September 1866.

Though Nikolai and Anton Rubinstein did much to advance music education in Russia, they were not without opponents. Anton's training was largely Western European; he was a late-Romantic as a composer. He wrote rather defensively that "passions are not national, therefore there can be no national opera. Attempts to write national music are doomed to spell failure."[18]

The group of composers known as the Russian Five disagreed. The Five—or *mogutchaya kutchka* as they had been dubbed by Vladimer Lomakin in 1867—included the composers Mily Balakireff (1837–1910), Alexander Borodin (1833–1887), Cesar Cui (1835–1918), Modest Musorgsky (1839–1881), and Nikolai Rimsky-Korsakoff. Balakireff, the leader of the Five and the one who had had the most extensive musical training, gave music lessons to the others. All dilettantes, they were convinced that formal training was harmful to artistic truthfulness; inspiration, not classroom training, was the key to musical genius.

The fledgling music schools soon had an intended impact on Russian musical culture. Tschaikovsky (1840–1893), among the first great Russian composers trained at Anton Rubinstein's music school, enrolled at the St. Petersburg Conservatory in 1863. In 1866, he moved to Moscow, where he became a theory instructor at Nikolai Rubinstein's new conservatory. In that capacity, one of his most important contributions was his textbook *Rukowodstwo k praktitcheskomu isucheniu garmonii* (introduction to the practical study of harmony; 1871), one of only four harmony manuals in Russian among more than fifty music texts published in that country during the nineteenth century.

Since then, both schools of music have provided musical training for important composers including Anatol Lyadoff (1855–1914), Sergei Lyapunoff (1859–1924), Mikhayl Ippolitoff-Ivanoff (1859–1935), Anton Arensky (1861–1906), Alexander Skryabin (1872–1915), Sergei Rachmaninoff (1873–1943), and Sergei Prokofieff (1891–1953). Another school of music, operated by the Moscow Philharmonic Society, contributed to the musical culture of that city in the later nineteenth century. Serge Koussevitzky was one of that institution's outstanding graduates.

Sergei Rachmaninoff, 1873–1943

As a boy, Rachmaninoff studied piano with Vladimir Demiansky and harmony with Alexander Rubets. His advanced studies began at the Moscow Conservatory in 1885. There he studied piano, first with Nikolai Zvereff and later with Alexander Siloti. Siloti was one of the great pianists of the age and had studied with Liszt. Rachmaninoff's work in composition was with Sergei Taneyeff (1856–1915) and Arensky. Taneyeff was a pupil of Tschaikovsky's and wrote textbooks on counterpoint and canon; Arensky was a pupil of Rimsky-Korsakoff's.[19]

In order for Rachmaninoff to qualify for the composition major, it was necessary for him to pass an examination that would permit him to move from the general music education curriculum (called "Musical Encyclopedia") to the "Composers' Division."[20] Rachmaninoff took that exam during the 1886–87 academic year.

As this year Tchaikovsky was an honorary member of the committee the examination bore rather a special character. My classmates one after another showed their papers, and each time Arensky glanced at the

Sergei Rachmaninoff

first page and frowned discontentedly, after which he gave an imploring look in my direction. . . . I handed my two pages of manuscript to Arensky. . . . He sent a quick glance over the first page, but without frowning. . . . "You are the only one," he said, "to grasp the sense of the correct harmonic change."

After this comforting information I went home, full of hope.

On the following day was the decisive meeting of the board of examiners. . . . Amongst the Professors . . . sat Tchaikovsky. The highest mark given was a five, which could, in exceptional cases, be supplemented by a plus sign. When I had finished, Tchaikovsky rose and busied himself with the examination journal. It was only after a fortnight that I heard what he had been doing with it: he had added three more plus signs to my mark, one on top, one below, and one behind.[21]

Rachmaninoff graduated as a pianist in 1891, then in 1892 as a composer. His opera *Aleko*, after Pushkin, captured for him the Great Gold Medal, the highest honor bestowed by the Conservatory. His work as pianist and composer was complemented by conducting, and here too, he demonstrated outstanding talent.

The 1890s witnessed the first flowering of Rachmaninoff's genius in scores such as the orchestral tone poem, *The Rock*, Op. 7, the First Piano Concerto (retroactively designated Op. 1), the beautiful *Trio elégiaque*, Op. 9, and the set of Five Pieces, Op. 3, which includes the famous Prelude in C-sharp minor. It was also during this decade, in 1893, that Tschaikovsky died, shortly after the premiere of his Sixth Symphony. Tschaikovsky's death was the inspiration for the *Trio elégiaque*: Taking the lead from Tschaikovsky himself, who had written his own A-minor Piano Trio, Op. 50 in memory of Nikolai Rubinstein, Rachmaninoff poured his most profound feelings into this three-movement piece dedicated to the man who had helped and encouraged his career and whose music Rachmaninoff admired so intensely. The first movement, with its ominous ostinato figures, its mood of profound despair, and its virtuosic writing for the piano, is an especially impressive example of the young composer's skill.

In 1895, Rachmaninoff completed his Symphony No. 1 in D minor. Its premiere was an abysmal failure. Shaken by the experience, Rachmaninoff decided to abandon his career in composition, but his psychiatrist, Dr. Nikolai Dahl, helped him to return to pen and score paper. Rachmaninoff expressed his gratitude in the Piano Concerto No. 2 in C minor (1900), which was published in the following year with a dedication to Dahl. Fittingly, it was this Piano Concerto that established Rachmaninoff as being among the finest of twentieth-century composers.

In 1902, Rachmaninoff married Natalie Satin. From 1904 to 1906, he was principal conductor at the Bolshoy Theatre. He gave up this post because it took too much of his time from composing. The happy consequence of his newfound time was the Second Symphony in E minor, Op. 27 (1907). The tender lyricism of its slow movement shows the depth of Rachmaninoff's affinity to Tschaikovsky's Western European Romanticism as well as his familiarity with post-Wagnerian musical styles in general.

In 1909, Rachmaninoff was invited to undertake a concert tour in the United States. On this tour, he featured his new Piano Concerto No. 3 in D minor, thereby distinguishing himself from the many other piano virtuosos who were traveling through the U. S. A. at the time. After his return to Russia, he became an official in the Imperial Russian Musical Society. During these last years in his native country, he continued his activities as a conductor and composer. Though his compositions from this period are relatively few, the Piano Sonata No. 2 in B-flat minor, Op. 36 (1913) and the Solemn Vespers, Op. 37 (1915) rank as masterworks.

The Vespers—along with his symphonic setting of Edgar Allan Poe's poem, the "Bells"—ensures Rachmaninoff a lasting place in the annals of choral music. Though nominally for mixed chorus, the fifteen movements of the Vespers frequently call for *divisi* chorus. Moreover, soloists are extracted from the chorus for additional obbligato lines. The texture is lush and Romantic, yet quite contrapuntal at times. Distinctive too is the fact that nine of the movements are based on traditional plainchant melodies for the all-night vespers liturgy in the Russian Orthodox Church.[22]

Rachmaninoff escaped the turmoil of the Revolution by concertizing in Scandinavia during most of 1917. In 1918, he settled in the United States, where he found countless opportunities for concert appearances. His compositions from this period are primarily works for his own use either as piano soloist or in combination with orchestra. The most important of these are the Piano Concerto No. 4 in G minor, Op. 40 (1927; rev. 1941), the *Variations on a Theme by Corelli* (1932), and the *Rhapsody on a Theme by Paganini* (1934). Standing as the culmination of the post-Wagnerian, Russian symphonic tradition is the Third Symphony, Op. 44 (1936; rev. 1938). Rachmaninoff's last composition was the set of *Symphonic Dances* (1940).

Of the late works, the most often performed is the *Rhapsody on a Theme by Paganini*.[23] The score may have begun with a scenario. In 1937, Rachmaninoff himself proposed to Michel Fokine a balletic version of the work based on the life of the legendary virtuoso Nicolo Paganini. The production, called "Paganini: Fantastic Ballet in Three Scenes," had its premiere at Covent Garden on 30 June 1939.

Whether Rachmaninoff envisioned the ballet from the outset or not, the score certainly embodies dramatic elements. In its overall form, the *Rhapsody* consists of an Introduction followed by the variations. For his theme, Rachmaninoff turned to

Paganini's *Ventiquattro capricci per violino solo*, Op. 1 (twenty-four capriccios for solo violin; 1820) from which he took the tune of the last one for his principal subject. The twenty-four capriccios suggested the idea of twenty-four variations. Rachmaninoff used a second theme, the *Dies iræ* of the Roman Catholic Requiem Mass, to represent the character of Mephisto. This macabre tune is announced in the piano part in Variation X (Poco martelato), and in the ensuing variations Rachmaninoff writes what amounts to a set of double variations. The highlight of the work is Variation XVIII (Andante cantabile), where the theme of Paganini's capriccio is inverted at a slower tempo and set within a languid Romantic harmonization. In the final variation, the *Dies iræ* tune is recalled by the full brass and strings.

Despite the dramatic undercurrents of the piece, its overall design closely resembles a conventional three-movement piano concerto prefaced by an introduction that hints at the theme to come; however, this concerto is not built of three distinct movements. Rather, its movements follow without pause. Thematic transformation and cyclic recollection of themes provide organic unity and dramatic continuity.

The bulk of the Third Symphony was composed in 1935 and 1936. Minor revisions were made in 1937, and the revised edition was published two years later.[24] The Third Symphony is not only Rachmaninoff's most impressive composition in that genre, but it is also a strikingly effective synthesis of techniques developed by both Wagner and native Russian composers, especially Tschaikovsky.

Sergei Prokofieff, 1891–1953

Prokofieff's mother was a pianist; hence, his childhood was accompanied by her performances of the repertoire for that instrument, especially Beethoven and Chopin. Prokofieff's training began in 1902, when he began studies with Reyngold Glière.

At the suggestion of Alexander Glazunoff (1865–1936), Prokofieff entered the St. Petersburg Conservatory. Glazunoff's colleagues on the faculty included Anatol Lyadoff (1855–1914) and Nikolai Rimsky-Korsakoff (1844–1908).[25]

The musical influences that contributed to the formation of Prokofieff's mature style were diverse but included many Russian composers. The works of the "Mighty Handful" exerted an impact as did the compositions of more progressive composers like Skryabin, Debussy, and Strauss. The adventurous harmonic style of Skryabin, especially the superimposed fourths of his distinctive "mystic chord" (i.e., C, F-sharp, B-flat, E, A, D), was an important precedent for Prokofieff's experimentation, and Prokofieff's symphonic poem *Rêves* (dreams; 1910) is dedicated to Skryabin.

In 1908, Prokofieff made his debut as a pianist and began conducting classes with Nikolai Tcherepnin (1873–1945), a composer whose importance has not yet been sufficiently explored.[26] The compositions for piano, especially the five piano concertos (1911–1932) and the ten piano sonatas (1909–1953; the Tenth was left incomplete), established Prokofieff's reputation as a composer; however, his scores also include symphonies, operas, ballets, and film scores.

In 1914, Prokofieff composed the *Scythian Suite* for Sergei Diaghileff's Ballets Russes. Unfortunately, the ballet was never given. The *Classical Symphony* (1917), which was popularized by Prokofieff's friend Sergei Koussevitzky, is an important early example of Neoclassicism. These two pieces were among the few items that Prokofieff took with him when he left Russia to come to the United States in 1918. World War I had set his homeland into a state of chaos, and the civic unrest in the aftermath of the October Revolution created countless obstacles to his work.

Prokofieff's career as a composer for the stage took a turn for the better in 1919, when the Chicago Opera Company commissioned the *Love for Three Oranges* (1921).[27] Following the close of the opera season, Prokofieff relocated to Paris, where he wrote another theatrical work, *Le pas d'acier* (step of steel; 1925) for the Ballets Russes.

Following Diaghileff's death in 1929, Prokofieff's connections with Paris began to erode, and he resumed concertizing in the Soviet Union. As a composer, he was in an awkward position: Although he tended to be experimental, Russian society after the Revolution of 1917 grew increasingly conservative. In 1932, the Central Party formulated a resolution "On the Reconstruction of Literary and Artistic Organizations," which established the Union of Soviet Composers. It was to this Union that Prokofieff was forced to apologize in 1948 after the purges of Andrei Zhdanov. Prokofieff was condemned as a "formalist." In the new regime, "social realism" was the only acceptable style: one that included prominent melodies (preferably Russian folk songs), nationalistic themes, and accessible story lines.

Prokofieff performed as a pianist in the USSR in 1927 and again in 1929; he eventually settled in Moscow in 1934. Doubtless he was encouraged by a commission from the Bolshoy Ballet that resulted in the score of *Romeo and Juliet* (1938). It was at this time that his collaboration with the film directors Alexander Faint-simmer (also "Feinzimmer") and Sergei Eisenstein began. His music for Faint-simmer's *Poruchik Kizhe* (*Lieutenant Kijé*) scored an immediate success despite the fact that it was written "only after the film had been completely planned out."[28] *Alexander Nevsky* (1939) was a genuine collaboration, and the music and the film progressed hand-in-hand. Later, Prokofieff made the soundtrack into a cantata in seven movements. The piece deals with a Russian nationalist of the thirteenth century, Prince Alexander of Novogorod, who defeated invading Swedish forces. The Prince later received the appellation Alexander Nevsky owing to the fact that the principal battle with the Swedes took place on the Neva, a forty-six-mile river connecting Lake Ladoga with the Gulf of Finland. The Neva freezes in winter, and the colossal battle scene of the film takes place on the ice. *Alexander* is a classic piece of social realist art and one of Prokofieff's most powerful scores. The parody of Western European plainchant, ominously scored in the low brass, reveals the tense

music style

relationship between the invading Teutonic forces and the Russians (appropriate for both the thirteenth- and twentieth-century circumstances!); the energetic melodies and brilliant scoring of the music for the Russians reveal Prokofieff's genuine commitment to national music; and the contralto solo, as she mourns over "The Field of the Dead," is a heartfelt depiction of the catastrophes that are a consequence of any war.

Perhaps as a result of his interest in film scores, Prokofieff turned his hand to music for theater. In 1943, he completed his five-act opera (after Leo Tolstoy) *War and Peace*. Here too, he produced a compelling example of social realist art.

Prokofieff's theatrical instincts are also apparent in his score of *Peter and the Wolf* (1936), a symphonic poem for children. The story, which is supposed to be narrated during the performance of the orchestral music, was written by Prokofieff himself. The various characters—Peter, the Bird, the Duck, the Cat, Grandpa, the Hunters, and the Wolf—are each assigned specific instruments and motifs. Peter is represented by the strings; the Bird by the flute; the Duck by the oboe; the Cat by the clarinet; Grandpa by the bassoon; the Wolf by French horns; and the Hunters by percussion. Prokofieff has constructed his tale so that it naturally leads to a fascinating and complex combination of instruments.

On 5 March 1953, the death of Josef Stalin occupied the world's attention; thus, the composer's death on that same day was largely overlooked by the press.

Music in the Socialist State: Dmitri Shostakovich, 1906–1975

The career of Dmitri Shostakovich reflects the impact of politics on art in an unprecedented way. The evolution of his style may be construed as evidence of totalitarian suppression, but the information presently available suggests a different picture.

Shostakovich's earliest musical training was from his mother, who happened to be a professional pianist with a conservatory training. His first experiences as performer and composer were at the keyboard. His earliest compositions were written in the wake of the October Revolution of 1917. These early pieces are already openly and deliberately political. In his memoirs, Shostakovich recollects:

> There was nothing extraordinary about [my childhood]. . . .
> They say that the major event in my life was the march down to the Finland Station in April 1917, when Lenin arrived in Petrograd. The incident did take place. . . . But I don't remember a thing. If I had been told ahead of time just what a luminary was arriving, I would have paid more attention, but as it is, I don't remember much.
> I remember another incident more clearly. It took place in February of the same year. They were breaking up a crowd in the street. And a Cossack killed a boy with his saber. It was terrifying. I ran home to tell them about it.

There were trucks all over Petrograd, filled with soldiers, who were shooting. It was better not to go out in those days.

I didn't forget that boy. And I never will. I tried to write music about it several times. When I was small, I wrote a piano piece called "Funeral March in Memory of the Victims of the Revolution." Then my Second and Twelfth Symphonies addressed the same theme. And not only those two symphonies.[29]

Dmitri Shostakovich

In addition to his "Funeral March," Shostakovich, as a boy, also composed a "Hymn to Liberty." Neither of these compositions was the result of pressure from the regime. Though the Party's views of Shostakovich and his music changed as he matured and came to occupy a prominent position in international cultural affairs, they were certainly not interested in his youthful scribbling; nevertheless, his natural inclination, even as a child, was to react to political and social events through music. The nationalistic aspects of his works were a sincere expression of his own deeply personal views. In many of his works, these views are concealed so that his meanings will be apparent only to the skillful and insightful musician.

Shostakovich's formal musical training began in 1919 when he entered what at that time was called the St. Petersburg Conservatory. The name changed as the city's name became "Petrograd," from 1914 to 1924, then "Leningrad" in 1925. There, he studied piano with Leonid Nikolaeff and composition with Maximilian Steinberg (1883–1946), who had been a student of Rimsky-Korsakoff and Glazunoff. Glazunoff was on the faculty of the Conservatory during Shostakovich's student years, so the younger composer knew at first hand what a class with the "Russian Brahms" was like. In his memoirs, Shostakovich relates the following amusing anecdote:

Glazunov didn't let composers off lightly on the exams. . . . He . . . could argue long and hard about whether a student should get a 3 or a 3- or perhaps a 2+.

There was an examination on the fugue. Glazunov gave the theme and I had to write a fugue with a stretto. I sat and puffed over it, I was soaked with perspiration, but I couldn't do that stretto. You could kill me, but it didn't work. I thought there was a catch in it, maybe there wasn't supposed to be a stretto. So I handed in the fugue without one, and I received a 5-. I was hurt. Should I go and talk to Glazunov? That wasn't done, but on the other hand, it looked as though I hadn't passed well enough. I went to see him.

Glazunov and I began looking it over and it turned out that I had incorrectly copied down the theme. I got a note wrong. That's why I couldn't do the stretto. That miserable note changed everything. If I had written it down correctly, I could have done all kinds of stretti. At a fourth, or a fifth, or an octave. I could have written canon by augmentation or diminution or even a retrograde canon. But only on the condition that I had the theme copied correctly, and I had made a mistake.

But Glazunov didn't change my grade, instead he scolded me. I remember his lecture, word for word, to this day: "Even if you had mistaken that note, young man, you should have realized that it was a mistake and corrected it."[30]

Shostakovich completed his conservatory studies in 1925. His graduation piece, his First Symphony, had its premiere in Leningrad in 1926 and was acclaimed by the critics. Overnight, Shostakovich came onto the musical scene as a phenomenon. Soon after, Bruno Walter led the first German performance in Berlin, and Leopold Stokowski gave the American premiere in November of 1928. In every case, the symphony was enthusiastically received.

The success of the First Symphony led to a commission from the Soviet government for a work commemorating the tenth anniversary of the Revolution: the Second Symphony (1927), which bore the designation *To October*. The Third Symphony also had a political theme and was called the *Mayday Symphony*. Neither work was successful. The Fourth Symphony followed shortly after, but it was withdrawn and did not receive its first performance until 1961, presumably in a much revised version.

Owing perhaps to the failure of his Second, Third, and Fourth Symphonies, Shostakovich turned his attention to music for the theater in the early 1930s. He wrote the opera *The Nose* (after Gogol), as well as the ballets *The Age of Gold* and *The Bolt*. In these works, the influence of Musorgsky is apparent. Shostakovich was always fascinated by this music, and in 1939, he revised *Boris Godunoff*. Other Musorgsky projects included an edition (1959) of *Khovanshchina* and an orchestration (1962) of the *Songs and Dances of Death*.

At the age of twenty-seven, Shostakovich achieved operatic fame with *Lady Macbeth of the Mzensk District* (1932). The premiere in St. Petersburg in 1934 was a grand success. For two years, *Lady Macbeth* played to packed houses in both Soviet and Western European cities until Stalin saw it in 1936. As Shostakovich recalls, that changed the entire situation.

On January 28, 1936, [Viktor Kubatsky and I] went to the railroad station [in Arkhangelsk] to buy a new *Pravda*. I opened it up and leafed through it—and found the article "Muddle Instead of Music." I'll never forget that day; it's probably the most memorable in my life.

That article on the third page of *Pravda* changed my entire existence. It was printed without a signature, like an editorial—that is, it expressed the opinion of the Party. But it actually expressed the opinion of Stalin, and that was much more important.

There is a school of thought that holds that the article was written by the well-known bastard Zaslavsky, but that's another matter entirely. The article has too much of Stalin in it, there are expressions that even Zaslavsky wouldn't have used; they were too ungrammatical. . . . It's clear that this is a genuine pronouncement of our leader and teacher. There are many places like that in the article I can distinguish with complete confidence.

The title—"Muddle Instead of Music"—also belongs to Stalin. The day before, *Pravda* had printed the leader and teacher's brilliant comments on the outlines of new history textbooks, and he talked about muddles there too.

This text by the Leader of the Peoples and Friend of Children was printed over his signature. Obviously, the word "muddle" stuck in his mind, something that often happens to the mentally ill. And so he used the word everywhere. . . . From that moment on I was stuck with the label "enemy of the people. . . ."[31]

Shostakovich regained favor in 1937 with his Fifth Symphony. This nationalistic work commemorating the twentieth anniversary of the Revolution supposedly reflects Shostakovich's reaction to "justified criticism." Beyond these general concessions to social realism, the work has no program, nor does it use Russian folk music.

Prior to the premiere of the Fifth Symphony, it was heard by censors of the Soviet Party in a private concert in Leningrad.[32] The Fifth Symphony is, in some ways, a document of social realism. Its thematic materials are easy to follow: The first theme is conspicuous for its dotted rhythms and wide leaps; the second strain is equally distinctive, with its plaintive, legato theme set against a homophonic accompaniment featuring dactylic rhythms. The use of imitation in the statement of the first theme is important, as it is in the developmental process in general. The movement is a clearly defined sonata form. The clarity of the first movement is paralleled by equally accessible structures in the others; nevertheless, the piece is not what Shostakovich claimed it was, and the Soviet authorities may have overlooked key features of the piece. Galina Vishnevskaya explains:

In that "joyous, optimistic" finale—beneath the triumphant blare of the trumpets, beneath the endlessly repeated A in the violins, like nails being pounded into one's brain—we hear a desecrated Russia, violated by her own sons, wailing and writhing in agony, nailed to the Cross, bemoaning the fact that she will survive her defilement.[33]

Shostakovich continued in the favor of the regime, and he was awarded the Stalin Prize in 1940 for his Quintet for piano and strings. He won a second Stalin Prize for his Seventh Symphony (1942). The Seventh was actually written during the siege of Leningrad in World War II, and so, it too has nationalistic associations.

Shostakovich's increasing fame led to a visit to the United States in 1949. A second visit was undertaken in 1959. In the meantime, the composer had been admitted to the Order of Lenin in 1956, the occasion of his fiftieth birthday. In 1966, for his sixtieth birthday, he was named "Hero of Socialist Labor"—the only composer to have received this award.

Additional works of importance include the Twenty-Four Preludes and Fugues, Op. 87 (1951), written to celebrate the life of Bach and modeled directly after his two volumes of preludes and fugues, *Das wohltemperierte Klavier* (the well-tempered keyboard; 1722 and 1746).[34] In each piece, Shostakovich pays fitting tribute; but the A-major Prelude and Fugue is a glorious example both of Shostakovich's contrapuntal skill and his virtuosic technique. The prelude is a concise, contrapuntal essay exhibiting remarkable clarity of line. The fugue, exquisitely simple in its musical materials, is an ebullient fantasy on an A-major triad. Arpeggios slide one over another, in an apparently endless cascade of sound; still, the harmonic structure is surprisingly simple.

In his politically inspired pieces, Shostakovich has taken a strong stance against violations of human rights. His abhorrence of anti-Semitism is clear in the five-movement String Quartet No. 8 in C minor, Op. 110 (1960). He wrote this in the wake of a visit to Dresden to compose the score for *Five Days and Five Nights*, a film that recounts the bombing of that city during World War II. Within the quartet, Shostakovich uses his own name as a motif (D, S, C, H = D, E-flat, C, B-natural). It is the principal subject in the outer fugal movements (both Largo), but it appears in various guises throughout the work.

Noteworthy too is the *Babi Yar Symphony* (No. 13; 1962), which is scored for baritone solo, male chorus, and orchestra. Yevgeny Yevtushenko penned the texts of the symphony, which protests the Nazi massacre of the Jews and, by inference, Soviet anti-Semitic policies.[35]

Also inspired by the poetry of Yevtushenko is *The Execution of Stepan Razin*, Op. 119 (1964). Razin was a rebel, who, in 1670, led the serfs in an anti-tsarist uprising. He was captured and beheaded in the public square in Moscow. Shostakovich's skill at orchestration is clear in this colorful work for bass, mixed chorus, piccolo, two flutes, two oboes, English horn, three clarinets, bass clarinet, two bassoons, contrabassoon, four horns, three trumpets, three trombones, tuba, timpani, triangle, tambourines, whip, cymbals, drum, tam-tam, bells, xylophone, celesta, harp (at least two), piano, violins 1 (at least twenty), violins 2 (at least eighteen), violas (at least sixteen), 'celli (at least fourteen), and double basses (at least twelve). An astoundingly refined score, it displays many characteristic features, including ostinatos, asymmetrical rhythms, modal melodies, declamatory vocal lines, and dramatic use of percussion. The tolling church bells after Razin's execution are terrifying.

In Shostakovich's life and works, the tension between politics and art, between personal inclination and civic duty, resulted in music that transcends its circumstances. His message, at once human, warm, and caring, is, at the same time, abstract. It alerts all citizens of this world to the importance of political structures, governmental agencies, and, most importantly, society's need for art as a source of inspiration, guidance, and hope.

Notes

1. Sadly, Senator Joseph R. McCarthy (1908–1957), the Republican senator from Wisconsin from 1947 to 1957, made claims that the State Department had been subverted by Communists. Playing on the public's fear, he maneuvered himself into the position of chairman of the Government Operations Committee. Among the musicians who were accused of Communist sympathies during the McCarthy era was none other than Aaron Copland—along with Hanns Eisler, who was eventually compelled to leave the country despite the support of influential composers such as Leonard Bernstein, David Diamond, Roy Harris, Walter Piston, Roger Sessions, and Randall Thompson.
2. For a detailed biography see Jaroslav Vogel, *Leos Janáček: His Life and Works*, trans. G. Thomsen-Muchova and rev. Karel Janovický (New York: Norton, 1981).
3. John K. Novak, "Janáček's *Nursery Rhymes* as a Compendium of His Compositional Style," *College Music Symposium: Journal of the College Music Society* 39 (1999), 43.
4. Novak, "Janáček's *Nursery Rhymes*," 44.
5. Leos Janáček, *O lidové písni a lidové hudbé* (about folksong and folk music); cited in Novak, Janáček's *Nursery Rhymes*, 47.
6. Otto Deri, *Exploring Twentieth-Century Music*, (New York: Holt, Rinehart and Winston, 1968), p. 45.
7. Cymbalom players in the U.S.A. are usually amateur entertainers who play in ethnic ensembles. Most conservatories and colleges neither own nor teach the instrument. In Europe, cymbalom players are usually found in bars or *Weinstuben*. Nevertheless, cymbalom is required by Stravinsky in *Renard*, the *Ragtime for Eleven Instruments*, in the second version of *Les noces*, in Boulez's score for *Éclat*, and in various other standard works of the contemporary repertoire. Failing an authentic cymbalom, an upright piano with hammers capped with thumb tacks approximates the sound quite well.
8. The photograph of the Academy can be found in Ferenc Bónos, *Béla Bartók: His Life in Pictures and Documents* (New York: Belwin Mills, 1972), plate 26, p. 44.
9. Pictured in Bónos, *Bartók: His Life in Pictures*, plates 29 and 30, p. 44.
10. János Demény, ed., *Béla Bartók Letters*, trans. Péter Balabán and István Farkas (London: Faber and Faber, 1971), p. 17.
11. For details, see Halsey Stevens, *The Life and Music of Béla Bartók* (New York: Oxford, 1964), pp. 9, 15, 40–41 respectively.
12. Demény, *Letters*, pp. 21–23.
13. See Constant Vauclain, "Bartók: Beyond Bi-modality," *The Music Review* 42 (August–November 1981), 242–251.
14. The activities of Bartók's American years are recounted in Agatha Fassett, *The Naked Face of Genius* (Cambridge, Massachusetts: Riverside Press, 1958). The book reveals much about Bartók's character; however, there is little discussion of his music.

15. See Mark A. Radice, "Bartók's Beethoven Parodies," in *The Music Review* 42 (August–November 1981), 252–260.

16. Philip Pomper, *The Russian Revolutionary Intelligentsia* (New York: Thomas Y. Crowell, 1970), pp. 112–113.

17. Anton Rubinstein, *Autobiography of Anton Rubinstein* (New York: Haskell House, 1969), p. 91.

18. M. D. Calvocoressi and Gerald Abraham, *Masters of Russian Music* (New York: Alfred Knopf, 1936), p. 119.

19. For details concerning all aspects of Rachmaninoff's career, see Barrie Martyn, *Rachmaninoff: Composer, Pianist, Conductor* (Brookfield, Vermont: Gower, 1990).

20. For details, see Oskar von Riesemann, *Rachmaninoff's Recollections Told to Oskar von Riesemann*, trans. from German by Dolly Rutherford (New York: Macmillan, 1934), pp. 59–60.

21. Riesemann, *Rachmaninoff's Recollections*, pp. 60–61.

22. See Geoffrey Norris, *Rachmaninoff* (New York: Schirmer Books, 1994), p. 150.

23. David Cannata, *Rachmaninoff and the Symphony* (Innsbruck: Studien Verlag, 1999), p. 58, suggests that Rachmaninoff used the word "rhapsody" in the title because "he was too astute a professional to overlook the immense popularity enjoyed by Gershwin's *Rhapsody in Blue.*

24. For compositional history, see Cannata, *Rachmaninoff and the Symphony*, pp. 119–125; analysis pp. 125–130. Particularly interesting is Cannata's observation that here, as in the First and Second Symphonies, Rachmaninoff uses "fugato sections to confirm the tonic key in any given tonal design. . . . With the Third Symphony, Rachmaninoff placed such a fugato section in the Finale" thereby resolving the double tonic conflict (between A and D) that pervades the structure of all three of its movements.

25. The childhood and conservatory years are covered in his memoirs; however, the memoirs do not go beyond the year 1909. See David H. Appel, ed., *Prokofiev by Prokofiev: A Composer's Memoir*, trans. Guy Daniels (Garden City, New York: Doubleday, 1979).

26. Not to be confused with his son Alexander Nikolayevich Tcherepnin (1899–1977), who was also a composer. The senior Tcherepnin moved to Paris in 1921 and worked with Diaghileff. Alexander studied there with Bohuslav Martinů (1890–1959).

27. Concerning the premiere performance of *Love for Three Oranges* and the critical reaction to it, see Harlow Robinson, *Sergei Prokofiev* (New York: Viking Press, 1987), pp. 168–169.

28. Robinson, *Sergei Prokofiev*, p. 278.

29. Dmitri Shostakovich, *Testimony: The Memoirs of Dmitri Shostakovich*, ed. Solomon Volkov, trans. Antonia W. Bouis (New York: Harper and Row, 1979), pp. 6–7. The accuracy of these memoirs has been questioned by Richard Taruskin. See his article "The Peculiar Martyrdom of Dmitri Shostakovich: The Opera and the Dictator," *New Republic*, issue 3,870 (20 March 1989), 34–40. Though she does not assail the accuracy of Volkov's information, Shostakovich's widow, Irina, whom he married in 1962, decries Volkov as an opportunist. See her article "An Answer to Those Who Still Abuse Shostakovich"; trans. Irina Roberts, *New York Times* (Sunday 20 August 2000), p. 27f.

30. Shostakovich, *Testimony*, pp. 50–51.

31. Shostakovich, *Testimony*, pp. 113–115.

32. Galina Vishnevskaya, *Galina: A Russian Story*, trans. Guy Daniels (New York: Harcourt Brace Jovanovich, 1984), p. 212.

33. Vishnevskaya, *A Russian Story*, p. 213.

34. In imitation of Bach, Shostakovich has written one prelude and fugue for each of the major and minor keys of the twelve tones of the chromatic scale.

35. Details are provided in Jeffrey W. Baxter, "A Descriptive Analysis of the Yevtushenko Settings of Dmitri Shostakovich," (D.M.A. diss., University of Cincinnati, 1988), 115 p.

Chapter 3

A Wandering Interlude: Stravinsky, Part I

Stravinsky (1882–1971) was Russian by birth, and his childhood was filled with Russian music, since his father, Feodor Ignatievich, was the principal bass soloist of the Imperial Opera House in St. Petersburg. Glinka, Musorgsky, and Tschaikovsky were his daily diet; however, his parents had hoped Igor would pursue a career in law.

The story of Stravinsky's life is not limited to any one location or nation: He left Russia in 1910 to settle in Paris, where the Ballets Russes, under the administration of Serge Diaghileff, was performing his work. He left France in 1914 in order to escape the disruption caused by World War I. In 1920 he returned from Switzerland to Paris, only to leave for the United States in 1940 because of World War II. Until 1968, he lived in California, but from then until his death, he lived in New York City.

The sources of information about Stravinsky are diverse: He wrote an autobiography that was published in English by Simon and Schuster in 1936; his musical aesthetics are explained in his *Poetics of Music*, six lectures he gave at Harvard University that were published by Harvard University Press in 1947; with Robert Craft, his personal secretary from 1948 until his death, Stravinsky compiled *Conversations with Igor Stravinsky* (1959), *Memories and Commentaries* (1960), *Expositions and Developments* (1962), *Dialogues and a Diary* (1963), *Themes and Episodes* (1966), and *Retrospectives and Conclusions* (1969). In 1972, Craft published his *Stravinsky: The Chronicle of a Friendship, 1948–1971*.

Stylistically, Stravinsky's music was constantly changing. The Russian period, which extends to the completion of *Les noces* in 1923, overlaps with the neoclassical period, which began in 1919 with the score of *Pulcinella*. The neoclassical works spill over into the serial works that he began writing after his meeting with Craft, an advocate of the music of Anton Webern especially.

Igor Stravinsky

Though he never undertook a conservatory training, Stravinsky did study piano as a boy, and between 1902 and 1908, he worked privately with Rimsky-Korsakoff. Under Rimsky's supervision, Stravinsky completed his Symphony in E-flat, Op. 1. This four-movement work shows influences of Glazunoff, Tschaikovsky, Wagner, and Rimsky. Formal designs, such as the sonata-form first movement, are conservative, but effectively employed.

After having orchestrated a couple of dances of Chopin's *Les sylphides* for a production by the Ballets Russes, Stravinsky produced his first full-length ballet, *L'oiseau de feu* (firebird; 1910). He capitalized on the exoticism of this Russian ballet in Paris: The story of Prince Ivan's dual rescue, first of the Firebird and then of the lovely young Princess, not only draws on Russian folklore but also provides opportunities for Russian sets and costumes. Stravinsky uses folksongs to complement this stage setting, but he had no concern for folkloric research: He simply took them from Rimsky's collection of *One Hundred Russian Songs* (1876). When he composed *Petroushka* for the 1911 season of the Ballets Russes, his casual attitude was his undoing, since he mistook a copyrighted song, Emile Spencer's "Elle avait un' jambe en bois," (she had a wooden leg) for a folktune.[1]

Stravinsky used his folksongs well: The tuneful, Eastern European melodies characterize the mortal persons of the scenario. Chromatic melodies and harmonies are used for the magical characters, such as the Firebird and Kastchei. In the case of the former, the tunes are Romantic, lyrical, and Chopinesque. For Kastchei and his retinue, they are irregular in meter and phrasing. The evil ogre Kastchei also merits distinctive orchestration featuring winds, especially brass, and percussion—what most would consider Stravinsky's characteristic style.

Petroushka, with its polytonal motif associated with the puppet who gives the ballet its name, and *Le sacre du printemps* (rite of spring; 1913) cemented Stravinsky's reputation in France. Because both *L'oiseau de feu* and *Petroushka* included bold new musical materials—angular melodies, irregular phrases, changing meters, emphasis on percussion and winds, deemphasis of lyricism and the strings—Stravinsky had no way of anticipating the reaction to *Le sacre*. In his autobiography, he tells us:

> The complexity of my score had demanded a great number of rehearsals, which [Pierre] Monteux had conducted with his usual skill and attention. . . . Demonstrations, at first isolated, soon became gen-

eral, provoking counter-demonstrations and very quickly developing into a terrific uproar. During the whole performance I was at Nijinsky's side in the wings. He was standing on a chair, screaming "sixteen, seventeen, eighteen"—they had their own method of counting to keep time. Naturally the poor dancers could hear nothing by reason of the row in the auditorium and the sound of their own dance steps. I had to hold Nijinsky by his clothes, for he was furious, and ready to dash on to the stage at any moment and create a scandal. Diaghileff kept ordering the electricians to turn the lights on or off, hoping in that way to put a stop to the noise. . . . Oddly enough, at the dress rehearsal, to which we had, as usual, invited a number of actors, painters, musicians, writers, and the most cultured representatives of society, everything had gone off peacefully, and I was very far from expecting such an outburst.[2]

Notes

1. See Eric Walter White, *Stravinsky: The Composer and His Works*, 2d ed. (Berkeley and Los Angeles: University of California Press, 1979), p. 200.
2. Stravinsky, *Autobiography* (New York: Simon and Schuster, 1936), pp. 46–47.

Chapter 4

The Transformation of Late Romanticism in France

The critical reaction to *Le sacre* can only be understood in light of the French musical landscape at the turn of the century, which was dominated by a handful of opera composers.

Save for the years that he spent in England during the Franco-Prussian War, 1870 to 1874, Charles Gounod (1818–1893) was France's leading musical figure from the mid century until his death. His most popular works, his *Messe solennelle de Ste Cécile* (1855) and the operas *Faust* (1859) and *Roméo et Juliette* (1867), demonstrate refinement and skill.[1] His harmonies are rich and varied, and his melodies are shapely and memorable. Too often, he relies on hackneyed gestures, banal phrasing, and tawdry orchestration. His music makes an immediate impression, but becomes tedious in the long run.

Camille Saint-Saëns (1835–1921) was a composer and performer of immense influence. His teaching at the École Niedermeyer from 1861 until 1865, in addition to his role as a founding member of the Société National de Musique in 1871, added to his prestige. His scores of the Organ Symphony (No. 3 in C minor; 1886), *Carnaval des animaux* (carnival of the animals; 1886), and concertos for various instruments and orchestra (five for piano, three for violin, and two for 'cello), are models of formal clarity and idiomatic writing. In 1877, he demonstrated a similar flair for theatrical and vocal composition with his opera *Samson et Dalila*. Fauré and Ravel were among his students, and Ravel's concept of form stems from his influence.[2]

An equally popular figure was Jules Massenet (1842–1912), who won the Prix de Rome in 1863. He wrote more than thirty operas, incidental music to many plays, and several ballets.[3] His smaller works include over 200 songs, song cycles, motets, part-songs, and the like. His treatment of *Manon* was the operatic highlight of the 1884 season, and *Werther* scored another success in 1892. Today Massenet is best known for orchestral excerpts from his operas *Le Cid* (1885) and *Thaïs* (1894).

Massenet's vocal writing reveals the influence of Wagner. Contours derive from the French language, and whatever there is of traditional melody stems from the music inherent in the text. Periodic structures and meters are relaxed; hence, formal plans are fluid.

In 1878, Massenet joined the composition faculty of the Paris Conservatoire. With the death of Ambroise Thomas, Massenet's former teacher, in February of 1896, the directorship became vacant. It was offered to Massenet, but he declined; moreover, he decided that the time was right for a change, and so, resigned from the Conservatoire. His almost twenty years of teaching produced important pupils such as Henri Malherbe, Charles-Gaston Levadé, and Florent Schmitt.

Belgian by birth—and less important than Massenet in the eyes of the general populace of nineteenth-century France—César Franck (1822–1890) was, nevertheless, one of the most important of France's late-Romantic composers. Most of his works are for organ solo, but he also wrote excellent chamber music, including the Piano Quintet (1879), the Sonata (1886) for violin and piano, and the String Quartet (1889).[4] Franck composed several symphonic poems and the Symphony in D minor (1888) for orchestra.

Compositionally, Franck's style is linear. Chromaticism results from complex combinations of lines, each pursuing its own logic. The individual lines, too, are noteworthy in their construction: Franck preferred highly integrated scores, and he frequently employed a "germ cell" of three or four notes, which would then be manipulated in various ways to construct extended ideas. Though the lines are long, *cantabile*, and Romantic, they are actually composed, like a mosaic, of innumerable melodic fragments. This technique of thematic generation and transformation is Franck's hallmark. The cyclic recurrence of themes and their contrapuntal combination are also standard features. His most important pupils were Vincent D'Indy, Louis Vierne, Georges Bizet, and Claude Debussy.

D'Indy (1851–1931) was Franck's most enthusiastic advocate. A composer of note, D'Indy was devoted to church music, and he was the guiding force behind the Schola Cantorum, a conservatory he founded (1896) along with Charles Bordes and Alexandre Guilmant. Initially, they had hoped only to expose the public to first-rate performances of ecclesiastical music, but their efforts expanded to include the training of church musicians.

Ultimately, their purposes blended with those of the monks at the abbey of St. Pierre de Solesmes, who worked to restore the Gregorian repertoire of the Roman church. In 1889, they began publication of *Paleógraphie musicale*, consisting of facsimiles of early chant manuscripts, along with commentaries on transcription and performance. Pope Pius X charged the monks with the compilation of the Vatican Edition, the official texts of the chants used until the Second Vatican Council allowed the vernacular in Catholic liturgies. *Paleógraphie musicale* is complemented by the *Revue grégorienne*, a periodical exploring musical and sociological aspects of plainchant.

An important contemporary of D'Indy was Gabriel Fauré (1845–1924).[5] From 1854 until 1865, he studied at the École Niedermeyer, where Saint-Saëns was among his teachers. Fauré pursued the training for a church musician: keyboard, organ, improvisation, composition, and choral studies. From 1866 until his death, he was one of the leading church musicians in France. His major posts were at St. Sulpice and the Church of the Madeleine.

Fauré was influenced by Saint-Saëns's approach to pattern forms. His mentor's interest in music history also had an impact upon Fauré's musical orientation: The Pavane (1887) is one of Fauré's most refined works as well an early example of the neoclassical revival that became widespread around the time of World War I.

Today, Fauré's fame rests primarily upon his *Requiem* Mass, much of which was composed soon after the death of his mother in 1888. From 1905 until 1920, he was the director of the Paris Conservatoire. His greatest achievements as a composer can be seen in his chamber pieces, especially the Second Piano Quintet (1921) and his numerous song cycles. The late song cycles, such as *Mirages* (1919) and *L'horizon chimérique* (imaginary horizon; 1921), suggest the increased importance of nuance and reserve that led to his three-movement String Quartet in E minor (1924), his final work and, possibly, his *magnum opus*. His students included Ravel, Charles Koechlin, Jean Roger-Ducasse, Georges Enesco, and Nadia Boulanger.

Claude Debussy, Maurice Ravel, and Impressionism

Debussy (1862–1918) and Ravel (1875–1937) contributed decisively to the musical styles of early twentieth-century France.[6] Both are associated with the school of painting called Impressionism, but recently, Debussy has been related to the French poets known as Symbolists. The leading figures in this movement were Paul Verlaine, Stéphane Mallarmé, Henri de Régnier, Maurice Maeterlinck, Paul Claudel, and Paul Valéry.

The Symbolists communicated through suggestion rather than statement. Allusion, allegory, and metaphor were their vehicles for expression. Symbolist works create an ambiance rather than a situation; they evoke a sympathy rather than a conclusion, and ambivalence and ambiguity are integral elements.

Debussy was personally acquainted with many of the most important Symbolist writers, and for his early song settings, he frequently turned to their poems. The *Ariettes oubliées* (forgotten tunes; 1888), the *Trois mélodies* (three melodies; 1891), and both volumes of *Fêtes galantes* (gallant celebrations; 1891, 1904) use Symbolist poems by Verlaine. The *Prélude à l'après-midi d'un faune* (prelude to the afternoon of a faun; 1894), inspired by Mallarmé's poem with that title, was the first of Debussy's works to win acclaim. Even in the twilight years of his career, Debussy remained intrigued by these writings, and his last set of songs was the *Trois poèms de Mallarmé* (1913).

Although Debussy was born thirteen years before Ravel, their careers unfolded more or less simultaneously. Ten years after completing his studies at the Paris Conservatoire, Debussy came into the public's eye in 1894 with the previously mentioned *Prélude*. Those ten years were packed with musical experiences: study in Rome from 1885 until 1887 as the Conservatoire's prizewinner, visits to Bayreuth in 1888 and 1889, and contacts with exotic music at the Paris Exhibition of 1889.

Though Ravel tried repeatedly to win the Prix de Rome, he failed on every occasion; nevertheless, he scored a popular success with his *Pavane pour une Infante défunte* (pavane for a dead princess; 1899). It was published first as a piano solo, then in an orchestral version (1910). By comparison, Debussy's best known piece, "Clair de lune" (moonlight), is the third movement of his four-movement *Suite bergamasque*. Though it was written in 1895, it was not published until 1905.

The musical materials of Debussy and Ravel are similar, but the ways in which they applied them are different. Both were fascinated by exoticism. Debussy evokes the Orient in his "Pagodes" from *Les estampes* (prints; 1903) and *Khamma* (1912); ancient music provided the mystique in scores like the *Danse sacree et danse profane* (sacred dance and secular dance; 1904), the ever-popular "Cathédral engloutie" (sunken cathedral) from the first book of Preludes (1910), and the *Six épigraphes antiques* (six antique epigraphs; 1914); Hispanic flavor pervades the pages of "La Puerta del Vino" (the gate of wine) from the second book of Preludes (1913); and his three late sonatas for chamber ensembles were inspired by the eighteenth-century composer Jean Philippe Rameau. For French nationalists, Rameau became a *cause célèbre* and an alternative to German musical hegemony. Heard in this context, Debussy's "Homage à Rameau" in the first set of *Images* (1905) assumes new significance.

One of Debussy's principal concerns was meter. In the nineteenth-century music that he would have known in his formative years—Wagner, Verdi, Tschaikovsky, Brahms, Musorgsky, and their contemporaries—several different tendencies are apparent: Meter may be regular (unmercifully so in the ballets of Tschaikovsky), or it may be less intrusive (as in the *recitativo* passages in Verdi's operas), or it may be intrusive but unpredictable (as in Musorgsky's works, or the 5/4 movement of Tschaikovsky's *Pathetique Symphony*). Even in "Clair de lune," Debussy takes pains to obscure its 9/8 meter: Rests appear on beats that are normally accented; subdivision of the beat changes constantly; and ties connect disparate subdivisions.

While its principal tonality, D-flat, is clearly indicated in the key signature, the frequent appearance of A-natural (first in measure 2 as part of a fully-diminished-seventh chord on A, then again in measure 6 as part of a dominant-seventh chord on F) undermines D-flat and suggests instead the key of B-flat. The frequent appearance in the ensuing measures of F-flat and C-flat further weakens tonal stability. The excursion into C-sharp minor (the enharmonic respelling of

D-flat minor) introduces sequencing that creates temporary leading tones of purely local significance. The harmonic ambiguity of the score corresponds to and enhances its rhythmic ambiguity.

"La Puerta del Vino," (Preludes, Bk. II) is another piece in D-flat. The rhythm of the *habanera* (a Cuban dance in slow duple meter that became popular in nineteenth-century France) pervades the left hand. Above this pattern, the right hand plays a tonally unpredictable melody using the same metrically elusive proliferation of rests, ties, changing subdivisions—and, in this case, little-note figuration—that obscures the meter of "Clair de lune."

In both "Clair de lune" and "La Puerta del Vino," a piano with three pedals—the conventional *damper* and *una corda* pedals now complemented by the *sostenuto* pedal—is presumed. The sophisticated mechanism of the late nineteenth-century piano reflects the growing importance of tone color as an element equal to harmony and melody.

Debussy's experimentation with rhythms and timbres is apparent in his works for larger ensembles too. Especially noteworthy are the three Nocturnes (1899) for orchestra, *Pelléas et Mélisande* (1902), and *La mer* (the sea; 1905). In all of these, instrumentation is used like glitter. Special sonorities highlight peaks in melodies or points of structural significance. The sound of the triangle, for example, may call attention to the apex of a crescendo that has taken place over the course of many measures. Here too, the sound of a bass drum may lend emphasis, but these fleeting sonorities are held in reserve for special effects. Among the late works, the Sonata (1915) for flute, viola, and harp attests to Debussy's sensitivity to nuances of timbre.

Ravel began his training at the Conservatoire in 1889 and studied there until 1895. In 1897, he returned for further study until 1900. His association with the institution continued until 1905. By that time, he had all the requisite training along with a portfolio including two masterpieces, the *Pavane pour une infante défunte* and the String Quartet in F.

At the time Ravel's career got underway, Debussy's style was already a known commodity; hence, some critics saw Ravel's music as an imitation of Debussy: Each wrote a single, early, string quartet; each had a penchant for the piano; each was fascinated by things Spanish (Was Ravel's *Rapsodie espagnole* a mere imitation of Debussy's *Ibéria*?); and Symbolist/Impressionist imagery—like water—figures prominently in the works of both (Ravel's *Jeux d'eau* and Debussy's *Reflects dans l'eau*, for example).

One feature that differentiates the two composers is that Ravel wrote many of his works twice: first as pieces for piano solo, later as orchestral works. The case of the *Pavane* has already been mentioned. The *Valses nobles et sentimentales*—inspired by the music of Schubert—were piano pieces in 1911, but orchestrated within a year's time. The *Tombeau de Couperin*, consisting of a Prelude, Fugue, Forlana, Rigaudon, Minuet, and Toccata, appeared in piano and orchestral versions in 1917. Such parallel scores are foreign to Debussy's *œuvre*.

Maurice Ravel

In considering just these few titles, another difference between Debussy and Ravel becomes clear: The latter's interest in music history—already in evidence in his 1895 score for piano entitled *Menuet antique*—predisposed him toward classical pattern forms. The Sonatine (1905) in F-sharp for piano solo hearkens to the eighteenth century as does his *Menuet sur le nom de Haydn* (1909).

As a student of Fauré and a close friend of Nadia Boulanger, Ravel could not have avoided a tour of the annals of music history. His exposure to early music—probably stimulated by the proximity of Wanda Landowska as well—influenced his own style. The elegance of line, the carefully balanced formal designs, the superbly idiomatic writing for all instruments, the attention to details of all sorts—these features suggest a composer of Classical rather than Romantic sensibilities. Though titles of pieces in collections like *Miroirs* (1906) and *Gaspard de la nuit* (1908), after prose poems by Bertrand, suggest poetic forms and program music, Ravel remained a composer of refined moderation.

On one occasion, Debussy and Ravel were colleagues in misery, owing to their commissions from Serge Diaghileff and the Ballets Russes. Debussy's *Jeux* (games; 1913) was hardly noticed because it shared the season with Stravinsky's *Le sacre du printemps*. Ravel suffered a similar humiliation with the ballet *Daphnis et Chloé* (1912): When Diaghileff arrived in Paris in 1909, he requested a piece from Ravel; but when Ravel played a piano reduction of the piece for him, Diaghileff found it disappointing and wanted to drop the project. It was only through the intercession of his publisher, Durand, that Ravel's score went into production, with the principal roles danced by Vaslav Nijinsky and Tamara Karsavina.

In 1928, Ravel visited the United States. During that tour he gave over thirty concerts, including a program on which he conducted the Boston Symphony Orchestra, then under the direction of his friend and colleague Serge Koussevitzky. (In 1922, at Koussevitzky's request, Ravel had orchestrated Musorgsky's *Pictures at an Exhibition*.) 1928 was also the year in which Ravel wrote the piece by which he is known: *Bolero*.

The bolero is a Spanish dance in a moderate triple meter that originated during the late eighteenth century. Usually danced by a man and woman with castanets, each of the three sections of a classic bolero concludes with a dramatic gesture called the *bien parado*, in which one arm is curved over the head while the other is placed across the chest in what looks like an empty embrace. Ravel's *Bolero* was written for Ida Rubinstein, who gave its premiere in Paris in 1928 with choreography by

Bronislava Nijinsky. Within a year, it had its American premiere by the New York Philharmonic under Arturo Toscanini. Subsequently, it was used in almost every conceivable context from Broadway shows to film scores, in every possible arrangement from two pianos to jazz band.

In 1932, Ravel wrote his last major composition, a setting of three poems by Paul Morand for baritone and orchestra entitled *Don Quichotte à Dulcinée*. Soon after, he began to feel the debilitating effects of Pick's disease: He lost motor control, was in intense pain, suffered partial paralysis, and became severely depressed. He had surgery in December of 1937, but he never regained consciousness. He died on the 28th of that month.[7]

Notes

1. Concerning his operas, see Steven Huebner, *Operas of Charles Gounod* (New York: Clarendon Press, 1990).
2. Two recent biographies are Brian Rees, *Camille Saint-Saëns: A Life* (London: Chatto and Windus, 1999); Stephen Studd, *Saint-Saëns: A Critical Biography* (Madison: Fairleigh Dickinson, 1999).
3. Demar Irvine's biography, *Massenet: A Chronicle of His Life and Times* (Portland, Oregon: Amadeus Press, 1994), is outstanding.
4. The organ works are discussed in Viktor Lukas, *A Guide to Organ Music* (Portland, Oregon: Amadeus Press, 1989), pp. 119–123.
5. See Edward R. Phillips, *Gabriel Fauré: A Guide to Research* (New York: Garland, 2000).
6. Debussy's style is examined in Richard S. Parks, *The Music of Claude Debussy* (New Haven, Connecticut: Yale, 1989). Some discussion of Ravel's idiom is included in Arbie Orenstein, *Ravel: Man and Musician* (New York: Columbia, 1975). See also James R. Briscoe, *Claude Debussy: A Guide to Research* (New York: Garland, 1990); and Orenstein, *A Ravel Reader: Correspondence, Article, Interviews* (New York: Columbia, 1990).
7. The diagnosis of Pick's disease is indicated in Paul Griffiths, *Thames and Hudson Encyclopedia of Twentieth-Century Music* (London: Thames and Hudson, 1986), p. 147.

Chapter 5

Music in Spain:
Manuel de Falla, 1876–1946

Ravel's fascination with Spanish culture stemmed from his Basque heritage, but political and social conditions in early twentieth-century Spain were not conducive to musical culture. Spain's defeat in the Spanish-American War and the nation's loss of colonies in the Americas compromised its political and economic stability. A brief period of prosperity came during World War I, when Spain, as a neutral country, experienced a surge of activity in its shipyards, manufacturing, and industry. Musically, the war took a tragic toll, since one of its victims was the composer and pianist Enrique Granados (1867–1916), who died aboard the SS *Sussex* when it was sunk on 24 March 1916. Granados was a champion of Spanish culture, and he had used national themes in his twelve *Danzas espanolas* (Spanish dances; 1892–1900) and in his two volumes of piano pieces called *Goyescas* (1912, 1914), which he used in 1916 in an opera of the same title.

After World War I, the government changed approximately twice each year. In 1923, General Miguel Primo de Rivera sidestepped the Spanish monarchy and placed himself at the head of a military government. Though he instituted economic reforms, his social policies were dictatorial and repressive. He suspended his reign of martial law in 1927, but his support had eroded, and he was forced to resign on 28 January 1930. Spain's government then became known as the Second Republic, and during the ensuing years, hostilities between Loyalists and Communists led to the Spanish Civil War (1936–1939). Germany, advancing the cause of General Francisco Franco as dictator, used the war as an opportunity for testing new military tactics, including the first saturation bombing in history. The German forces, collaborating with Franco, chose the Basque town of Guernica as their target.

The story of Guernica is well known (largely on account of Pablo Picasso's huge canvas—approximately 12′ × 26′) depicting the horrors of the event. Picasso began the picture just two days after the bombing and, fueled by righteous indignation, he completed it in several weeks' time. Ironically, the work was commissioned for the Spanish pavilion of the 1937 World's Fair, where it was viewed by thousands. At the time Picasso painted *Guernica*, he was a resident of Paris. Like many other Spaniards, he had left his native land in disgust. During Franco's dictatorship, Spain's leading musical talents fled across the globe: Joaquín Nin-Culmell (b. 1908) to the United States, Pablo Casals (1876–1973) to Puerto Rico, Roberto Gerhard (1896–1970) to England, and Manuel de Falla to South America.

Manuel de Falla, 1876–1946

De Falla first studied piano with his mother. His progress was rapid, and he soon began work in harmony, counterpoint, and composition. When the time came, he enrolled at the conservatory in Madrid, where his composition teacher was Felipe Pedrell. Pedrell was a skillful composer intrigued by the lyric theater; however, his greatest impact was as a musicologist. His interests were broad, and he wrote essays on theoretical and practical issues such as solfège, musical terminology, and the performance of Beethoven's piano sonatas, as well as historically oriented studies such as his history of the festival of Elche, his bio-bibliographical dictionary of Spanish, Portuguese, and Latin-American composers, and his monograph on Tomás Luis de Victoria. He investigated folk music, and his *Cancionero musical popular espagnol* (compendium of popular Spanish songs; 1922; 2d ed., 1936) was widely circulated.

De Falla's interest in keyboard music was lifelong, but his work with Pedrell from 1901 until 1904 shifted his focus to composition. He wrote several *zarzuelas* (lyric theater pieces with spoken dialogue) and managed to get some performed. He made his mark with *La vida breve* (the short life; 1905), based on a libretto by Carlos Fernández Shaw. With it, de Falla won first prize in a competition hosted by the Real Academia de Bellas Artes de San Fernando.

La vida breve shows influences of Italian *verismo*. The cast focuses on three characters: the beautiful young Salud; her beloved, Paco; and Carmela, the object of Paco's affections. In working out this love triangle, Paco abandons Salud. She then confronts Paco, who is about to marry Carmela. During an intense exchange, Salud falls to the ground, dead.

Despite the flaws of the scenario, Falla created a lyric theater piece that captured the imaginations of his audience. The sets, which include a panoramic view of Granada with the Alhambra in the distance, played a crucial role in its success. Equally picturesque is the music, which employs elements of Andalusian folk music, Flamenco, guitars, castanets, and memorable tunes. In the first scene of Act II, de Falla goes beyond stereotypes of Hispanic music in his Flamenco concert and Spanish dance. In *La vida breve*, de Falla combines refined orchestration with a clearly tonal idiom. The music is distinctive and powerful because of its colorful ethnic elements; furthermore, it can be produced with limited resources.

In *La vida breve*, de Falla came closer to traditional opera than in any other of his lyric theater pieces. Ironically, the first production was in a French translation made by Paul Milliet. De Falla had moved to Paris in 1907. There he befriended Paul Dukas, Debussy, Ravel, Isaac Albéniz, and Joaquin Turina. The premiere on 1 April 1913 was at the Municipal Casino in Nice, a Mediterranean seaport town in southeastern France. It was given in Paris on 30 December of that same year at the Opera Comique. With the outbreak of World War I in 1914, Falla returned to Spain, where the work was heard in Spanish for the first time on 14 November in Madrid.[1]

El amor brujo (love—the magician; 1915) is a mixture of recitations, songs, and dances. De Falla wrote it with the dancer Pastora Imperio in mind. *El sombrero de tres picos* (the three-cornered hat) is a revision of an earlier *farsa mimica* (pantomime) entitled *El corregidor y la molinera* (the magistrate and the miller's wife; 1917). It combines ethnic dances, such as the *farruca*, *fandango*, and *jota*, with folk songs in a hybrid product that is neither opera nor ballet in the traditional sense. *El retablo de Maese Pedro* (Master Peter's puppet show; 1923) is based on a segment from Cervantes' *Don Quixote* in which the Man of La Mancha and his Page are entertained with a puppet show based on the story of Don Gayferos and Melisendra. In de Falla's piece, which was written for the salon of the Princesse Edmond de Polignac, two sets of puppets are required: large ones representing the characters in the novel, and smaller ones representing the characters of the puppet show.[2]

When he left Spain in 1939, he was already at work on *Atlántida*, which is another hybrid including solo and choral vocal music, exquisite orchestration, and scenery; yet, it has more in common with oratorio than with opera. De Falla worked on *Atlántida* until his death, producing over three hundred pages of music based on Jacint Verdaguer's poem by the same title. The score might be described as a scenic cantata dealing with a mythological history of Spain, from its origin as a land mass until the time of Columbus. De Falla's score shows influences of Spanish folk music, classical Spanish literature, and the traditional sacred music of Spain, from the Mediæval and Renaissance eras. The choral movement "Praise the sea," which uses a text by Alfonso the Wise (reg. 1252–1284), has the character of sacred music. The score as de Falla left it is hardly a performable work. Fortunately, de Falla's pupil Ernest Halffter (1905–1989) was familiar enough with de Falla's style to make a completion of *Atlántida*. Halffter's performing version had its premiere at La Scala in 1962, but various alterations have since been applied to his score; hence no two performances are identical.

Of de Falla's instrumental works, the most important are *Noches en los jardines de Espagna* (nights in the gardens of Spain; 1915), a concerto-like piece for piano and orchestra, and his Concerto (1926) for harpsichord, flute, oboe, clarinet, violin, and 'cello. This piece, which de Falla worked on for four years, was crucial in the revival of harpsichord playing. The premiere took place on 5 November 1926 with Wanda Landowska at the harpsichord and de Falla conducting. Though he dedicated the work to her, she apparently had not come to grips with its difficulties at the time of the premiere. In the Concerto, the influence of Stravinsky's neoclassicism is apparent, as is de Falla's fascination with the music of his favorite harpsichordist, Domenico Scarlatti (1685–1757), who spent most of his career in Spain and Portugal.

De Falla's final years were plagued with hardship. Disappointed with his country and disgusted by Franco's dictatorship, he left Spain in October 1939 and fled to Argentina. He was already in his sixties and he lacked the strength to begin anew in the musical circles of Buenos Aires. As a consequence of the war, he received no royalties from his published works. When the war ended, the Spanish government extended an official invitation to de Falla to return to Spain, but he would not. It was a cruel bit of irony that following de Falla's funeral on 19 November at the Cathedral of Córdoba, his sister, Maria del Carmen, arranged to accompany his coffin back to Spain, where it was placed in the crypt of the Cathedral of Cadiz on 9 January 1947.

Notes

1. An excellent and heavily illustrated discussion of de Falla's activities in Paris and the premiere of *La vida breve* can be found in Gonzalo Armero, ed., *Manuel de Falla: His Life and Works*, trans. Tom Skipp (Madrid: Edicioines Opponax, 1996), pp. [47]–78.
2. A photograph of the salon of Princesse de Polignac with audience, and scenery for the premiere on 25 June is given in Armero, ed., *Manuel de Falla*, p. 176. De Falla was emphatic about the instrumentation: It must be limited to 2 first violins, 2 seconds, 2 violas, one 'cello, and one double bass, with harpsichord. "Only in this manner can the sound of the harpsichord be balanced with the rest of the orchestra." Ibid, p. 178.

Chapter 6

Music in Latin America

The search for musical materials independent of Western European clichés of the nineteenth century led nationalist composers around the world to investigate the musics of their native lands; however, the prominence of Spanish, Portuguese, and Italian cultures in South America could not be evaded by composers like Heitor Villa-Lobos (1887–1959), Silvestre Revueltas (1899–1940), Carlos Chávez (1899–1978), Alberto Ginastera (1916–1983), and Astor Piazzolla (1921–1994). With the exception of Villa-Lobos, these composers were trained in traditional academic institutions; hence, the classical heritage was more natural to them initially than any of their national musics. In many cases, too, it was difficult or impossible to determine exactly what the musical practices of ancient Native Americans might have been. Although some, like Chávez, attempted to unravel the mystery by investigating contemporaneous folk musics of the Huicholes, Series, and Yaquis, it is probable that the music he heard had already been affected by centuries of European influences.

Popular idioms provided additional alternatives. Some of these popular styles, such as the *chôros*, were already a synthesis of European and local musical materials—in this case, imported dances and songs performed by instrumental ensembles and soloists at fairs and other social events. This genre, which became popular in the late nineteenth century, combined traditional instruments like the flute, clarinet, and trombone, with folk instruments like *cavaco*, guitar, *chocalos*, and other, percussion, instruments.[1] These mixed genres are a musical reflection of the mixed races of South America: the *mestizos*. The term sometimes refers to people of mixed racial strains, often a synthesis of Native American, European, and African backgrounds; but it is also used to refer to pure-blooded Native Americans who adopt European customs and clothing. In musical discourse, *mestizo* style refers to synthetic musics like the *chôros*.

Villa-Lobos was fascinated by the music of Brazil, which he knew from practical experience: As a young man, he was one of the popular musicians called *chorões*. His father, Raul, was an amateur 'cellist, and he gave Heitor his first music lessons on that instrument, which remained his primary performance medium. The instrument is featured in many of his works, and in his nine *Bachianas Brasileiras* (1930–1945) for various instrumentations, Villa-Lobos employs an ensemble consisting exclusively of 'celli in the First and Fifth.

Music became for Villa-Lobos a passport to the world. He toured Brazil as a concert pianist. This took him to remote regions of the country and put him in touch with many regional musical dialects. Soon, he became hooked on folk music, and in 1912, he made his first field trip into the interior of Brazil to collect this repertoire.

After the first concert in Rio de Janeiro (November 1915) devoted exclusively to his music, Villa-Lobos became a sensation. Among his earliest admirers was the pianist Artur Rubinstein, for whom Villa-Lobos wrote his virtuosic piano solo, *Rudepoema* (1926). Simpler technically, but equally interesting musically, are the eight pieces of the *Prole do bebê* (the baby's family; 1918), a series of vignettes about dolls that uses children's folk songs. Various dolls—Caucasians with fair complexions, *mestizo*, brunette, *mulatto*, and black—are depicted in this suite of ethnic diversity.

From 1923 until his return to Brazil in 1930, Villa-Lobos was in Paris. There, his music was greeted with great enthusiasm.[2]

The fifteen *chôros* of Villa-Lobos (1920–1928) are his most distinctive blending of European and South American styles.[3] Written for various scorings ranging from solo guitar (No. 1; 1920) to orchestra, band, and chorus (no. 14; 1928), they use dissonant counterpoint, polymeters, polytonality, and multiple layers of syncopation, as well as popular dance rhythms like those of the *maxixe* and the *samba*.

Musical complexity in these pieces often rises to an astounding level, and anyone expecting easygoing background music scented with exotic perfumes will likely be disappointed. For those interested in a musical adventure, however, Villa-Lobos's more demanding works, like his single-movement *Quintette en forme de chôros* (1928) for flute, oboe, cor anglais, clarinet, and bassoon are highly recommended.

Villa-Lobos is probably the most prolific composer since Telemann, and to date, no one has attempted a thematic catalog of his complete works.[4] When he died, he left at least twelve symphonies and seventeen string quartets, thereby surpassing Beethoven in both genres.

For Mexico, 1899 was a jackpot year. Carlos Chávez was born on 13 June, and Silvestre Revueltas was born on 31 December. Revueltas's works, which include film scores such as *Redes* (waves; 1937), *Música para charlar* (music for talking; 1938), and *La noche de los Mayas* (night of the Mayans; 1939), reveal a man of the modern world.

Revueltas knew of cultural and technological affairs in the United States, since much of his academic training took place there. From 1913 until 1918, he studied at St. Edward College in Austin, Texas.[5] From 1918 until 1920, he was a student at the Chicago Musical College, and he returned to that city for studies in violin from 1922 until 1926. From then until 1928, he was active as a concert artist and conductor in the South, especially Alabama and Texas.

At the time of Revueltas's sojourns in the United States, a bond of cooperation was growing between Mexico and the United States. Having survived the expulsion of General Porfirio Diaz in 1911, the liberal but ineffective presidency of Francisco Madero who was assassinated in 1913, and the tumultuous teens, when Emiliano Zapata, Pancho Villa, Victoriano Huerta, and other rebels vied for power, the United States joined eight Latin American countries in 1915 to organize a stable government in Mexico. In 1917, Venustiano Carranza and a new constitution offered signs of hope, but Carranza, too, proved unable to control rival political factions and was assassinated in 1920. At this point, Alvaro Obregón was elected president. The United States supported his administration, which was eager to reconcile American and Mexican conflicts. His successor, Plutarco Calles, called for constitutional reforms, a rehabilitation of the Mexican economy, and a reduction of the power of the Roman Catholic Church. Soon after Obregón's reelection in 1928, he was assassinated by a disgruntled papist; nevertheless, the modernization of Mexico was underway. During the 1930s, Mexico tended toward liberal Socialism, and railways and other institutions were nationalized. Surprisingly, Mexico supported the Spanish Loyalists during the Civil War. In 1936, Franklin Roosevelt consolidated diplomatic progress by his Good Neighbor policy, which facilitated cultural interaction of the two nations.

Carlos Chávez also benefited from increasingly congenial relations with the United States. Returning from his trip to Europe in 1922–23, he stopped briefly in New York City. His European tour put him in touch with recent music by Schönberg, Stravinsky, and Les Six, but the musical scene in New York City impressed him too. Soon, he decided to make an extended visit to the Empire State. During that visit, from 1926 until 1928, he met most of the important musicians resident in New York City at the time: Henry Cowell, Roy Harris, Edgard Varèse, and Aaron Copland.

When Chávez returned to Mexico, he gave the first performances of the new repertoire he had learned. In the summer of 1928, filled with enthusiasm and surrounded by eager colleagues, he was appointed by the government as director of the Orquesta Sinfónica de Mexico. In this capacity, Chávez had an ideal situation for advancing his program of reforms in Mexican musical culture. Expansion of his influence came with his appointment as director of Mexico's national conservatory of music in that same year. From 1929 until 1935, Revueltas was the assistant conductor to Chávez. Initially, the relationship was a congenial one, and Chávez encouraged Revueltas to compose. Later, they became rivals, and Revueltas organized his own ensemble, the Orquesta Sinfónica Nacional.

Carlos Chávez

Of Revueltas's three string quartets (1930–1931) and roughly a dozen orchestral tone poems, the most frequently performed is *Sensemayá* (1938), which was inspired by the poem "Chant for Killing a Snake" by the Afro-Cuban writer Nicolás Guillén.

Mayombe—bombe—mayombe!
Mayombe—bombe
The snake with its glassy eyes
comes and coils around a tree.
The glassy-eyed snake
coiled around and around the tree.

Originally, Revueltas had wanted a vocalist with chamber orchestra, but he changed the plan and wrote a purely instrumental work with an impressive array of percussion including tympani, piano, xylophone, claves, maracas, raspador, gourd, small Indian drum, bass drum, high and low tom-toms, cymbals, high and low gongs, glockenspiel, and celesta. This emphasis on percussion may have been influenced by the Cuban mulatto composer Amadeo Roldán (1900–1939). In his six *Rítmicas* (1930), Roldán not only explored Afro-Cuban rhythms, but in the fifth and sixth, wrote for an ensemble composed exclusively of percussion, the first composer to do so.

Sadly, Revueltas died before realizing his potential. A dissolute lifestyle combined with poverty and alcoholism led to his death on 5 October 1940, the day after the premiere of his children's ballet *El renacuajo paseador* (the travelling pollywog).

Revueltas's disputes with Chávez did not distract the latter from his work even momentarily. He wrote symphonic works, chamber music, ballets, choral pieces, and music for solo piano in abundance, despite his responsibilities as conductor of the Orquestra Sinfónica, a post that he held until 1949, when he was succeeded by José Pablo Moncayo.

In the fall of 1932, Copland visited Chávez in Mexico for four months.[6] One of the results was Copland's *Short Symphony* (1934), which was premiered by and dedicated to Chávez. Another was Copland's first striking example of Americana—albeit South Americana—*El Salón México*. Copland's numerous professional visits to Mexico, in 1947, '53, '62, and '72, were also noteworthy.[7]

Of Chávez's symphonies, the second, entitled *Sinfonia India* (1935) is the best known. The Indian themes, to which the title refers, grow out of the changing-meter Introduction: The first theme is a tune of Huichol Indians from Nayarit, the second and third are Yaqui tunes from the Sonora region, and the concluding theme of the entire symphony is a Seri Indian melody. Structurally, Chávez uses sonata form as the basis of this piece, but the development of themes takes place immediately rather than being reserved for a separate portion of the work. The third theme serves as the slow movement, and the final theme is positioned within a recapitulatory passage.

In this piece and other works, Chávez used modes, pentatonic scales, quartal harmonies, changing meters, and repetitious motifs, stylistic elements that he felt were inherent in the music of Native Americans. Though ethnomusicologists may question the accuracy of Chávez's suppositions, the issue seems irrelevant: The musical idiom that Chávez achieved is distinctive and sincere, and it will endure with or without archival validation.[8]

Copland's liaisons with Chávez and Mexico made him an ideal cultural attaché for Inter-American affairs during the Second World War. As a member of the cultural committee to Latin America organized by Nelson Rockefeller, Copland's

> four-month mission included lecturing on American music in person and on the radio, performing his own music, investigating local talent (especially with an eye for composers who would make good candidates for in-kind visits to the United States), and . . . promoting cultural relations in the context of the nation's Pan-American wartime efforts.[9]

As a talent-scout, Copland surveyed the South American musical landscape in considerable depth. He identified many promising young composers, such as Camargo Guarnieri (Brazil), José María Castro and Juan Carlos Paz (Argentina), Domingo Santa Cruz (Chile), Hector Tosar (Uruguay), José Ardéval and Gilberto Valdés (Cuba), Antonio Esteves (Venezuela), and Hector Campos-Parsi (Puerto Rico).[10]

As the head of the composition department at the Berkshire Music Center (i.e., Tanglewood), Copland had opportunities to invite many of these composers to share their works with young American students. The most prominent guest selected from among the established composers was Villa-Lobos. From the younger group, Copland helped to bring Campos-Parsi, Tosar, and Ginastera, among others.

Ginastera was a problematic composer. The first problem had to do with the pronunciation of his name. Though he allowed that the G might be pronounced like the J in "Jose," his preference was to pronounce it in the Italian manner, like the G in "Giovanni."

The second problem with Ginastera had to do with his musical style and the Argentinean government. Early works, like the ballets *Panambí* (1935) and *Estancia* (the big ranch; 1941) used nationalistic elements in a conventional idiom. *Panambí*, the composer's official Opus 1, is a story of love and magic based on Guaraní Indian legends in a scenario by Felix L. Errico. Its emphasis on prehistoric ritual and ceremony owes a debt to Stravinsky's *Le sacre du printemps*.

Estancia, a series of tableaux devoted to Argentine rural life, was commissioned by Lincoln Kirstein and the American Ballet Caravan. Because the Caravan was discontinued in 1942, the premiere of *Estancia* was delayed for ten years; however, Ginastera's four-movement suite that was taken from it made a favorable impression at its premiere in 1943.

In its complete version, *Estancia* includes recitations of three poems from José Hernández's *Martin Fierro*.[11] In these texts, which are ruminations about the *gaucho*'s way of life, first at dawn, then at around noon, and finally at night, the guitar is a poetic image. Ginastera picks up on the idea in the piano part by using the pitches of the open strings of the guitar: E-A-D-G-B-E.

The *Estancia Suite* consists of four scenes, "Los trabadores agricolas" (the farmers), "Danza del trigo" (dance of the wheat), "Los peones de hacienda" (workers of the ranch), and "Danza final" (final dance). In the ballet, this last scene is danced only by the men, and in such an energetic way as to exhaust the dancers. The last man able to carry on the dance is the winner. This type of dance (an example of the *malambo*, characterized by changing meters of 3/4 and 6/8) is an element of the *gaucho* tradition that pervades the score of *Estancia*.

Ginastera's works of the '30s and '40s exhibit strongly nationalistic elements. During the '50s and '60s, his style became more experimental. He used modified serial techniques, experimented with classical forms of Western music, employed *Sprechstimme*, and began writing operas.

His First Piano Concerto (1961), a commission from the Koussevitzky Foundation, is a striking work. The first movement begins with a serial cluster that becomes the basis of a wild cadenza for piano and orchestra. The serial premise is developed in ten variations and a coda. The second movement is a pointillistic scherzo (*allucinante*, or "hallucinating") in the conventional A-B-A plan, but with an introduction and coda. The third movement, Adagissimo, contrasts with the fourth movement, a furious Toccata that brings the work to its close. The juxtaposition of the third and fourth movements was suggested by the contrast between the final two movements of Beethoven's Ninth. In fact, Ginastera's Second Piano Concerto (1972) uses a twelve-tone row derived from the dissonance with which Beethoven begins the Finale (i.e., a tutti B-flat major chord played as an appoggiatura against a single A—scale degree 5 in the key of D). The Second Piano Concerto also alludes to Ravel's Piano Concerto in D for left hand alone, since the second movement of Ginastera's piece is written in the same manner.

Opera does not appear in Ginastera's output until the 1960s; then, in rapid succession, he composed *Don Rodrigo* (1964), *Bomarzo* (1967), and *Beatrix Cenci* (1971). In their scenarios, these works show affinity to early twentieth-century Expressionism, especially Berg's operas *Wozzeck* and *Lulu*. The symmetrical design of *Don Rodrigo*, with three acts of three scenes each, separated by interludes, stems from Berg's design of *Wozzeck*. The explicit sex, violence, and psychological cruelty of *Bomarzo* led the mayor of Buenos Aires to cancel its premiere there, which was to have taken place in August of 1967. This may account for its subsequent success in

New York and Washington, D.C., as well as Ginastera's decision to leave Argentina and move to Geneva for the remainder of his life.

In 1975, he composed the *Turbæ ad Passionem Gregorianam* (mob choruses for the Gregorian Passion), which uses plainchant for the soloists and extended vocal techniques for the polyphonic choruses of the mob scenes. Its contrast of monody and polyphony is similar to that in the three Passion settings of Heinrich Schütz, which Ginastera may have known, but Ginastera's work is a theatrical, rather than practical, composition.

Ginastera composed some noteworthy chamber music too, especially his three string quartets (1948, '58, '73). The Second String Quartet is a watershed work in which he used neo-Expressionistic and modified serial techniques for the first time. The Third String Quartet requires a soprano soloist, an idea that, according to Ginastera, was inspired by Schönberg's Second String Quartet in F-sharp, Op. 10. At the time of his death, Ginastera was at work on a fourth quartet—this one requiring a baritone soloist to sing the text of Beethoven's "Heiligenstadt Testament."

Ginastera's estate included more than his music. He was active as a teacher, and his influence continued through his students. One of the most fascinating of them was Astor Piazzolla (1921–1992), who was born in Mar del Plata, Argentina, relocated to New York City with his Italian parents at the age of four, returned to Argentina in 1937, and changed residences occasionally throughout his life.

Piazzolla's initial contact with Ginastera is one of those stories that seems too bizarre to be true. It was the piano virtuoso Artur Rubinstein who brought it about: Rubinstein was visiting Buenos Aires in 1942. Piazzolla went to his hotel, found his room, and played a sample of his music for Rubinstein. Impressed, Rubinstein tried to arrange for Piazzolla to study with Juan José Castro, but Castro's schedule was full. He recommended that Piazzolla study with Ginastera. At this point, the twenty-six-year-old Ginastera had no teaching experience; nevertheless, Piazzolla continued his studies with Ginastera for the next five years.[12]

At the same time he was studying with Ginastera, Piazzolla was acquiring valuable practical experiences performing with many ensembles (including that of Anibal Troilo), writing incidental music for films and such, and doing arranging for any paying customers. He also composed a symphony that was premiered by Fabien Sevitzky.[13]

Piazzolla wrote in a wide variety of genres. In early works like his Suite (1943) for harp and strings and the Suite (1949) for oboe and string orchestra, he made an effort to write in the respected Western European genres.[14] He was embarrassed about ethnic idioms and instruments. As a mature composer, however, his tangos won him fame. Piazzolla elevated the tango to a higher level, as Chopin had done with the *mazurka*. His tangos contain striking dissonances, chromaticism, virtuosity, counterpoint, jazz, and other elements that were alien to the genre. Sometimes he changed the conventional instrumentation, going so far as to add electric guitar.

Among Piazzolla's more astonishing tangos is one for 'cello and piano called *Le grand tango* (1982; rev. 1990) written for Mstislav Rostropovich. The piece—not a commission—was the spontaneous result of Piazzolla's admiration. Piazzolla sent it to Rostrapovich, but the 'cellist did not look at it until eight years later. When he did, he arranged a rehearsal with Piazzolla, made changes in the 'cello part, and took the piece into his repertoire.[15]

The tango as a genre already had a long and varied history by the time of Piazzolla's activity. Both a song and a dance, the tango has a mixed background, but certainly one of the most important elements is the habanera. Like the tango, it is in duple meter, usually with dotted rhythms on the first beat with the second divided into two equal units.

Old-style tango, known as *canyengue*, originated during the late nineteenth century among immigrants from Italy. These tangos were often vocal pieces with octosyllabic recitations flavored by contemporaneous European salon music. This was the music of *mestizos*, of the downtrodden and illiterate, and it had no lofty cultural associations; consequently, it was viewed condescendingly by society's upper crust. The *canyengue* interacted with the *milonga*, a genre that dates back to the mid-nineteenth-century *gauchos*. Comparable to Texas Blues, the *milonga* is often sentimental and moody. Rhythmically, it tends to be complex in its juxtaposition of duple-compound-meter guitar accompaniments with poetically inspired rhythms in the vocal parts. The *tango canción*, as the name implies, is always sung. In the early twentieth century, the texts almost invariably viewed "love and life in highly pessimistic, fatalistic, and often pathologically dramatic" ways.[16]

Many early tangos are scored for a trio of flute, violin, and guitar. Sometimes accordion replaced the guitar. In the early twentieth century, the trio was frequently altered to include violin, bandoneon, and piano. During the 1930s, popular bands and radio orchestras made this music into a commercial commodity. The fluid rhythms of the older styles were simplified into a square meter of two quarter notes per measure, and the subtle inflections of *milonga* melodies were regularized in the strongly rhythmic tangos of the 1920s and '30s. This type of tango was the prevalent type during Piazzolla's formative years, and Piazzolla was himself a bandoneon player.[17] Piazzolla is now internationally known as the composer who developed the *nuevo tango*—the new tango; but when he did, he was considered a sort of musical heretic. In fact, his "tangos" were so shocking that, in order to avoid controversy, he referred to them as "music of Buenos Aires."

Piazzolla's change of heart about his ethnic popular music is another one of those stories that seems too bizarre to be true. It was the French pedagogue Nadia Boulanger who brought it about.

Notes

1. The *cavaco* is a four- to six-stringed instrument with frets of Portuguese origin. Its smaller version, called *cavaquinho* or sometimes *machete*, was taken by sailors to Hawaii,

where it is known as the *ukulele*. There are many different types of *chocalos* (rattles); some are made of wood, others of metal or other materials. Dried gourds are frequently used.

2. Gerard Béhague, *Music in Latin America: An Introduction* (Englewood Cliffs, New Jersey: Prentice Hall, 1979), p. 186. For a detailed discussion of these and other issues, see Béhague's *Heitor Villa-Lobos: The Search for Brazil's Musical Soul* (Austin, Texas: Institute of Latin American Studies, 1994).

3. Some sources reckon a total of sixteen by counting the *Introdução aos chôros*.

4. David Appleby comes close in the list of works and discography in *Heitor Villa-Lobos: A Bio-Bibliography* (New York: Greenwood Press, 1988).

5. An all-male college founded in 1876.

6. See Howard Pollack, *Aaron Copland: The Life and Work of an Uncommon Man* (New York: Henry Holt, 1999), pp. 223–228.

7. Pollack, *Aaron Copland*, p. 226.

8. Chávez was the Charles Eliot Norton Lecturer at Harvard University during the 1958–59 academic year. His æsthetics are advanced in the series of lectures entitled *Musical Thought* (Cambridge, Massachusetts: Harvard, 1960).

9. Pollack, *Aaron Copland*, p. 228.

10. This listing gives only highlights from Pollack's more extensive roster. See his *Aaron Copland*, pp. 228–233.

11. The only complete recording of *Estancia*, including the poetic recitations, is by Gisèle Ben-Dor with the London Symphony Orchestra. The complete score of *Panambí* is on the same recording: (London: Conifer Records, 1998), CD 75605-51336-2. In the several instances where Ginastera's suites differ from the original scores, Ben-Dor uses the more brilliant readings of the suite versions.

12. María Susana Azzi and Simon Collier, *Le grand tango: The Life and Music of Astor Piazzolla* (New York: Oxford, 2000), p. 29. This fascinating book is the most extensive study of Piazzolla available, but it suffers from small print and a general lack of precision. This and other references to Ginastera are not properly indexed.

13. Fabien (1891–1967) was the nephew of Serge Koussevitzky. Like his uncle, Fabien was a double bassist and conductor. In order to avoid confusion, Serge suggested the truncated name "Sevitzky." Fabien emigrated from Russia with his wife, Maria, in 1923. They settled first in Mexico, but moved in that same year to the U.S.A. From 1923 until 1930, he played in the Philadelphia Orchestra. His principal career, after naturalization in 1928, was as director of the Indianapolis Symphony Orchestra from 1937 until 1955.

14. The dates here are taken from Miguel Ficher et al., *Latin American Classical Composers: A Biographical Dictionary* (Lanham, Maryland: Scarecrow Press, 1996), pp. 272–273. Cliff Eisen's article for the *New Grove Dictionary*, 2d ed., asserts that Piazzolla's works number at least 750; however, no work list is provided. (See vol. 19, p. 701.). Azzi, *Le grand tango*, likewise lacks a work list.

15. I have deduced the dates from Azzi, *Le grand tango*, pp. 228–229.

16. Gerard Béhague, "Tango," *New Grove Dictionary of Music and Musicians*, 2d ed. (London: Macmillan, 2001), vol. 25, pp. 73–75.

17. A square accordion operated with buttons.

Chapter 7

Nadia Boulanger, 1887–1979

Teaching and music were in Nadia Boulanger's blood from childhood. Her father, Ernest Boulanger, was a composer of operas and choral music as well as a faculty member of the Paris Conservatoire, as his father had been before him.[1] Her mother, Raïsa Myschetsky, was a soprano whom Ernest met during his tour of Russia in 1874. After moving to Paris, she studied voice with him, and later they married.

The Boulanger home in Montmartre was a haven for artists. Gounod, Massenet, and Fauré were frequent visitors, along with the librettist Jules Barbier. Juliette Nadia Boulanger had a younger sister, Lili, who was born in 1893. The entire family, including young Nadia, devoted their energies to the girl's musical education. Their efforts were successful, and Lili was the first woman to win the Prix de Rome. Her talent was manifested primarily in a handful of psalm settings and the cantata *Faust et Hélène*, but she died in 1918 before her potential could be realized.

In 1896, Nadia entered the Conservatoire. Having had private organ lessons with Louis Vierne, she was comfortable at the keyboard, and her skills at accompanying and sightreading became legendary. By 1898 she had won first prize in the solfège class.[2]

When Ernest Boulanger died in 1900, Nadia had a new motivation for success: She had to support her family—or at least, contribute to the economic resources. At thirteen, she entered the piano accompaniment class in the fall of 1900 (youngest in the class). In 1901 she won second prize in harmony class, and then, in 1903, she took the first prize.

She continued private organ studies with Alexandre Guilmant. Fauré, who was organist at the Church of the Madeleine at the time, frequently called upon Nadia when he needed a substitute. At about this same time, she began composition lessons with Andre Gédalge, Fauré's assistant. She was simultaneously auditing Fauré's composition classes and was formally admitted to these several years later. Her circle of friends included the composers André Caplet, Marcel Dupré, Enesco, Koechlin, Ravel, and Schmitt, as well as the music historian and organist Joseph Bonnet. Her Conservatoire days ended in July 1904. By then she had won the prizes in composition, fugue, accompaniment, and organ.

In that same year, Boulanger began teaching. Performance commitments also filled her time, and she participated in programs of contemporary and early music in addition to substituting for Fauré at the Madeleine.

She continued to audit classes at the Conservatoire, especially the composition class of Charles Marie Widor. Her diligence paid off, and in 1908 she won the Prix de Rome competition: To her disappointment, it was the *second* prize. In that year, she composed the eight songs entitled *Les heures claires* (the hours of light) in collaboration with the pianist Raoul Pugno.[3]

1909 marked the first full season of Serge Diaghileff's Ballets Russes. He garnered financial support from the Princesse Edmond de Polignac, a woman whose voracious appetite for things artistic put her in proximity not only with Diaghileff, but also with Jean Cocteau, Stravinsky, Fauré, de Falla, and, of course, Nadia herself.[4]

The premiere of *L'oiseau de feu* must have been an inspiration to Boulanger, who spotted at once the genius of its creator.[5] Her own compositional efforts at the time were again in collaboration with Pugno. This time, the project was a more ambitious one. In February of 1914, the Opéra-Comique committed to a November production of *La ville mort*, an opera based on a novel by Gabriele D'Annunzio with a libretto by the author himself. The score was pulled from rehearsal in August of 1914 when France mobilized for war.[6]

Most composers are also conductors. It was for the purpose of introducing one of her own compositions that Boulanger wielded a baton on stage for the first time: This was in April of 1912, when she conducted excerpts of her Prix de Rome cantata, *La sirène* (siren; 1908). Boulanger went on to become the first woman to direct leading orchestras throughout Europe and the United States.[7]

During the war, Boulanger worked generously for social welfare programs: Lili and Nadia both raised money to support struggling musicians. Much of the funding came from American donors. These were important contacts for Boulanger, and in later years, when she visited the United States, many of these same individuals continued their benefactions. In France, a group called La Société Régénératrice (Society for regeneration [of morals]) called for help from Boulanger, who responded with a powerful piece for piano solo, *Vers la vie nouvelle* (toward the new life).[8] The international Walter Damrosch—German by birth, a United States citizen by naturalization, and an admirer of French culture—spotted an opportunity to contribute, and founded the American Friends of Musicians in France.[9] Damrosch gave free concerts in France during the war, and for one of these, he selected Saint-Saëns's Third Symphony for organ and orchestra. Boulanger was the soloist; the concert was a success; and the affiliation among Boulanger, Damrosch, and the United States was confirmed. Boulanger's American friends were

Nadia Boulanger

among the most influential people in the nation. Besides Damrosch, there were: the architect Whitney Warren; William Kissam Vanderbilt, the grandson of Cornelius Vanderbilt and founder of the Vanderbilt clinic; Henry Clay Frick, the colleague of Andrew Carnegie and later president of U. S. Steel, who bequested his art collection, his mansion on 5th Avenue, and an endowment of $15 million to the city of New York; and John D. Rockefeller. To these illustrious names, others famous primarily at the windows of early-twentieth-century bank tellers could be added. When World War I came to a halt in November of 1918, the bonds of friendship between Boulanger and her Americans continued.

With the return of peace, the pianist Alfred Cortot joined with August Mangeot to found the École Normale de Musique. Boulanger was invited to join the faculty—along with Wanda Landowska, one of the most active advocates of the early music movement at the time. Mangeot, who was also editor of the *Monde musical*, asked Boulanger to be a critic for his journal. As a result, she had access to most concerts, composers, performers, and arts organizations. It was a chance for her to broaden her horizons as well as to exert her own influence in shaping the musical landscape.

In 1921, Francis Casadesus, acting as principal administrator, assembled a faculty featuring Boulanger, Paul Vidal, Isidore Philipp, Lucien Capet, André Hekking, and Marcel Grandjany. From that year until 1979, Boulanger was at work at the École de Fontainebleau, a summer program primarily for foreign students, that was housed in the Louis XIV wing of the royal château in the town of Fontainebleau. In 1953, she became its general director.

The list of Boulanger's students—both at Fontainebleau and later during her visits to the United States[10]—contains some of the most prominent figures in twentieth-century music: Douglas Moore, Virgil Thomson, Copland, Marc Blitzstein, Lennox Berkeley, Roy Harris, Roger Sessions, Ross Lee Finney, Soulima Stravinsky, Elie Siegmeister, Elliott Carter, David Diamond, Claudio Spies, Ned Rorem, Gian Carlo Menotti, Karel Husa, Thea Musgrave, George Wilson, Don Harris, Easley Blackwood, Luise Talma, Daniel Pinkham, Piazzolla, Julia Perry, and Quincy Jones.

Boulanger became a musical guide for many aspiring American musicians. George Gershwin had hoped to be admitted to her studio, but she declined. Sessions and Copland, who jointly sponsored concerts of new music in New York, regularly consulted with Boulanger on programming.[11] The journal *Musical America* sent Irving Weil to interview her and report on her musical activities.

Performers too, many of them legendary now, eagerly solicited her advice: Ruth Slenczynska, Yehudi Menuhin, and Constantin (i.e., Dinu) Lipatti were among them.

Composers in Europe also sought Boulanger's opinions. Stravinsky became one of her closest friends, and he sometimes sent her copies of new works before they had been published or performed. In 1935, when Dukas died, his position as chair of composition at the Paris Conservatoire was taken over jointly by Boulanger and Stravinsky. In 1932, she was inducted to the Legion of Honor.[12]

Boulanger combined her roles as conductor and teacher. For her, the podium was a vehicle for setting the musical standards of the musicians who performed with her; it was also a venue for forming the musical standards of the general public. She had great success with her performances of Bach cantatas—unfamiliar repertoire at the time; Fauré's Requiem was hardly known outside of France until she popularized the piece in Great Britain and the United States; she dusted off the Monteverdi madrigals and let the public hear a bit of the early Italian Baroque; she even conducted Heinrich Schütz's austere but fascinating *St. Matthew Passion.*[13]

Her podium proselytizing included the modernists, too. She obtained a commission from the Princesse de Polignac for Lennox Berkeley's *Dithyramb and Hymn.* In 1937, during a visit to the United States, she obtained from Mr. and Mrs. Robert Woods Bliss a commission for Stravinsky to write the Concerto in E-flat, now known as *Dumbarton Oaks*, the name of their mansion. Boulanger conducted the premiere on 8 May 1938.

With the outbreak of World War II, Boulanger fled to the United States. Stravinsky had done the same. Boulanger's friend Serge Koussevitzky was already well established as the conductor of the Boston Symphony. Many of her older American friends were still on the scene. She waited out the war teaching at Peabody, the Longy School, and Edgewood College; cavorting with Vera and Igor Stravinsky; performing and premiering new works—like Stravinsky's Sonata for two pianos. At war's end, she decided to go back to France: She arrived there in January of 1946, and was appointed Professor of *accompagnement* at the Conservatoire National de Musique, a position that she held until her retirement in 1957. From that time until her death, she continued teaching at her home in Paris and at the summer school at Fontainebleau. Remarkably, the musics of her various students reveal no familial similarities. The graduates of the "Boulangerie" maintained their individuality. In all probability, many of her students had experiences with her like the following one involving Piazzolla's discovery of his distinctive gift:

"This music is well written," she told him, "but it lacks feeling." . . . She asked him what music he played in Argentina. Piazzolla reluctantly admitted it was the tango. "I love that music!" she exclaimed. "But you don't play the piano to perform tangos. What instrument *do* you play?" . . . Piazzolla could barely bring himself to tell her it was the bandoneon. Boulanger reassured him: she had heard the instrument in

Kurt Weill, and said that even Stravinsky appreciated its qualities. Finally, Boulanger persuaded Piazzolla to play one of his tangos on the piano. . . . At the eighth bar she stopped him, took him by his hands, and told him firmly: "This is Piazzolla! Don't ever leave it!" In later recollections, he was always to describe the moment as something like an epiphany: "She helped me find myself."[14]

Notes

1. The most detailed biography is Léonie Rosenstiel, *Nadia Boulanger: A Life in Music* (New York: Norton, 1982), pp. 12–13.

2. Rosenstiel, *Nadia Boulanger*, p. 38.

3. The poems were written by Emile Verhaeren. They are, in order, "Le ciel en nuit s'est déplié," "Avec mes sens, avec mon cœur," "Vous m'avez dit," "Que tes yeux claires, tes yeux d'été," "C'était en Juin," "Ta bonté," "Roses de Juin," and "S'il arrive jamais." They are recorded in *Lieder und Kammermusik: Nadia Boulanger* (Germany: Trouba Disc, 1993), TRO-CD 01407.

4. For a photograph of Nadia with Princesse de Polignac, see Jerome Spycket, *Nadia Boulanger*; trans. M. M. Shriver (Stuyvesant, New York: Pendragon Press, 1992), p. 78. Boulanger's activities at de Polignac's salon are examined in Jeanice Brooks, "Nadia Boulanger and the Salon of the Princesse de Polignac," *Journal of the American Musicological Society* 30 (fall 1993), 415–468.

5. Rosenstiel, *Nadia Boulanger*, pp. 90–91.

6. Selections from the opera were presented by the Paris Radio in 1955. See Spycket, *Nadia Boulanger*, p. 130. Before turning her attention to *La ville mort*, Boulanger had composed several chansons: "Larme solitaire," "Ne jure pas!," "Mélancolie," and "Pour toi," all translations of poems by Heinrich Heine, and one on a text by Georges Delaquys entitled "Chanson." Most of the works that were published during her lifetime were issued by Heugel et Cie.

7. Her experience as the first woman to conduct the Boston Symphony Orchestra is detailed in Rosenstiel, *Nadia Boulanger*, p. 289. In 1939, she also conducted the New York Philharmonic, the Philadelphia Orchestra, and the National Symphony.

8. The piece was published privately by Mme. Rivachovsky. See Rosenstiel, *Nadia Boulanger*, p. 131. Its opening ostinato figures are irregular in their melodic contours. The ensuing section is an ominous dialogue between bass and soprano with hand crossings over incessant arpeggio figures that change subtly as the piece progresses. Three staffs—*à la* Debussy—are used in the score.

9. Walter Damrosch is probably best known as the man responsible for the construction of Carnegie Hall. He also conducted the New York Symphony, the New York Oratorio Society, and the Metropolitan Opera.

10. She taught at the Longy School in Cambridge, Massachusetts, and the Peabody Conservatory in Baltimore, among others.

11. Rosenstiel, *Nadia Boulanger*, p. 225.

12. Roger-Ducasse actively sought the award on her behalf. See Spycket, *Nadia Boulanger*, p. 81.

13. Boulanger's performance of the Fauré *Requiem* at Queen's Hall on 24 November 1936 was its premiere in that country. See Rosenstiel, *Nadia Boulanger*, p. 267. She recorded selections from Monteverdi, and many of these have been reissued. For the Schütz, originally an *a capella* work, she composed instrumental accompaniments. Ibid., p. 268.

14. Azzi, *Le grand tango*, p. 51.

Chapter 8

The Years of World War I: Stravinsky, Part II

The score of *Les noces* (weddings) gave Stravinsky more trouble than anything previously. When he began it in 1914, he envisioned a large orchestra like that of his earlier ballets. Wartime economics and his removal to Switzerland contributed to his decision to rethink the piece, and in 1917, he rescored it for two cymbaloms, pianola, harmonium, and percussion in addition to the solo vocal and choral forces. In 1923, he decided on the definitive version: four pianos, percussion, solo voices, and chorus.

During the compositional process, Stravinsky had his first encounter with the music of Domenico Scarlatti and the neoclassical movement. In April of 1917, he, Diaghileff, Picasso, and Massine went to Italy for a production of *The Good-Humored Ladies* with Scarlatti's music orchestrated by Vincenzo Tommasini. Not long after, at the suggestion of Diaghileff, Stravinsky assembled various pieces by Giovanni Battista Pergolesi and other Baroque composers, orchestrated them, and worked the pieces into the ballet *Pulcinella* (1919). "Stravinsky at first thought that [Diaghileff was] mad. At the time he knew little of Pergolesi's music except the *Stabat Mater* and *La serva padrona*, neither of which interested him in the least."[1] Still, the excitement of the four performances of *The Good-Humored Ladies*, staged in Rome at the Teatro Costanzi to aid the Italian Red Cross, the special settings provided by Giacomo Balla for *L'oiseau de feu*, which was also featured on the opening program, Stravinsky's first meeting with Pablo Picasso—all of these proved too enticing for Stravinsky. He assumed, at least for a time, the temperament of Italy.[2]

Musically, Stravinsky has inserted his own *persona* into these Baroque scores. No one could mistake this music for authentic Italian Baroque repertoire; nevertheless, Stravinsky did make certain adjustments to suggest the sound world of eighteenth-century Italy: His orchestra excludes clarinets; soprano, tenor, and bass vocal soloists are required, and they sing in Italian. Most important, Stravinsky displays an economy and sleekness that his earlier music had lacked. This last idea influenced virtually all of his later scores.

The characters of *Pulcinella* are based on improvised, stereotyped characters of Italian *comedia del'arte*. This approach enabled Stravinsky to break free from the dramatic conventions of the nineteenth century, which too often belabored details. Stravinsky's scenarios present us with freeze-frame pictures. This abstract conception of theater pervades many of Stravinsky's later dramatic works, such as *Oedipus Rex* (1927) and *The Rake's Progress* (1951).

Les noces, in all three versions, includes another abstract element: Stravinsky's first extensive use of the octatonic scale. This scale, composed of alternating whole steps and half steps, is an artificial scale. While the octatonic scale may focus on a single pitch as its tonal center, that pitch may change easily. The insistence—by repetition—upon one leading tone's movement to a focus pitch results in a score in which a limited collection of motifs provides the fundamental melodic ideas. These motifs are expanded or contracted by additive rhythms; consequently, the score is unified by its steady pulse, but the meters and tonal orientation change constantly. Stravinsky piles layer upon layer, motif upon motif, meter upon meter, and constructs a score of dazzling complexity and intricacy.

Stravinsky spent World War I in Switzerland so that he could continue his work. There, in the fall of 1915, he met Charles Ferdinand Ramuz, a Swiss novelist who wrote in French. Ramuz, even though he knew no Russian, made the French poem for *Les noces* based upon Stravinsky's explanations of the original, Russian texts. Next they began work on *Histoire du soldat* (the soldier's tale; 1918).

The underlying principle of *Histoire* was simplicity. The cast would include only a handful of characters; the instrumental ensemble would be modest; and the production would have to be flexible enough to work in a small theater—perhaps even a public meeting hall or some similar facility.

The *dramatis personæ* include the narrator, the soldier, and the devil. Another character, the princess, is a silent role for a dancer. The instrumental ensemble consists of clarinet, bassoon, cornet *à pistons*, trombone, violin, double bass, and a percussionist who plays two side drums, bass drum, cymbals, tambourine, and triangle. The music is about half an hour in duration.

Histoire du soldat incorporates popular elements along with parodies of classical works, especially in Part Two. After the "Soldier's March," which was heard earlier in Part One, the "Royal March" is a virtuosic showpiece for cornet using the rhythms of a Spanish *paso doble*, a popular, march-like dance in moderate duple meter. In scene V, the Princess (hitherto in a neurostatic state) awakens from her profound slumber to dance, in succession, a tango, then a waltz, and finally, a ragtime. Later in the scene, Stravinsky parodies the well known Lutheran chorale tune "Ein feste Burg ist unser Gott" in both the "Little Chorale" and the "Great Chorale."

Notes

1. Eric Walter White, *Stravinsky: The Composer and His Works*, 2d ed. (Berkeley and Los Angeles: University of California Press, 1979), p. 283.
2. Stravinsky's empathy with Italy was not as transient as this passage might suggest: His funeral service took place in Venice on 15 April 1971, and he was buried on the island of San Michele, near the grave of Diaghileff.

Chapter 9

An Italian Interlude: Music at the Time of Stravinsky's Visit

In the opening decade of the twentieth century, Italy, more than any other country, was bogged down by the fetters of lingering Romanticism. Giuseppe Verdi (1813–1901) not only lived past the close of the nineteenth century, but he continued to write into the final decade of that century: His last opera, *Falstaff*, dates from 1893; his magnificent set of sacred choral works, the *Quatro pezzi sacre* (four sacred pieces), was completed still later, in 1898. It would be both unfair and inaccurate to suggest that Verdi's style remained stagnant. Indeed, his late works reveal new, interesting ideas: The unusual instrumentations that he uses in *Otello* (1887) show that he became increasingly sensitive in using timbre for characterization. Striking, too, is the artificial scale (*scala enigmatica*) consisting of the tones C, D-flat, E, F-sharp (ascending) / F (descending), G-sharp, A-sharp, B, C that he used as the basis of his "Ave Maria" in the *Pezzi sacre*. The remarkably elegant voice leading of this score, incidentally, was inspired by the music of Giovanni Pierluigi da Palestrina. These progressive and neoclassical elements of Verdi's music, however, had little impact on Italian music at the close of the century. The great crowd-pleasers—*Rigoletto* (1851), *Il trovatore* (troubadour; 1852), and *La traviata* (the wanton woman; 1853)—were more powerful as anchors in the past than his late works were as enticements into the future.

Verdi's headlock on Italian musical style was complemented by the power over Italian musical culture exercised by Giulio Ricordi (1840–1912). Casa Ricordi, the family publishing business, issued the staples of Italian Romantic opera. Their catalog included the works of Rossini, Donizetti, and Bellini. Verdi joined their ranks in the 1840s—a development that left other Italian music publishers in a state of delirium. As the nineteenth century progressed, Ricordi absorbed numerous smaller publishers including Ferdinando Artaria e figlio (1837), Gaetano Longo (1840), Giorgio Del Monaco (1887), Giovanni Gualberto Guidi (1887), Francesco Lucca (1888), and Escudier di Parigi (1889). In the twentieth century, Ricordi took over the firms of Alessandro Pigna (1902), Carlo Schmidt (1902), Beniamino Carelli (1905), Breyer di Buenos Aires (1924), and W. Mocchi (1929).[1]

Upon Verdi's death, Giacomo Puccini (1858–1924), who had already scored box office hits with *Manon Lescaut* (1893), *La bohème* (1896), and *Tosca* (1900), became the chief living composer in Ricordi's stable. These scores were soon followed by *Madama Butterfly* (1904), *La fanciulla del West* (girl of the [golden] west; 1910), *La rondine* (sparrow; 1917), and *Il trittico* (triptych; 1918), a series of three operas including "Il tabarro," "Suor Angelica," and "Gianni Schicchi." He was nearly done with *Turandot* when he died in 1924. Franco Alfano (1875–1954) made a completion, which was edited by Arturo Toscanini (1867–1957) and premiered by him in 1926.

Puccini had an uncanny ability to capture the essence of a personality or a character's mood in a concise musical portrait. Anger, humor, tenderness—he communicated each of these affections in a strikingly powerful yet concise way. Toward the end of the first act of *La bohème*, for example, Mimi and Rudolpho are trying to decide their plans for the evening. As one possibility after another is put forth, the diatonic A-major tonality of Mimi's previous aria, "Si, mi chiamono Mimi," gives way to rapidly changing and unpredictable harmonies that reflect the mental states of the two characters. This keen understanding of characters is not restricted to musical details. Consider that in the original libretto of *La bohème*, Illica and Giacosa had no biographical aria for Rudolpho. The addition of "Che gelida manina," probably at Puccini's recommendation, not only gives the tenor a magnificent aria in the first act, but it also makes believable the fact that the shy, delicate Mimi should open her heart to Rudolpho and reveal intimate personal details.

Puccini's operas are effective not only because of the aptness of the musical gestures that he associates with each of his characters, but also because of his keen sense of dramatic timing. Recollections of important motifs appear at the very moment where they will be most effective. These happen in a natural, almost conversational way—not in the symphonic manner that governs motivic recollections in Wagner's music dramas.

Telling, too, is Puccini's melodic gift. In the final act of the opera bearing her name, Manon's soliloquy "Sola, perduta, abbandonata" shows that by his mid thirties, Puccini had mastered a natural, clear, comprehensible declamatory style.[2]

In terms of form, Puccini's "arias" hardly merit the term. The words—often written by his principal librettists Luigi Illica and Giuseppe Giacosa, but sometimes by others—generate the forms. Puccini's music is never forced to conform to the requirements of some preconceived design. Melodies are often enforced through doubling by the entire first violin section; nevertheless, most of Puccini's music has a solid, contrapuntal structure in two parts. Sometimes, the harmonies are ingenious; at other times, unexpected; sometimes, downright adventurous.

The main reason why Puccini could, with impunity, employ advanced techniques such as dissonant harmonies, non-functional use of traditional sonorities,

Gian Carlo Menotti

and acrid instrumentation, was the presence of a strong scenario. The opening of Act II of *La bohème*, for example, includes chord streams, rapid changes in texture and meter, sudden dynamic shifts, and other elements that might be disconcerting in purely instrumental music. Within the context of the story, however, based on Henry Mürger's novel *Scènes de la vie de bohème*, these elements make sense, since we presume to be looking in on the town square of the Latin quarter. The diversity of the music is simply a reflection of the diversity of events taking place. (It is hard to imagine that Stravinsky did not have this scene in mind when he wrote the opening tableau of *Petroushka*.)

The continuation of the Puccini manner in the later twentieth century is most clearly apparent in the operas of Gian Carlo Menotti (b. 1911). He followed in Puccini's footsteps as a student from 1923 until 1927, at the Milan Conservatory. When his family emigrated to the United States of America, he continued work at the Curtis Institute in Philadelphia with Rosario Scalero. Menotti taught there from 1948 until 1955, but by that time his reputation had grown so much as a consequence of his scores for the *Medium* (1946), the *Consul* (1950), *Amahl and the Night Visitors* (1951), and the *Saint of Bleeker Street* (1954), that he left his teaching post. *Amahl* has the distinction of being the first opera written specifically for production on television, in which capacity it was tremendously successful. In 1958, he instituted the Spoletto Festival of Two Worlds, primarily for the presentation of his own works. Menotti writes his own librettos. He also wrote the libretto for *Vanessa* (1958) by Samuel Barber (1910–1981). In addition to Menotti's operas—of which these are just a few—he has written instrumental music, including four concertos and a symphony.

At the time Puccini wrote *La bohème*, the dominant type of Italian opera was *verismo* (realism). In retaliation against Ricordi, in 1888, the smaller firm of Sonzogno initiated a competition for young Italians. The rules restricted the scope of the operas to a single act. The most important opera stemming from the Concorso Sonzogno was *Cavalleria rusticana* (rustic chivalry), produced in Rome in May of 1890, by Pietro Mascagni (1863–1945).

Mascagni's music for *Cavalleria rusticana* is simple and direct. His characters are common people whose tragic lives we might read about in a newspaper. The basis of Mascagni's scenario was a short story by the same name written by Giovanni Verga, a native of Sicily, who wrote sympathetically about poverty and adversity in Sicily and Calabria, where droughts, poor transportation, earthquakes, and illiteracy hindered economic development.

Owing to the brevity of *Cavalleria rusticana*, it is usually paired with another one-act opera to provide a full evening's entertainment. Traditionally, another brutally realistic opera, *I pagliacci* (the clowns; 1892) by Ruggero Leoncavallo (1857–1919), is the companion piece. Together, these two operas represent the apex of Italian *verismo*.[3]

Puccini was well aware of the verist composers. He had been Mascagni's roommate when they were both students of Amilcare Ponchielli (1834–1886) at the Milan Conservatory. The influences of *verismo* are most apparent in Puccini's score of "Il tabarro." His operas reveal many other influences, too, for Puccini "studied carefully the scores of his leading contemporaries: Debussy, [Richard] Strauss, Stravinsky, Schönberg, and Hindemith."[4] Of the Strauss works, Puccini knew at least *Salome* (1905), which he heard Strauss conduct in Naples in 1908, and *Der Rosenkavalier* (bearer of the rose; 1911). Puccini was so taken with *Rosenkavalier* that he decided to try something along those lines himself: The result was *La rondine*.

Wagner was another important influence. In August 1889, Ricordi sent Puccini to Bayreuth to attend a performance of *Die Meistersinger*. He was there again in 1912 to experience *Parsifal*. He must have known *Die Walküre* as well: It is difficult to imagine that Turandot's pleading with her father to spare her from marriage to Calaf was not inspired by Brünnhilde's comparable address to Wotan just before he agrees to encircle her sleeping body with a ring of fire.

Ottorino Respighi (1879–1936) was also a prolific composer of opera. The comic *Re Enzo* of 1905 was first in the line of dramatic works from his pen that included *Semirama, Marie-Victorie*, the marionette opera *La bella dormante nel bosco* (sleeping beauty), *Belfagor, La campana sommersa* (the sunken bell), *Maria Egiziaca, La fiamma* (the flame), and *Lucrezia*. When Respighi died on 17 April 1936, the last-named opera was nearly complete: A brief portion of the final act remained to be done. This list excludes his realizations of operas by old Italian masters; he was particularly fascinated with the works of Claudio Monteverdi, and he made arrangements of both *Orfeo* and *Lamento di Arianna*. At a time when composers were seeking new styles of expression, Respighi's antiquarian work pointed the path to untapped resources from which he and many of his contemporaries drew.

The stream of operas coming from Italy in the early twentieth century resulted in an almost total neglect of instrumental music there. Respighi was unique among the Italians because he was equally active in the fields of instrumental music and opera. Having come to symphonic music from opera, however, his works are naturally dramatic and colorful. Subtle control over the panoply of changing textures and sonorities characteristic of Respighi's music was clearly his goal in the symphonic poems that he was to write during his Roman period. According to Elsa Respighi's biography of her husband, the programs of his Roman triptych were written after the fact; hence, it is clear that instrumentation is an integral element rather than a means for depicting programmatic details.

The manner in which Respighi cultivated his understanding of the subtleties of instrumental composition was a curious one. At about the time he completed his studies at the Liceo Musicale in his native Bologna, he began playing violin and viola there in the orchestra of the Teatro Communale. An impressario from the Imperial Theater in St. Petersburg visited Bologna and recruited Respighi for the Italian opera season (1900–01) in Russia; he returned to Russia in the following year for another engagement with the same orchestra. During his stay in Russia, Respighi learned the language fluently. As a keen cultural observer, he was inclined, after his experiences there, to show interest in Russian cultural activities. He worked with Serge Diaghileff on the ballet *La boutique fantasque* (the fantastic shop; 1919), for example. While in Russia, he visited Rimsky-Korsakoff. Rimsky, having perused several of the scores that the young Italian had brought, dismissed the rest of the would-be students and devoted the rest of the day to his new pupil. Respighi took only a few lessons from the Russian master, but they had lasting consequences.

In 1913, Respighi was appointed professor of composition at the Conservatorio di Santa Cecilia in Rome. The move from Bologna to Rome was a difficult one and, although Rome is the city in which he spent most of his productive years, Respighi was initially upset by the change of environment.

Despite the fact that his restless mood made it difficult for him to work, he composed the well known symphonic poem *Fontane di Roma* (fountains of Rome; 1916). The creation of this masterpiece was a cathartic experience. His misgivings about Rome arose primarily from fear, and, having overcome this inhibition for city life, he went on to produce two more symphonic poems related to his new home. These were *Pini di Roma* (pines of Rome; 1924) and *Feste Romane* (Roman festivals; 1928). It is upon this Roman triptych that Respighi's fame rests. Brilliant young conductors of the day including Arthur Nikisch, Serge Koussevitzky, Fritz Reiner, and, above all, Arturo Toscanini programmed these orchestral showpieces on their concert tours; consequently, Respighi quickly established an international reputation.

Respighi's prowess as an orchestrator was unsurpassed by any. Puccini, himself an orchestrator of the first rank, acknowledged this when he asked Respighi to attend a rehearsal in preparation for the Italian premiere in 1919 of *Il trittico*. Puccini was unhappy with the effect achieved by his own scoring of the orchestral reference to Frugola's cat in "Il tabarro." Having heard the passage, Respighi revised it to the satisfaction of his friend and colleague.

Respighi himself played violin and piano. His Sonata (1917) for those instruments is a unique and exquisite contribution to the chamber music repertoire. Its harmonic idiom stems from the late-Romantic era. Although Respighi's works from the year 1919 onward uniformly reflect his fascination with plainchant, no trace of it can be detected in the Violin Sonata. The chant-related works appear only after his marriage to Elsa Olivieri-Sangiacomo on 13 January 1919. She had completed a course on this topic shortly before their marriage. Respighi picked up on her enthusiasm for this music. In her words—"It became quite a craze with him." The Violin Sonata, completed before Respighi's experiments with chant melodies, modal scales, counterpoint, and harmonies, therefore represents the culmination and conclusion of his first style period.

Formally, the Sonata is a mixture of Classical and Baroque features. The three-movement layout typical of late eighteenth-century sonatas is retained, but the final movement is a ciaccona. (So, too, is the Finale of the three-movement Concerto *in modo misolidio* for piano and orchestra.) Respighi became familiar with this type of variation on a recurring harmonic or melodic pattern in slow triple meter no later than 1908. In that year, he arranged sonatas of Locatelli, Tartini, Veracini, Valenti, Vivaldi, and Porpora, and he perpared an edition of a ciaccona by Vitali that was frequently performed by the violinist Arrigo Serato, to whom, along with the pianist Ernesto Consolo, Respighi's Sonata is dedicated.

The Violin Sonata, which was published by Ricordi in 1919, remained one of Respighi's personal favorites: He used it on his own concert tours, including an Italian tour with his wife (21 January–6 February 1921), during his second American tour (1927), and during a tour of Spain (February 1929). His only other important chamber work is the *Quartetto Dorico* (quartet in Dorian mode; 1925).

Respighi must have been a formidable pianist in order to have performed pieces such as his *Tre preludi sopra melodie Gregoriane* (three preludes on Gregorian melodies; 1922) and the Piano Concerto (1925) in the Mixolydian mode. The former pieces are more widely known in their orchestral version, *Vetrate di chiesa* (church windows; 1927), where Respighi provided titles for each of the three preludes: "La fuga in Egitto" (flight into Egypt), "San Michele Arcangelo" (St. Michael the Archangel), "Il mattutino di Santa Chiara" (The Matins of St. Clare). He also added a fourth movement, the colossal "San Gregorio Magno" (Saint Gregory the Great).

The first movement conjures up the exotic world of the middle East with its 5/4 meter and Phrygian mode. The last movement, replete with an introduction that includes tolling bells, introduces the plainsong of the "Gloria" from the *Missa de angelis* on muted horns. The theme is passed to the organ for an impressive solo, then to full brass, and then to the orchestral tutti for a powerful conclusion.

Also active in the early part of the century were Ildebrando Pizzetti (1880–1968), Gian Francesco Malipiero (1882–1973), Alfredo Casella (1883–1947), Goffredo Petrassi (b. 1904), and Luigi Dallapiccola (1904–1975). As a group, they show in their works an international attitude and an openness to new techniques.

Pizzetti was keenly interested in the flexible declamation of Wagner and Debussy, but this in light of the Italian *bel canto* heritage. He wrote a number of expressive unaccompanied choral works bearing testimony to his conviction that vocal polyphony offered expressive riches on a plane with the Romantic style. He was an intelligent music critic, too, though rather harsh in his estimation of Puccini's works.

Malipiero's music is now little known, but he is remembered for his pioneering editions of the music of Claudio Monteverdi. In 1913, he went to Paris, where he befriended Alfredo Casella, became interested in the music of Debussy, and heard Stravinsky's *Le sacre du printemps*. Between 1920 and 1964, Malipiero wrote eight string quartets.

Casella spent much of his career in France, where he studied with Fauré and became acquainted with Ravel. Casella's early works show their influences along with those of Mahler and Strauss. When Casella returned to Italy in 1915, he took a position at the Liceo di Santa Cecilia in Rome, where he taught, performed, and promoted contemporary music. During World War I and for a few years after, Casella's style became acerbic. His three-movement Sonatina, Op. 28 (1916) for piano, is one of his best pieces. At the time, it was considered a highly dissonant and unapproachable work; however, those familiar with the works of Bartók will find striking similarities. Casella's lively rhythms, changing meters, ostinato patterns, reiterated sonorities (especially major and minor seconds) and flexible forms result in a composition that could easily be mistaken for early Bartók. 1926 marked a turning point in Casella's career. In that year, he completed the neoclassical score of *Scarlattiana* for piano and orchestra, inspired by the music of Domenico Scarlatti.

Goffredo Petrassi's long career began during the mid century. From 1939 to 1959, he was a faculty member of the Conservatorio di Santa Cecilia; subsequently, he taught at the Accademia di Santa Cecilia. During the 1930s, he was strongly influenced by Stravinsky, Hindemith, and Casella. In his later works, he abandoned tonality and focused on chamber pieces and orchestral works.[5]

Luigi Dallapiccola, born in the Austro-Hungarian province of Istria in 1904, was the earliest Italian composer to take an interest in Serialism. His father's outspoken opposition of the Austrian government led to the family's deportation to Graz until the end of World War I. Luigi resumed studies in Florence in 1922, and eventually became an influential teacher. He taught composition at the Conservatory of Florence from 1930 until 1967, and during the summers of 1951 and 1952, at the Berkshire Music Center, where Luciano Berio (b. 1925) was among his students.

Dallapiccola's serial style came to maturity during the late 1930s in the *Tre laudi* (three songs of praise; 1937) for high voice and thirteen instruments. His one-act opera *Volo di notte* (night flight; 1940) is based on a text by St. Exupery. In it, Dallapiccola's music complements the scenario depicting a pilot's encounter with infinity, achieved by means of technology. The notion of material and spiritual progress through technology links *Volo di notte* with earlier philosophies of the Italian *Futuristi*.

More important is the one-act opera *Il prigioniero* (the prisoner; 1948). In this powerful work, Dallapiccola realized for the first time the full potential of music as a vehicle for his expression of outrage against fascism and social injustice.[6] For the setting of *Il prigioniero*, Dallapiccola turned to European history and focused on the oppressive reign of the Hapsburg Emperor Philip II, during which, as a result of acquisitions in the Western Hemisphere, Spain was at the height of its power and affluence. During the Spanish Inquisition, Philip exploited the ecclesiastical courts of the Roman Church as a means of controlling his political rivals and silencing his enemies. Philip was particularly ruthless in his persecution, first of the Moriscos in Spain, and then of the Protestants in the Netherlands. Revolts erupted there beginning in 1567, and for the remainder of his reign, Philip was plagued with the Protestant issue.

The characters of *Il prigioniero* are archetypes rather than individuals. This abstract approach to drama not only set Dallapiccola's opera apart from the highly specified characters of Italian *verismo*, but it also enabled Dallapiccola to present a broadened vision of the dialectic between prisoner and oppressor. As he noted, "it seemed necessary to leave out the name of the imprisoned . . .; if it were left in, the problem would be presented as an individual one, whereas it is one that is common to nearly all men."[7] Accordingly, the characters are identified merely as: the Prisoner, the Mother, the Jailer, the Grand Inquisitor, and two Priests.

The opera, which lasts less than an hour, is scored for a large orchestra with mixed chorus, organ, and offstage brass and percussion, but Dallapiccola uses rather little orchestral tutti. Instead he extracts constantly changing chamber groups from the larger ensemble. His sense of instrumental color is remarkably refined, and timbres evoke subtle moods and atmospheres.

According to the composer, *Il prigioniero* contains three principal twelve-tone rows.[8] These rows are associated with prayer, hope, and freedom, respectively. Dallapicolla also uses smaller motifs throughout the score. The first of these, sounded as the top notes in the three dissonant chords that open the opera, represents *Roelandt*, the large bell in the tower of Ghent. This bell was used in the sixteenth century to signal the peasants to begin their revolt against Charles V and his son Philip II. Ironically, the bell signifies death as well, since Charles V subsequently ordered the citizen who rang the bell to be hanged from its clapper. Another important motif is associated with the word *fratello* (brother). The prisoner explains to his mother as follows:

quando il Carceriere
pronunciò finalmente una parola:
"Fratello." Dolcissima parola
che mi diede ancor fiducia nella vita.

(then the jailer
finally uttered a single word:
"Brother." That sweetest word
which restored my confidence in life!)

The tone rows of *Il prigioniero* are highly profiled: The Prayer theme, for example, generally ascends in thirds and fourths in its first half, and concludes with a melodic arc in the second half; the Hope theme, on the other hand, is anguished and angular. It begins with a chromatic ascent of four tones, then expands in a chromatic wedge, alternating tones below and above the fulcrum notes. The Freedom theme surges upward for its first nine pitches and settles downward in repose in the final three notes. Dallapiccola usually states the rows in a clear, linear context, and he often picks them up immediately in some permutation—such as the Mother's inverted statement of the Hope theme immediately after the Prisoner's first statement of it. Dallapiccola's twelve-tone method is liberal, and he does not hesitate to toggle between two tones in order to accommodate the text; nevertheless, the total chromatic spectrum is well represented in any given segment of the score. In all three rows—as well as others that appear intermittently—Dallapiccola reveals his *bel canto* heritage in producing an unusually singable Serialism.

Il prigioniero contains self-quotations (in the choral music of scene four, "Domine, labia mea aperies") taken from Dallapiccola's *Canti di prigionia* (songs of captivity; 1941). He wrote these pieces in protest to Mussolini's announcement on 1 September 1938 that Italy would be organizing anti-Semitic campaigns—a clear threat to Dallapiccola, whose wife was Jewish.

Work on *Il prigioniero* was interrupted by several projects, among them, the Chaconne, Intermezzo, and Adagio (1945) for solo 'cello. The piece, commissioned by the 'cellist Gaspar Casadó, uses serial procedures liberally, especially in the last

EXAMPLE 2
Twelve-tone Rows in Dallapiccola's *Il prigioniero*

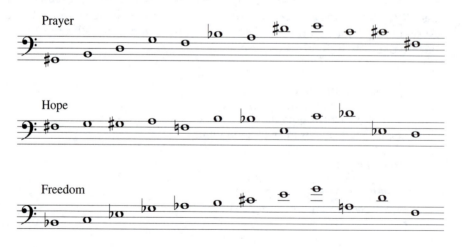

movement. For most of its pages, the score exhibits moderate use of dissonance and deliberate allusions to tonality.

The *Quaderno musicale di Annalibera* (musical notebook of Annalibera; 1952) is a strictly dodecaphonic work. It consists of eleven contrapuntal movements in contrasting characters, but all based on a single row. The extensive use of canon recalls various works by Bach, especially the *Canonic Variations on "Von Himmel hoch, da kom' ich her,"* the canonic movements of the *Goldberg Variations,* and those of *Die Kunst der Fuge* (art of the fugue), and Dallapiccola cites Bach's name (i.e., B-flat, A, C, B-natural=H, but here transposed to E-flat, D, F, E-natural) at the opening of the piece. Bach frequently wrote pieces for his family members and assembled them into notebooks; similarly, Dallapiccola assembled these eleven pieces for the eighth birthday of his daughter, Annalibera. (Her name celebrates the fact that Florence had just been freed from the Germans at the time of her birth.)

Dallapiccola also experimented with neoclassicism. His two *Tartiniana* (1951, '56) for violin and orchestra are good examples. The *Tartiniana seconda* is also available in an arrangement for violin and piano.

Notes

1. Claudio Sartori, *Dizionario degli editori musicali italiani* (Florence, 1958), pp. 130–132.
2. Ironically, this aria was one of the cuts that Puccini allowed to be made. The passage was restored by Toscanini for the thirtieth-anniversary productions given at La Scala during the 1922–23 season.
3. Among Mascagni's later operas, *L'amico Fritz* (1891) and the exotic *Iris* (1898) merit attention; however, neither of them achieved quite the box-office appeal that *Cavalleria rusticana* continues to enjoy.
4. William Ashbrook, *The Operas of Puccini* (Ithaca, New York: Cornell University Press, 1985), p. 5.
5. The most convenient source in English for further information relating to Petrassi is J. S. Weissmann, "Goffredo Petrassi and His Music," *Music Review* 22 (1961), 198–211.
6. For Dallapiccola's own discussion of the work, see his article "The Genesis of the *Canti di prigionia* and *Il prigioniero:* An Autobiographical Fragment," *Musical Quarterly* 39 (July 1953), 355–372.
7. Luigi Dallapiccola, "Notes on my *Prigioniero,*" brochure for *Il prigioniero* (New York: London Records, Inc., Decca Record Co, Ltd., 1975).
8. Luigi Dallapiccola, "Notes on my *Prigioniero,*" brochure for Decca LP recording OSA 1166 (New York, 1975).

Chapter 10

Back in France: Les Six

In November of 1917, the mezzo-soprano Jane Bathori performed songs by six composers in a recital. That was the first time that works by "the six" had been heard on the same program. There are few similarities of musical style that relate these composers. Rather, the group's identity sprang from an alliance against Debussy, Ravel, and Wagner, whom the young musicians saw as a past to be evaded. The eccentric Erik Satie (1866–1925) became their musical and æsthetic role model. The nickname *Les Six* was coined in January 1920, by the critic Henri Collet, who listed Georges Auric (1899–1983), Louis Edmond Durey (1888–1979), Arthur Honegger (1882–1955), Darius Milhaud (1892–1974), Francis Poulenc (1899–1963), and Germaine Tailleferre (1892–1983), relating them to the Russian Five of the nineteenth century. Collet had chosen the six names mainly because the composers knew one another, were friends, and frequently were combined on concert programs. As spokesman, *Les Six* had the *enfant terrible* of early twentieth-century French theater, Jean Cocteau. Cocteau admonished: "Musicians ought to cure music of its convolutions, its dodges and its tricks, and force it as far as possible to keep in front of the hearer." He also recommended as models "the music halls, the circus, and American negro bands," saying "all of these fertilize an artist just as life does." Of *Les Six*, only Milhaud, Honegger, and Poulenc have held firm ground in concert life.

Milhaud was the most highly trained of the group.[1] His teachers included Widor,[2] Gédalge, and Dukas. Milhaud was also the most prolific of the group, and his *œuvre* includes fifteen operas, eighteen symphonies, thirteen choral works, eighteen string quartets, five organ pieces, over two hundred *mélodies*, and dozens of miscellaneous pieces for radio, film, and other media.

Milhaud traveled extensively, and from 1916 until 1918, he was in Rio de Janeiro. This South American sojourn inspired the *Saudades do Brazil* (souvenirs of Brazil; 1921) for piano solo, some of which he later orchestrated. The easy tunefulness of these pieces, their attractive and often intricate rhythms, and their brevity and formal directness have made them equally accessible to professional musicians and casual listeners.

Milhaud had known about Jazz only indirectly: His score of 1919 entitled *Le boeuf sur le toit* (The ox on the roof) had already introduced jazzy elements. In 1922, he visited Harlem and heard real Jazz. This stimulated him to compose what many consider his masterpiece, the symphonic poem *La création du monde* (the creation of the world; 1923). Here the plaintive, opening melody of the saxophone shows Milhaud's melodic invention to great advantage. Milhaud's score was originally presented as a ballet accompanied by seventeen solo instruments, with Fernand Léger's costumes and stage decorations, which were inspired by African art. The choreography was by Jean Borlin.

That same melodic gift is apparent in Milhaud's more intimate pieces, such as the *Deux petits airs* (two little songs; 1918) on texts by Mallarmé. In the second, the unusual meter of ten beats to the measure reflects the prose-like style of Mallarmé's verse, while providing Milhaud ample opportunity to construct impressively elegant musical lines.

Milhaud seems to have reveled in his musical dexterity, and, as though at once to flaunt his skill and mock the tradition of the art song, he composed several sets of songs on banal texts: In his *Machines agricoles* (farm machines; 1919), he set descriptions of farm machinery from an agricultural catalog; in the *Catalogue de fleurs* (flower catalog; 1920), he set poems of Lucien Daudet, which approximate descriptions of flowers that might be found in a gardening catalog. These compact pieces range in length from seven measures (*Le bégonia*) to twenty-six measures (*L'eremus*). As in all of Milhaud's music, his extraordinary control is complemented by a wry sense of humor, urbane wit, and a keen sense of irony.

Among *Les Six*, Honegger was the odd man out.[3] Though born in Le Havre, his parents and citizenship were Swiss. He went to Switzerland during World War I to serve in the military; hence, he was a foreigner among the French. He lived in Paris for a while and studied at the Paris Conservatoire, but his outlook was deeply serious. The sarcastic witticisms, irony, and clever allusions of his French colleagues were alien to him in the final estimation.

Because of his circumspect attitude, he was less prolific than Milhaud. Of his large works, the oratorio *Le roi David* (King David; 1921) and his symphonic poem *Pacific 231* (1923) are the best known. The oratorio, which contains extensive portions for narrator, is an appealing and highly idiomatic score. Some of its movements are easily excerptable and can be performed by choirs of intermediate abilities. The tone poem, inspired by a locomotive, was hailed as a groundbreaking work. It is surely one of the most powerful of the many early twentieth-century examples of *musique méchanique*.

For *Pacific 231*, Honegger composed two companion pieces: *Rugby* (1928) and *Symphonic Movement 3* (1933). The set results in a three-movement symphony, both in terms of musical materials and overall duration. Interestingly, when Honegger

Arthur Honegger

came to write his five symphonies, it was the three-movement plan that he preferred.

Honegger's First Symphony (1930) was written at the request of Koussevitzky, who had given the first performance of *Pacific 231* in Paris in May of 1924. Later in that same year, when he became the principal conductor of the Boston Symphony, Koussevitzky renewed his request for a piece, and between December of 1929 and March of 1930, Honegger completed this masterpiece. Of the three movements, the central Adagio is perhaps the most impressive. The structure of this movement is a hybrid design. Honegger begins with a bass line using a chromatic scale ascending from F-sharp by one semitone each measure. During the movement, this bass line is repeated twice in slightly varied form. At the third and final statement of the chromatic scale, Honegger reverses its direction and has it descend to the final F-sharp of the movement. In between these three statements of the recurring bass line are two episodes in which the *basso ostinato* is temporarily set aside. These episodes exhibit a remarkable shift in instrumentation, too, and they contain delicate filagree for brass and woodwinds. The result is an ingenious combination of *basso ostinato* with rondo and codetta.

Honegger's remaining symphonies are all late works: The Second was completed in 1941, the Third and Fourth in 1946, and the Fifth in 1951. Of these, only the Third has programmatic associations. Honegger's title, *Symphonie liturgique* (liturgical symphony), derives from the fact that its three movements are inspired by the Requiem Mass of the Roman Church. The first movement bears the title "Dies iræ," the second "De profundis," and the third, "Dona nobis pacem"; however, there are no plainchants in any of the movements. The work has been widely performed not only because of its anti-war sentiments, but also for its brilliant orchestration.

Honegger's Fifth Symphony bears the title *Di tre re*, but any search for ecclesiastical allusions to the three Magi will be fruitless. The title refers to the tympani strokes on the tone D (i.e., *re*) that conclude each of the three movements. In the central movement, Honegger employs a design similar to that of the First Symphony. Three of the five segments are Adagio, and the two episodes are Allegretto.

The music of Poulenc has fared better than that of his cohorts.[4] His social connections with Diaghileff, Boulanger, Stravinsky, and the Princesse Edmond de Polignac, to cite just a few, set him in a good position to advance his musical cause. Nevertheless, social connections have never been a substitute for talent, and Poulenc possessed lots of that.

He came from a cultivated family, and he was erudite even in his boyhood. His principal musical mentors were his piano teacher, Ricardo Viñes, who gave premieres of many Debussy scores, and the prolific and cosmopolitan Charles Koechlin (1867–1950), with whom he studied from 1921 to 1924. Poulenc had two lessons with Koechlin each week during the school year. Aside from his own studies, this constituted his entire musical education.

Poulenc's potential became apparent in the 1919 score of *Le bestiaire ou cortège d'Orphée* (the bestiary; or, the cortege of Orfeus) a set of six songs on poems by Guillaume Apollinaire scored for solo voice, flute, clarinet, and string

Francis Poulenc

quartet. The idea of such a song cycle integrated with chamber music scoring probably came from Schönberg's *Pierrot lunaire* (moonstruck Pierrot; 1912). At Stravinsky's suggestion, Poulenc, using his own scenario, composed *Les biches* (the little darlings; 1924) for Diaghileff and the Ballets Russes. This score marked the establishment of Poulenc's characteristic style.

Poulenc was fascinated by the music of Bach. This interest is reflected in his *Concert champêtre* (rustic concerto; 1928) for harpsichord and orchestra, and, even more, in the G-minor Concerto (1938) for organ, tympani, and strings. The Concerto is modeled after the G-minor Prelude and Fugue (S. 542) of Bach and was premiered by Boulanger.

As a pianist, Poulenc accompanied vocalists throughout his career. Practical experience gave him a keen understanding of the singer's art, which is evidenced in over a hundred songs. Some, like the *Trois chansons* (three songs; 1947) on texts by Garcia Lorca, use poems of the highest caliber. Others, like the *Chansons gaillardes* (spicy songs; 1926), are utter trash. Poulenc wrote them only to prove that pornography could also be set to music.

Poulenc's skill at setting texts was proved most tellingly in his score of the *Dialogues des Carmélites* (dialogues of the Carmelites; 1956), the gruesome story of a convent of nuns who, during the French Revolution, are sentenced to death. The tale focuses on Blanche de la Force, who initially tries to escape the guillotine, but rejoins her community at the moment of truth. During the executions, they sing the *Salve Regina* in unison as the voices dwindle one by one.

Poulenc wrote a considerable amount of sacred music. His *Gloria* (1959) for soprano, mixed chorus, and orchestra, which was commissioned by the Koussevitzky Foundation, has become a staple of contemporary choral repertoire. The scores of the *Litanies à la Vierge noire* (Litanies to the black Virgin; 1936) and the *Ave verum corpus* (hail true body; 1952) are major contributions to the literature for women's chorus. His *Stabat Mater* (1950) for soprano, chorus, and orchestra, is probably his choral masterpiece.

Notes

1. In addition to biographical information, Roger Nichols, *Conversations with Madeleine Milhaud* (London: Faber, 1996) provides abundant photographs from the family collection.
2. See Viktor Lukas, *A Guide to Organ Music* (Portland, Oregon: Amadeus Press, 1989), pp. 131–133.
3. Honegger's *I Am a Composer*, trans. William O. Clough (New York: St. Martin's Press, 1966), and Harry Halbreich, *Honegger*, trans. Roger Nichols (Portland, Oregon: Amadeus Press, 1999) are the two best sources in English.
4. For an overview of literature on Poulenc, see George R. Keck, *Francis Poulenc: A Bio-Bibliography* (New York: Greenwood Press, 1990). For detailed discussion of the music, see Keith W. Daniel, *Francis Poulenc: His Artistic Development and Musical Style* (Ann Arbor, Michigan: UMI Research Press, 1982).

Chapter 11

France Revisited, 1920–1940: Stravinsky, Part III

With the conclusion of World War I, Stravinsky returned to France to pick up his career where it had left off; but the composer who went back to Paris was a different man. The terse, abstract style he acquired during the war continued in the Octet (1923) for winds, *Oedipus Rex* (1927), *Apollon musagète* (Apollo leader of the muses; 1928), the Duo concertante (1932) for violin and piano, and the Concerto in E-flat (*Dumbarton Oaks*; 1938).

Oedipus Rex, a two-act opera based on Sophocles, took Stravinsky into another realm of abstract theater: in this case, language. Cocteau's French libretto was translated into Latin by Jean Daniélou (ironic, since Sophocles wrote in Greek). By using Latin, Stravinsky gained several advantages: a liberal approach to declamation, a monumentality that corresponded with his envisioned staging, and emancipation from theatrical conventions.

Stravinsky's penchant for classical subjects, no doubt stimulated by work on *Oedipus Rex*, was exquisitely manifested in his next score, the two-act ballet, *Apollon musagète* for string orchestra. The work was a commission from the Elizabeth Sprague Coolidge Foundation, which was organizing a festival of contemporary music to be held at the Library of Congress. The commission stipulated a piece of about one half-hour, requiring not more than six dancers. Unable to depict all nine muses, Stravinsky selected three for the ballet: Calliope (muse of poetry), Polyhymnia (muse of gesture), and Terpsichore (muse of the dance). In his biography of Stravinsky, Eric Walter White gives the following comments about the style of *Apollon musagète:*

> The music for this *ballet blanc* [had to be] diatonic in character and . . . all extrinsic effects of instrumental contrast and variety [had to] be avoided. [Stravinsky] set aside the ordinary orchestra with its various

instrumental departments because of its heterogeneous character. He also felt that ensembles of woodwind and brass had been sufficiently exploited in recent years and decided to use only a string orchestra. This was to be a sextet with 1st and 2nd violins, violas, 1st and 2nd cellos, and double-basses.[1]

Stravinsky had decisive ideas about production. In the title role he envisioned Serge Lifar, a friend of Diaghileff's and a dancer with the Ballets Russes. Less than a month after its American premiere, *Apollon* was presented in Europe, with Lifar as Apollo, using choreography by George Balanchine. Diaghileff described the ballet as "an amazing work, extraordinarily calm, and with greater clarity than anything he has so far done; [with] clear-cut themes, all in the major key; somehow music not of this world, but from somewhere above."[2]

The *Dumbarton Oaks Concerto* was the result of another American commission, this one from Mr. and Mrs. Robert Woods Bliss. Their lovely home, with gardens designed by Beatrix Farrand, was frequently the site of artistic events.[3] Stravinsky's concerto was intended as an occasional piece to celebrate their thirtieth anniversary. Stravinsky visited Mr. and Mrs. Bliss when he was writing the concerto. Perhaps the propriety and elegance of their home suggested to him the idea of this neoclassical score inspired by Bach's *Brandenburg Concertos* (ca. 1721). In good Baroque fashion, Stravinsky limited his ensemble to a total of fifteen instrumentalists. In formal aspects, too, he conformed to the general design of the Baroque concerto: a three-movement plan with fast outer movements framing a relaxed central movement. The premiere will be remembered as one of the golden moments for women in the history of twentieth-century music: At the time (8 May 1938), Stravinsky was seriously ill with tuberculosis. Unable to conduct, he deputized Boulanger to take his place. Mrs. Bliss, who heard the piece many times subsequently, always considered Boulanger's performance definitive.

Stravinsky composed his next score, the Symphony in C, during a period of transition. He began it in France in 1938; by the time he wrote the fourth and final movement, he was in California. Relying on his experiences from World War I, Stravinsky determined that his best course of action would be to leave France for a settled environment where he could continue his creative work. By this time, he had a considerable number of benefactors in the United States. His reputation was growing steadily, partly owing to the presence of Koussevitzky on the podium of the Boston Symphony Orchestra. Boulanger, likewise, was an important advocate for Stravinsky. The disruption of European artistic organizations at the outbreak of World War II was an inconvenience, to be sure; but, it was a stimulus for Stravinsky to seek his fortunes in the most propitious context: the United States.

Notes

1. Eric Walter White, *Stravinsky: The Composer and His Works*, 2d ed. (Berkeley and Los Angeles: University of California Press, 1979), p. 341.
2. White, *Stravinsky*, p. 342.
3. For information about the gardens, see Diana Balmori, Diane Kostial McGuire, and Eleanor M. McPeck, *Beatrix Farrand's American Landscapes: Her Gardens and Campuses* (Sagaponack, New York: Sagapress, 1985).

Chapter 12

La jeune France, *Olivier Messiaen, and Homiletic Music*

Among the French artistic organizations disrupted by the Second World War was a recently formed one known as *La jeune France* (young France). The group initially consisted of four composers: Yves Baudrier (b. 1906), Daniel Lésur (b. 1908), André Jolivet (1905–1974), and Olivier Messiaen (1908–1992). Though each of these composers wrote in a distinctive style, they were united by their antipathy toward the sardonic and often superficial music of *Les Six*. "They sought to restore to music a more human and spiritual quality, combined with a seriousness of intention so sadly lacking in much of the French music of the interwar years."[1]

The spirituality of *La jeune France* is not always conventional Christianity. Jolivet's early piano pieces entitled *Mana* (1935) take their inspiration from Eastern cult objects that were given to him by his teacher Edgar Varèse (1883–1965). Varèse, who had emigrated to the United States in 1915 and achieved notoriety with his score of *Amériques* (1921), returned to Paris for the years from 1928 to 1933. During that time, while working on the score of *Ionization* (1931), he accepted a limited number of students. He became an important figure in the avant-garde until he virtually stopped writing for more than a decade after the completion of "Density 21.5" (1936) for solo flute. Jolivet's studies with Varèse lasted from 1930 until 1933.

Jolivet's spiritually oriented pieces from around this time include the *Cinq incantations* (five incantations) for flute, the *Danse incantatoire* (incantational dance) for orchestra (both 1936), and the *Cinq danses rituelles* (five ritual dances; 1939) for orchestra. His later works, however, especially his concertos for trumpet, violin, 'cello, harp, piano, percussion, and ondes martenot, seem little related to his earlier mysticism.

The most important figure in the group was undoubtedly Messiaen. Messiaen was progressive and eclectic in his music, but ironically, he was strictly orthodox in his Roman Catholic faith. As a consequence of the integral connection between his faith and his music, his life was a Janus-faced existence that looked equally to the past and to the future. Indeed, his contemplation of things eternal and his efforts to explore these mysteries in music led him to certain ideas about rhythm and duration that have no precedent or parallel in Western European musical thought.

As a student at the Paris Conservatoire, Messiaen was most influenced by Marcel Dupré and Dukas. Upon completion of his training, Messiaen took the position of organist at the church of the Sainte Trinité in Paris, a post that he held until his death.[2] His earliest work to become a staple in the repertoire is *Le banquet céleste* (celestial banquet; 1926). Its ephemeral and serene music progresses at such a glacial pace as to preclude any perception of rhythm or meter. In it, many characteristic traits of Messiaen's style are already apparent, among them the use of the octatonic scale, one of the various symmetrical scales that Messiaen eventually codified as the "modes of limited transposition" in his treatise *La technique de mon langage musicale* (the technique of my musical language; 1944).[3] The final sonority of the piece is a dominant-seventh chord in the key of F-sharp, the key signature that Messiaen uses for the piece; however, the octatonic scale he uses does not contain F-sharp. In place of the tonic, he prolongs the dominant sonority and reinforces it on a very low pedal tone so that its harmonically open conclusion is a suggestion of eternal ecstasy. This musical detail embodies a theological concept: that in the Eucharist, Christians have a foretaste of the eternal kingdom of God. Concerning such unfulfilled tonal implications, Paul Griffiths has observed that "atonality is for Messiaen a medium of mystery. . . . To discover within that medium some familiar signposts is to find amiableness even in the most inscrutable doctrines of Christianity."[4]

Messiaen probably invented the modes of limited transposition in the course of his organ improvisations at Sainte Trinité, and they became increasingly important in his scores of the 1930s. Noteworthy among these are the four-movement symphonic suite, *L'Ascension* (1933) which Messiaen realized in two versions, one for orchestra, another—with an alternate third movement—for organ solo; *La nativité du Seigneur* (nativity of the Lord; 1935), a nine-movement suite also for organ solo; the *Poèmes pour Mi* (poems for me; 1936), which are dedicated to the composer's first wife, the violinist and composer Claire Delbos, and *Les corps glorieux* (mystical bodies; 1939), an organ cycle that Messiaen describes as "seven brief visions of the life of the resurrected." *La nativité du Seigneur* is important for its explanatory preface, in which Messiaen articulated for the first time his theories of the modes of limited transposition. At this point, they numbered only five, and their numbering is at odds with that in *La technique de mon langage musicale;* nevertheless, their critical roles, both as a means of expression and as building blocks in his music, are unequivocally established.

In their exploration of spirituality, the composers of *La jeune France* frequently turned to non-Western sources. In this search, Messiaen discovered the theoretical writings of the thirteenth-century Indian theorist Śârngadeva, whose

EXAMPLE 3
Messiaen - Modes of Limited Transposition

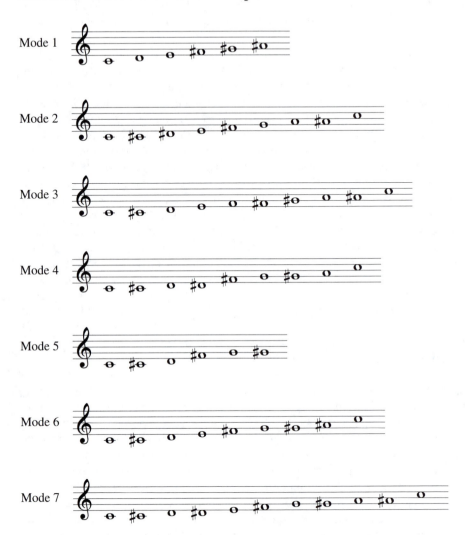

treatise *Sangîta-ratnakâra* (ocean of music) explored music in all of its manifestations and aspects. Messiaen was intrigued by the rhythmic patterns, or *deçî-tâlas,*
identified in Śârngadeva's work.[5] These non-Western materials give Messiaen's
music an exotic and mystical nature. To these elements, Messiaen added allusions
to birdsongs—a topic first apparent in "Dieu parmi nous" (God among us), the

ninth and final movement of *La nativité du Seigneur*—and the imitation of rain-drops—such as may be heard in "Le jardin du sommeil d'amour" (the garden of the slumber of love), the sixth movement of his *Turangalîla-symphonie* (1948).

The outbreak of World War II led not only to the dissolution of *La jeune France,* but also to an interruption of Messiaen's career: He was conscripted to service, but owing to his poor eyesight, he was assigned to a post at Verdun as a paramedic. In May of 1940, the Germans invaded. After a futile flight to Nancy, Messiaen was captured and interned at Görlitz, in Silesia, in a Nazi camp known as compound VIIIA.[6]

Music has often been a means for confronting despair. Within the confines of compound VIIIA, Messiaen composed what has become his most widely known work, the *Quatuor pour la fin du temps* (quartet for the end of time; 1941). For Messi-aen, the composition of this quartet was a means of preserving his mental health.[7] The unusual instrumentation was the consequence of circumstances: Among the prisoners at the camp were the violinist Jean Lee Boulaire, the clarinetist Henri Akoka, and the 'cellist Etienne Pasquier.[8] The only 'cello available was missing one string. Boulaire and Akoka had been allowed to keep their instruments when they entered the camp. For these two and the handicapped 'cellist, Messiaen first wrote what is now the fourth movement, "Intermède." The remainder of the quartet (save for the third movement, "Abîme des oiseaux") includes piano—an upright piano in disrepair. The first performance was given on 15 January 1941 with the composer at the piano assisted by his three friends. For Messiaen, it was the musi-cal experience of his life. Approximately five thousand inmates listened with a concentration and perception that the composer experienced neither before nor afterwards.

At the head of the score, Messiaen wrote verses 1 through 7 of chapter 10 of the Revelation of St. John the Divine:

> I saw an angel full of strength descending from the sky, clad with a cloud and having a rainbow over his head. His face was like the sun, his feet like columns of fire. He set his right foot on the sea, his left foot on the earth and, standing on the sea and on the earth, he raised his hand to the sky and swore by Him who lives in the centuries of centuries, saying: "There shall be no more Time, but on the day of the seventh Angel's trumpet the mystery of God shall be accomplished."[9]

The relationship between Messiaen's personal religious views and his music is a complex one. He once stated:

> The first idea that I wished to express—and the most important—is the existence of the truths of the Catholic faith. I've the good fortune to be a Catholic; I was born a believer, and it happens that the Scriptures struck

me even as a child. So a number of my works are intended to bring out the theological truths of the Catholic faith. That is the first aspect of my work, the noblest and, doubtless, the most useful and valuable; perhaps the only one which I won't regret at the hour of my death.[10]

For Messiaen, composition was a vocation. His music making was part of his religious life. The composition and performance of the quartet within a concentration camp was paradoxical. He never composed a traditional setting of the Ordinary of the Mass—though the *Messe de la Pentecôte* (Pentecost Mass; 1950), with its outer movements flanking the Offertoire, Consécration, and Communion is clearly a set of organ pieces to accompany that ritual. In a discussion of his *Trois petites liturgies de la Présence Divine* (three little celebrations of the Divine Presence; 1944), however, he pointed out that "I've imposed the truths of the Faith on the concert room, but in a liturgical sense . . . . I thought of performing a liturgical act, that is to say, transporting a kind of [religious] Office, a kind of organized act of praise into the concert room." He concludes that he has "taken the idea of the Catholic liturgy from the stone buildings intended for religious services and . . . installed it in other buildings not intended for this kind of music and which, finally, have received it very well." In the case of the quartet, the "organized act of praise" elevated and consecrated Messiaen's surroundings, making the camp a sanctuary and his very imprisonment an action of devotion.

Messiaen's theological views pervade the complex musical idiom of the quartet. He reminds us that "most of the arts are unsuited to the expression of religious truth: only music, the most immaterial of all, comes closest to it."[11] Again, irony confronts us, since Messiaen effaces this "immateriality" by the programmatic titles for each of the quartet's eight movements; furthermore, each title is accompanied by a detailed prose explanation.[12]

That a concentration camp could not, for Messiaen, negate the presence of God in all things and in all places, found a natural parallel in the music of birds and the sounds of drops of water that could be heard even within the barbed-wire enclosures of the camp. In order to appreciate these sounds in the quartet and other works, it is helpful to note Messiaen's observation that:

> The phenomenon of nature is . . . beautiful and calming, and, for me, ornithological work is not only an element of consolation in my researches into musical aesthetics, but also a factor of health. It's perhaps thanks to this work that I've been able to resist the misfortunes and complications of life.[13]

The irony here is twofold: Messiaen not only attaches material meanings to immaterial music by invoking nature's sounds, but in so doing, he acknowledges the power of time. The composer himself noted that "all of God's creations are enclosed in Time, and Time is one of God's strangest creatures because it is totally opposed to Him who is Eternal by nature, to Him who is without beginning, end, or succession."[14]

Messiaen suggests the ending of time through musical materials. Sometimes he constructs themes based upon non-retrogradable rhythms (i.e., palindromic patterns in which time past and time future are identical). Repetitious figures and rhythmic cycles are employed—especially in the first movement—to provide coherence. Though such cycles are presented by 'Sârngadeva, they are not unique to his theory; in fact, similar rhythmic structures appear in Western Europe's rhythmic modes as well as in the later isorhythmic motets of the Ars nova. In the first movement, Messiaen uses panisorhythmic structures combining dissimilar cycles of durations and sonorities. Paul Griffiths has estimated that the cycles as they appear at the beginning of the piece would not come into alignment again for approximately two hours.[15]

Litanies, which have played an important part in Christian liturgies since the fifth century, also influenced Messiaen's score.[16] Their repetitious structure induces a sort of spiritual intoxication in which one becomes oblivious to the world and to time. Messiaen's use of recurrence—particularly the links between the second and seventh movements, and the fifth and eighth—enhances this sense of timelessness. Finally, the eight-movement plan is significant. "Seven is the perfect number, the creation of 6 days sanctified by the holy Sabbath; the 7th day of repose extends into eternity and becomes the 8th day of indefectible light, of unalterable peace."[17]

In the *Quatuor,* Messiaen used previously composed music for the fifth movement, "Louange à l'éternité de Jésus" (paean to the eternity of Jesus), and the last movement, "Louange à l'immortalité de Jésus" (paean to the immortality of Jesus). The former is drawn from the *Fête des belles eaux* (celebration of beautiful water; 1937), scored for six ondes martenot, the latter from the *Diptyque* (1930) for organ solo.

In the years following the war, Messiaen attracted important students, including Pierre Boulez (b. 1925) and Yvonne Loriod (b. 1924). Boulez attended Messiaen's classes during his years of study at the Paris Conservatoire (1942–1945). Loriod, a pianist, was a pupil in Messiaen's harmony class. She soon attracted his attention with her keen rhythmic sense and fine tone. For her, he wrote the *Visions de l'amen* (visions of the amen; 1943), a suite of seven movements for two pianos. The part for Loriod is a virtuosic showpiece replete with bird songs, tintinnabulations, and decorative writing, while the second part provides the harmonic foundations and principal themes of the pieces. As in many of Messiaen's multi-movement scores, cyclic recollection plays an important role; specifically, the serene theme of the opening movement, "Amen de la crèation," returns in the final "Amen de la consommation." Within these framing movements, the composer provides symmetrically balanced essays on Christian acceptance of the Divine will, with the central movement, "Amen du désir," acting as the fulcrum. It has been remarked that this movement "represents . . . the convulsive energy with which creation strives to be united with its creator."[18] For Loriod, Messiaen also composed the *Vingt regards sur l'enfant Jésus* (twenty contemplations of the infant Jesus; 1944).

Though Messiaen's compositional and academic work flourished in the years following the war, his personal life was marked with hardship. His wife, Claire, was grievously ill, and the condition rendered her an invalid until her death in 1959. His patience and fidelity were rewarded, however, and in 1962, he married Yvonne Loriod.

In the works that Messiaen wrote following the war, there is a general trend toward longer pieces and larger ensembles. His ten-movement *Turangalîla-symphonie* (1948), for example, requires large orchestra, solo piano, and ondes martenot. This symphony uses recurring themes, refrain structures, and variation processes to explore various aspects of love, ranging from the erotic to the Divine. It contains some of Messiaen's most energetic music, such as the vast symphonic scherzo, "Joie du sang des étoiles" (joy of the blood of the stars). As an antithesis to this music, Messiaen provides the exquisite and very nearly static sonorities of the sixth movement, "Jardin du sommeil d'amour" (garden of the sleep of love). In this impressive essay on serenity, the ondes martenot plays a vital role, a role that proves what a valuable asset electronic instruments can be.

More expansive still is the score of *La Transfiguration de notre Seigneur Jésus-Christ* (the Transfiguration of our Lord Jesus Christ; 1969), for a huge orchestra plus seven soloists (piano, 'cello, flute, clarinet, xylorimba, vibraphone, marimba), and a mixed chorus of over a hundred voices. The text is drawn principally from the account of the Transfiguration in St. Matthew, chapter 17. Commentaries relating to the transvestiture from this mortal flesh to glorified bodies are drawn from the epistles of Paul, the psalms, the Wisdom of Solomon, and the *Summa theologica* of St. Thomas Aquinas.

Further expansion of resources occurred in his opera, *Saint François d'Assise,* which Messiaen began in 1975. The project, which occupied him for over eight years, was undertaken reluctantly at the request of Rolf Liebermann, the chief administrator of the Paris Opéra at the time.

The apogee of Messiaen's musical discourses on celestial topics is the score of *Éclairs sur l'au-delà* (illuminations of the beyond; 1987), his last major work. It was commissioned by the New York Philharmonic Orchestra. When he accepted the commission, Messiaen had no idea of the size or instrumentation of the composition that would result.[19] As the piece materialized, it grew into an eleven-movement symphony of about seventy minutes duration. The pages of *Éclairs sur l'au-delà* contain many familiar musical gestures as well as the customary musical materials: bird songs, Indian rhythms, non-retrogradable rhythms, modes of limited transposition, ametrical dotted notes, programmatic instructions, scriptural allusions, emphasis on prime numbers, and symmetrical structures oriented around a central fulcrum.

In many of its movements, *Éclairs sur l'au-delà* seems to recall earlier works: Two of its serene movements, the fifth, "Demeurer dans l'amour" (abide in love), and the ninth, "Le Christ, lumière du Paradis" (Christ, the beacon of Paradise), recall the "Louange" movements of the *Quatuor pour la fin du temps.* The ninth movement, "Plusieurs oiseaux des arbres de vie" (various birds of the tree of life), recalls in its virtuosic bird songs for eighteen wind instruments the more modest scores of "Abîme des oiseaux" in the *Quatuor pour la fin du temps* and the whimsical *Merle noir* (blackbird; 1951) for flute and piano.

One particularly influential experimental work is Messiaen's set of piano pieces, *Quatre études rythme* (four rhythmic etudes; 1950). Of these, "Mode de valeurs et d'intensités" (modes of duration and intensity) is of chief importance, since it organized not only pitch, but also attack, duration, and register. This experiment, which Messiaen never repeated, provided the foundation for total Serialism as a compositional principle.

Messiaen and his music have been controversial. Paul Henry Lang, who was generally astute, perceptive, and fair in his criticism, found his music garish. Messiaen's colleagues at the Paris Conservatoire respected him with reservations: He was, after all, a mystic, part of the fringe element, and, perhaps, a bit too eccentric. In spite of these reservations, Messiaen has achieved a place of enduring significance in the annals of music history. His sincerity, complexity and simplicity, his eclectic views of music and sound, commingled with his vast imagination—assisted, he would say, by Divine grace—produced an idiom that is without precedent.

Three Students from Messiaen's Studio: Pierre Boulez, Iannis Xenakis, and Mikis Theodorakis

Great teachers have the ability to suppress their own egos so that the identities of their students can surface. In listening to representative works by these three composers, one does not hear the shadow of Messiaen, and even among the three, stylistic similarities are less conspicuous than differences. Nevertheless, each of these students reveals links with Messiaen's vision and his philosophy of the role of the artist.

Pierre Boulez

Boulez studied with Messiaen at the Paris Conservatoire during the final year of his degree program, then with René Leibowitz, a devoted disciple of Schönberg. The Polish-born Leibowitz also studied with Webern and Ravel. During the late '40s and most of the '50s, Boulez was active primarily as a conductor. His concert series called Domaine Musical (founded in 1954 as Concerts du Petit-Marigny and renamed in the following year) featured contemporary music. In 1964, he made his debut in the United States. From 1971 until 1977, he was the principal conductor of the New York Philharmonic, where he did much for modern music, in addition to bringing to the orchestra a degree of accuracy that had been lacking under his flamboyant predecessor, Leonard Bernstein.

Since 1974, Boulez has been working with experimental techniques, electro-acoustical music, computer music, and other avant-garde processes. Most of these experiments have taken place at the Institut de Recherche et de Coordination Acoustique/Musique (IRCAM), which he organized in Paris at the request of Georges Pompidou, president of France at the time.[20] The facility, which opened in 1977, was complemented by the Ensemble InterContemporain for the performance of modern music. Boulez became its director.

Boulez has been influential as a teacher and lecturer, especially at the International Darmstadt Festivals (1955–1960), Harvard University (1962–63), and the Academy of Music in Basel (1960–1966). He has been able to advance his radical ideas at the Darmstadt Festivals in particular. The program was founded in 1946 by Wolfgang Steinecke, and the United States, eager to promote cultural interchange between the erstwhile enemy states, did much both financially and administratively to support its work. Leibowitz, Messiaen, Hans Werner Henze, Karlheinz Stockhausen, Bruno Maderna, Luigi Nono, Luciano Berio, Henri Pousseur, John Cage, Brian Ferneyhough, and other mavericks have lectured there, but none with more frequency than Boulez, who dominated the Darmstadt pulpits for a full decade beginning in 1955. The various trends explored at these new-music festivals are available for consideration in the pages of the yearbook *Darmstädter Beiträge zur neuen Musik* (Darmstadt periodical for new music; 1958–).

An interesting feature of Boulez's music is the way in which he sometimes shifts the traditional focus from harmony and counterpoint to rhythm. In his *Livre pour quatuor* (book for quartet; 1949), the harmonic structure moves at a glacial pace in comparison to the constantly changing durations within the lines. In this respect, Boulez's early style has a certain affinity to the Minimalism of the late century. During the 1950s, he experimented with total Serialism in scores such as his *Polyphonie X* (1951) for eighteen instruments.

During the late '50s and '60s, Boulez investigated Aleatory music. *Alea* is the Latin word for dice; hence, works written in an aleatoric manner are chance pieces. In fact, there is very little left to chance in many of these pieces. Instead, performers are invited to make decisions—about tempos, how many times to repeat a particular section, how long to continue an improvisational passage, and so forth. In this context, it would be more accurate to speak of "indeterminate" music. (Another term frequently used—more accurate than "aleatory," to be sure—is "mobile form" music.) Boulez was influenced by literary models, especially Symbolist writers like Mallarmé.

Indeterminacy appears in *Pli selon pli* (fold upon fold; 1962) for soprano and orchestra, which is a synthesis of song cycle and tone poem. Each of its five pieces is based upon a poem by Mallarmé, ranging from early to late poems; however, the poems per se are not sung. At the opening, a line is sung, and here and there words are set to music. Most of the text is transformed into purely musical elements. The number of syllables in a line, the number of lines in a stanza, and other details, are paralleled in the music; but this is done without recourse to the actual words. In all of the movements, Boulez uses a highly pointillistic style that isolates sonorities as individual musical events. Within this stylistic context, his decision to eschew conventional text setting was probably a prudent one.

Boulez's attention to precise moments and musical events led to his distinctive and highly instructive manner of conducting. Listening to Boulez's interpretations of classics—Debussy's *La mer,* or Bartók's *Bluebeard's Castle,* for example—is always a revelation. The clarity of lines, the accuracy of intonation, the precision of the rhythms, the exacting realization of dynamics, and the fastidious attention to tempos are indications of a perfectionism that may possibly account for the fact that Boulez has completed rather few compositions in recent years. Given his preference for mobile forms, it hardly seems possible that he should fix in print a final, definitive version of anything. Among the few works that Boulez has completed in recent years, *Rituel* (1974) for large orchestra is noteworthy. Its title, however, seems to be an ironic self-commentary on its status as a fixed composition, as well as on certain of its formal and structural aspects.

Written as a memorial for Maderna, *Rituel* is designed for eight highly profiled ensembles: (1) solo oboe, (2) two clarinets, (3) three flutes, (4) four violins, (5) wind quintet, (6) string sextet, (7) wind septet, and (8) fourteen brass instruments. A percussionist assists the first seven groups, and two percussionists combine with the eighth. The odd-numbered sections are more formalized movements in a slow tempo, whereas the even-numbered sections are improvised at a moderate tempo. The conductor coordinates the progression of movements in a sort of *messa di voce* where more and more instruments join in, building to the crux of the work; then the process is reversed, and the instruments taper off. This process is supported by the percussion, which functions roughly as a rhythmic ostinato. The constructive elements of *Rituel*—unification through a rhythmic motif and alternating movements in disparate tempos—suggest the influence of Berg: the Invention on a rhythm in Act III of *Wozzeck,* and the tempo scheme of his *Lyric Suite.* Because of its structural clarity, *Rituel* is a good choice for the first encounter with Boulez.

Iannis Xenakis

During World War II, Iannis Xenakis (1922–2001), an engineering student at the University of Athens, joined the Greek Resistance. He helped organize demonstrations that regularly ended in violence. Following the German evacuation, when Greece was plunged into the agony of civil war, he aligned himself with the Communists fighting for an independent Greece. During a skirmish with the British, an explosion shattered the left side of his face and destroyed his left eye. Sentenced to death by the Greek right-wing post-war regime and forced underground, Xenakis fled from Greece with a forged passport in September 1947. He made his way to Paris, where he began working illegally for the architect Le Corbusier.

The contact was a critical one for Xenakis's aesthetic orientation, and throughout his career, architecture inspired his music and vice versa. As the principal architect for the Couvent de St. Marie de la Tourette from 1954 until 1957, he designed transparent exterior walls, fusing the use of glass with the musical concept of polyphony. Later, his score of *Metastaseis* (1954) provided the model for his internationally acclaimed Philips Pavilion for the 1958 Brussels World Fair.[21]

Xenakis's diverse interests engendered equally diverse compositional techniques. His initial forays into composition led him to experiment with recorded sounds subjected to various transformations. The radical aspects of this procedure should not obscure the fact that it is a logical outgrowth of nineteenth-century thematic transformation; in his transformations, Xenakis merely used technologically assisted metamorphoses. This idiom appears in his *Diamorphoses* (1957) and *Concrète P. H.* (1958).

In 1951, Xenakis met Messiaen, who advised him to take the things he knew—his Greek heritage, science, and architecture—and to incorporate them into his music. Inspired by mathematics and physics, Xenakis invented what he called "stochastic music" in 1954.

The word stochastic, defined as "governed by the laws of probability," derives from the Greek word *stokhos*, meaning "to aim, to guess." Essentially, the word stochastic denotes random events, but it also implies the law of large numbers, a principle discovered by the Swiss mathematician Jacques Bernoulli. This law posits that the more numerous the phenomena, the more they tend towards a determinate end. When Xenakis used the term stochastic music, he referred to a non-deterministic music, composed with the aid of probability theory governed by statistics of the mathematics of large numbers. These stochastic techniques and processes are restricted to the realm of the composer's responsibility and are not relegated to the performers, as is the case with aleatory composition. At first experimenting with various kinds of distributions, such as the Gaussian, Poisson, and uniform distributions, Xenakis soon incorporated more complex twentieth-century mathematical principles into his music: Markovian chains, game theory, theories of sieves and of sets, symbolic logic, and group theory. Originally calculating copious mathematical formulæ and operations manually, Xenakis was among the first to recognize the implications of computer technology for facilitating musical composition. His research into computer technology, undertaken in 1957, came to fruition in 1962 with *ST/48-1.240162.* "ST" indicates "stochastic"; "48" shows the number of instruments required; "1" stands for the first composition with this instrumentation; and the last digits mark the date of the composition: 24 January 1962.[22] Subsequent works also composed with computer assistance and likewise scored for traditional instruments include *ST/10, ST/4, Morisma/Amorisma,* and *Atrées.*

Xenakis's engineering and architectural background furnished a unique blueprint for his musical compositions: In the embryonic stage of his works, the coordinates of pitch and time were expressed in graphic format, not in musical notation. These compositional drafts were visual representations of sounds both seen and heard. Once the musical detail was finalized, Xenakis converted the composition into conventional musical notation. Working from his scores, it is possible to reconstruct detailed views of his music by plotting the pitches in graphic format: time in measure numbers on the X-axis against pitches in semitones on the Y-axis. Frequently this reconstruction process exposes an itinerary of musical events in the form of fascinating shapes, which are visually lost in traditional musical scoring, and which cannot be detected by the ears alone. Sketches of this sort permit a more comprehensive understanding of the spatial, registral, and textural dimensions of Xenakis's music. They also reveal the new musical forms—the architecture—created through the implementation of mathematics.[23]

Words are critical in Xenakis's music. Many of his compositions have Greek titles that encapsulate particular philosophical messages otherwise cryptically embedded in the music. Some titles describe the mathematical theories at the heart of the work. *Pithoprakta* (probability; 1956) contains the first musical phrase known to be based on probability theory; his orchestral pieces based on game theory, both scored for two orchestras in competition with each other, are appropriately entitled *Duel* (1959) and *Stratégie* (1962).

Of the more than 150 works in Xenakis's output, twenty-five use sounds or words articulated by the human voice. Sometimes it is impossible to discern the meaning of the "texts" without elucidation. In *Nuits* (nights; 1967), for example, that extraordinary human cry scored for twelve *a capella* voices, the text consists entirely of phonemes either invented by Xenakis or taken from the Sumerian and ancient Persian languages.[24] On the other hand, *Pu wijnuej we fyp* (1992) is a linguistic transformation. Based on Arthur Rimbaud's poem "Le dormeur du val," Xenakis's transformed text for this piece for *a cappella* children's choir is a one-to-one mapping of alphabet letters. This process transforms the French text into a non-existent language, thereby providing a game through which Xenakis invites children to discover the beauty of the poem and of mathematics simultaneously.[25]

The exigencies of war constituted a crucial aspect of Xenakis's existence from which his intellectual and artistic impulse cannot be separated. The spectacle of night skies illuminated by explosions found resonance in his futuristic sound and light shows. Featuring music accompanied by lights, mounted on high steel cables and laser beams, to project light in three-dimensional space, he fashioned the *Polytope de Montréal* (created for the French Pavilion at the 1967 Montreal Exposition), the *Polytope de Cluny* (1972), and *La légende d'Er* (1977). For the massive open-air exhibit, *Persepolis*, commissioned for the 1971 Shiraz Festival of Arts and Music in Iran, Xenakis assaulted the surrounding Persepolis hillsides with huge petroleum fires, strings of car headlights, and processions of children carrying torches, all directed and coordinated by the composer from the palatial ruins of Apadana, at the source of the music. The universal theme of man's inhumanity to man is evidenced most overtly in the sounds of his orchestral works, in which musical elements, such as dynamics, percussion, and rhythm simulate vigorously and passionately, the frenzy of combat. As the action and the pain of the battlefield are transformed into sound, the music conjures visions of confrontations: great blocks of chords, explosions, bullets whistling overhead, silences pregnant with frantic anticipation.

Understanding Xenakis's music requires knowledge of mathematical concepts that lie outside the musical canon. This is the fundamental challenge that has hindered musicians in confronting his works; nevertheless, his music is vibrant with contradictions. It is based on mathematics and science, yet it bears witness to the composer's intensely personal experiences. It is inspired by twentieth-century concepts, yet it is tied culturally and historically to the history of Greece. It employs formalized and codified stochastic techniques and processes, yet these seem violently alien to the human spirit. This juxtaposition of opposites triggers a ferocity, a kind of power and energy reminiscent of that generated by molecules crashing into each other when the heat is turned up. Indeed, at each step of a musical journey the interpreter and listener are challenged—intellectually, emotionally, and psychologically—to be in the fire.

Mikis Theodorakis

Messiaen's studio included another Greek composer, Mikis Theodorakis (b. 1925), whose childhood encounters with music were largely Byzantine chant and liturgical musics of the Greek Orthodox church. In 1942, he entered a contest to compose a *troparion* (a hymn in honor of some saint). He submitted his *Troparion to Kassiani,* won the contest, and thus began his career as a composer.

In 1943, Philoktitis Economidis accepted Theodorakis into his composition class at the Athens State Conservatory. Economidis was also director of the Athens Choral Ensemble and the Conservatory Orchestra, and he allowed Theodorakis to serve as his assistant. The repertoire that the young composer studied included Bach, Mozart, Beethoven, Wagner, Franck, and Hindemith among others.[26]

Along with his growing musical interests, Theodorakis discovered his proclivity toward political activism: He was deeply committed to the United All-Greek Youth Organization, which included cultural as well as political meetings among its activities. Another member with whom Theodorakis became friendly was Xenakis. Both young men were involved in the Resistance movement against the invading Fascist and Nazi forces (1941).[27]

As a Greek nationalist, Theodorakis became interested in the musics of his native land. To the distinctive musical materials that he had encountered in Byzantine chant, he added two characteristically Greek ingredients: *demotic* songs and *rebetic* music. The demotic songs were heavily influenced by the *klephetic ballads* stemming from the late eighteenth century. These ballads are comparable to the Mediæval *chansons de geste*. Their subjects are usually the deeds of the mountain chieftains (*Klephts*) who fought to expel the Turks from Greek lands. *Rebetic* music originated in hashish joints, the Greek counterpart to nineteenth-century British opium dens. This music was often dreary and despondent—along the lines of American Blues. The instrument commonly used to accompany these songs was a descendant of the rebec and the related *rabab*. Both are stringed instruments with long necks and pear-shaped backs. The Greek version of the instrument is the *bouzouki*, which eventually was subject to electronic amplification like the guitar. The bouzouki has become, in fact, modern Greece's equivalent to the guitar of Pop music.[28]

Theodorakis, a leftist Socialist who has been concerned about class distinctions in musical circles, has tried to bridge this gap by forming a musical synthesis of four nationalistic elements: Byzantine chant, demotic music, rebetic music, and contemporary styles of Pop music (*laik*), and he has called upon the poets of modern Greece to join with him in effecting a comparable synthesis in their poetry.

The combination of music and drama has always attracted Theodorakis; consequently, he has written many song cycles, oratorios, and ballets. In the life of the general populace of the twentieth century, however, the most vibrant, intimate, and compelling form of lyric theater has been the film score. Theodorakis has written more than twenty. Some of his most important triumphs include the scores for the film *Z* (a dramatization of the assassination of Grigoris Lambrakis) and his phenomenally successful sound track of 1964, for Michael Cacoyannis's film version of Nikos Katzanzakis's novel *Zorba the Greek.*

Theodorakis is a prolific writer and composer. (His autobiography occupies four volumes!) He has also published many essays on topics such as Greek folk music, music education, and the Lambrakis Youth Movement.[29]

The music of Theodorakis has been slow to gain acceptance in the United States. Linguistic difficulties account in part for this phenomenon; however, the composer's political views have been equally problematic. Efforts to introduce his music were made by influential people, such as Dimitri Mitropolous. Mitropolous was conductor of the Minneapolis Symphony Orchestra from 1936 until 1949, and then of the New York Philharmonic from 1950 until 1957, when he turned the post over to his protege, Leonard Bernstein. In 1953, Mitropolous tried to arrange for a performance of Theodorakis's music in Salt Lake City, but when news of the composer's Communist sympathies became known, the performances were canceled. Since the melt-down of the Iron Curtain, his music has become more accessible, particularly via arts organizations in erstwhile East Germany, where his political affiliations are viewed positively.

In his native land too, Theodorakis's music has often been suppressed because of his politics. This was the case in the years following World War II, when Greece was in the balance between democracy and communism. In 1945, Greek radio came under national control. Anyone who owned a radio was required to register with the national broadcasting company and pay radio taxes.[30] Broadcasts were closely supervised, and leftists like Theodorakis were denied access to the airwaves. After the 1967 military coup, he was imprisoned; but international outrage forced his release in 1970, and he has remained active in Greek politics and culture since then.

Modern Greek poetry has provided the impetus for many of Theodorakis's works. For some, he has used acknowledged masterpieces by contemporary writers such as George Seferis, Iannis Ritsos, and Odysseas Elytis. Elytis, who won the Nobel Prize for literature in 1979, reflected upon his days in the Greek resistance against the Fascists and Nazis in his poem *Axion esti* (praise be; 1959). As soon as it was published in 1960, Elytis sent the poem to the composer, who was living in Paris at the time. Theodorakis was intrigued by the quasi-liturgical format of the poem, which is apparent in its title, the opening words of the Greek Orthodox Eucharistic liturgy. The completed setting, which was not performed until 1964, is an oratorio in three parts for baritone and bass soloists, mixed chorus, and orchestra including piano, guitar, and drums, as well as the traditional Greek instruments *bouzouki* and *santouri* (a trapezoidal hammered dulcimer). The singers act at times as narrators, as cantors, or sing in a popular style as chorus leaders approximating a modern equivalent to the *koryphaios* of ancient Greek drama.

Despite many interesting moments, overall, the score suffers from excessive repetition of simplistic ideas (in the manner of Orff), as, for example, in movement 13, "Ich ziehe in ein Land hinab."[31] The score is further weakened by an overly long text, which consists only of selections from Elytis's poem, and a musical setting too often constrained by considerations of text declamation. This last difficulty is especially apparent in the choral writing, which is frequently in unison or simply spoken in rhythm.

The strongest parts of *Axion esti* are the purely instrumental Intermezzo in Part II, which not only shows the Greek instruments to good advantage, but also contains some interesting melodies influenced by Byzantine chant and treated in two-part imitation, and all of Part III. This concluding segment uses a choral refrain with intervening episodes for solo voices, but it has a certain energy that stems from Theodorakis's use of *tsamikos* rhythm. The *tsamikos* is a traditional, all-male dance in moderate triple meter. In the course of the Finale, this dance refrain gains momentum with each repetition and begins to resemble the kind of energy that Theodorakis had achieved in his score for *Zorba the Greek.*

Among the later works, *Liturgy No. 2* (1982) is particularly attractive. Commissioned by the Dresden Kreuzchor, *Liturgy* is an adaptation for *a cappella* chorus of an earlier song cycle entitled *Ta lirika. Liturgy* is modeled after the Greek Orthodox all-night vigil and thus begins with a Vespers prayer and concludes with a Matins prayer. The texts of the fourteen movements include ten by the composer's friend Tasos Livadhitis and four of his own poems, including an elegy for Anne Frank. This extraordinarily touching work is dedicated to the memory of children killed in wars.[32]

Theodorakis's Seventh Symphony (1983) uses solo vocalists, chorus, and orchestra in setting texts by Iannis Ritsos and Iorgos Kouloukis in a four-movement symphonic plan. The second movement, "The Execution of Athena," is a haunting setting of Kouloukis's poem recounting the execution of a young woman by that name at the concentration camp of Makronissos in 1949. Theodorakis was interned there along with Kouloukis and Athena. One morning, the guards dragged the young woman to the wall and shot her to death. The inmates observed that she had been carrying two oranges and that the juice of the oranges mingled with her blood at the execution. In his musical setting of this powerful poem, Theodorakis superimposes different strands of melody inspired by Byzantine chant. The effect is very close to certain passages in Stravinsky's *Les noces.*

Though recognition was slow in coming, in February of 1993, Theodorakis was appointed as the musical director of the State Radio Orchestra and Choir of Greece. He has written a vast amount of music including over 700 songs and 100 large works in various genres. The 1990s were years of touring and concertizing for him, and his combination of Greek traditional musics, Pop, and classical elements, in creating music pervaded by his sense of social responsibility may provide a viable model for future composers.

Notes

1. Robert Sherlaw Johnson, *Messiaen* (Berkeley and Los Angeles: University of California Press, 1975), p. 10.
2. Because so many of Messiaen's important works are for the organ, and since he is meticulous in specifying the registration to be used, a knowledge of this instrument is helpful in understanding the actual sounds he intended to be heard. The specifications are given in the appendix of Peter Hill, ed., *The Messiaen Companion* (Portland, Oregon: Amadeus Press, 1995), pp. 526–529.
3. (Paris: Leduc, 1944; English trans., Leduc, 1957).
4. Paul Griffiths, *Olivier Messiaen and the Music of Time* (Ithaca, New York: Cornell University Press, 1985), p. 88.
5. The 120 *deçî-tâlas* are given as Appendix II in Johnson, *Messiaen,* pp. 194–198.
6. Silesia is a region in central Europe in the upper valley of the Oder River. Prior to World War II, it was shared by Poland, Czechoslovakia, and Germany, the last of these holding the largest portion of the territories. In accordance with the terms of the Potsdam Agreement of 1945, Germany ceded its claims in Silesia to Poland.
7. Johnson, *Messiaen,* p. 61.
8. Olivier Messiaen, *Quatuor pour la fin du temps* (Paris: Durand, n.d.), Preface.
9. In the Preface to the score, Messiaen cites this text in French and goes on to remark concerning the piece that "Il a été directement inspiré par cette citation de l'Apocalypse. Son langage musical est essentiellement immatériel, spirituel, catholique." (It was inspired directly from this citation from the Apocalypse. Its musical language is essentially ephemeral, spiritual, catholic.)
10. Claude Samuel, *Conversations with Olivier Messiaen,* trans. Felix Aprahamian (London: Stainer and Bell, 1976), p. 2.
11. Samuel, *Conversations,* p. 7.
12. An accurate English translation of these commentaries is provided in Melvin Berger's *Guide to Chamber Music* (New York: Dodd, Mead, and Company, 1985), pp. 279–280.
13. Samuel, *Conversations,* p. 10. The birdsongs used by Messiaen are cataloged in Johnson, *Messiaen,* pp. 198–208.
14. Samuel, *Conversations,* p. 11.
15. Griffiths, notes for *Messiaen: Quatuor pour la fin du temps.* DGG CD 423-247-2, p. 3.

16. s.v. "Litany," in *The New Harvard Dictionary of Music*, ed. Don M. Randel (Cambridge, Massachusetts: Belknap Press of Harvard University Press, 1986), p. 452.
17. The Arabic number "8" is itself a representation of eternity, since it is a plane rendering of a three-dimensional Möbius strip.
18. Peter Hill, "Piano Music I," *The Messiaen Companion* (Portland, Oregon: Amadeus Press, 1995), p. 80.
19. Paul Griffiths, notes for *Éclairs sur l'au-delà*. Myung-Whun Chung cond., Orchestre de l'Opéra Bastille (Deutsche Grammophon CD 439-929-2, © 1994), p. 3. Discussion of the piece is, of course, absent from Griffith's book, which was published in 1985.
20. For a contextual discussion of IRCAM and Postmodern aesthetic criticism, see Georgina Born, *Rationalizing Culture: IRCAM, Boulez, and the Institutionalization of the Musical Avant-Garde* (Berkeley and Los Angeles: University of California Press, 1995).
21. For details concerning the structural parallels, see André Baltensperger, *Iannis Xenakis und die stochastische Musik: Komposition im Spannungsfeld von Architektur und Mathematik* (Bern: Haupt, 1996).
22. Nouritza Matossian, *Xenakis* (London: Kahn and Averill, 1990), p. 160.
23. Some examples of Xenakis's sketches appear in his treatise *Formalized Music: Thought and Mathematics in Composition* (Bloomington: Indiana University Press, 1971).
24. Matossian, *Xenakis*, pp. 206–207.
25. For this insight, I am grateful to Radu Stan of Éditions Salabert.
26. George Giannaris, *Mikis Theodorakis: Music and Social Change* (New York: Praeger, 1972), p. 29.
27. An Italian invasion in 1940 was repelled by Greek forces.
28. Typically, the instrument is with three strings tuned D-A-D.
29. Most of these are available only in Greek; however, his "Plan for the Reorganization of Greek Music," which is cosigned by Argyris Kounadis, Iannis Xenakis, Iannis Papaioannou, Dimitris Chorafas, and Phivos Anoyiannakis, is included as Appendix II (pp. 294–297) of Giannaris, *Mikis Theodorakis: Music and Social Change*.
30. Giannaris, *Mikis Theodorakis: Music and Social Change*, p. 112.
31. Titles and numbers as they appear on Theodorakis, *Axion esti* (Berlin Classics, 1992), CD 0093522BC.
32. The *Liturgy No. 2* has been recorded by the Dresden Kreuzchor under the direction of Martin Fläming (Berlin Classics, 1995), CD 0011282BC.

Chapter 13

Germany and Austria until the Fall of the Third Reich

Gustav Mahler's early death in 1911 left the musical scene in Germany and Austria in the first half of the twentieth century under the domination of one figure: Richard Strauss. Joseph Goebbels, Hitler's minister of propaganda, made this fact eminently clear in 1935, when he founded the Music Council (Musikkammer-senat) and appointed Strauss as its president. The Music Council consisted of eminent musicians who were charged with the regulation of all artistic activity. Its power extended to concert life, music criticism, instrument building, music publishing, professional music organizations, and even audience development. An important part of the Music Council was the Music Examining Agency (Musikprüfstelle), which weeded out *entartete Musik*—degenerate music.

Strauss's involvement with these government programs was viewed as a prudent move by most musicians—though after the war it led to his being charged at the Nuremberg trials as a Nazi conspirator. In the last decades of the nineteenth century, Strauss had established his reputation as a brilliant composer, orchestrator, and conductor with his seven tone poems. By the time of his appointment to the presidency of the Music Council, he had conducted at Bayreuth, Munich, Berlin, and Vienna. As a conductor, he was highly regarded, especially for his interpretations of Wagner. He confirmed his position as Germany's leading composer in the first quarter of the twentieth century with the scores of *Salome* (1905), *Elektra* (1909), and the neo-Romantic *Der Rosenkavalier* (bearer of the rose; 1911).

Salome and *Elektra* contained all of the principal musical elements that led to the Expressionistic styles later cultivated by Schönberg, Berg, and Hindemith. Strauss's scores are filled with "progressive details of all sorts, including tone clusters, whole-tone scales, extreme vocal leaps, purposefully distorted declamation, and many passages in which the harmony and orchestration were daring for their time."[1]

The texts of both operas, by Oscar Wilde and Hugo von Hofmannsthal respectively, are often disjunct. Lines in the librettos are emotional outbursts rather than lucid thoughts, and sometimes the succession of words is ungrammatical, even by the most liberal standards.[2] Strauss's music is correspondingly erratic, since it emphasizes momentary emotional states. Within this context, two or three notes, played at a certain dynamic level, with a particular articulation, in a certain register, become one of the structural foci in a larger composition. This style paved the way for "event music."

Strauss exerted a powerful influence on many young composers in the early twentieth century. Berg, for example, who heard the Austrian premiere of *Salome* in 1906, was "so strongly affected by the work that he attended six more performances in Vienna the same year."[3]

Despite racist policies of the National Socialist Party, Strauss frequently worked with Jews. Stefan Zweig, his librettist for *Der schweigsame Frau* (the silent woman; 1935), was a Jew. Hofmannsthal, the librettist for *Elektra, Der Rosenkavalier*, and other works, was part Jewish; and so was Strauss's daughter-in-law. The composer's complacency with the Nazis reflects a certain simplemindedness that appeared intermittently throughout his career: first, the use in the Finale of *Aus Italien* of a copyrighted song that he erroneously thought to be a folk tune; then, the inadvertent setting of stage directions as texts to be sung; later, insensitive remarks to his friend Gustav Mahler; worse, conducting in Bruno Walter's place when he was removed from his post at the Leipzig Gewandhaus because he was a Jew; more offensive still, his substituting at Bayreuth for Toscanini, who refused to perform for Nazis; and so on. The anti-Semitic activities of Strauss's later career are quite astonishing since, as a young man, he had had cordial professional and personal relationships with Jewish musicians, many of whom he actively supported.

Arnold Schönberg

The Early Years

Of Strauss's Jewish musical colleagues, perhaps the most important was Schönberg (1874–1951).[4] Born in Vienna to a family of orthodox Jews, as the oldest of three children, he took a job in 1891 as a bank teller after the death of his father so that he could help out with family expenses. He kept that post until 1895, when he explored his musical talents seriously. He studied from time to time with Alexander Zemlinsky (1871–1942), whose sister, Mathilde, he married in 1901.

In that same year, through the recommendation of Strauss, Schönberg obtained an appointment to the Stern Conservatory in Berlin. He moved there with Mathilde, but they decided to return to Vienna in 1903. Schönberg began teaching privately, and in 1904, Alban Berg (1885–1935) and Anton Webern (1883–1945) became his pupils.

It was at about this time that Schönberg's first important works, most of them programmatic, were given in public. The string sextet *Verklärte Nacht* (transfigured night, 1899) had its premiere in 1903. This tone poem, based on a poem by Richard Dehmel, is in an effusive, late Romantic style largely derivative of Wagner (especially *Tristan und Isolde*) and Strauss. Schönberg himself conducted the premiere of his vast orchestral tone poem *Pelleas und Melisande* (1903) in 1905.

After these expansive essays in Romanticism, the relative austerity of the First Chamber Symphony (1906) and the String Quartet No. 1 in D minor (1905) came as a shock. In the former, highly condensed symphonic movements are fused into a continuous movement for fifteen solo instruments. The quartet, though it includes the traditional four movements of Sonata, Scherzo, Adagio, and Rondo, is also played without break. Cyclic recurrence (the main theme group in the Scherzo, the second theme group in the Adagio, and both in the Rondo) provides further unification.

The premiere was given by the renowned Rosé Quartet on 15 February 1907. Josef Arnold Rosé founded the ensemble in 1883; from 1905 until 1920, the reconstituted ensemble included Rosé, Paul Fischer, Anton Ruzitska, and Friedrich Buxbaum. Their interpretations were highly regarded, but their work was brought to a tragic halt when Rosé and Buxbaum fled to England upon the Nazis' takeover of Austria in 1938. Rosé continued concertizing until his death in 1946.[5]

While composing the quartet, Schönberg was also working on the score of *Gurrelieder*. Franz Schreker conducted the premiere in Vienna on 23 February 1913. The majority of the piece was completed during 1900–1901, but the orchestration took the next ten years. The *Gurrelieder* is a dramatic oratorio of gargantuan proportions, a worthy companion of the contemporaneous *Symphony of 1000* by Mahler. The public response to *Gurrelieder* was enthusiastic. At its conclusion, Schönberg was acclaimed with a standing ovation, but he was irate about not having been invited to conduct the performance and convinced that he was unappreciated in Vienna.[6] He stormed out of the theater without even acknowledging the applause.

A look at the score will quickly show why the public responded so positively to the *Gurrelieder*: King Waldmar's aria, "Du wunderliche Tove," is as sumptuous as any of Wagner's *Wesendonck Lieder* in its seemingly endless melodies and lush chromatic harmonies. The orchestral interlude that follows has all of the emotional power of a Strauss tone poem, and the orchestration shows the incredible skill that Schönberg had acquired as a result of orchestrating thousands of pages of popular music and operettas to supplement his income. In short, the score gave Schönberg's Viennese audience exactly the sort of music that they were accustomed to. There is, however, one important innovation in the score of the *Gurrelieder*, and that is the first appearance in Schönberg's music of *Sprechstimme*. The term means, literally, "speaking voice"; however, in practice, *Sprechstimme* is halfway between speech and song. Exact pitches and durations are indicated on a conventional staff, but these are rendered in something like the delivery used by popular entertainers like Marlene Dietrich or Rex Harrison (*recte:* Reginald Carey).

In all probability, the idea for *Sprechstimme* came from the realm of popular music. Schönberg worked in a cabaret in Berlin from 1901 to 1903, and was familiar with popular styles. Yvette Guilbert (*recte:* Emma Laure Esther Guilbert, 1865–1944), a chanteuse who, by 1891, was a leading personality in Parisian *cafés-concerts,* and who toured England, Germany, and the United States, used this sort of dramatic speech-song delivery. It has been noted that "She turned every song into a miniature drama."[7] Schönberg saw the potential of this style of singing, particularly in instances where every word was critically important and required clear delivery. Schönberg used *Sprechstimme* to create little dramas in his song cycle of twenty-one poems, *Pierrot lunaire* (moonstruck Pierrot; 1912) for soprano, flute/piccolo, violin/viola, clarinet/bass clarinet, 'cello, piano.[8]

For Schönberg, the years before World War I were fruitful ones in which he produced some of his most important Expressionistic works. These scores, often full of anxiety and frustration, parallel the Angst of Schönberg's personal life. His marriage was a stormy one, and his wife was romantically involved with a young artist, Richard Gerstl. Schönberg knew the man well and admired his paintings. A painter himself, Schönberg was very much attracted by Gerstl's Expressionistic style and even took some lessons with him.[9] Gerstl found his position within this romantic triangle impossible, and after Webern convinced Mathilde to leave Gerstl and return to Schönberg and their two children, Gerstl committed suicide on 4 November 1908. "The twenty-five-year-old painter had . . . burned all personal evidence of his existence . . . thrown a noose around his neck and, finally, plunged a knife into his chest. . . . It was a situation that . . . was destined to prove disastrous to all concerned."[10]

Schönberg explored his feelings in a more creative way than Gerstl, especially in the two musical dramas *Erwartung* (expectation; 1909) and *Die glückliche Hand* (the lucky hand; 1913).[11]

Erwartung is one of Schönberg's finest and most original creations. This monodrama is based on a text by Marie Pappenheim, at the time, a medical student at the University of Vienna and friend of Zemlinsky's. Her poem consists of fragmented phrases that suggest events rather than providing linear narrative. Schönberg's score is replete with stage directions. The following samples will show both the envisioned setting and the poetic style.

[The edge of a forest. Moonlight paths and fields; the forest high and dark. Only the first trees and the beginning of the broad path still light . . . a woman approaches.]

> The night is so warm.
> I'm afraid . . . what heavy air blows . . .
> Like a storm that stands . . .
> So horribly calm and void . . .
> But here it is at least light . . .
> The moon was bright a moment ago . . .
> Oh! still the cricket . . . with his love song . . .

Don't speak . . . It's so sweet beside you . . .
the moon is in the twilight . . .
You're a coward . . . Don't you want to look for him?
Die right here!
How oppressive this silence is . . .
The moon is risen . . . does it see into this?
I, alone, in the suffocating shadows.
I'll sing so that he hears me.

Much of the tension in both the text and music arises from the dialectic between *hallucination* (an ungrounded and unrealistic horror in face of the present) and *memory* (an unrealistic and idealized recollection of imagined security and contentment). In the course of the drama, a further conflict arises between *reality* and *self-deception*. As the story unfolds (at least, to the extent that we can make sense of it as a story), self-deception replaces hallucination as the protagonist struggles to ignore the corpse. *Memory*, initially a vehicle to escape from the present, becomes the agent for exposing the crime at hand. Memory demands the identification of a guilty party, a motive for the crime, and a victim. At the same time, *dementia* diverts any reasonable conclusion.

Schönberg's musical technique mirrors the text as well as its progressive, scientific influences. Musical climaxes are coordinated with high points of psychological stress. An atonal harmonic idiom, devoid of tonal stasis, complements the sense of unsettled emotion. Athematic setting of the text mirrors the fragmentary nature of the prosody. At the same time, lush orchestration enhances the Romantic imagery of the text, with its frequent references to moonlight, trees and shrubs, breezes, and so forth. Certainly, these images could have provided idyllic topoi for any Romantic composer; yet, in the context of *Erwartung*, they are horrific images that provoke terror.

Schönberg, and the Expressionists generally, could not have achieved their artistic goals without reference to concurrent developments in the newly emerging discipline of psychoanalysis. At the time, Vienna was the center for research in this area, and Sigmund Freud was the forward-looking personality around whom likeminded intellects gathered.

Sigmund Freud, 1856–1939

Born in Freiberg (now in Czechoslovakia), Freud and his family moved to Leipzig to escape anti-Semitic riots. He attended the University of Vienna from 1873 until 1881. He later worked there with Ernest Wilhelm von Brücke on neurological research. In 1886, Freud established a private practice in Vienna, where he devoted his principal attention to the treatment of nervous disorders. His first publication, written in collaboration with Josef Breuer and published in 1893, was a study of the physical origins of hysterical disorders. A more detailed investigation of the topic was published as *Studien über Hysterie* (studies of hysteria; 1895). In this volume, Freud discussed undischarged emotions associated with forgotten traumas. Therapy included hypnosis. Freud's study of infantile cerebral paralysis of 1897, was his final publication on neurology. From that time onward, he became increasingly interested in disorders not caused by organic malfunctions of the brain. He had already named the field "psychoanalysis" in 1896.

From 1895 until 1900, Freud explored the potential of free association, word slips, and other involuntary clues for the identification of mental mechanisms of repression and resistance, as well as the operation of various unconscious processes. Dream analysis became increasingly important, and he published a treatise on that topic in 1900. He subsequently identified the Oedipal complex, an erotic attachment of a child toward the parent of the opposite sex, which results in an antipathy toward the parent of the same sex.

In 1902, Freud was appointed professor at the University of Vienna, where Marie Pappenheim certainly would have known him personally and been aware of his work. Freud's founding, in 1910, of the International Psychoanalytic Association was a major advance for the discipline. His work progressed at break-neck speed until the advent of the Third Reich. In 1938, Freud left Austria. His last major work, *Moses and Monotheism* (1939) clearly shows Freud's concern for the plight of the Jew in Western European society in addition to his experiments in applying psychoanalysis within a broader assessment of cultural history. He died in London on 23 September 1939.

Schönberg and the Crisis of Being

Schönberg's life was a hard one: As a Jew in an anti-Semitic society, he was an outcast. In 1898, he converted to Lutheranism, but his change in loyalty proved pointless.

Schönberg's acerbic personality did little to endear him to important and powerful people. He was stubborn, inflexible, and often arrogant. While no one would deny his genius, even his most enthusiastic adherents would have to admit that he often brought hardships upon himself. In a letter of 7 March 1910 to Emil Hertzka, then director of Universal Editions, the young Schönberg wrote:

> My [painting] is highly praised by experts. . . . You might be able to get one or the other well-known patron to buy some of my pictures or have his portrait done by me. . . . Only you must not tell people that they *will* like my pictures. You must make them realize that they cannot but like my pictures, because they have been praised by authorities on painting; and above all that it is much more interesting to have one's portrait done by or to own a painting by a musician of my reputation than to be painted by some mere practitioner of painting whose name will be forgotten in 20 years, whereas even now my name belongs to the history of music.[12]

This same, egotistical bravado surfaces in Schönberg's letter of 19 March 1910 to Karl Wiener, then President of the Academy of Fine Arts, Vienna, who was trying to get an appointment for Schönberg as professor of composition. Wiener's efforts earned the following ungracious reaction:

> I assume your only reason for hesitating to appoint me to the Academy staff is that you are . . . afraid of protests from that section of the public which keeps on forgetting . . . *who* I am and what abilities I have, and this although I have proved it a hundred times. This although I have so often shown both what people can learn from me and what people do learn from me, namely how to develop one's own talent in the way most suited to it. . . . Anyone who wants to study modern music will learn from me all that can be learnt: based on a solid classical foundation, right up to the latest achievements in our art. . . . I take it for granted that you know you cannot find a more suitable teacher for the Academy than myself and that the only reason why you could not risk engaging me is that you do not wish to expose yourself to . . . criticism.[13]

In another letter to Hertzka, written on 31 October 1911, the none-too-modest Schönberg declared flatly:

> You cannot imagine how famous I am here. . . . I am known to everyone. I am recognized from my photographs. People know my biography. . . . So if you would lend a bit of a hand, we should see some results soon. Now please print my work!!! I am certain it's good!!![14]

Schönberg's personal circumstances and Expressionistic musical style seem to have arrived at an impasse at precisely the time World War I broke out. During the years 1915 and 1916, he served in the Austrian army. From 1917 until 1922, he worked on the score of an oratorio entitled *Die Jakobsleiter* (Jacob's ladder). Though the piece is nominally "unfinished," the portions that were completed are extensive, and they contain much that is simply astonishing. The solo vocal writing, which shows the influence of Mahler's Eighth Symphony, makes unprecedented demands on the soloists for range, endurance, dynamic control, and intonation.

Among Schönberg's instrumental works, the String Quartet No. 2 in F-sharp minor, Op. 10 (1908), the Three Piano Pieces, Op. 11 (1909), the Six Little Piano Pieces, Op. 19 (1911), and the Five Pieces for Orchestra, Op. 16 (1909) are important. The third movement of this last set is entitled "Farben" (colors), and it is Schönberg's first use of *Klangfarbenmelodie* (tone color melody). Though precedents for such music can be found—Wagner's Prelude to *Das Rheingold*, for example—Schönberg's use of *Klangfarbenmelodie* was more self-conscious than earlier, more instinctive applications of the concept. Schönberg coined the term in his *Harmonielehre* (harmony manual; 1911), where he explains it as a melody that derives its identity from changing timbres rather than changing pitches.

Schönberg realized that his evolving musical style would not be accessible to the public; accordingly, in 1918, he organized the Verein für musikalische Privataufführungen (society for private musical performances). This organization was one of the earliest advocacy groups for contemporary music. Its members were required to show identification for all events, and they were prohibited from showing any reaction, positive or otherwise. Scores were studied prior to the programs, and pieces that were of an advanced nature would be played twice. Critics were barred from the society's events.

In 1923, Schönberg began composing serial music. His first forays into this style were in the Five Piano Pieces, Op. 23, and the Serenade, Op. 24. The latter piece is interesting in its combination of a twelve-note row with eleven-syllable lines of a Petrarchan sonnet. The first fully dodecaphonic score is that of the Piano Suite, Op. 25, in which Schönberg associates his own modern compositions with the mainstream of German music history. Its five movements are Prelude, Gavotte, Musette, Menuett, and Gigue.

In 1923, Schönberg's adulterous first wife, Mathilde, died. Gertrud Kolisch, the sister of his student Rudolf Kolisch, met Schönberg through her brother, who was a violinist. In 1922, Rudy had founded a professional quartet that was at the forefront of modern chamber music performance until 1939. They gave the premiere performances of Schönberg's Third and Fourth String Quartets as well as that of Berg's *Lyric Suite*, Webern's Trio and Quartet, and Bartók's Fifth. Schönberg's frequent meetings with Kolisch—both Rudy and Gertrude—led to affection, then from affection to his marriage to Gertrude in 1924.

By 1924, Schönberg became the chair of the composition department at the Prussian Academy of Arts in Berlin. No doubt, Schönberg thought at the time that his years of travail were over, that his career would proceed in a fashion appropriate for his genius, and that he and his family would live happily ever after; but, in the eyes of the Third Reich, the Christianized Schönberg was still a Jew. In fact, they were right: Schönberg was proud of his heritage, and the years from 1930 until 1932 were occupied largely with the composition of his opera-oratorio, *Moses and Aaron*.

In this colossal work, Schönberg, who wrote the libretto himself, deals with the role of the artist in a society gone amok; thus Moses, the seeker of truth and servant of the Most High, must endure the insane scene of the worship of the golden calf in Act II. Schönberg did not set the final portion of his libretto—possibly because there was no need to set anything more than he already had. In any event, the year 1933 found him stripped of dignity and denied the rewards of his accomplishments. He was expelled from his post at the Academy. He fled first to France, where he converted back to Judaism, then to the United States. By 1934, he settled in California, where he found employment, first at the University of Southern California, and from 1936 until his retirement in 1944, at the University of California at Los Angeles. Writing from the U.S.A. to Berg, Schoenberg commented that "my return to the Jewish religion took place long ago and is . . . demonstrated in . . .

Moses and Aaron, . . . but especially in my drama *Der biblische Weg*" (the biblical way).[15]

Schoenberg was apprehensive of life in the United States: He lamented "there's no knowing how disregarded, slighted, and without influence I may be there."[16] Nevertheless, his American years were peaceful and productive. The Violin Concerto, Op. 36 (1936), the Second Chamber Symphony, Op. 38 (1939), the Organ Variations on a Recitative, Op. 40 (1941), and the Piano Concerto, Op. 42 (1942) are among his important instrumental works from the period. As in the early stages of his career, Schoenberg continued to use music as a way to deal with psychological trauma. His horror at

Arnold Schoenberg

the brutality of the Third Reich is powerfully expressed in his *Survivor from Warsaw*, Op. 46 (1947), for speaker, men's chorus, and large orchestra.

What is, perhaps, conspicuous in Schoenberg's American works is a certain relaxation of the aggressive dissonance of his serial works of the 1920s. In part, this fact is a result of a different approach to the treatment of the row, which, in his works of the 1940s, frequently functions as a *cantus firums* that retains recognizable musical details. Schoenberg's renewed interest in traditional tonal repertoire, as evidenced by the arrangements he made between 1932 and 1934, of concertos by Georg Monn and George Frederick Handel, may have been a further factor in his modification of serial techniques.

On 2 August 1946, he suffered a near fatal heart attack, but he recovered and went on to write more music—including the String Trio, Op. 45 (1946), which was Schoenberg's musical response to his circumstances as "one whose life was coming to a close on soil far from his native land and the culture of his youth."[17] His health continued to decline, and he died on 13 July 1951.

Schönberg's Pupils: Alban Berg and Anton Webern

Schönberg was a teacher for most of his life. Whether at the Stern Conservatory in Berlin, his private studio in Vienna, the Prussian Academy of Arts in Berlin, at USC, or UCLA, he constantly worked with young musicians. The results of this process led him to write many textbooks, including the previously mentioned *Harmonielehre*, in addition to such titles as *Style and Idea* and *Structural Functions of Harmony*.[18]

Alban Berg

Of Schönberg's students, many went on to professional careers in music. Two, however, are of singular importance: Alban Berg (1885–1935) and Anton Webern (1883–1945). Berg's lessons with Schönberg began in October 1904. By 1908, he had completed what we might consider his diploma piece, the Piano Sonata, Op. 1. In this work, Berg's inclination toward Romanticism is clear; nevertheless, his ingenuity is apparent in his approach to form. The Sonata is a tonal work; yet its melodies and harmonies are so chromatic, that the delineation of polarized key areas within the exposition and their reconciliation within the recapitulation as a consequence of intervening developmental techniques is simply impossible. Berg saw the problem and chose simply to replace one musical parameter (key) with another (tempo); hence, the three themes of the exposition are assigned precise tempos that return in the recapitulation. Berg originally planned a three-movement work; however, he could find no suitable material for the second and third movements. Schönberg, in a bit of wonderfully practical advice, simply indicated to Berg that if there is nothing further to say, the piece is done.

The five songs for soprano and large orchestra known as the *Altenberg Lieder*, Op. 4 (1912) are impressive.[19] Of them, the last, which Berg calls a passacaglia, is important because its treatment of the repeated line presages many of the procedures of Serialism.

Of Berg's large works, his opera *Wozzeck* (1922) is especially important. Using materials from Georg Büchner's incomplete play *Woyzeck*, Berg assembled his own, tightly structured libretto of three acts with five scenes in each. The structural organization of the individual scenes and the larger acts is impressive: The scenes of the first act yield a suite; those of the second, a symphony in five movements; those of the third, a series of inventions on specific musical figures. Berg himself was quick to point out that the structures of the opera are unimportant in comparison to their impact on listeners, whether they are conscious of them or otherwise.

His *Lyric Suite* (1925) for string quartet is a six-movement work in increasingly disparate tempos. For its tonal materials, it uses a row consisting of the tones F, E, C, A, G, D, A-flat, D-flat, E-flat, G-flat, B-flat, B. The row alludes to Berg's mistress, Hanna Fuchs-Robettin. The score was published as a purely instrumental string quartet, but in fact, Berg withheld a part for solo soprano—hence, the title *Lyric Suite*. He also quotes the *Tristan* chord, notorious from that opera written by Wagner during his affair with Mathilde Wesendonck.

Berg was at work on his opera *Lulu* when he received a commission from Louis Krasner to write a violin concerto. This turned out to be his last completed work. In the "magic square" showing the tone row of the Violin Concerto, the original row (known as the "prime" form and abbreviated as P) is shown across the top in Arabic numbers with C being 0 and B being 11. To get the numbers in the

EXAMPLE 4A
Magic Square for Berg's Violin Concerto

G B♭ D F# A C E G# B C# D# E#

7	10	2	6	9	0	4	8	11	1	3	5
4	7	11	3	6	9	1	5	8	10	0	2
0	3	7	11	2	5	9	1	4	6	8	10
8	11	3	7	10	1	5	9	0	2	4	6
5	8	0	4	7	10	2	6	9	11	1	3
2	5	9	1	4	7	11	3	6	8	10	0
10	1	5	9	0	3	7	11	2	4	6	8
6	9	1	5	8	11	3	7	10	0	2	4
3	6	10	2	5	8	0	4	7	9	11	1
1	4	8	0	3	6	10	2	5	7	9	11
11	2	6	10	1	4	8	0	3	5	7	9
9	0	4	8	11	2	6	10	1	3	5	7

Triads:
    minor: (0, 3, 7)
    augmented: (0, 4, 8)
    major: (0, 4, 7)
    diminished: (0, 3, 6)

Lydian scale: $\hat{1}, \hat{2}, \hat{3}, \hat{4}, = (0, 2, 4, 6)$

left-hand column, we perform (in base 12) the *opposite* operation between the first number and each of the following numbers in P: 7 *plus* 3 yields 10; 7 *minus* 5 yields 2, etc. Conversely, 7 *minus* 3 yields 4; 7 *plus* 5 yields 12 (0 in base 12). These numbers give the inversion (I) of the row when read from top to bottom. The lines from right to left form the retrograde (R) forms of the rows in their various transpositions. Reading the numbers of any column from bottom to top yields the retrograde inversions (RI). Indications such as P-7, R-9, and so forth indicate the prime form starting on G (i.e., 7 in the chromatic scale) and the retrograde transposed (i.e., add 2 to each value) to start on A (i.e., 9 in the chromatic scale).

Berg constructed this tone row with several purposes in mind. First, the row demonstrates a nostalgic longing for the sonorities of functional harmony—of sweetness remembered but now lost. The final four notes also form a structural link with the quotation of the chorale tune "Es ist genug," which begins with an ascent through a tritone. Berg took this chorale from Bach's cantata S. 60, *O Ewigkeit, du Donnerwort* (o eternity, you word of thunder).

Magic squares are useful for identifying manipulations of pitch sets. In this case, Berg has used minor $(0, 3, 7)$, augmented $(0, 4, 8)$, major $(0, 4, 7)$, and diminished $(0, 3, 6)$ triads extensively. Any configuration of tones that can be reduced to one of these sets of integers therefore represents one of these triads. In P-0, for instance, the third, fourth, and fifth numbers are the set $(7, 11, 2)$. By subtracting 7, we get $(0, 4, 7)$, the numerical equivalent of a major triad. The final four tones $(11, 1, 3, 5)$, when put in simple form by subtracting eleven, correspond to $(0, 2, 4, 6)$, which are the first four notes of a Lydian-mode tritone. In this piece, the various

EXAMPLE 4B
Alban Berg-Violin Concerto-Row

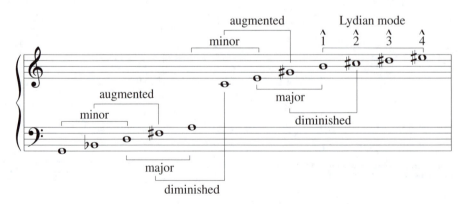

EXAMPLE 4C
Alban Berg, Violin Concerto. Chorale and text of J. S. Bach, "Es ist genug"

Es ist genug: Herr, wenn es dir gefällt,	(It is sufficient: Lord, if it please Thee,
So spanne mich doch aus.	Then from this life release me.
Mein Jesus kommt; nun gute Nacht,	My Jesus comes: Now good night,
o Welt!	o world!
Ich fahr' in's Himmelshaus,	I go to my heavenly home,
Ich fahre sicher hin mit Frieden,	I journey forth in peace as
Mit grosser Jammer bleibt darnieden,	Those below remain in great distress.
Es ist genug, es ist genug.	It is sufficient, it is sufficient.)

Chorale "Es ist genug" from J. S. Bach, Cantata S. 60, *O Ewigkeit, du Donnerwort*

types of triads are easy to recognize, but in pieces using pitch sets that are foreign to tonal music, these mathematical operations can reveal manipulations that might not be apparent to the ear or eye.

Berg wrote this concerto in memory of Manon Gropius, the daughter of Alma Mahler and Walter Gropius as well as a close friend of Berg's. At the time of her death, she was a youthful beauty of eighteen. Berg, a sensitive man by nature, was devastated. His choice of this tune, used in the Lutheran church as a funeral hymn, fits within the larger historical context of the piece. Certain Corinthian folk songs are also quoted for similar, personal reasons.

Anton Webern began his career as a musicologist in the classes of Guido Adler at the University of Vienna (1902–1906).[20] His historical work focused on the music of Heinrich Isaac (ca. 1450–1517), particularly the *Choralis Constantinus*, a setting of liturgical texts for the church year in which Isaac used elaborate counterpoint, dense canons, and complex proportional manipulations. Webern's own music, though characterized by its brevity, is equally intricate.

Webern studied with Schönberg from 1904 until 1908. Like Berg, he produced a diploma piece: his Passacaglia, Op. 1 (1908) for orchestra. From the time he completed his studies with Schönberg until 1934, Webern made his living as a conductor, first in Prague, then in Vienna, and in various other locations. The Nazis considered Webern and his music antithetical to German culture; hence, he was forced to confine himself to editing and teaching.

In his earliest characteristic works, Webern tended to use sparse textures, small ensembles, and compact musical gestures. He first used serial techniques in his *Drei gesitliche Volkslieder* (three spiritual folksongs; 1924). Like Schönberg, he was fascinated by the music of Bach; consequently, he orchestrated the six-part Ricercar from the *Musical Offering* (1747).

Webern went on to write a body of works that contained the elements of what came to be integral Serialism. The focus in this repertoire on individual timbres, registers, dynamic levels, attacks, articulations, and so on, laid the foundations for pointillism and event music. Even in Webern's works for large ensembles, such as the Chamber Symphony (1928) and the Variations (1940) for orchestra, the sound of the full ensemble is rare.

Webern's career was brought to an abrupt halt when he was shot—obviously in error—by a soldier on 13 September 1945. Ironically, the war had officially ended by the time of Webern's assassination.

Anton Webern

Music inside the Reich: Carl Orff, Wolfgang Fortner, and Hans Pfitzner[21]

Orff (1895–1982) spent virtually his entire career in Munich, the city of his birth and death. He completed his studies at the Munich Academy of Music in 1914. In 1920, he began work with Heinrich Kaminski (1886–1946), who was a musical autodidact—and an eccentric one at that. Early on in Kaminski's career, the music of Bach, Beethoven, and Brahms exerted the most important influences. Kaminski's approach to the arts became increasingly philosophical, and he was concerned largely with questions of emotion and meaning in music. His approach to music stands in bold contrast to Orff's utilitarian and practical orientation.

In 1924, Orff met Dorothee Günther and with her, founded a school that taught music rudiments through active participation. His characteristic compositions function on a visceral level. Ostinatos, repeated melodic or rhythmic motifs, and a simplistic harmonic vocabulary are typical. Phrase structures and periodic structures are deliberately direct—almost naïve. The rhythmic mannerisms of Orff's style are also noteworthy. The tyranny of the bar line seems to have been an endless source of inspiration for Orff. Metrical patterns in his music are basic, and complex beat divisions are rare.

Though he composed a fair amount of music in his early years, Orff's reputation was established only in 1937, with the premiere of *Carmina Burana*. Scored for a large orchestra, mixed chorus, small chorus, boys' choir, and soloists, it is a setting in twenty-five movements of goliardic poetry of the thirteenth century. The majority of the movements are for chorus. Also significant is the related work, *Catulli carmina* (1933; rev. 1943) which is similar in scoring, text, and effect. All of Orff's significant compositions are "theatrical" works, nevertheless, one is hard pressed to identify one that would accord with the typical features of either opera or oratorio.

Orff Schulwerk combines music making with instruments, the human voice, extemporization, movement, and aural perception. Orff's techniques are especially useful because they can be implemented from the first encounter, regardless of the individual's previous musical training or experience.

Carl Orff

Wolfgang Fortner (1907–1987) was probably the most gifted of the composers who worked within the Reich. His music from the 1930s and '40s is mostly instrumental. In these, his contrapuntal skills and keen sense of form are apparent. After the fall of the Reich, Fortner began writing dramatic works including operas, ballets, and pantomimes. In his very late works, such as *Damals* (at that time; 1977), he combines mime, narration, and two vocalists with harpsichord, guitar, piano, and live electronics.

Hans Pfitzner (1869–1949) taught at the Stern Conservatory in Berlin from 1897 until 1907; served as director of music for the city of Strasbourg and director of its Conservatory of Music from 1908 until 1918; taught at the Berlin Academy of Arts from 1920 until 1929; and was a faculty member of the Munich Academy of Composition from 1929 until 1934.[22] By the advent of the Reich, he was a well-respected and eminent presence in musical circles.

A prolific and skillful composer, he wrote in almost all genres and media, but his many chamber pieces are probably his most important achievements. His only score that has anything like an enduring place is the opera *Palestrina* (1917). The problem with Pfitzner's music is that it was written by him: He enthusiastically supported the Reich, and he attacked progressive composers, critics, and musicians, whom he considered enemies of the Reich and the German musical tradition. Since his chamber pieces are ideologically neutral, they may, at some point, reenter concert repertoire.

Notes

1. Crawford and Crawford, *Expressionism in Twentieth-Century Music* (Bloomington: Indiana University Press, 1993), p. 33.
2. Freud's work must have been familiar to Hofmannsthal when he wrote the libretto of *Elektra*, which is "one of the first works of art in which psychoanalytical findings are used consistently." Crawford and Crawford, *Expressionism in Twentieth-Century Music*, p. 34.
3. Crawford and Crawford, *Expressionism in Twentieth-Century Music*, p. 34.
4. He changed the spelling of his name to "Schoenberg" after leaving Germany in 1933.
5. Rosé's daughter Alma was not so lucky. A violinist herself, she was captured by the Nazis and sent to Auschwitz. There, she managed to buy time—like Scheherazade—by entertaining her captors. She organized a women's orchestra, and she and her musicians were allowed to live in exchange for their music. She died of a sudden illness in 1944. See Richard Newman and Karen Kirtley, *Alma Rosé: Vienna to Auschwitz* (Portland, Oregon: Amadeus Press, 2000). p. 432.
6. See Schönberg's letter of 6 February 1913 to Emil Hertzka in *Arnold Schoenberg's Letters*, pp. 37–38.
7. Elaine Brody, *Paris, The Musical Kaleidoscope: 1870–1925* (London: Robson Books, 1988), p. 108.
8. Only five instrumentalists are required, since the instruments separated by the virgules never play simultaneously.
9. For a sampling of paintings by Schönberg, Gerstl, and other Expressionists active in Vienna, see Jane Kallir, *Arnold Schoenberg's Vienna* (New York: Galerie St. Etienne and Rizzoli International Publications, 1984). Concerning Gerstl's personal relationship with the Schönbergs, see especially p. 23.

10. Kallir, *Arnold Schoenberg's Vienna*, p. 28.
11. Schönberg wrote the text of *Die glückliche Hand* himself; hence, its allusion to Gerstl is not surprising. Kallir (*Arnold Schoenberg's Vienna*, p. 32) objects that the "tendency to see [*Erwartung*] as a direct reflection of the [Gerstl affair], . . . since Schoenberg did not write the text, . . . is farfetched. Pappenheim, after receiving the commission, went off to Traunkirchen to execute it, and it appears that the composer had little, if any, direct input in the formulation of the plot." Though Schönberg may have had little "direct input," Pappenheim could easily have gotten information from other, mutual acquaintances.
12. Arnold Schoenberg, *Arnold Schoenberg Letters*, selected and ed. Erwin Stein, trans. Eithne Wilkins and Ernst Kaiser (New York: St. Martin's Press, 1965), pp. 25–26.
13. Schoenberg, *Arnold Schoenberg Letters*, p. 27.
14. Schoenberg, *Arnold Schoenberg Letters*, p. 30.
15. Schoenberg, *Arnold Schoenberg Letters*, p. 184.
16. Schoenberg, *Arnold Schoenberg Letters*, p. 184.
17. Michael Cherlin, "Memory and Rhetorical Trope in Schoenberg's String Trio," *Journal of the American Musicological Society* 51 (fall 1998), 562.
18. *Style and Idea* (New York: Philosophical Library, 1950); *Structural Functions of Harmony* (New York: Norton, 1954).
19. The texts are aphoristic poems that were written by Peter Altenberg for the flip sides of picture postcards.
20. Kathryn Bailey, *The Life of Webern* (Cambridge, England: Cambridge University Press, 1998) is both readable and reliable. Technical aspects are examined in Bailey, *Twelve-Note Music of Anton Webern: Old Forms in a New Language* (Cambridge, England: Cambridge University Press, 1991).
21. For additional Reich composers, see Michael H. Kater, *Composers of the Nazi Era: Eight Portraits* (New York: Oxford, 2000).
22. For details, see John Williamson, *Music of Hans Pfitzner* (New York: Oxford, 1992).

Chapter 14

Music in Great Britain

The foundation for modern Britain was laid during the reign of Queen Victoria (1837–1901). Domestic advances included continued urbanization, extension of the vote to laborers and farmers (women were still unable to vote), formation of the first trade unions, and efforts toward a national educational system.

Foreign policy focused on preservation and expansion of Britain's imperial holdings. In 1839, the first Opium War with China enabled Britain to establish a system of naval bases there. More important still was the establishment of Hong Kong as a British colony.

Later in the century, Benjamin Disraeli (1804–1881) played an important role in this process of expansion. During his second tenure as prime minister (1874–1880), he annexed many areas around the globe—including portions of South Africa; arranged for Queen Victoria to be proclaimed Empress of India (1877); forced Turkey to cede Cyprus to Britain; reduced Russian influence in the Balkans; and strengthened the British presence in the Mediterranean. This last accomplishment was fortuitous. The Suez Canal Maritime Company, originally an independent Egyptian concern operated in conjunction with French support, was in desperate need of funds by 1875. They sold huge blocks of stock to finance the operation of the canal, which had opened to navigation on 17 November 1869. Disraeli saw the opportunity and seized it. Using government funds, he bought controlling interest in the company, and, as a consequence, established a means to supervise all navigation between the Mediterranean and the Red Sea. In addition to these new lands, Britain maintained its older, established colonies, especially Australia, Canada, and New Zealand.

The administration of these vast and diverse holdings precluded cultural isolationism; accordingly, non-Western influences are apparent in the music of many British composers. The extent to which ethnic musics are authentic or stereotyped is, of course, variable. Of the British composers active in the first half of the twentieth century, Gustav Holst was the most powerfully stimulated by the creative prospects of cultural diversity. It is to his life and works that we now turn our attention.

Gustav Holst, 1874–1934

Holst's mother, Clara Lediard, was a pianist, and the family included other musicians; hence, it seemed quite natural that in 1893 he decided to enter the Royal College of Music, where he studied piano, organ, theory, and composition. Composition studies were with Sir Charles Villiers Stanford (1852–1924). In addition, Holst played the trombone and had a good deal of practical pit experience. 1895 marked the beginning of his friendship with Ralph Vaughan Williams.

Holst took a position as music director of St. Paul's Girls' School in Hammersmith in 1903. Later, he held other teaching positions simultaneously at the Royal College of Music and Reading College.

Holst's early works were heavily influenced by Wagner.[1] According to the composer's daughter, Wagner's spell over Holst came to its zenith in the one-act theater piece, *The Youth's Choice* (1902). Holst soon realized that his Wagnerian imitations were futile. Holst found a fruitful alternative in English folksong, and several scores inspired by folksong resulted. The *Somerset Rhapsody* (1907), based on tunes from that region, is a miniature concerto for oboe *d'amore*, an antiquarian curiosity newly revived by the early music movement.

At the same time he worked on the *Somerset Rhapsody*, Holst completed his first opera, *Sita*, which is based on Hindu epic poetry. *Sita* was another blind alley. The music was still too much influenced by Wagner, but instead of Teutonic legends, Holst turned to the colorful legends of India—in this case, the *Ramayana*, an epic poem about Rama (the seventh incarnation of Vishnu), whose wife, Sita, is abducted by a demon. Rama ultimately recovers Sita and is restored to his kingdom.

Although Holst made little progress toward a personal musical idiom, he nevertheless discovered in the religious writings of India (which he translated himself) a treasure trove that would serve him well. In 1907, he began work on the solo songs from *Rig Veda*. Vedas are the sacred texts of the Hindus. There are four vedas: the *Yajur Veda, Sama Veda, Atharva Veda*, and the *Rig Veda*. The *Rig Veda* is the oldest of these, and was written in Sanskrit before 1000 B.C.E.

The *Rig Veda* contains 1,028 hymns to various Hindu deities. Holst must have been attracted to these texts not only because of their timeless and picturesque images, but also because his mother had been a theosophist. From her, Holst inherited a respect for spirituality—a respect that he shared with Vaughan Williams. Holst often chose contemplative texts as the basis of his vocal compositions, but he generally avoided liturgical Christian texts. The pinnacle of Holst's compositions based on the sacred writings of the Hindus were the four series of *Rig Veda* hymns that he composed between 1908 and 1912. The first series is for mixed chorus and orchestra and consists of (1) "The Battle Hymn," (2) "To the Unknown God," and (3) "The Funeral Hymn." The second series is for women's chorus and orchestra and includes (1) "To Varuna," (2) "To Agni," and (3) "Funeral Chant." The pieces of the third series, for women's chorus and harp, are (1) "Hymn to the Dawn," (2) "Hymn to the Waters," (3) "Hymn to Vena," and (4) "Hymn of the Travelers." The fourth series is for men's chorus and orchestra and consists of (1) "Hymn to Agni," (2) "Hymn to Soma," (3) "Hymn to Manas," and (4) "Hymn to Indra."

Holst's *Rig Veda* hymns create an ephemeral quality through their scoring and dynamics, joined with a distinctive harmonic style and unusual voicings. Holst does not use any particular scale consistently, but rather, uses scales containing *pien* tones (i.e., substitution tones) so that scale forms are variable. This results in an unpredictability that seems appropriate and natural for these texts. In the *basso ostinato* figure that dominates much of the "Hymn to the Unknown God" (Series I, no. 2), for example, Holst fills in an octave between E_1 and E_2 with the pitches E, D, C, B, A-sharp, G-sharp, F-natural, E. The pitch content is incompatible with E minor, E major, or the Phrygian mode. The half-step motion in the lowest voice repeatedly suggests a Phrygian cadence; however, the whole-step motion expected in the upper voices with this cadence formula is missing as Holst places a B-flat in the soprano (above the F-natural in the bass), which moves by half-step to B-natural (above the E in the bass). Harmonies lack traditional functional relationships; nevertheless, the chord successions are natural and fluid.

Unusual meters are also employed to good effect. These rhythms are often a byproduct of Holst's fidelity to the accentuation of the texts themselves. In the "Hymn to Agni" (Series II, no. 2), Holst uses various combinations of 3+2 and 2+3 within a quintuple time signature; perhaps the most bizarre meter is the 21/8 time used in the "Hymn to the Waters" (Series III, no. 2).

Other compositions flavored by Holst's interests in non-Western cultures include the opera *Savitri* (1908), *Beni Mora*, an "Oriental Suite" (1910), *Two Eastern Pictures* (1911) for women's chorus and harp, and the *Japanese Suite* (1915), written for the dancer Michio Ito, who apparently supplied Holst with some of the themes.

Holst's most widely performed work is undoubtedly his seven-movement symphonic poem, *The Planets* (1917). Earth is excluded from the score, as is Pluto. (It was not discovered until 1930 by the American astronomer Clyde William Tombaugh.) The premiere of *The Planets* took place in 1918 under the baton of Adrian Boult.

The score of *The Planets* requires four flutes, three oboes, three clarinets, bass clarinet, three bassoons, double-bassoon, six horns, four trumpets, three trombones, two tubas, timpani, celesta, percussion, two harps, organ, strings, and optional S-A chorus. Despite the large orchestra, the score shows that Holst had made progress in breaking free of the Wagnerian style. Particularly significant is the fact that there are no thematic links among its movements. In this respect, *The Planets* exhibits an almost classical approach to symphonic composition. Novel aspects include the bitonal passages in the third movement ("Mercury, the Winged Messenger") and the last movement ("Neptune, the Mystic"). The Finale fluctuates between the tonalities of E-minor and G-sharp minor. Toward the end of the movement, the wordless women's chorus enters giving the piece that ethereal quality that Holst typically evoked in his music for women's voices. The opening movement, "Mars, Bringer of War," is intriguing for its use of strings played *col legno* (with the wooden part of the bow) to create a percussive rather than lyrical string sound.

In 1919, Holst composed *The Hymn of Jesus* for double chorus, semi chorus, and orchestra. The text is Holst's own translation from the Greek of the Apocryphal Acts of St. John. In this work, Holst employed two plainchant melodies, *Vexillia regis prodeunt* and *Pange lingua gloriosi*; however, they do not permeate the harmonic and melodic fabric of the piece. Holst conducted its premiere in 1919.

Neoclassicism appeared in Holst's works in the early 1920s with the *Fugal Overture* (1922) and the *Fugal Concerto* (1923) for flute, oboe, and strings. The composer's daughter, Imogen Holst, notes that:

[The *Fugal Overture*] gives the impression that [Holst] had . . . set out to write an intellectual exercise. He had never heard of neo-classicism: Stravinsky had not yet written his Octet for Winds, nor had Hindemith begun work on his Kammermusik Op. 36. If Holst's *Fugal Overture* seems to coincide with the . . . "back-to-Bach" movement, it is not because he had allowed himself to be drawn into following a new fashion, but because his own inquiring mind had led him up that particular path at that particular moment.[2]

The *Fugal Concerto* conforms to the traditional, eighteenth-century, three-movement plan. The Double Concerto (1929) for two violins is another work in a three-movement plan. In these pieces, Holst used modest resources. The reduction of doubling orchestral instruments forced a new attention to the individual parts. Sometimes the linear movements result in polytonality.

Standing in contrast to these compositions of absolute music is the orchestral tone poem *Egdon Heath* (1927). Egdon Heath was an area in Dorchester near the home of Thomas Hardy and the site of the action in many of his writings. Holst visited the area in Hardy's company while composing this piece, which is dedicated to Hardy and opens with a quotation from *The Return of the Native*. The score is highly coloristic and requires a large orchestra, but *tutti* passages are few, and dynamics are subdued. The orchestral magnificence of *The Planets* is supplanted here by unprecedented nuance and subtlety.

Holst composed two operas during the 1920s. The first was his one-act opera, *At the Boar's Head* (1924). In this score, the bar scenes from Shakespeare's *Henry IV* are combined with folk music that Holst had collected. His last opera was *Tale of the Wandering Scholar* (1930).

Perhaps the finest of Holst's late works are the twelve *Humbert Wolfe Songs*, Op. 48 (1929) for voice and piano. The musical gestures are highly refined, sometimes resembling the manner of Henri Duparc (1848–1933). The songs are strikingly economical—the fifth song ends with unaccompanied solo voice—yet, their affective message is clear despite their sparseness. In all of the songs, the melodic lines, though tuneful, are unpredictable; the same is true of the chord successions. Holst's subtle musical gestures are skillfully matched both to the prosody of the English words and the sentiments of the poems, which are thought provoking. The apparent simplicity of the music anticipates the style of Britten, who knew the songs, performed them frequently, and recorded them with Peter Pears.

Certain of Holst's works have become popular favorites. Among these are his *Three Festival Choruses*, which include "Let all mortal flesh keep silence" (Picardy) and "Turn back, O man." His two band suites are performed with equal frequency. They are the three-movement Suite No. 1 in E-flat (1909) and the Suite No. 2 in F (1911). The former opens with a chaconne in which the ground bass migrates to other voices, appears in inversion, and is manipulated in many ingenious ways. The concluding movement of the Second Suite was arranged by Holst for orchestra in the *St. Paul's Suite* (1913). Another important piece for band is *Hammersmith* (1930), a two-movement work that Holst later arranged for full orchestra.

Ralph Vaughan Williams, 1872–1958

Ralph [pronounced *Rāfe*] Vaughan Williams was born in the town of Down Ampney.[3] His childhood studies of music included strings, keyboard, and harmony—the harmony text used was one by Sir John Stainer (1840–1901). He came from a well-to-do family of scientists, clergy, and legal professionals. In 1890, he entered the Royal College of Music as a student of Sir Charles Hubert Hastings Parry (1848–1918). From 1892 until 1895, he was an undergraduate at Trinity College, Cambridge, where his composition teacher was Charles Wood. He received the Mus. B. in 1894, and the B.A. (in history) in 1895. Upon completion of his degrees, he returned to the Royal College of Music to study composition with Stanford.

Eager to expand his horizons, he went to Berlin in 1897, to work with Max Bruch (1838–1920). Bruch had received an honorary doctorate from Cambridge in 1893; in addition, he conducted the Liverpool Philharmonic from 1880 until 1883. Bruch's ties with Great Britain must have made him an appealing mentor for any young English composer. Furthermore, Bruch's practical approach was congenial to Vaughan Williams, who later quoted with pride Bruch's maxim "You must not write eye music, you must write ear music."[4] Vaughan Williams lived up to this motto. In fact, he wrote not a single score that was anything less than viable music for real musicians, nor did he waste a drop of ink on chimerical musical contraptions. In 1908, he went to Paris to study with Ravel, who likewise encouraged a practical approach to music. Vaughan Williams relates that Ravel chided him for composing without the piano: "How," he asked, "can you invent new harmonies?"[5]

In 1919, after a four-year tour of duty in France, Vaughan Williams joined the faculty of the Royal College of Music. His strong nationalistic sentiments led him to the folk music of his native land beginning in 1903.[6] The folk influence bore its first fruits in the solo song "Linden Lea," an arrangement of a tune from Dorset. (This was Vaughan Williams's first published work.) More ambitious folk-inspired compositions include *The Fen Country* (1904) and the two *Norfolk Rhapsodies* (1907). He was proud of England's heritage, and his

Ralph Vaughan Williams

knowledge of this tradition is reflected in works like the *Fantasia for Double String Orchestra on a Theme of Thomas Tallis* (1910), the *Five Mystical Songs* (1911) for baritone, chorus, and orchestra, the Mass in G Minor (1922), and the *Five Tudor Portraits* (1935).

As a Bach enthusiast, Vaughan Williams had a keen sense of polyphony. His contrapuntal style, however, includes touches of the English Renaissance manner—particularly apparent in the Mass in G minor. The modal character of Renaissance music was reinforced by the numerous irregular melodies that Vaughan Williams examined in selecting tunes for the English Hymnal (1906), which he edited; one such melody was that assigned to the Lenten hymn (no. 92), "When rising from the bed of death." The text was written by John Addison.[7] The melody, a Phrygian tune by Thomas Tallis (ca. 1505–1585), was composed for Archbishop Matthew Parker's Psalter of 1567. Vaughan Williams's ingenious variations on this tune, his manipulation of motifs within it, and his inventive exploration of unusual modal inflections in its harmonization became the basis of the *Fantasia on a Theme of Thomas Tallis*. The final touch of genius was the piece's unusual scoring for double string orchestra and solo string quartet.

Most of Vaughan Williams's early works are vocal compositions. The song cycle *Songs of Travel* (1904; after texts by R.L. Stevenson), the setting of Walt Whitman's poem *Toward the Unknown Region* (1905) for chorus and orchestra, and the song cycle *On Wenlock Edge* (1909) for tenor, string quartet, and piano after A. E. Housman's "A Shropshire Lad" are characteristic.

Vaughan Williams was never a practicing Christian. As a youth, he was an atheist; later, he mellowed to agnosticism. Despite his work as editor of the English hymnal and as a church organist, and despite his voluminous output of sacred music, his relationship with the church was ambivalent. In selecting texts for his

Example 5
Tallis Phrygian Melody used by Vaughan Williams in his Fantasia

Third Mode Melody (D.C.M.)

Thomas Tallis, c. 1510–85
(*rhythm slightly simplified*)

vocal works, however, he preferred spiritual poems. Among the most moving of his spiritual compositions are the *Five Mystical Songs* for baritone, mixed chorus, and orchestra (1911), the oratorio *Sancta civitas* (holy city; 1926), *Dona nobis pacem* (grant us peace; 1936), and the Christmas cantata, *Hodie* (today; 1954).

Folksongs were pressed into service in a number of ecclesiastical works. Some eventually appeared in his *Fantasy on Christmas Carols* (1912) for mixed chorus, baritone soloist, and orchestra. Others made their way into his 1928 edition of the *Oxford Book of Carols*.

In the score of the *Dona nobis pacem*, a cantata for soprano and baritone, chorus, and orchestra, he combined text fragments from the Ordinary of the Roman Catholic Mass with poetry by Walt Whitman, one of the composer's favorite poets. In combining a Mass fragment with newly created poetry, Vaughan Williams anticipated Benjamin Britten's *War Requiem* as well as Leonard Bernstein's *Mass*.

Vaughan Williams was active as a conductor, and his scores give evidence of his practical experience. His nine symphonies span the period from 1903, the year in which he began his First Symphony (*Sea Symphony*), to 1957, the year of his Ninth Symphony. The First Symphony (1909) is a choral symphony with texts by Whitman. The Second Symphony, the *London Symphony*, is a soundscape of metropolitan London complete with the carillon of Westminster.[8] The premiere of the Third Symphony, the *Pastorale Symphony* (1922) was an important musical event for Vaughan Williams. The conductor, Adrian Boult, won a triumph with the piece, and he and Vaughan Williams formed an enduring friendship. Happily, Boult's recordings of Vaughan Williams's music give us an authentic performance tradition.

The Seventh Symphony is a unique score. Vaughan Williams was attracted by the possibilities of the moving picture, and, at the urging of Ernest Irving, he agreed to compose a score for the film *Scott of the Antarctic* concerning the explorations of Captain Robert Falcon Scott. This later became the basis of the highly coloristic *Sinfonia Antarctica* (1952). The instrumentation of this five-movement symphony includes wind machine and organ as well as solo and choral women's voices. The organ part is conspicuous, especially in the "Landscape" movement. (In the event that an organ is not available, the cuts indicated in the score may be observed.)

Each of the movements is headed with a provocative quotation—some from poetry, some from Scripture, and some from Scott's journals. These citations suggest the mood of each movement. Since much of the music in the symphony derives from the film score, the formal designs of the movements are generally free, programmatic forms. The conventional sonata form is not used. In his melodic and harmonic style, too, Vaughan Williams uses a more progressive idiom often based upon octatonic configurations.

In addition to his nine symphonies, Vaughan Williams composed important tone poems such as *The Lark Ascending* (1914) for violin and orchestra, and *Flos Campi* (meadow blossom; 1925) for viola, orchestra, and wordless chorus. He contributed significantly to almost every genre during his long and prolific career.

To the world of opera, he contributed five works. Though rarely performed, they contain much fine music. The earliest of these, *Hugh the Drover* (1914), is heavily influenced by folksongs. Because of the war, it did not get a performance until 1924. *Sir John in Love*, a comedy after Shakespeare, followed in 1929. The one-act *Riders to the Sea* (1932) is a serious work influenced by French Impressionism.

Another comedy, *The Poisoned Kiss*, was completed in 1936. *Pilgrim's Progress* (1951) was the composer's last opera.

Of the five, perhaps the finest is *Riders to the Sea*, based almost verbatim on a play by John M. Synge. The score features female solo roles, women's chorus—both on-stage and off-stage—and a small orchestra of about thirty-four players, including *cor anglais*, bass clarinet, bass drum, and "sea-machine." Synge owes much to the ephemeral manner of the French Symbolists; but whereas the French are willing to forgive the lack of action in the score for *Pelléas et Mélisande*, the dreamy inactivity of *Riders to the Sea* has kept it from establishing a place in the operatic repertoire. Vaughan Williams's only theatrical music that remains in the repertoire is the instrumental Fantasia on "Greensleves" from *Sir John in Love*.

The ISCM was helpful in establishing Vaughan Williams's reputation. His works were featured on their programs in 1924, '25, '29, and '31. In 1932, he was invited to lecture at Bryn Mawr College in Pennsylvania. This was his first visit to the United States. In the autumn of 1954, he was invited to Cornell University. These lectures were published, along with a fifth, given at Yale University in December of 1954, under the title *The Making of Music*.

In his *Serenade to Music* (1938), written to honor the conductor Sir Henry Joseph Wood, Vaughan Williams may well have written his finest work. The text, set for sixteen soloists and orchestra, is drawn from the scene of Portia's garden in the first scene of the final act of Shakespeare's *The Merchant of Venice*. The elegant, late-Romantic style of this piece is apparent from the outset, in the exquisite orchestral prelude featuring an expansive melody for concertante violin. The full ensemble of soloists enters before the prelude reaches its cadence, and throughout the piece, Vaughan Williams carefully dovetails its various subsections to conceal the fact that he has written concertolike showpieces for each of his soloists.

Benjamin Britten, 1913–1976

Britten began composing when he was eight and started composition lessons with Frank Bridge (1879–1941) when he was twelve. These lessons were more than a passing episode; Bridge forever remained the object of Britten's esteem, friendship, and admiration—both on account of his musicianship and his personal integrity.

In 1930, Britten entered the Royal College of Music where he studied composition with John Ireland (1879–1962) and piano with Harold Samuel and Arthur Benjamin. Britten graduated in 1934, the same year in which his Fantasy Quartet, Op. 2 for oboe, violin, viola, and 'cello was featured on an ISCM concert in Florence.

The ISCM continued to advance Britten's music, and they featured his Suite for Violin and Piano at their 1936 conference in Barcelona, and his *Variations on a Theme of Frank Bridge* at their 1938 meeting in London. The theme of this last work, by the way, was taken from the second of Bridge's *Three Idylls*.

In 1939, Britten left England with Peter Pears, a young tenor whom he had met in 1937. The two men were inseparable for the rest of their lives, and Pears built his international reputation on his interpretations of Britten's scores. After arriving in the United States, they shared an apartment in Brooklyn with Wystan Hugh Auden for a short time. For the next three years, Britten and Pears lived in a home in Amityville, Long Island.

While in the United States, Britten received a commission to compose a work celebrating the Japanese Imperial Dynasty. The score that resulted was the *Sinfonia da Requiem* (1940). The political tensions between Japan and the West led to the retraction of the commission, but the piece had already been composed. Sir John Barbirolli led the New York Philharmonic at its premiere in March, 1941.

In 1942, Britten decided that he had to return to England. Shortly before his departure, he attended a performance of the *Sinfonia* by the Boston Symphony under Serge Koussevitzky. Britten met with him after the performance, and the discussion focused on the young composer's plans. During the late 1930s, Britten just happened to have completed a series of compositions that were theatrical.[9] In 1941, he wrote his first opera, *Paul Bunyan*, to a libretto by Auden. The piece had a disappointing premiere at Columbia University that same year. (Britten revised the score in 1974.)

Equipped with this experience, the time was right for the composition of a full-length opera. The Koussevitzky Foundation provided a grant that enabled Britten to devote his attention to what many consider his finest opera, *Peter Grimes*.[10] The premiere in June 1945 at the Sadler's Wells Theatre was a triumph. Leonard Bernstein led the American premiere at Tanglewood in August of 1946.

The libretto by Montague Slater is based on a poem by George Crabbe called "The Borough." The action of the opera is divided into three acts, each arranged according to a pattern: orchestral prelude, first scene, orchestral interlude, second scene. This symmetrical arrangement was highly successful in *Peter Grimes*, and Britten used a similar format later in *The Turn of the Screw* (1954).

The story involves the fisherman, Peter Grimes, who cannot afford a man to work with him but needs help nonetheless. He hires a boy, William Spode, as his apprentice. While returning from a fishing trip, Grimes and Spode are blown off-course. They drift at sea for three days without water, and the boy dies. After he returns to port, Grimes is suspected of foul play. In a court ruling, the boy's death is pronounced "accidental," but suspicions linger. The school teacher, Ellen Orford, finds another apprentice for Grimes, a boy named John.

Act II scene i takes place outside the church on Sunday morning, just as the service is beginning. Ellen notices that John's clothing is torn and that he is bruised. She interrogates the boy against the backdrop of the liturgy. The juxtaposition of the liturgical texts with Ellen's questioning is disconcerting. It also anticipates the combination of the Roman Catholic Requiem Mass with the anti-war poetry of Wilfred Owen in the score of Britten's *War Requiem* (1961).

In scene ii, the boy tries to climb down the cliff with Grimes to get to the fishing boat. He falls to his death on the rocky coast.

In Act III, Ellen and Captain Balstrode, a retired merchant skipper, find Grimes alone on his boat. Realizing that Grimes has no hope of escaping justice, he suggests to Grimes that he sail his boat out to sea and scuttle it. In the dense fog of the night, Grimes meets his end. As dawn breaks, the villagers go about their business, oblivious to the multiple tragedies that have taken place.

The opera is a landmark in the history of British lyric theater. The score is remarkable in its diversity: excellent choral music (the canonic "Old Joe has gone fishing" in Act I scene ii, and the aforementioned church scene), ensemble numbers (the amusing trio of the two nieces with Swallow in Act III scene i), and orchestral music are effectively mixed with solo song. Particularly striking among the solo numbers are Grimes's monologues in Act I scene ii ("Now the Great Bear and Pleiades") and in Act II scene ii ("In dreams I've built myself some kindlier home").

Britten's writing for solo voice alternates between passages that are unpredictable yet highly melodic, and others that are an intensely personal sort of recitative. These solo vocal styles appear in the operatic works, the songs, and the chamber pieces with voices, such as the *Canticle II, Abraham and Isaac* (1952).

Britten's next three operas, *The Rape of Lucretia* (1946), *Albert Herring* (1947), and his realization of *The Beggar's Opera* (1948), were written for the English Opera Group.[11] In these, the general tendency is toward smaller casts, chamber orchestras, and less-costly productions. *The Rape of Lucretia*, for example, consists of a cast of six characters and a small orchestra of twelve instrumentalists. The score of *The Beggar's Opera*, one of many examples of Britten's affinities for the music of the Baroque era, is similarly economical. Subsequent operas include *Let's Make an Opera* (1949), *Billy Budd* (1951), *Gloriana* (1953), *Turn of the Screw* (1954), *Midsummer Night's Dream* (1960), *Owen Wingrave* (1971), and *Death in Venice* (1973).

Though none of Britten's later operas achieved the fame of *Peter Grimes*, each has distinctive features that show the composer's imagination and the freshness with which he approached each new undertaking. *Let's Make an Opera* is intended to show children how operas are composed. Part I of the piece is a discussion among six children and five adults about requirements of sets, costumes, and music. Part II is the actual opera, "The Little Sweep." Between the first and second parts, the audience learns four choruses that they sing in Part II. *Billy Budd* is unique for its all-male cast, unusual orchestration (including drums, bugles, and saxophone), and for the unaccompanied monologue that concludes the opera. *Turn of the Screw* uses preludes and interludes in the manner of *Peter Grimes*; however, these instrumental portions are now much condensed and arranged for a chamber orchestra. The orchestral portions of the opera introduce twelve-note themes that are varied in each of the sixteen scenes. *Midsummer Night's Dream* was the first twentieth-century opera to include a role (Oberon) for countertenor. Britten wrote the part for Alfred Deller, who sang its premiere in 1960.

In 1948, Britten established the Aldeburgh Festival, an annual festival that takes place during June. Though Britten's own music is featured, recent programs have included a wider variety of music.

In addition to his operas, Britten wrote many excellent songs. Noteworthy among the song cycles are *Les illuminations* (1939; texts by Rimbaud) for voice and string orchestra; *Serenade* (1943; texts by Cotton, Tennyson, anonymous fifteenth-century writers, Jonson, and Keats) for tenor, horn, and strings; and *Nocturne* (1958; texts by Shelley, Tennyson, Coleridge, Middleton, Wordsworth, Owen, Keats, and Shakespeare) for tenor, bassoon, harp, horn, tympani, English horn, flute, clarinet, and string orchestra. Among the songs for voice and piano, the *Seven Sonnets of Michelangelo* (1940) and *A Charm of Lullabies* (1947; texts by Blake, Burns, Greene, Randolph, and Philip) are outstanding.

Most of Britten's choral works are functional pieces that are within the grasp of community choruses, school or church choirs, and amateur groups. Some especially attractive compositions of this type include the two volumes of *Songs for Friday Afternoons* (1934), *A Ceremony of Carols* (1942), *Hymn to St. Cecilia* (1942), *Rejoice in the Lamb* (1943), and *St. Nicholas* (1948). More complex are the scores of the *Spring Symphony* (1949) and the *Cantata academica* (1959), the *War Requiem*, and the eight mediæval lyrics entitled *Sacred and Profane* (1975) for *a cappella* chorus.

The *Songs for Friday Afternoons*, for children's voices and piano, were written for a school where Britten's brother was headmaster. The singing classes were held on Friday afternoons. Though the songs are simple, the piano accompaniments are packed with musical interest and offer challenges even to the finest player. Perhaps the most amusing of these pianistic extravaganzas is the song "There was a monkey climb'd up a tree." The concluding song, "Old Abra'm Brown is dead and gone" is a strict canon. In the closing measures, the canonic theme appears in augmentation—like one of Ockeghem's mensuration canons—to produce a hair-raising effect.

Ceremony of Carols is written for treble voices in three parts, with a harp part written specifically for Osian Ellis, replete with a stunning solo interlude. The *Spring Symphony* consists of fourteen texts about spring, organized within the traditional, four-movement symphonic framework. The fourth movement includes both text and music of the Mediæval English *rota* "Sumer is icumen in." The *Cantata academica* was written for the 500th anniversary of the University of Basle and has a Latin text by Bernhard Wyss. The premiere performance was given by the Basle Chamber Orchestra and Choir conducted by Paul Sacher on 1 July 1960. For the *Cantata*, Britten wrote in a formal, academic style: twelve-tone Serialism. The *Cantata* proves that it is possible for a composer to retain a characteristic style even within a dodecaphonic context.

The *War Requiem* occupies a special place in Britten's output. In the *Requiem*, Britten produced a masterpiece to equal *Peter Grimes*. The *War Requiem* was commissioned for the rededication of St. Michael's Cathedral, Coventry. The original fourteenth-century structure was destroyed, along with most of the city, during an eleven-hour bombing in November, 1940. The new cathedral, constructed beside remnants of the original, was consecrated in 1962.

For the text of the Requiem, Britten used the Latin Mass for the Dead; this he combined, by way of ironic commentary, with anti-war poems by Wilfred Owen, who was killed in France shortly before the end of World War I. In setting these texts, Britten chose two distinctly different ensembles: The Latin liturgical texts are set formally for soprano soloist, chorus, and large orchestra; by contrast, the poems of Owen are set for solo tenor and/or baritone with the accompaniment of a chamber orchestra.

The juxtaposition of ancient and modern texts, large and small ensembles, and male and female voices are only the most obvious of the conflicts that fill the score of the *Requiem*. The opening movement, "Requiem æternam," is barred in changing meter with irregular subdivisions of the beat. The text is intoned on an unchanging, augmented fourth between C and F-sharp. The overall effect suggests unmetered, plainchant recitation. The neo-Gregorian element of the movement is reinforced by the setting of the "Kyrie" with which it concludes. The music of this "Kyrie" returns at the conclusion of the second movement, the "Dies iræ," and again at the conclusion of the sixth and last movement, the "Libera me."

The construction of this choral refrain, another example of conflict between ancient and modern, is sheer genius. Lines in F-sharp minor grind against lines in the Phrygian mode on E-sharp. Dissonances are repeated and extended until, almost magically, the two tonal planes converge in the last bar on a simple, root-position, F-major chord. The dynamic level is subdued, and one strains to hear; but the potency of the harmonies prevails.

By contrast to the chantlike opening movement, the "Dies iræ" is strident and strongly rhythmic, though much of it is in 7/4 meter. The movement is interrupted by gentle moments, such as the "Recordare" and the "Pie Jesu"; the latter again employs the F-sharp minor/Phrygian bimodality.

The third movement, the "Offertorium," consists of two hymns, each ending with the refrain *Quam olim Abrahæ promisisti et semini ejus*. These words receive a lively treatment in fugal texture with changing meters and elaborate contrapuntal devices. The leading voice states the subject in G major; the answer is a real one beginning on D. Next, Britten introduces the subject in inversion on A. The *recto* form is then stated on A. Subject and inversion next appear on the tone E, but now the gap between entries is reduced. For the remainder of the fugue, the subject appears in *stretto* at various tonal levels in both *recto* form and inverted form. The return of the *Quam olim Abrahæ* text at the end of the movement is a varied restatement of the original fugue, beginning with the inverted form of the subject. The *recto* form enters as a counterpoint. The section concludes with both forms of the subject in *stretto*.

In the fourth movement, the "Sanctus," texture emerges as the key element. Britten divides the voices into eight parts, but the text is to be chanted freely. The

EXAMPLE 6
Britten, Modal counterpoints of the "Kyrie," *War Requiem*

passage begins at a *pianissimo* dynamic level in the second basses and gradually expands to include all parts at a *fortissimo* level. In the *Hosanna in excelsis* refrain, Britten returns to a metrical setting of the text. The ensuing "Benedictus" is set for soprano solo and chorus. Next, the *Hosanna* appears in a varied restatement. With the exception of the concluding three measures, the fifth movement, the "Agnus Dei," is for chorus in unison.

The concluding movement, "Libera me," begins in the tempo of a funeral march. The impact is frightening—not so much for the fear of death itself as for the pervasive atmosphere of dementia. The piece turns from these anguished sounds as the chorus of boys sings the hymn "In Paradisum deducant te angeli" (may the angels lead you into paradise). Chorus in eight parts, singing a single subject and its inversion, leads to the final statement of the F-sharp minor/Phrygian motif for the words *Requiescant in pace, Amen* (may they rest in peace).

Britten's chamber compositions begin with the previously cited *Fantasy Quartet*, Op. 2. He also composed three string quartets. The first of these was completed in 1941. The Second String Quartet (1945) is unusual because of its concluding chaconne—a design rarely encountered in chamber music. The Third String Quartet (1975) contains leftovers from his opera *Death in Venice*. The concluding movement of this five-movement work is also built on a ground bass.

In addition to the quartets, the *Lachrymæ, Reflections on a Song by John Dowland* (1950) for viola and piano and the *Metamorphoses after Ovid* (1951) for solo oboe are noteworthy. Britten's friendship with Mstislav Rostropovich resulted in the Sonata (1961) for 'cello and piano, and three Suites (1964, '67, '72) for 'cello solo.

Britten wrote relatively little orchestral music. In addition to the *Variations on a Theme of Frank Bridge* and the *Sinfonia da Requiem*, noteworthy orchestral works include the *Simple Symphony* (1934), the Piano Concerto (1938), the Violin Concerto (1939), and the 'cello Symphony (1963). The *Simple Symphony* includes passages from Britten's childhood compositions. The 'cello Symphony was written for and premiered on 12 March 1964 by Rostropovich with Britten conducting.

Britten composed many excellent works for young musicians. In addition to the *Songs for Friday Afternoons* and *Let's Make an Opera*, his score for the documentary "The Instruments of the Orchestra," should be noted. Published separately as *Young Person's Guide to the Orchestra* (1946), it may be performed with or without narration. *Young Person's Guide* is a set of variations and a final fugue, all based on a rondeau theme from Henry Purcell's incidental music to the play *Abdelazar*. At the opening, Britten states the theme with orchestral *tutti*. He then breaks the orchestra into its choirs, restates the theme with some variation, and then reunites the *tutti* ensemble. In the ensuing variations, he goes through the orchestra in score sequence (i.e., flutes, oboes, clarinets, bassoons, etc.) writing astonishingly idiomatic variations for each instrument. After completing his review of percussion instruments (the last choir to be demonstrated), he writes a fugue, in which the instruments enter in the exact order in which they had appeared. When the full ensemble is playing this remarkable fugue, Britten retrieves Purcell's theme and states it in its pristine form amidst this fantastic counterpoint.

Additional pedagogical scores of note include the setting of Psalm 150 (1962), scored for voices in two parts with the accompaniment of any available treble, bass, keyboard, and percussion instruments, and the *Gemini Variations* (1964). The variations were written for two Hungarian youngsters, twins who both played piano. In addition, one played flute, the other violin. Accordingly, Britten composed a set of twelve variations and a fugue, using solo violin, solo flute, solo piano, violin and flute duet, violin and piano duet, flute and piano duet, and piano duet. Britten took the theme of the *Gemini Variations* from the music of the Hungarian music educator Zoltán Kodály.[12] Britten also made arrangements of early music, especially that of Henry Purcell.

Michael Tippett, 1905–1998

Tippett decided on a career as a composer relatively late in life; he had not even had lessons on an instrument until his late teens, when he began piano studies. In 1923, he entered the Royal College of Music and studied composition with Charles Wood (1866–1926) and C. H. Kitson, and piano with Aubin Raymar. His conducting classes were with Malcom Sargent and Adrian Boult. Two years after his graduation in 1928, he undertook additional studies with Reginald Owen Morris. These lessons, focusing on counterpoint, continued until 1932. From 1940 until 1951, Tippett was the music director of Morley College.

Perhaps it was Tippett's late start in composition that made him reluctant to put his compositions before the public eye until the late 1930s: His first important publication did not come until the appearance of the Concerto (1939) for double string orchestra.[13] The Concerto reveals many characteristic features: the bristling rhythms of the outer movements; the high regard for traditional genres and forms, such as the *ritornello* structure of the first movement, the sonata-rondo design of the last movement, and the overall plan of three movements; the intense lyricism of the central movement; and the overriding importance of counterpoint.

It was Tippett's oratorio *A Child of Our Time* (1941) that established him as a major figure.[14] For its text, he turned to T. S. Eliot, who agreed to write a libretto; however, on seeing Tippett's draft, Eliot decided that Tippett should complete the poem himself. This he did, and he wrote the texts for all of his subsequent vocal works.

The title comes from Oedon von Horvath's novel *Ein Kind unserer Zeit*, the story of a young soldier fighting for an empty cause. The more immediate content of the oratorio is based upon an event that took place in 1938, shortly before the outbreak of World War II. Ian Kemp gives the following details:

> Herschel Grynspan was the son of a Polish Jew who had settled in Germany before the First World War. Grynspan left his native Hanover in 1936, intending to emigrate to Palestine. But in fact he went to Paris, living there with an uncle and aunt. In August 1938 he was served with an expulsion order by the French authorities . . . and from that date his uncle sheltered him illegally. On 3 November he received a postcard from his sister telling him of his family's arrest and deportation, and of their suffering on the Polish frontier. . . . On 7 November, Grynspan bought a revolver and walked in to the German Embassy in Paris. . . . He protested about the treatment of Jews at the Polish frontier and then fired five shots, two of which hit [Ernst] vom Rath. Grynspan made no attempt to escape.

Michael Tippett

. . . Vom Rath died the day after that. The Nazis used the assassination as the pretext to unleash a pogrom of unparalleled brutality. . . . On that night—the infamous Crystal Night of 9 November, so-called by the Nazis because of the acres of broken glass lying in German cities the following morning—there were thousands of arrests and beatings all over Germany and Austria, synagogues were burned, some people were stoned to death, shops were attacked and plundered.[15]

A Child of Our Time is a protest against totalitarianism; it is also Tippett's statement concerning the nature of humanity. According to his view, each individual carries elements of light and of darkness. He avoids the words "good" and "evil," and value judgments find no place in his thinking. The score of *A Child of Our Time* is headed with a citation from Eliot's *Murder in the Cathedral*: "The darkness declares the glory of light." This maxim distills the essence of Tippett's understanding of humanity. In his libretto, Tippett implies that the individual becomes a whole person only through an awareness of both aspects of the human psyche.

The oratorio is scored for soprano, contralto, tenor, and bass; chorus; and an orchestra of double woodwinds plus English horn, contrabassoon, four horns, three trumpets, three trombones, tympani, cymbals, and strings. It includes five American spirituals: "Steal away to Jesus," at the conclusion of Part I, "Nobody knows the trouble I see, Lord," "Go down Moses," and "O, by and by, I'm going to lay down my heavy load," all contained in Part II, and "Deep river," which concludes Part III.

According to the composer, the piece is Passion music. In this particular case, the passion happens to be that of Herschel Grynspan—or any individual overwhelmed by circumstances. In using the spirituals, Tippett found a meaningful counterpart to the Lutheran chorale melodies of Bach's music for the Passion. The spirituals also invite a broader audience, including people of other races. A careful study of the libretto shows that Tippett intended the work to speak to all people, and so we find references not only to the plight of the slave in the old South, but also to "Pogroms in the east," and "lynching in the west," as well as allusions to the Passion music of Bach.[16] The score of *A Child of Our Time* reveals Tippett as a first-rate composer, a formidable librettist, and a profound thinker.

Tippett continued to explore issues in his first opera, *The Midsummer Marriage* (1952). Dark and light are used again to represent conflicting forces, forces that must simply be understood as dualities of various sorts. In Tippett's opera, these dualities stem from diverse sources: the conflicts between tradition and innovation, young and old, male and female, and between social classes. On a personal level, the opera explores the disparity between the image that an individual projects to the world (Jung's *persona*) and the inner person. Tippett has kept these conflicts vague so that the tale may be interpreted in many ways.

The libretto shows the influence of psychiatry, particularly the branch of psychiatry developed by Freud's pupil Carl Jung (1875–1961) and designated by him as "analytical psychology." In essence, the story of the opera is a dream.

In the dream, the groom-to-be (Mark) and the bride-to-be (Jennifer) have a parting of ways on the summer morning of their marriage. Jennifer and Mark go off to learn of the unknown aspects of their own personalities: At first, she goes into light and he into darkness; then the roles are reversed.

A sort-of Greek chorus that sings and dances looks on throughout all three acts of the opera. In addition to the "hero" and "heroine," we have Jungian archetypes: the She-Ancient and He-Ancient. Presumably, these nameless representatives of an older generation are "parents." They give advice, warn of dangers, and behave in a generally parental manner, though the precise meaning of what they say is never clear. The She-Ancient and He-Ancient are characters representative of Jung's collective unconscious.

Tippett presents quite a different case in the character of King Fisher. He is Jennifer's father. He is not a genuine individual, but a *persona*—according to Jung, a personality acted out primarily for public consumption. King Fisher, who typifies a strong-willed, tough, crass businessman accustomed to having his way, is strongly opposed to the marriage. King Fisher is assisted in his attempts to stop the marriage by Bela, his secretary, and her boyfriend, Jack, who is a mechanic. Bela and Jack represent the physical world, its inertia, and the means that enable us to confront and sometimes to overcome that inertia. Both are obedient, reliable, and know their place. When King Fisher, a man who can only function in the conscious world, attempts to assert his power in the unconscious world through the assistance of Sosostris, a clairvoyant, his impotence is manifest. As King Fisher unveils Sosostris, who has never been seen by human eyes, he discovers his daughter, Jennifer. He falls to the ground dead as Mark and Jennifer turn to face him. The Ancients and the chorus comment on the death of King Fisher in an extended ensemble.

The fire dance that follows represents the carnal passion between Mark and Jennifer, who sing an extended canonic duet. Mark's psychological conflicts stemming from the impending marriage have been purged through the dream sequence; he addresses Jennifer saying, "after the visionary night, the senses purified, my heart's at rest." Jennifer alludes to the objection of her obdurate father to the marriage, and indicates that she could have loved "even my father, had he lived." Mark comforts her and presents her with the wedding ring. A choral epilogue brings the opera to a close.

Tippett's unusual libretto for *Midsummer Marriage* had important musical consequences. Because most of the opera's action takes place in a dream, the composer was not restricted to a well-reasoned story line. There is time for the action to relax, so that parenthetical ideas—both philosophical and musical—can be explored. Ensembles, choruses, and dance numbers are both pervasive and integral. Tippett made a suite from the opera's dances, *Ritual Dances from The Midsummer Marriage*, which was first performed by the Basle Chamber Orchestra, conducted by Paul Sacher, in 1953.

Tippett continued his exploration of psychological dialectics in his subsequent operas, *King Priam* (1961), *The Knot Garden* (1969), *The Ice Break* (1976), and *New Year* (1988). *King Priam* was commissioned by the Koussevitzky Foundation.

In addition to the Concerto for double string orchestra, noteworthy orchestral works include Tippett's *Fantasia on a Theme of Handel* (1941) for piano and orchestra, the First Symphony (1945), the *Fantasia Concertante on a Theme of Arcangelo Corelli* (1953) for string orchestra, the *Divertimento on "Sellinger's Round"* (1954) for chamber orchestra, the Concerto (1955) for piano and orchestra, the Second Symphony (1957), the Concerto (1963) for orchestra, written to celebrate Britten's fiftieth birthday, the Third and Fourth Symphonies (1972, '77), and the Triple Concerto (1979) for violin, viola, 'cello, and orchestra.

The orchestral works demonstrate Tippett's high regard for music of earlier masters as well as his careful attention to traditional pattern forms. The Divertimento on "Sellinger's Round" was commissioned by and dedicated to Paul Sacher, who led the premiere in 1954. The Second Symphony marked a turning point in Tippett's style; quartal harmonies are used more extensively in this score than in any previous composition. The Third Symphony, Tippett's only symphony with vocal resources, uses a text by the composer, which is scored for soprano soloist. The Fourth Symphony, commissioned by the Chicago Symphony and premiered by them under Georg Solti in 1977, is a single movement including a conventional introduction, exposition, and first development (=first movement), a slow movement, a second development, a Scherzo with two trios (one paraphrasing a string fantasia by Orlando Gibbons), a third development, and a recapitulation. This conflation of formal components yields an expansive symphonic sonata of remarkable cohesion.

Tippett's chamber works include four excellent string quartets (1935, 1942, 1946, 1978). The First String Quartet was originally a four-movement plan. In 1943, Tippett discarded the first two movements and replaced them with a single movement. The first movement is a sonata allegro form, the second, a lyrical movement in three sections, and the Finale is a fugue that includes an early instance of additive rhythm in Tippett's scores.

The Second String Quartet is the most traditional. It consists of four movements in the sequence Allegro, Andante, Scherzo, Allegro. The outer movements are sonata forms. The second movement is a fugue. The traditional balance of movements in chamber works of the eighteenth century is upset here owing to the intensity of the concluding movement.

The Third String Quartet consists of five movements in which the odd-numbered movements are fugues and the even-numbered movements are more expressive and melodious. The odd-numbered movements are further distinguished by their fast tempos; the *cantabile* movements represent a rhythmic relaxation.

The Fourth String Quartet consists of a single movement with subsections. The main motivic material appears in the opening slow section. Many of the musical gestures in the Fourth Quartet are reminiscent of those in the late quartets of Beethoven, works that Tippett studied repeatedly.[17]

The subtle formal balances explored by Tippett in his four quartets also occupied his attention in his five sonatas for piano (1937, 1962, 1973, 1979, 1984). The First Sonata (rev. 1942; 2d. rev. 1954) is a four-movement work with the tempo indications Allegro, Andante, Presto, and Rondo giocoso con moto. The Second Sonata is one continuous movement. The Third Sonata conforms most nearly to the Mozartian model, having three movements. In this case, the tempo indications are Allegro, Lento, and Allegro vivace.

Tippett's late vocal works include *The Vision of St. Augustine* (1965), a cantata for baritone, chorus, and orchestra, and the song cycle, *Songs for Dov* (1970), for tenor and chamber orchestra. *The Vision of St. Augustine* is based on psychoanalytical procedures.

Jung's therapeutic process places a great deal of emphasis on word associations. A stimulus word is suggested to the patient; the patient's response then reveals the "complexes" active in the patient's psyche. For the central text of *The Vision of St. Augustine*, Tippett employed Latin excerpts from the *Confessions* of St. Augustine. Key passages from this text are sung by the baritone soloist, but progress is by phrases, phrase fragments, or even single words. These scraps of text correspond to stimulus words.[18]

The responses to the stimulus words appear in *The Vision of St. Augustine* as choral passages. The Latin texts for these responsive passages draw upon St. Ambrose's hymn "Deus, creator omnium" and the Vulgate version of the Bible. In preparation for the composition of *The Vision of St. Augustine*, Tippett conducted research to determine the traditional conceptions of what "celestial" music might be like. The result of this research was his treatise, *Music of Angels*.[19]

Tippett found that angelic song supposedly employs *glossolalia*, which are vocal outbursts accompanying a state of ecstasy. In his score, Tippett frequently extends the final vowel of text in a free, melismatic setting. This procedure has precedent in Western music in the *jubilus*—the melisma on the concluding "a" of the word *alleluia*—of classical plainchant.

Important musical consequences also resulted from the notion that angelic choirs are constituted by enormous numbers of voices singing in unison. Rather than observing the traditional division of voice types into soprano, alto, tenor, and bass, Tippett sometimes writes for a unison choir with an expansive range. The score of *The Vision of St. Augustine* is one of Tippett's most progressive ones. The use of ostinato patterns and the superimposition of ostinatos of conflicting durations lead to remarkable complexities.

Tippett's works reveal a synthesis of tradition and innovation as well as an impressive coordination of musical materials, interdisciplinary interests, and an acute sense of social responsibility. In this respect, Tippett's compositions represent not only one of the most compelling contemporary musical idioms, but equally, a philosophy of contemporary life.

British Music since the Mid Century: The Manchester School

Between the First and Second World Wars, three composers were born whose works have come to occupy a central position in contemporary repertoire. These composers are (Peter) Alexander Goehr (b. 1932), Harrison Birtwistle (b. 1934), and Sir Peter Maxwell Davies (b. 1934).

Goehr's father, Walter Goehr, fled from Germany during the Reich years. Alexander Goehr became affiliated with Birtwistle and Davies during their student days at the Royal College of Music, Manchester, where they studied with Richard Hall.

Walter Goehr was himself a distinguished musician. He studied with Schönberg and was among the earliest advocates of Serialism. As a conductor, he did much to advance the cause of modern music, and he gave premieres of many important scores—including Tippett's *Fantasia on a Theme of Handel*.

Alexander Goehr went from his studies at Manchester to private instruction with Messiaen. Goehr's Capriccio (1958) for piano is dedicated to Messiaen's wife Yvonne Loriod. Post-serial methods are apparent in most of his scores. Of these, the most important are his instrumental works, especially the Violin Concerto (1962), the Little Symphony (1963), and the *Romanza* (1968) for 'cello.

Post-serialist constructive features are also apparent in the music of Birtwistle.[20] His principal instrument is the clarinet, and he has demonstrated an affinity for woodwinds. His first major work, *Refrains and Choruses* (1957), is scored for woodwind quintet. His compositions also reveal a fascination with music history. The *Monody for Corpus Christi* (1959) for soprano and three instruments reinterprets the *Ars antiqua* in its emphasis on the single line, flexible scoring, and topical origins within the liturgical year of the ancient Christian church.

Birtwistle has written a considerable amount of dramatic music, such as *The Mark of the Goat* (1966), a cantata for children, *The Versions of Francesco Petrarca* (1966), for baritone, chamber ensemble, school orchestra, and mime, and *Punch and Judy* (1967), an opera that was commissioned by the English Opera Group. The premiere of *Punch and Judy* took place at the Aldeburgh Festival in 1968. Francis Routh took a grim view of the piece and summed it up as a "miscalculation . . . : the ugliness of orchestral sound palls quickly on the ear, while the scoring and instrumentation combine to make the singers inaudible. Stephen Pruslin's text is equally savage and aggressive."[21]

Chronometer (1971) is one of the many metronome/clock scores that became almost a trend in the last quarter of the twentieth century. Based on tapes of the sounds of clocks—the oldest extant in England, the ticking of Big Ben, and so forth—the assembly of over one hundred "time markers" was submitted to electronic manipulation to produce a tone poem of about one half-hour in length. The various superimpositions of the sounds of clocks result in a layering of strata, in strettos, augmentations, diminutions, and all of the devices associated with the most artfully wrought scores in the Western European tradition. There is, as well, more than a hint of the Minimalist movement, which was already underway.

Birtwistle's concerns with time and with music as a temporal art are also apparent in *The Triumph of Time* (1972). The score of this tone poem for large orchestra was influenced by the drawing of the same name by the sixteenth-century artist Pieter Bruegel. Relationships such as foreground activity to background (i.e., small segments of time contrasted with longer segments), discrete events as opposed to continuous events, and stasis as opposed to metamorphosis, are scrutinized from a musical perspective.

The founding of the London Sinfonietta in 1968—a chamber ensemble with conductor—gave Birtwistle the vehicle for many of his finest works. *Verses for Ensembles* (1969) was the first of his scores for them. It was followed by *Silbury Air* (1977), *Carmen arcadiæ mechinicæ perpetuum* (1978; for the tenth anniversary of the Sinfonietta), and the *Secret Theatre* (1984). In all of these works, Birtwistle explores sounds as instantaneous events, as events within an ongoing sequence, as elements within a vertical simultaneity, as part of a ritual, and as a vehicle for interaction with "others," i.e., an audience who may or may not understand what is being performed.

Of the Manchester School, Sir Peter Maxwell Davies has emerged as the most significant member—a fitting state of affairs, as he is the only one of the three who was actually born in Manchester.[22] His interest in World musics is reflected in his Master's thesis, which deals with the rhythmic organization of Indian *ragas*. Davies went on to advanced studies, working in Rome with Goffredo Petrassi during the 1957–58 academic year. In 1962, he went to Princeton University, where his mentor was Roger Sessions. There, he also worked with Earl Kim and Milton Babbitt.

Music history has had a crucial impact on many of Davies's works, such as his scores of the *Alma Redemptoris Mater* (1957; the title of one of the four Marian antiphons) for wind sextet; *Prolation* (1958) for orchestra; *Veni Sancte Spiritus* (1963; one of the four Mediæval sequences retained by the Council of Trent); *L'homme armé* (1968; the most popular of all early Renaissance *cantus firmi*) for speaker and chamber ensemble. The most extensive of his historically inspired scores is the opera *Taverner* (1969). The topic of the opera is the life and times of John Taverner (ca. 1490–1545), one of England's greatest Reformation-era composers. The "In nomine" of Taverner's *Missa Gloria tibi Trinitas æqualis* became the basis of many instrumental variations written in Great Britain during the sixteenth and seventeenth centuries, and Davies revisited the idea in two large scores, the *Fantasia on an* In nomine *of John Taverner* (1962) for orchestra and the second *Fantasia on John Taverner's* In nomine (1964). Both scores are of exquisite craftsmanship. The second Fantasia uses music from the first act of the opera and exhibits total control of technique, meaningful appreciation of Renaissance polyphony, and a sense of connectedness of past and present.

In 1967, Davies and Birtwistle founded a chamber ensemble that included the vocalist Mary Thomas. The ensemble included the five players needed for Schönberg's *Pierrot lunaire* with the addition of a percussionist. The group was originally called the Pierrot Players, but they later changed their name to the Fires of London. For them, Davies wrote many fascinating works, among them, the *Vesalii icones* (1969).

The piece takes its name from the work of Andreas Vesalius, a sixteenth-century Flemish scholar who held the chair of anatomical studies at the University of Padua from about 1537 until 1546. In 1543, he compiled his best-known work, *De humani corporis fabrica* (concerning the makeup of the human body). The treatise is important, not only as a contribution to medical sciences, but equally for its "perfect blend of format, typography and illustration."[23] Davies happened to purchase a facsimile of the Vesalius treatise—probably the edition issued jointly in 1934 by the New York Academy of Medicine and the Library of the University of Munich under the title *Icones Anatomicæ of Andreas Vesalius*, since this is the only publication of the engravings that uses the word "icons" in the title.[24] Though this term may refer generally to any image, figure, or picture, in religious circles, the word is most often used to designate an image or picture of Jesus, Mary, a saint, or some other holy person. In his note to the score, Davies states:

> The idea of eventually making a set of fourteen dances based on the illustrations to Vesalius came to me when I bought a facsimile edition of the *de Humani Corporis Fabrica* a few years ago; the idea of superposing the Vesalius images on the fourteen stations of the Cross (slightly modified to include the Resurrection) came much later, and was the direct stimulus to composing the work.[25]

The music of the *Vesalii icones* superimposes three different types of music: (1) traditional religious music, especially plainchant, (2) popular music—including a parody of Victorian hymnody, which Davies views as the ultimate blasphemy; and (3) entirely new music of his own invention. The chamber ensemble requires the addition of a dancer. The piece responds to three conceptions of the human anatomy: (1) the anatomical drawings (i.e., "icons") of the Vesalius treatise; (2) the stations of the cross; and (3) the dancer's body. These three levels correspond to the layout, typography, and illustrations that were so remarkable in the original Vesalius edition published in Basel by Johannes Oporinus in 1543.[26]

The *Vesalii icones* was preceded by other theosophical works in Davies's output, especially the *Alma Redemptoris Mater* (1957; a wind sextet based on the plainsong Marian antiphon as well as the polyphonic setting of this melody by the fifteenth-century composer John Dunstable) and *Antechrist* (1967) for piccolo, bass clarinet, violin, 'cello, and three percussionists.[27] In these works, citation, parody, and paraphrase are tools for investigation and exploration of religious truths, and so, musical distortion ought not to be equated with mockery. The instrumentation of the *Vesalii icones* includes flute (doubling alto flute and piccolo), basset clarinet in A or clarinet in A, percussion (one player), piano, autoharp, viola, and 'cello.

Davies added the Resurrection to the conventional sequence of stations, but there is a tradition for its inclusion. "Devotion to the Passion of Christ . . . became widespread during the 12th and 13th centuries, [and] was promoted by many veterans of the Crusades who erected tableaux at home representing various places they had visited in the Holy Land."[28] The number of stations was only stabilized in 1731 under Pope Clement. Indeed, many "modern theologians and liturgists emphasize the fact that Christ's death and Resurrection ought not to be dissociated, and some think the devotion of the Way of the Cross is psychologically and theologically incomplete if it terminates without reference to the Resurrection."[29] Davies concludes his *Icones* with a riddle, however, because the Resurrection in this case is of the "Antichrist." Noteworthy, too, is the fact that

> the triumph of Antichrist comes to the sound of a foxtrot, for during this period the foxtrot was an obsessive image in Davies's music, an image of total corruption. Commercial music is itself a betrayal of all the art's powers to present new, stretching experiences; and the commercial music of the past, having no part in Davies's own life since he was not born until the foxtrot era was in decline, is an invitation to indulge in fake nostalgia, the most unreal of emotions. . . . In this case . . . a problem of honesty at the very heart of the art is smilingly exposed.[30]

The format that Davies gave the score also deserves comment. The piece contains fifteen distinct movements, each concluded with a double-bar line and headed with an Arabic number and legend indicating the dramatic action of the station. It is significant, however, that the measures are counted consecutively throughout all movements for a total of 491 (not counting repeats) and a playing time of about forty minutes. The reason for this probably stems from the fact that the devotion of the Way of the Cross obtained for the believer an "indulgence." These indulgences are "authoritative grants from the Church's treasury for the remission or payment in whole (plenary indulgence) or in part (partial indulgences) valid before God, of the debt of temporal punishment after the guilt of sin has been forgiven."[31]

One of the canonical conditions for obtaining the indulgence is that the ritual of the Way of the Cross cannot be interrupted except for the purpose of Confession or receiving the Eucharist. At the same time, the ordinances for execution of the ritual indicate that "to gain the indulgence, it is necessary . . . to move from station to station . . . and to meditate upon the subject of Our Lord's Passion and death."[32] This movement would not be executed by individuals in a congregation, but rather, by a priest or other clergyman; hence, Davies's implementation of a dancer was suggested by the history of the ritual per se. The composer has thus changed the context of a religious ritual while retaining and reinterpreting its significance.

Like many composers of the Second Viennese school, Davies is intrigued by psychoanalytical studies. His psychodramas include two major song cycles: the *Eight Songs for a Mad King* (1969), based on texts by Randolph Stow and by the deranged King George III himself, and *Miss Donnithorne's Maggot* (1974), again with a text by Stow. Both cycles are scored for soloists—baritone in the former and mezzo-soprano in the latter—and the Fires of London.

The music of the *Eight Songs* is unrelentingly ugly and abrasive; nevertheless, it demonstrates Davies's wonderful sensitivity to tone color, fluidity of rhythm, tempo, and meter, and his knack for exploring the potential of the human voice—even in ugly songs. In *Miss Donnithorne's Maggot*, Davies depicts the world of Miss Eliza Emily Donnithorne (the model for Charles Dickens's Miss Havisham in *Great Expectations*).

Miss Donnithorne was born in India in 1827, became engaged in 1856, but was abandoned by her intended on her projected nuptial day. She died in 1886, but during the thirty years after her catastrophic moment, she lived as though the clock had stopped.

In the *Miss Donnithorne* cycle, Davies ameliorates his style—although the ideas remain as harsh as ever. (One even encounters the f—— word!) As in so many of his other compositions, a thorough knowledge of music history is presumed: The Prelude is followed by the "Maggot," that by a "recitative," then her "Dump," a nocturne for instruments alone, her "Rant," another "recitative," and we end with her "Reel." The *dump* is a seventeenth-century instrumental *lamento* often based on a recurring harmonic pattern. During that same era, the *rant* was a lively dance in duple meter; and the *reel* was a dance for couples in an energetic duple meter. The final dance, in which Miss Donnithorne becomes aroused upon the imagined return of her lover, provides not only the erotic conclusion of the cycle, but also the exit music for the actress/singer, who, amidst cascades of confetti, pirouettes off stage for a carnal encounter with her paramour.

In the *Vesalii icones* and both of these song cycles, Davies consolidates the worlds of chamber music, lyric theater, and dance. The chamber ensemble and the dance band exchange identity; the stage and the psychiatrist's office become synonymous; the present-day musician and the nostalgic image of Elizabethan minstrels become consolidated. In astounding ways, these and other antitheses merge.

In 1974, a commission from the Philharmonia Orchestra initiated Davies's symphonic works. He originally wrote a single movement called "Black Pentecost." The title came from a poem by George Mackay Brown about the deserted farms of the Orkney valley, where Davies lived at the time. The movement grew into the four-movement First Symphony (1976), which is permeated by images of the sea and Scotland's northwestern coast. The sea, and its various wave forms in particular, inspired his Second Symphony (1980) as well. In the Third (1984), Davies created musical parallels to the architectural theories of Brunelleschi, Alberti, Pietro della Francesca, and Leonardo. The Renaissance use of vanishing points, for example, provided a paradigm for tonal focus. The buildings themselves suggested sleek, linear structures, which Davies approximated in his counterpoint, limited in this symphony to not more than five parts—more often three, or two.[33]

The Fourth Symphony (1989) stands apart in its scoring for chamber orchestra. Since 1985, Davies has been the associate conductor and composer-in-residence for the Scottish Chamber Orchestra, and this was his first symphony for them. As in his previous symphonies, he retains the traditional four-movement plan, but here the movements proceed without break. The concise Fifth Symphony (1994) consists of episodes of contrasting characters and tempos. The Sixth (1995; for the 50th anniversary of the UN) is a larger piece in three movements that incorporates elements of an older concert overture, *Time and the Raven*. The Seventh Symphony (2000) is the final element in Davies's symphonic cycle, which includes the previous six. Like the Fourth Symphony, its textures are contrapuntal but limited to several voices. The Finale draws on motifs from the previous three movements, but the conclusion is written so that it can lead either to the beginning of this symphony or the opening of the First Symphony. Davies is currently at work on his Eighth Symphony (2001), the *Antarctic Symphony*, which was commissioned by the British Antarctic Survey. One of the terms of the commission was an actual visit to the Antarctic; hence, the composer has, in fact, seen those landscapes that Vaughan Williams had only imagined in his work by the same title.

The ten Strathclyde Concertos for various solo instruments and combinations thereof were written for the principals of the Scottish Chamber Orchestra. The tenth of these is, logically, a concerto for orchestra. Currently, Davies is at work on a series of string quartets.

Notes

1. Imogen Holst, *The Music of Gustav Holst and Holst's Music Reconsidered* (New York: Oxford University Press, 1986). See especially chapter 23: "Following Where Wagner Led," pp. 134–135.
2. Imogen Holst, *The Music of Gustav Holst*, p. 58.
3. Ursala Vaughan Williams, *R. V. W.: A Biography of Ralph Vaughan Williams* (New York: Oxford University Press, 1984), xv.
4. Ralph Vaughan Williams, *The Making of Music* (Ithaca, New York: Cornell University Press, 1955), p. 17.
5. Vaughan Williams, *The Making of Music*, p. 23.

6. A list of the folksongs collected by Vaughan Williams is in Michael Kennedy, *The Works of Ralph Vaughan Williams* (London: Oxford University Press, 1964), pp. 646–681.

7. In the 1906 English Hymnal, the melody is associated with the following text: "When, rising from the bed of death,/O'erwhelmed with guilt and fear,/I see my Maker face to face,/O how shall I appear/If yet, while pardon may be found/And mercy may be sought,/My heart with inward horror shrinks,/And trembles at the thought;" | "When thou, O Lord, shalt stand disclosed/In majesty severe,/And sit in judgment on my soul,/O how shall I appear?/But thou hast told the troubled mind/Who does her sins lament/The timely tribute of her tears/Shall endless woe prevent." | "Then see the sorrow of my heart,/Ere yet it be too late;/And hear my Saviour's dying groans,/To give those sorrows weight./For never shall my soul despair/Her pardon to procure,/Who knows thine only Son has died/To make her pardon sure."

8. Regarding the symphonies, see Michael Kennedy, *The Works of Ralph Vaughan Williams*, 2d ed. (New York: Oxford, 1980). See also Elliot Schwartz, *The Symphonies of Ralph Vaughan Williams* (Amherst: University of Massachusetts, 1964).

9. Incidental music for plays: *The Ascent of the F 6* (1937; Auden and Christopher Isherwood), *The Seven Ages of Man* (1938; Montague Slater), *Old Spain* (1938; Slater), *On the Frontier* (1939; Auden and Isherwood), *Johnson over Jordan* (1939; J. B. Priestly). Film scores: *The King's Stamp* (1936), *Coal Face* (1936), *Night Mail* (1936), *The Line to Tchierva Hut* (1937), *Calendar of the Year* (1937), *The Savings of Bill Blewitt* (1937), *Around the Village Green* (1937), *Village Harvest* (1937), *The Way to the Sea* (1937), *Love from a Stranger* (1937), *The Tocher* (1938), *H.P.O.* (1939), and *Advance Democracy* (1939). Music for Auden's radio script: *Hadrian's Wall* (1938).

10. The Koussevitzky Foundation was organized by Serge Koussevitzky in 1942 in memory of his wife, Natalie, to provide financial assistance to composers. Britten's *Spring Symphony*, Albert Roussel's Third Symphony, Bartók's Concerto for Orchestra, Messiaen's *Turangalîla Symphony*, and Husa's Sonata for Violin and Piano are among the commissioned works.

11. Britten, Eric Crozier, and John Piper formed the group in 1947. In 1975, it was reorganized and named the English Music Theatre Company. The Company terminated in 1980. Regarding specific productions, see Eric Walter White, *Benjamin Britten: His Life and Operas* (Berkeley and Los Angeles: University of California Press, 1970). Concerning these three operas, see Norman Del Mar, "The Chamber Operas," *Benjamin Britten: A Commentary on His Works from a Group of Specialists*, ed. Donald Mitchell and Hans Keller. (New York: Philosophical Library, 1952), pp. 132–185.

12. Regarding the music for children, see Peter Evans, *The Music of Benjamin Britten* (Toronto: J. M. Dent, 1979), chapter 13, "Music for Children."

13. Tippett's unpublished works are listed in Ian Kemp, *Tippett: The Composer and His Music* (New York: Da Capo, 1984), p. 498.

14. Reception history of the oratorio is detailed in Kenneth Gloag, *Tippett: A Child of Our Time* (Cambridge, England: Cambridge University Press, 1999), pp. 89–95.

15. Kemp, *Tippett*, pp. 151–152.

16. Kemp, *Tippett*, p. 173, musical example no. 51.

17. Comparisons of related passages in Beethoven and Tippett quartets are given in Meirion Bowen, *Michael Tippett* (London: Robson Books, 1982), pp. 126–130.

18. For a different interpretation of the sources of Tippett's poetic collage technique, see Kemp, *Tippett*, p. 401.

19. Meirion Bowen, ed. *Music of Angels: Essays and Sketchbooks of Michael Tippett* (London: Eulenberg, 1980).

20. Robert Adlington gives an overview of Birtwistle's works up to the 1998 score of *Harrison's Clocks* for piano in the *Music of Harrison Birtwistle* (Cambridge, England: Cambridge University Press, 2000), 242 p.

21. Francis Routh, *Contemporary British Music: The Twenty-Five Years from 1945 to 1970* (London: Macdonald, 1972), p. 315.

22. Details on Davies in Mike Seabrook, *Max: The Life and Music of Peter Maxwell Davies* (London: Gollancz, 1994) and Carolyn J. Smith, *Peter Maxwell Davies: A Bio-Bibliography* (Westport, Connecticut: Greenwood, 1995).

23. J. Saunders and Charles D. O'Malley, *The Illustrations from the Works of Andreas Vesalius of Brussels* (Cleveland: World Pub. Company, 1950), p. 16.

24. The 1934 edition was the last to use the original sixteenth-century wood blocks, which were destroyed during World War II. See Saunders and O'Malley, *The Illustrations from the Works of Andreas Vesalius*, p. 10.

25. Peter Maxwell Davies, *Vesalii icones* (New York: Boosey and Hawkes, 1978), preface.

26. Oporinus had already achieved some notoriety owing to his printing of the first Latin edition of the *Koran*. It was only through the intercession of Martin Luther that the civil authorities agreed to release the printer from the jail sentence he had earned by this. Concerning Oporinus, see Saunders and O'Malley, *Vesalius*, pp. 21–22.

27. Both works are discussed in Paul Griffiths, *Peter Maxwell Davies* (London: Robson Books, 1981).

28. B. Brown, "Way of the Cross," *The New Catholic Encyclopedia* (New York: McGraw-Hill, 1967), vol. 14, p. 832.

29. Brown, "Way of the Cross," vol. 14, p. 834.

30. Griffiths, *Peter Maxwell Davies*, p. 67.

31. P. F. Palmer, "Indulgences," *The New Catholic Encyclopedia* (New York: McGraw-Hill, 1967), vol 7, p. 482.

32. Brown, "Way of the Cross," vol. 14, p. 835.

33. Davies's own lucid discussion of paradigms and musical correspondences appears as the jacket note for the recording of Symphony No. 3; cond. Edward Downes (BBC Artium LP REGL560, © 1985).

Chapter 15

The Musical Maturity of the United States

By the end of the nineteenth century, the United States could boast of composers, performers, concert halls, and opera houses on a par with those in Europe; nevertheless, a distinctive American school of composition was lacking. Composers writing at that time relied heavily on German Romanticism, and many of them actually studied in Germany. Some of the most important figures were John Knowles Paine (1839–1906), the first professor of music at Harvard (1875); Horatio Parker (1863–1919), a student of Rheinberger's in Munich from 1882 to 1885, and, after 1894, professor of music at Yale; George Whitfield Chadwick (1854–1931), who studied in Leipzig and Munich, and who became the director of the New England Conservatory in 1897; Mrs. H. H. A. Beach (1867–1944); and, perhaps the most Europeanized of the lot, Edward MacDowell (1860–1908), who studied in Paris, Wiesbaden, and Frankfurt, and whose first professional position was as a faculty member at the Darmstadt Conservatory. In 1896, MacDowell was appointed the first professor of music at Columbia University, a post he held until 1904.

The works of these composers exhibit exquisite craftsmanship, but in many cases, a dearth of original thinking. Too often, their intention seems to have been merely to demonstrate that they can do what the Europeans do equally well. It is both ironic and sad that the first composer who spoke with a genuinely American voice felt that his music was so far beyond the comprehension of the musical establishment that he turned to an alternate career as an insurance salesman. He was tremendously successful in this capacity, but had Charles Ives attempted to conform to prevailing musical tastes, he would probably be forgotten today. It was his decision to strike out on the path less traveled "that has made all the difference."

Charles Edward Ives, 1874–1954

George Ives, Charles's father, led the Brigade Band of the First Connecticut Heavy Artillery during the Civil War. His music making was necessarily practical, and his tastes were not limited by artificial boundaries. He loved hymns, spirituals, dance music, patriotic songs, band music, and sentimental parlor-room songs. George was also an experimentalist; his natural curiosity led him to investigate acoustical phenomena, quarter tones, and other techniques long before these became fashionable. The senior Ives taught Charles to play the piano, violin, and cornet, and gave him his first instruction in harmony, counterpoint, and ear-training. The instruction was well rewarded, and the younger Ives paid touching tribute to his father's musical guidance in the twelfth of his *114 Songs*, "A Sound of a Distant Horn."

In 1889, at fourteen, Charles became the organist of the First Baptist Church of Danbury, Connecticut. From 1898 until 1900, he was organist at the First Presbyterian Church in Bloomfield, New Jersey, and from 1901 until 1902 he served the congregation of Central Presbyterian Church in New York City. These experiences were crucial for Ives, since throughout his career, hymnody of the Christian church provided him with a rich musical treasure trove from which he drew consistently—in direct quotation, paraphrase, or subtle suggestion.

Perhaps Ives's predilection for the homely melodies of hymns, pedestrian march tunes, and common dance melodies is best understood from the perspective set forth by Ralph Waldo Emerson, whose work Ives admired. In his essay on art, Emerson noted that:

> The artist must employ the symbols in use in his day and nation to convey his enlarged sense to his fellow-men. Thus the new in art is always formed out of the old. The Genius of the Hour always sets his ineffaceable seal on the work and gives it an inexpressible charm for the imagination. . . . No man can quite emancipate himself from his age and country, or produce a model in which the education, the religion, the politics, usages and arts of his times shall have no share.[1]

Ives's music is rich in associations, but his use of existing music is never reduced to the level of an arrangement. Citations always have a spiritual and affective motivation. Both the "ineffaceable seal" and the "inexpressible charm" distinguish his scores and reveal his unique genius.

Many disregard Ives's music, thinking that it was only his hobby, and that he was not in control when he set his pen to paper. Although Ives made his livelihood in the insurance business from 1898 until 1930, he had had a formal academic training in music at Yale University from 1894 until his graduation in 1898. At Yale, Ives studied composition with Horatio Parker and organ with Dudley Buck.

Ives was frustrated by Parker, who was unsympathetic to his innovative ideas. That Ives had mastered traditional harmony and counterpoint by the time he completed his studies at Yale is apparent in scores from this period. It was common in composition classes then, as now, for students to write pieces in the style of some well-known composer. Parker frequently used this exercise, and some of Ives's most charming songs were the result. The collection of *114 Songs* (1922) contains four French songs ("Qu'il m'irait bien," "Elégie," "Chanson de Florian," and "Rosamunde") and four German songs ("Weil' auf mir," "Du alte Mutter," "Feldeinsamkeit," and "Ich grolle nicht"). The second and third of the German songs are equipped with optional English texts, though it is apparent that the melodies were designed to accommodate the German poems.[2]

The third German song, "Feldeinsamkeit," is a fine example of Ives's neo-Romantic manner. The composer he imitates is probably Brahms. The song is in common meter. The accompaniment consists primarily of sixteenth-note arpeggio figures in D-flat major, though many altered tones are employed for coloristic purposes. A brief introduction sets the dreamy mood of the piece before the voice enters. The song is divided into three sections: The first concludes with the words ". . . von Himmels bläue wundersam umwoben"; the second, contrasting section concludes with the text ". . . und ziehe selig mit durch ew'ge Räume," whereupon the third section, a modified restatement of the opening, commences. For the return of the opening material, Ives has not only written in the word *rallentando*, but he has built one directly into the music. The sixteenth-note subdivisions give way to triplets, and the triplets in turn to duplets. The gradual slowing of the subdivision of the beat is unclear, though, because Ives ties the last note of the triplet to the first of the pair of eighth notes; furthermore, the single bar in which this takes place has been expanded from common meter to 3/2 time.

More ambitious compositions from Ives's late-Romantic period include the First Symphony (1898), a four-movement work in the conventional symphonic plan, and the seven-movement cantata, *Celestial Country* (1899). The text is based on a poem by Henry Alford and is scored for soprano, alto, tenor, and bass, chorus, string quartet, orchestra, and organ. The Cantata, which is unabashedly Romantic, had its premiere in 1902 at the Central Presbyterian Church in New York City. Ives must have liked the piece. When he compiled the *114 Songs*, he included two songs, "Naught That Country Needeth," and "Forward into Light" (in the Cantata, the second and sixth movements).

"Forward into Light" as it appears in the collection of 1922, reveals something of Ives's understanding of composition and its relationship to performance. In the piano accompaniment for the passage "All through youth and manhood," the pianist is asked to span a four-octave-plus range; moreover, in the middle of this span is a sixteenth-note tremolando on an E-major-seventh chord. The passage cannot be played as written. In this particular song, this disparity between written score and actual performance is, perhaps, understandable, since the accompaniment is a literal reduction of the original orchestral score; nevertheless, the fact that Ives did not make a piano arrangement is telling. He dealt with musical conceptions, not with performance limitations. His approach to music was more akin to the architect's approach to constructing a building than to the engineer's. Ives was concerned with the design and its significance rather than the details of the blueprint. That this conceptual approach dominated his thinking is shown conclusively by the fact that similar "impossible" passages appear regularly in other compositions that are not reductions of instrumental parts.

The reasons for Ives's conceptual approach are several. To begin with, most of his large works were not performed until many years after their composition. Consequently, "definitive" performing materials were, in many cases, never compiled. Composition scores frequently include alternative readings from which the performer must choose. Perhaps a more important reason is a philosophical one. Ives said:

> Some of the passages now played have not been written out, and I do not know as I ever shall write them out as it may take away the daily pleasure of playing this music and seeing it grow and feeling that it is not finished and the hope that it never will be.[3]

Along with the growth of the music that resulted from these conceptual scores, Ives hoped as well for a growth of the individual musician. In the Postface to the *114 Songs*, he explains his view of creativity and the average person in detail.

> Every normal man,—that is, every uncivilized or civilized human being not of defective mentality, moral sense, etc., has, in some degree, creative insight. . . . There are many, too many, who think they have none of it. . . . There are a few who think (and encourage others to think) that they and they only have this insight, interest, etc. . . . and that (as a kind of collateral security) they and they only know how to give true expression to it, etc. But in every human soul there is a ray of celestial beauty, . . . and a spark of genius. . . .
>   If this is so, and if one of the greatest sources of strength,—one of the greatest joys, and deepest pleasures of men, is giving rein to it in some way, why should not every one instead of a few, be encouraged, and feel justified in encouraging everyone including himself to make this a part of every one's life and his life, a value that will supplement the other values and help round out the substance of the soul?[4]

Ives viewed composer and performer as partners. As a result, he considered optional readings of a score as a strength rather than a weakness. In this respect, he was not an innovator, but a restorer. Some examples of the choices that Ives allows the performer to make can be found in numbers 1, 15, 21, 27, 33, 50, 53, 54, 57, 96, and 97 from the *114 Songs*; in the last movement of the Second Piano Sonata, where Ives allows either piano solo throughout or the addition of a flute in the last two pages; and in the third movement of *Three Places in New England*, where he writes a part that may be played on two harps, piano with two players, or piano and celesta. To these examples, others can be added.

In some instances, the performer may decide that some work cannot be performed at all. This would be an exceptional case, but Ives admits that possibility in the Postface of the *114 Songs*, where he states: "Some of the songs in this book . . . cannot be sung,—and if they could perhaps might prefer, if they had a say, to remain as they are,—that is 'in the leaf.'"

Ives demonstrated equal flexibility in transferring a score from one medium to another. Many of the songs also exist as instrumental pieces.[5] Likewise, many instrumental pieces exist in a variety of incarnations. The First String Quartet (1896), for example, consists of four movements bearing the designations "Chorale," "Prelude," "Offertory," and "Postlude."[6] Were these originally organ works that Ives later arranged for string quartet?

The first movement of the Quartet is a fugue based on Lowell Mason's "Missionary Hymn," associated with Reginald Heber's text "From Greenland's Icy Mountains."[7] (Ives revisited and transformed this movement as the third movement of his Fourth Symphony.) The fourth movement is based on the tune "Webb," ordinarily used for George Duffield's poem "Stand up for Jesus." Ives alludes to the hymn, both in the pitch content and in the tempo indication, *Allegro marziale*, which was suggested by the word "soldier." Themes from the second movement reappear in the fourth, which contains striking examples of polymeters: Duple march motifs are contrasted with material in triple meter.

Polymeters are frequently paired with bitonal or polytonal music. In his setting of Psalm 67 (1898) for double chorus, he juxtaposes women's voices in C with men's parts in G minor. Less progressive but equally impressive among the early Psalms is Psalm 90 (ca. 1894), for which he requires soprano and tenor soloists, double chorus, bells, and organ.[8] Each of the opening four measures of the organ part bears an inscription: (1) "The Eternities" and "Creation," (2) "God's wrath against sin," (3) "Prayer and Humility," and (4) "Rejoicing in Beauty and Work." The corresponding sonorities function as motifs in the course of the Psalm. This score is also distinctive for its tone clusters, a device that Ives used regularly.

The three *Harvest Home Chorales* were composed between 1898 and 1901, but the originals were lost. Ives put the pieces back together later; hence, the *Harvest Home Chorales* as we know them are probably quite different from the first versions. The pieces are amazingly difficult, not only because of their advanced harmonic idiom, but also because very few musical events are coordinated. The impression they give is of several ensembles progressing simultaneously, but independently. Bar lines are not used.

The first two decades of this century were the most prolific of Ives's compositional career. His most important orchestral works of this period include: the Second and Third Symphonies (1902, '04); the four-movement *Holidays Symphony* including (1) "George Washington's Birthday," (2) "Decoration Day" [=Memorial Day], (3) "The Fourth of July," (4) "Forefathers' Day" [=Thanksgiving Day], composed between 1904 and 1913; *Two Contemplations* (1) "The Unanswered Question," and (2) "Central Park in the Dark" (1906); *Three Places in New England*

(1) "The Saint-Gaudens in Boston Common," (2) "Putnam's Camp, Redding, Connecticut," and (3) "The Housatonic at Stockbridge," (1908–1914); and the Fourth Symphony (1909–1916).

The Third Symphony, entitled *The Camp Meeting*, includes subtitles for each of its three movements: (1) "Old Folks Gatherin'," (2) "Children's Day," and (3) "Communion." The score is rather tame, but it contains interesting passages, such as the misplaced accents in the march of "Children's Day," the occasional measures of 7/8 in "Communion," and the striking use of bells at the end of that same movement. The premiere, conducted by Lou Harrison in May of 1947, won the Pulitzer Prize for Ives.

The "Unanswered Question" is Ives's most popular work. It is scored for trumpet, four flutes, and string orchestra, though here too, certain substitutions are admitted. The music is divided into two levels: The winds exhibit greater rhythmic activity and a higher dissonance level; the strings (separated from the winds and placed offstage) are consonant and move at a much slower pace. Even without its provocative title, this piece is an alluring score; but the title does invite speculation that Ives was making a philosophical statement—not the first and by no means the last.

The four movements of the *Holidays Symphony* were composed separately; the last movement, "Forefathers' Day," was composed first, in the year 1904. The first movement, "George Washington's Birthday," was written next, in 1909; the second movement, "Decoration Day," dates from 1912; last, in the year 1913, Ives added the cacophonous third movement, "The Fourth of July." He indicated that the movements could be played separately or "lumped together as a symphony." "The Fourth of July," characteristic of Ives's outrageous, mature orchestral style, is peppered with patriotic tunes, but "The Battle Hymn of the Republic," "Columbia the Gem of the Ocean," and the call for "Reveille" are particularly prominent. The music contains startling contrasts in dynamics and orchestration, and glissandos for *tutti* strings. March rhythms appear throughout the movement, but these are invariably complicated by false accents, polymeters, and polytonality. The raucous celebration comes to a peak as the marching band plays "Columbia the Gem of the Ocean" against the backdrop of pealing bells of the village church.

The Fourth Symphony follows the traditional four-movement plan. The first is based on three hymn tunes: Mason's "Watchmen" and "Bethany" (the latter usually sung with the text "Nearer My God to Thee") in addition to "In the Sweet Bye and Bye." The main orchestra, which includes piano and chorus, is complemented in this movement by an off-stage ensemble of harp and strings. The second movement is one of Ives's most complex conceptions. It draws on many familiar melodies including "Marching through Georgia," "In the Sweet Bye and Bye," "The Turkey in the Straw," "Camptown Races," "Throw out the Lifeline," "Beulah Land," "Yankee Doodle," "Hollingside" (usually sung with the text "Jesus, lover of my soul"), and "Columbia the Gem of the Ocean." The third movement is a double fugue based on the first movement of the First String

Quartet. Here the melodies of Mason's "Missionary Hymn" and Oliver Holden's "Coronation" (usually sung with the words "All hail the pow'r of Jesus' name") are the fugue subjects. The movement concludes with a brief citation from Mason's "Antioch" ("Joy to the world"). The final movement is based on the tune "Bethany." The treatment is one of great complexity, in which the percussion instruments, the main orchestra, and the off-stage ensemble of harp and strings act as independent ensembles. Toward the end of the movement, wordless chorus is added.

In addition to the First String Quartet, Ives's important chamber works include four sonatas for violin and piano (1908, '10, '14, and '16 respectively) and a Second String Quartet (1913). The Second String Quartet contains three movements headed: (1) "Discussions," (2) "Arguments," (3) "The Call of the Mountains." The Quartet was a reaction against the concerts given by the Kneisel Quartet that Ives attended when he was living in New York.[9] He prefaced the score with the words "String Quartet for 4 men—who converse, discuss, argue, fight, shake hands, shut up—then walk up the mountain-side to view the firmament." The joking manner of this remark is continued in the tempo indications in the score. The piece quotes "Dixie," snatches from Tschaikovsky's *Pathetique Symphony*, and Ives's favorite, "Columbia the Gem of the Ocean."

Among Ives's piano works, the First and Second Sonatas (1908, '15) and the three Quarter-Tone Pieces (1924) are important. The second Sonata, known as the *Concord Sonata*, is an expression of Ives's homage to the New England Transcendentalists, who influenced his thinking so profoundly. The Sonata drew from earlier works including the *Orchard House Overture* (1904), the *Emerson Concerto* (1907), and the *Hawthorne Concerto* (1910). Ives thought the Sonata required some commentary, and so he wrote six essays, one devoted to each of its four movements, namely (1) "Emerson," (2) "Hawthorne," (3) "Alcotts," and (4) "Thoreau," in addition to a Prologue and an Epilogue. The set of essays and the Sonata were printed in 1920.[10] With the help of George F. Roberts, Ives revised the Sonata between 1940 and 1947.[11]

Much of the *Concord Sonata* lacks bar lines. Other features include polytonality, polymetrics, tone clusters, and, in the "Hawthorne" movement, sympathetic vibration of strings, created by holding down the black and white keys through the range of two octaves and a second. (The performer will need to cut a two-by-four to the length of 14.5 inches to accomplish this.) No matter how odd things may look on the page, most of these works can be performed with very rewarding results. Ives simply wants his musicians to think.

Though his career was cut short by his debilitating heart attack in 1918, Ives left a rich repertoire that embodies the symbols that were part of the American national heritage when he wrote. He did not attempt to emancipate himself from his age, country, education, religion, or politics; instead, he transformed and enlarged these values by interpreting them through his uniquely expressive musical language.

EXAMPLE 7A
"Missionary Hymn" used by Ives for one of the fugue subjects in
Symphony No. 4, third movement.

In moderate time   Lowell Mason, 1792–1872

EXAMPLE 7B

"Coronation," one of the hymn tunes used by Ives as a fugue subject in Symphony No. 4, third movement.

Edward Perronet, 1785, alt.
Stanza 5, John Rippon, 1787

C. M.
First Tune

CORONATION
Oliver Holden, 1791

Serge Koussevitzky, 1874–1951

In surveying the accounts of Koussevitzky's life, one aspect of his character emerges as the preeminent factor that led to his success, first as a double bassist, then as a conductor, and finally as the guiding hand that established what we now call Tanglewood and populated it with the most brilliant talents of the twentieth century. That characteristic was his indomitable will.

Moses Smith, the dean of Bostonian music critics during Koussevitzky's tenure as director of the Boston Symphony Orchestra and a personal acquaintance, relates an anecdote told by Vladimir Dubinsky, who knew Koussevitzky during his student years: "He was a lovely chap—amiable and congenial. . . . He was also ambitious and determined in his decisions, but very modest about his ability as a musician. . . . There was no limitation for him."[12] This observation sums up Koussevitzky's entire career: His congenial personality endeared him to persons of power and privilege; his ambition enabled him to identify his goals as a musician; his determination and energy led to the realization of those goals, even in circumstances where persons more gifted than he would have failed; his humility enabled him to recover from situations that others would have experienced as devastating and to put his ego aside in order to spot brilliance in aspiring musicians.

Koussevitzky's contact with classical music began when he was eight. In his village, Vyshny Volochek, there lived a woman named Maria Fedorovna Ropenberg, who had studied piano with Nikolai Rubinstein. The instruction she gave Koussevitzky consisted mainly of study of the works of Austro-German masters—Bach, Mozart, and Beethoven.[13] His enthusiasm grew, and he decided upon a career as a musician. He therefore left his home and set out for Moscow to confront whatever challenges might arise.

When Koussevitzky arrived there, Russia's capital had two conservatories. The Imperial Moscow Conservatory had been founded by Nikolai Rubinstein in 1864. Piotr Adamovitch Shostakovsky had been on the faculty of that institution, but resigned owing to disagreements with Rubinstein. Shostakovsky opened a rival school of music in 1878. He turned the institution over to the Moscow Philharmonic Society in 1883, but he remained as the director and professor of piano until 1898.[14]

Koussevitzky had hoped to enter the Imperial Moscow Conservatory, but the semester had already begun. Vasily Il'ich Safonov, the director from 1889 until 1905, refused even to entertain the notion of Koussevitzky's beginning studies at that time, and so turned the boy away without even hearing an audition. Shostakovsky received Koussevitzky with the same negative reaction, but after an emotional outburst by the youngster, Shostakovsky relented and allowed him to enter the program.

Koussevitzky had no money. There were only three vacant assistantships at the time, one in double bass. Koussevitzky decided in favor of that position. By good fortune, the double bass teacher happened to be Joseph J. Rambousek, a Czech of outstanding reputation and musicianship. Koussevitzky's other important teachers included Semion Kruglikov for harmony and Pavel Blaeremberg for counterpoint and composition.

In 1894, Koussevitzky put his skills to the test in public auditions: He won a place in the orchestra of the Bol'shoi Theater. When Rambousek died in 1901,

Koussevitzky was invited to become the professor of double bass at the Philharmonic School. All the while, he was active as a concert bassist and presented solo recitals—unheard of with this instrument—in Europe's major music centers. Owing to the paucity of solo repertoire for the bass, he turned his hand to composition. He gave the premiere of his Concerto in F-sharp Minor, Op. 3, for double bass and orchestra on 25 February 1905 in Moscow. His other original works for bass are the *Humoresque, Valse miniature,* and *Chanson triste.*[15]

1905 was a crossroads year, not only in Koussevitzky's career but also in the course of European politics: The Russo-Japanese War erupted when Japan broke off diplomatic relations with Russia on 6 February 1904. Two days later, in a surprise attack, the Japanese overpowered the Russian navy at Port Arthur. By May 1905, Admiral Togo had demolished the Russian fleet. Russia had been humiliated, and Japan had advanced to the status of a world power.

Russian authorities were on the defensive. Rimsky-Korsakoff, the leading composer in Russia at the time as well as a former naval officer, was openly critical of the country's cultural and governmental operations. His candor won him a dismissal from the St. Petersburg Conservatory. Several illustrious colleagues, including Koussevitzky, resigned in protest. In the autumn of 1905, he left for Berlin with his new wife, Natalya Konstantinovna Ushkova.

The move to Berlin stimulated his interest in conducting. Hugo Leichtentritt observed that:

> Arthur Nikisch...was one of Koussevitzky's main inspirations. Nikisch's passionate, improvisatory, rhapsodic manner, and his sensitivity to the magic of colorful sound struck a related chord in the nature of the young Russian musician. Moreover, Nikisch had no superior . . . in his rendering of Russian music.[16]

Two areas of musical endeavor seem to be of paramount importance in this quotation: first, the art of the virtuoso conductor; second, the advocacy of Russian music. Koussevitzky's personal response to the role of virtuoso conductor, as set forth by Nikisch, took place over a period of several years. Through the generosity of Joseph Joachim, a virtuoso violinist, one of Brahms's close personal friends, and at the time, director of the Berlin Hochschule für Musik, Koussevitzky was allowed, beginning in 1906, to direct the student orchestra.[17] (Koussevitzky's goal—to conduct the Berlin Philharmonic—had to wait until 23 January 1908.)

Koussevitzky's interest in modern music resulted in his founding, in 1909, of the Édition russe de musique, a publishing firm intended exclusively for the promulgation of contemporary Russian music.

Owing to the prominence of Berlin in international music circles, Koussevitzky had ample opportunities to see the other great conductors on the podium: Gustav Mahler, Felix Weingartner, Felix Mottl, and Ernst Schuch were among the legends whose conducting Koussevitzky saw at first hand.[18]

Koussevitzky had limited keyboard skills. In later years, during his tenure as the conductor of the Boston Symphony Orchestra, his critics argued that he took a long time to learn a new score, and that he only did so with the aid of a *répétiteur*.[19] During these sessions, Koussevitzky "practiced his conducting gestures before rows of empty chairs, arranged according to the pattern of a symphony orchestra . . . [and] . . . before a mirror."[20] Olin Downes, the leading music critic for the *New York Times* for much of Koussevitzky's career in the United States, made the following quip concerning the conductor's alleged inability to deal with a score directly:

> This writer would say, as regards Mr. Koussevitzky, that if he is unable to decipher and understand an orchestral partition, it is only a pity that there are not more conductors possessed of a similar abysmal ignorance. It may not be believed that such charges and explanations as those recorded would be made by supposedly serious and intelligent people. . . . But these things have been said time and again by those who should know better. . . . It is not necessary to defend Mr. Koussevitzky by refuting them.[21]

Koussevitzky's debut with the Berlin Philharmonic was both successful and distinctive. The repertoire consisted exclusively of contemporary Russian music. The oldest music was Tschaikovsky's *Romeo and Juliet Fantasy Overture* (1870; rev. 1880). The remainder of the program consisted of Rachmaninoff's C-Minor Piano Concerto (1901) with the composer as pianist, orchestral excerpts from the opera *Orestes* (1894) by Sergei Taneyev, and the premiere of Reinhold Glière's Symphony in C Minor (1907). Soon afterwards, Koussevitzky conducted in London, Paris, and Vienna.

For a time, Koussevitzky pursued a dual career as conductor and bassist. In the latter capacity, he appeared with Nikisch, Schuch, and Edouard Colonne. Debussy, a composer whose works Koussevitzky championed, and a personal friend of his as well, observed in an article for the 1 January 1914 issue of *La revue musicale* that under Koussevitzky's baton, the double basses had "an unexpected sonority. . . . It is truly this foundation, in turn solid, tumultuous, even intangible, on which all possible orchestral elements play freely, without fear."[22]

In 1915, Koussevitzky expanded his publishing firm by buying out the company of K. Gutheil in Moscow. Gutheil had already taken over the publishing business of F. Stellovski, which owned hitherto unpublished repertoire by Russian masters including Glinka and Dargomyzhky; thus Koussevitzky turned his sights to Russia's musical heritage.

Initially, Koussevitzky worked with an acquisitions committee that included Medtner, Rachmaninoff, and Skryabin. After the committee advised against accepting Stravinsky's *Petrushka* and Prokofieff's *Scythian Suite*, Koussevitzky dissolved the committee and made determinations himself. He took the score of

Le sacre du printemps and other Stravinsky pieces in addition to new works by Rachmaninoff and Skryabin. The firm had offices in both Russia and Germany in order to prevent unauthorized reprints. (At the time, Russian publishers had no contractual agreement with Western Europe in matters of copyright.)

Koussevitzky returned to Russia for the 1909–10 concert season. He and his wife presented a series of eight concerts with the orchestra of the Bol'shoy Theatre in Moscow, for which they were solely responsible. He supervised the artistic matters while she took charge of logistics. In St. Petersburg—approximately 400 miles to the Northeast—he took charge of the Concerts of the Russian Musical Society, repeating the programs of the Moscow series.

His Moscow debut on 27 October 1909 opened with what was to become one of Koussevitzky's signature pieces: Beethoven's *Egmont Overture*. This was followed by one of Bach's *Brandenburg Concertos* (whether the third or fourth is uncertain), the Overture to Weber's opera *Oberon*, and Chopin's First Piano Concerto in E Minor, with Leopold Godowsky as soloist.[23] In the 1910–11 season, Koussevitzky repeated this endurance test with his own orchestra of eighty-five selected players and, in Moscow, a chorus of 250 voices. Beethoven was the featured composer for the season. All nine symphonies, as well as the Fourth Piano Concerto and the Violin Concerto, were given. One of Koussevitzky's innovations (anticipating Tanglewood) was the introduction of discounted tickets for students.[24]

Closer still to the yet-distant vision of Tanglewood was the tour that Koussevitzky arranged for his orchestra during the 1909–10 season. He took his entire orchestra and hand-selected soloists on a voyage down the Volga River. The stops along the way included the major ports of Nizhniy Novgorod [=Gorky] and Samara, other large cities, like Yaroslavl, Kazan, Saratov, and Tsaritsyn [=Volgograd], as well as the smaller cities of Tver [=Kalinin], Rybinsk, Simbirsk [=Ulyanovsk], and Astrakhan.[25] The tour, which included nineteen concerts, was so successful that Koussevitzky repeated it in 1912 and 1914.

In 1917, Koussevitzky became conductor of the St. Petersburg Court Orchestra, the ensemble that subsequently became the Petrograd Philharmonic, and later, the Leningrad Philharmonic. He retained this post after the Bolshevik Revolution in October, and he remained as conductor until the end of the 1919–20 concert season. By that time, his possessions—home, land, and the Russian branch of his publishing business—had been nationalized. There was little to keep him in Russia.

From 1920 until 1924, Paris was his base of operation. In November of 1921, he founded the Concerts Symphoniques Koussevitzky, where he brought impressive contemporary scores to the public in outstanding performances. Honegger's *Pacific 231*, Ravel's orchestration of Musorgsky's *Pictures at an Exhibition*—made at Koussevitzky's request—and Stravinsky's Concerto for Piano and Orchestra were among these. For this last work, Koussevitzky prevailed on Stravinsky to make his debut as a pianist. Later, Stravinsky tried his skills as a conductor, leading his Octet for wind instruments at another one of the Koussevitzky Concerts. Aaron Copland's career had its beginning here, too. At the time, he was a student of Nadia

Boulanger's at the American School at Fontainebleau. Copland showed Koussevitzky his *Cortège macabre* (funeral march), and he agreed to perform it.

In 1924, Koussevitzky's accomplishments led to his induction into the French Legion of Honor. Now in his mid-forties and in his stride as a conductor, he made a sensation throughout Western Europe.

Pierre Monteux, conductor of the Boston Symphony Orchestra from 1920 until 1924, resigned in the spring of that year. The identification of a successor was cause for great debate, but Koussevitzky eventually won the post. His first concert, consisting of works by Vivaldi, Berlioz, Brahms, Honegger, and Skryabin, took place on 10 October 1924. He held the BSO podium for twenty-five years until 1949.

Koussevitzky championed new music and gave premieres of works by Samuel Barber, Bartók, Arnold Bax, Arthur Bliss, John Alden Carpenter, Chávez, Frederick Converse, Copland, Diamond, Lukas Foss, George Gershwin, Howard Hanson, Roy Harris, Edward Burlingame Hill, Paul Hindemith, Honegger, Jacques Ibert, Bohuslav Martinů, Menotti, Walter Piston, Prokofieff, Rachmaninoff, Gardner Read, Respighi, Albert Roussel, Florent Schmitt, William Schuman, Roger Sessions, Stravinsky, Ernst Toch, and Villa-Lobos.

Koussevitzky's programming balanced new and traditional repertoire. In an interview with the *New York Times*, he observed:

> I am neither a modernist nor a classicist. . . . The works of the great classic masters are absolutely indispensable to me, as musician and in my life. . . . But music is not a static art. Music is continually being made which is an expression of the period in which it appears. It is as necessary for us to know what is being done as to know and admire what has been done. As for the value of the new works, the conductor uses his best judgment. . . . He must leave the rest to the judgment of time.[26]

This elegant statement must have been prepared in advance. Koussevitzky arrived in the United States at New York harbor on 12 September 1924. At the time, his "English was practically non-existent. His German was makeshift. In French, which was his second language, . . . he was more plausible."[27] Language barriers notwithstanding, he immediately made his intentions clear. For the 1925–26 season, Koussevitzky dismissed approximately twenty BSO players. In the 1926–27 season, seven new musicians were brought on; six in the 1927–28 season; and six in the 1928–29 season.[28] The Boston Symphony Orchestra under Koussevitzky included fine performers from around the globe. In addressing the orchestra, he spoke French or used standard Italian terminology; when speaking to individuals, he used Russian, German, or broken English, depending upon the recipient of his comments.

Koussevitzky saw the need not only for new music but for new musicians as well. In 1936, he began giving annual summer concerts with the BSO at the Tanglewood estate in Lenox, Massachusetts. In anticipation of the 1938 festival, he engaged Eliel Saarinen to design the permanent concert hall accommodating 6,000 people and known as "The Shed." Permanent residence halls were constructed for the musicians and students. By 1940, the Berkshire Music Center was a reality. The Music Center comprised two student bodies: a small group of advanced students in the School for Advanced Study, known as the "Institute," and a larger group, not necessarily professionals, in the Department of Music and Culture, known as the "Academy." Saarinen designed a theater and a chamber music hall for the 1941 festival.

Koussevitzky chose Copland as Assistant Director of the Tanglewood Festival. Distinguished musicians who have taught there include Dallapiccola, Ginastera, Hindemith, Honegger, Martinů, Messiaen, Villa-Lobos, and many others. In the summer of 1940, Leonard Bernstein was a student there and studied conducting with Koussevitzky. In 1946, he became Koussevitzky's assistant conductor for the summer programs. At Tanglewood, Bernstein conducted his own *Jeremiah Symphony* as well as the American premiere of Britten's *Peter Grimes*, which had been commissioned by the Koussevitzky Foundation. Bernstein stepped in at short notice as the general director of Tanglewood when Koussevitzky died on 4 June 1951.

Many other students in Koussevitzky's conducting classes achieved distinction, especially Walter Hendl, Thor Johnson, Richard Duncan, Richard Korn, and Robert Whitney. Koussevitzky considered the social role of the conductor very important, and he was convinced that a conductor ought to set public standards of decency in dress and deportment.[29]

Koussevitzky became an American citizen in April of 1941. His wife died on 12 January 1942. He campaigned vigorously for Franklin Roosevelt in the election campaign of 1944. On 15 August 1947, he married Olga Naoumoff.

Filmed performances, numerous written accounts, and abundant sound recordings of Koussevitzky's conducting give a clear picture both of his technique and his musical style. Nicolas Slonimsky, for years a close personal friend and musical associate of Koussevitzky's, states that:

> Koussevitzky belonged to that school of conductors who first and foremost were guided by the intrinsic emotionalism of the music. . . . He underscored dramatic contrasts and sparkling manipulations of timbre. In lyrical passages, he often slowed the tempo down in order to recreate fully the expressive content of the melody. Koussevitzky always conducted with a baton and score. He possessed a stick technique that was both vigorous and attractive, and he knew, above all in Romantic music, how to communicate his wishes to the orchestra with expressive gestures.[30]

If any criticism can be leveled against Koussevitzky, it is that his gift for lyric expression sometimes obscured the desired effect of passages intended to be played *semplice*. Copland, after hearing Koussevitzky conduct *Appalachian Spring*, commented that "some of the parts that I thought were expressive of a certain American simplicity, Koussevitzky would tend to 'lean on.'"[31]

Through his activities as a conductor, educator, administrator, publisher, and benefactor, Koussevitzky contributed mightily to art music of the twentieth century.

Aaron Copland, 1900–1990

When Copland's parents emigrated from Lithuania, their name was "Kaplan," but somewhere between there and Brooklyn, the name came to be "Copland." Copland's childhood gave no hint that he would become America's leading composer by the age of forty. He did not display extraordinary precociousness, nor were his parents musical. His piano lessons only began when he was thirteen, but when they did, Copland progressed quickly. He later studied with Victor Wittgenstein and Clarence Adler.

Copland's training in composition began with Rubin Goldmark (1872–1936), the nephew of Karl Goldmark. Rubin was born in the United States and attended City College of New York. Later, he studied at the Vienna Conservatory. After completing his curriculum there, he returned to the United States, settled in New York City, and studied with Antonin Dvořák at the National Conservatory. In 1902, Goldmark opened a studio in New York. From 1924 until 1936, he headed the composition department at the Juilliard Graduate School.[32]

The topics of Goldmark's works anticipate the homely, American atmosphere that has come to be the hallmark of Copland's mature masterpieces. Goldmark's compositions, like the *Negro Rhapsody*, *The Call of the Plains*, and the *Requiem*, were prototypes for Copland's homely scores like *Appalachian Spring*, *Billy the Kid*, *Rodeo*, and the *Lincoln Portrait*. Goldmark taught other important American composers including George Gershwin (1898–1937) and Abram Chasins (1903–1987).

As a young man, Copland was progressive. He found that Goldmark was not particularly sympathetic to his experiments, and so he decided to try his luck at the newly founded American Conservatory at Fontainebleau. First he studied with Paul Vidal (1863–1931). Although Vidal was sympathetic to new ideas—he was a close friend of Debussy and the teacher of André Caplet (1878–1925)—Copland seems to have found him too conservative.

As it happened, Boulanger was also on the faculty at Fontainebleau. After his initial frustrations with Vidal, Copland found in her a congenial mentor. He so enjoyed the musical environment at Fontainebleau that he remained there from 1920 until 1924.

For Boulanger, who was an organist, Copland wrote his first orchestral masterwork, the Symphony (1924) for organ and orchestra. The premiere featured Boulanger, with Walter Damrosch conducting the New York Symphony. The

Aaron Copland

Symphony is a four-movement composition, but its two central movements proceed without break. Many characteristics of Copland's style are already present in this piece: the prominence of the interval of the fourth in melodic lines; a harmonic style that is not so much "sparse" as "spacious"; and melodies with successive leaps in the same direction.

Damrosch seems not to have understood the piece, but Koussevitzky had a different impression. Not only did he conduct the Symphony with the BSO, but he encouraged the recently founded League of Composers to take advantage of Copland's talents.[33] The following contemporary account gives the details relating to Copland's score called *Music for the Theatre* (1925).

At his Boston home one spring afternoon in 1925 the late Serge Koussevitzky said enthusiastically to me, "In Paris there has been living a young American, very talented; you should know about him." . . . "I could make up a very interesting program of new works, by Serge Prokofieff, Arthur Honegger, and Alexandre Tansman," he said eagerly; "a Russian, a Swiss, and a Polish composer—all good men—friends of mine. And I would like also to include this talented young American, Aaron Copland. He has been a pupil in Paris with Boulanger. He recently returned to this country. I would like him to write a work for us." . . .

Thus it came about that in 1925 the League of Composers commissioned the first work in its long history of awards. It may have been a good omen for Aaron Copland for it was the first assignment he received in what was to become a long list of honors.

This particular work was called *Music for the Theatre* and was completed in time for Dr. Koussevitzky to conduct its world *première* at Town Hall in November 1925. It has remained one of the very popular compositions in contemporary literature.[34]

Copland's star was on the ascendancy. He was the first composer in history to receive a Guggenheim Foundation grant. This grant extended from 1925 to 1927. During the years from 1927 to 1937, he was invited to lecture at the New School for Social Research. In 1935 and then again in 1944, he lectured at Harvard University. Copland was the distinguished Norton Professor at Harvard during the academic year 1951–52. Perhaps most important of all, he headed the composition program at Tanglewood from 1940 until 1965, and gave direction to some of America's most important musical talents.

It was Copland who made American music respectable throughout the world. Ives had already written works of distinction, but these were largely unknown. One scholar has explained that

Because of the unusual delay in the general public awareness of the music of Ives and Ruggles, Copland became for many the first composer whose musical Americanism was as distinctive in its idiom as the work of the major composers of Europe, and in time this became, to a degree, his international role.[35]

The Americanism in the score of *Music for the Theatre* is Jazz. Jazz rhythm gives the piece its characteristic sound; however, the Jazz in *Music for the Theatre* is stylized, and frequently relies on clichés. Odd, too, is the orchestration, which is overly elaborate.

Many of these problems were solved in the Concerto for piano and orchestra. The Guggenheim grant that Copland had received allowed him to concentrate on a large-scale work, and so, in 1926, at the suggestion of Koussevitzky, he set to work on the Concerto. The piece is a continuous movement with two sections, a slow opening followed by a faster one. Jazz rhythms play an important role, as do Blues notes (i.e., scale degrees 3, 7, and sometimes 5, have variable inflection), bent notes, and seventh chords, especially those that fall within the function of subdominant harmony, such as I^{b7} and IV^{b7}. Copland's style as seen in the Concerto is derived primarily from Blues, which tend—at least in the New Orleans and St. Louis styles—to be slow, sentimental, and more lyrical than Texas Blues. The dreamy, tender style of Blues is particularly apparent in the opening slow section of the Concerto. The instrumentation employs muted trumpets, saxophone, and other Jazz sonorities. In the Concerto, Copland achieved a synthesis of Jazz and his own characteristic style. The premiere took place in January of 1927. Koussevitzky conducted the BSO with Copland as pianist. This beautiful work, which is not played often enough, is one of Copland's most satisfying scores.

The Four Piano Blues were begun in 1926. The last of the set, "For John Kirkpatrick," was completed in that year. The first three pieces were written in 1948, '47 and '34 respectively. The set was published in 1949.

A much more progressive and individual style is apparent in the Piano Variations (1930), which Copland orchestrated for the Louisville Orchestra in 1957.[36] The piece contains a theme, twenty variations, and a coda. At the structural heart of the work is a four-note motif hammered out at the opening. (Copland instructs that the player should "strike each note sharply.") The Variations show the influence of Schönberg, especially in their pointillistic style, which eliminates the distinction between melody and accompaniment so that isolated musical events, such as pitches, register shifts, durations, timbres, and so forth, become focal elements. Copland gave the premiere on a League of Composers program in January of 1931. A similar style is apparent in Copland's *Statements* (1935) for orchestra.

After the Piano Variations, Copland wrote no major work for the instrument until his Piano Sonata (1941). Copland, who played the first performance of the work in Buenos Aires on 21 October 1941, made the following observations about the musical structure and character of the piece:

I always connect the *Piano Sonata* with my old teacher, Rubin Gold-mark. He thought of sonata form as music's highest goal. It was what a composer aimed for, even more than the fugue. One thinks of the sonata as dramatic—a kind of play being acted out with plenty of time for self-expression. It seems to me that my *Piano Sonata* follows that idea. It is a serious piece that requires careful and repeated study. There is considerable dissonance in it, yet the work is predominantly conso-nant. . . . Every note was carefully chosen and none included for orna-mental reasons. The *Sonata* lies somewhere between the *Variations* and *Our Town*. Its three movements follow a slow, fast, slow sequence and are separate in character, but with subtle relationships between them. . . . The first movement is a regular sonata allegro form with two themes, a development section characterized by disjunct rhythms and a playful mood, and a clear recapitulation in which the opening idea is dramatically restated. The second movement scherzo is rhythmically American—I never would have thought of those rhythms if I had not been familiar with jazz. This has to do with a dependence on the eighth note as the basic rhythmic element—very demanding for the pianist because the rhythmic units shift through 5/8, 6/8, 3/4, and 7/8. The third movement of the *Sonata* is free in form and farther from the classic sonata than the previous movements. . . . The *Sonata* does not end with the usual flash of virtuosic passages; instead, it is rather grand and massive.[37]

Copland's music of the 1920s and 1930s is demanding, not only for the per-formers but also for the listeners. Realizing this, he determined that it was neces-sary for composers to cultivate an audience for contemporary music. He therefore teamed up with Roger Sessions (1896–1985) for the Copland-Sessions Concerts, a contemporary music series that lasted from 1928 until 1931. In 1932 and 1933, Cop-land continued his promulgation of twentieth-century music at Yaddo, a festival that took place in Saratoga Springs, New York for a period of two weeks each year in September. The Yaddo festivals succeeded in calling attention to many young composers, and some older composers. There, the works of Charles Ives received their rightful recognition for the first time. In his autobiography, Copland gives the following information:

[Seven] Ives songs, performed by baritone Hubert Linscott with myself at the piano, were received with great interest—this was the first time a group of professional musicians were paying serious attention to Ives. It was a turning point in the recognition of his music. Arthur Berger was prophetic when he wrote in his review for the *Daily Mirror*: "His-tory is being made in our midst." . . .
. . . When I *did* investigate [the *114 Songs*], I was amazed. There we were in the twenties searching for a composer from the older genera-tion with an "American sound," and here was Charles Ives composing this incredible music—totally unknown to us!

. . . As Ives' music gradually emerged, it had an increasingly influential effect on younger composers and eventually on the position of the American composer in the international musical scene.[38]

The Yaddo Festival was discontinued during the years 1934 and 1935. When the festival resumed in 1936, Copland was no longer associated with it. The programs continued until 1940, were suspended until 1945, and resumed sporadically in 1946.

Copland's experiences with audience development led to a change in his style. One of the first scores to reflect this change was *El Salón México* (1936), which he composed after his visit to Mexico in 1932. *El Salón México* was Copland's first work to achieve international attention. The title alludes to the dance hall in Mexico City where Copland heard Mexican popular music. The themes that he used came from two collections of Mexican folk melodies, Frances Toor's *Cancionero Méxicano* and Ruben M. Campos's *El folk-lore y la música Méxicana*.[39] Copland's score captures the atmosphere of Mexico as perceived by a tourist. The premiere was given in 1936 by the Orquesta Sinfónica de México under Chávez.

In subsequent works, Copland explored a musical realm that was specifically American. Some important compositions of this type are *Billy the Kid* (1940), *Rodeo, Lincoln Portrait* (both 1942), *Appalachian Spring* (1944), and *Red Pony* (1948). *Billy the Kid* was written for Lincoln Kirstein's Ballet Caravan. The score continues in the manner of *El Salón México* insofar as it also uses folk melodies, in this case, American cowboy tunes. In 1940, Copland made a seven-movement suite that is more frequently heard than the complete ballet.

The *Lincoln Portrait* is scored for narrator and orchestra. The texts of the narrative portions, which begin after an extended essay for orchestra alone, are drawn mainly from various political speeches and writings of Abraham Lincoln which Copland found in Lord Charnwood's biography.[40] In addition, the narration includes biographical information about Lincoln. Although much of the music is written to *suggest* folksongs, only one actual folk melody, "Springfield Mountain," is used extensively.

Rodeo, like *Billy the Kid*, is a cowboy ballet. Perhaps Copland's interest in scenarios of this sort shows the influence of popular American cinema at the time, especially the work of John Ford, who began his long string of Westerns in 1939 with the film *Stagecoach*, starring John Wayne.[41] In the music of *Rodeo*, Copland used tunes that he had selected from song collections: *Our Singing Country* by John A. and Alan Lomax, and *Traditional Music of America* by Ira Ford.

Perhaps the finest of Copland's creations in the Americana manner is *Appalachian Spring*. The story line, which was drawn up by Martha Graham, deals with the "American Dream": A young couple in Pennsylvania have just finished their long-anticipated farm house. They are about to be married. A kindly neighbor and a fundamentalist preacher give the couple the benefit of their wisdom as they prepare to embark upon their new life together. Copland provided the following analysis of the piece:

(1) *Very slowly*—Introduction of the characters, one by one, in a suffused light.

(2) *Fast*—Sudden burst of unison strings in A-major arpeggios starts the action.

(3) *Moderate*—Duo for the Bride and Her Intended—Scene of tenderness and passion.

(4) *Quite fast*—The Revivalist and his flock. Folksy feelings—Suggestions of square dances and country fiddlers.

(5) *Still faster*—Solo dance of the Bride—Presentiment of motherhood. Extremes of joy and fear and wonder.

(6) *Very slowly* (as at first)—Transition scene to music reminiscent of the introduction.

(7) *Calm and flowing*—Scenes of daily activity for the Bride and her Farmer-husband. There are five variations on a Shaker theme. The theme—sung by a solo clarinet—was taken from a collection of Shaker melodies compiled by Edward D. Andrews and published under the title The Gift to be Simple. The melody I borrowed and used almost literally is called "Simple gifts" . . .

(8) *Moderate*—Coda—The Bride takes her place among her neighbors. At the end the couple are left "quiet and strong in their new house." Muted strings intone a hushed prayer-like passage. The close is reminiscent of the opening music.[42]

Appalachian Spring won the Pulitzer Prize in 1945.

There are no folksongs whatsoever in Copland's Third Symphony, which he began immediately after *Appalachian Spring* and completed in 1946, shortly before its premiere under Koussevitzky and the BSO. The themes are all original, but some have the character of folksong. The Symphony, which was commissioned by the Koussevitzky Foundation, is in four movements. The internal movements are a scherzo and trio, and a slow movement, respectively. The Symphony is unified by cyclic reappearance of the three main themes of the first movement (which, incidentally, is not in the traditional sonata form). The first and second themes reappear in the Finale; the third theme is stated in a rhythmically altered version in the third movement. The slow, third movement proceeds without pause into the Finale, which is introduced by the well-known "Fanfare for the Common Man." According to the composer,

The opening fanfare is based on Fanfare for the Common Man, which I composed in 1942 at the invitation of Eugene Goossens for a series of wartime fanfares introduced under his direction by the Cincinnati Symphony. In the present version it is played first *pianissimo* by flutes and clarinets, and then suddenly given out by brass and percussion. The fanfare serves as a preparation for the movement which follows.[43]

In an ingenious and effective coda, Copland combines the Fanfare theme and several variants of it with the principal theme of the first movement, while continuing the two themes of the Finale.

Copland did not produce a major vocal work until 1947, when he completed the score of *In the Beginning*, a setting for mezzo-soprano and unaccompanied mixed chorus, of the story of creation as told in the Book of Genesis. The music begins in a rather bare style, but becomes increasingly complex as the wonders of creation unfold.

In the Beginning was followed by the *Twelve Poems of Emily Dickinson* (1950), a set of songs for solo voice and piano accompaniment. Copland later orchestrated eight of these. Other important vocal works include the two volumes of *Old American Songs* (1950, '52) for voice and piano, which are based on traditional American tunes. The accompaniments are interesting and challenging. The first set includes: (1) "The Boatmen's Dance," (2) "The Dodger," (3) "Long Time Ago," (4) "Simple Gifts," and (5) "I Bought Me a Cat." The second set contains: (1) "Little Horses," (2) "Zion's Walls," (3) "The Golden Willow Tree," (4) "At the River," and (5) "Ching-a-ring Chaw."

Other vocal works range from Copland's only opera, *The Tender Land* (1953), which was commissioned to celebrate the thirtieth anniversary of the League of Composers, to the solo song for voice and piano, *Dirge in the Woods* (1954), and the *Canticle of Freedom* (1955) for chorus and orchestra.

Even after his return to an accessible compositional style, Copland continued to experiment with progressive idioms. From time to time, he used Serialism. One of the most successful of Copland's works in modified serial style is the vast Piano Fantasy (1957), a piece written as a single movement but with clearly discernible sections. Copland does not base his score on a twelve-note row; instead, he opens with a four-note set (reminiscent of the Piano Variations), which is immediately repeated and expanded to a ten-note row consisting of the tones: E-flat, B-flat, F, D-flat, B, F-sharp, A, G, D, C. The initial working of the row alternates steely, restless passages with sections of relative repose. The central section of the work has been described as a "Scherzo and trio" with new developmental passages at the return of the scherzo.[44] The final section leads to a more lyrical coda, in which the texture gradually thins out in order to bring contrapuntal statements of the row into relief.

Copland wrote *Connotations* for large orchestra in an effort to highlight the virtuosic playing of the New York Philharmonic's principals. At the time of its premiere in 1962, the orchestra had been under the direction of Leonard Bernstein since 1958. Early in his tenure as their conductor, Bernstein had anticipated the Philharmonic's relocation from Carnegie Hall to Lincoln Center, where they would perform in Philharmonic Hall. Copland, who had befriended Bernstein in 1937, was one of a select group of composers invited to write new works to be given during the 1962–63 inaugural season. Other composers who provided celebratory works included William Schuman (Eighth Symphony), Milhaud (*Ouverture Philarmonique*), Barber (*Andromache's Farewell*), Poulenc (*Sept répons de ténèbres*), Paul Hindemith (Concerto for Orchestra), and Hans Werner Henze (Fifth Symphony).

Connotations is one of Copland's few dodecaphonic compositions. (The others are his Piano Quartet, the Piano Fantasy, and *Inscape*.) The twelve chromatic tones of *Connotations* are heard at the outset of this single-movement work in a series of three chords, each with four notes, scored for brass. Copland indicated that the piece is like a chaconne, with variations based on the opening three chords and their implications.

In *Connotations*, Copland may well have been making an effort to keep pace with what he perceived as modern music; but, as Bernstein remarked, "when the musical winds blew past [Copland], he tried to catch up—with 12-tone music— just as it too was becoming old-fashioned."[45] Bernstein seems not to have been very much attracted to the piece, but he held a more positive view of the score of *Inscape* (1967), which Copland wrote on commission from the New York Philharmonic to celebrate its 125th anniversary.

Inscape is a companion piece to *Connotations*. They are related not only by their dodecaphonic style, but also, insofar as the source material for *Inscape* was sketched in 1963—immediately after *Connotations*. The important difference between the two is that in *Inscape*, Copland deliberately attempted to preserve tonal elements.

The word "inscape" was coined by Gerard Manley Hopkins, who intended the term to designate that inner essence underpinning all things, that imparts unity and significance to their external forms. The title suggests intimacy and introspection. These features are reflected in transparent counterpoint for two or three instruments, exposed solo lines, and dynamic nuances. Still, the piece begins and ends with a crashing, *fortissimo* chord containing eleven tones. Michael Steinberg has remarked that this sonority may be a "double tease . . . one addressed to his old teacher, Nadia Boulanger, who famously and vociferously disliked 12-tone music, the other aimed at some of his American colleagues who took their 12-tone orthodoxy terribly seriously."[46]

Other noteworthy compositions include the instrumental pieces an *Outdoor Overture* and *Our Town* (1938, '40) for orchestra, and *Quiet City* (1939; rev. 1940) for English horn, trumpet, and strings. All three works possess a tender, poetic simplicity that has ensured them an enduring place among orchestral masterpieces in miniature.

Copland wrote a handful of chamber works including the Sonata (1942) for violin and piano, an attractive, three-movement work that presents few difficulties for listeners or performers, the Piano Quartet (1950), a complex score using modified serial techniques, the Nonet (1960) for three violins, three violas, and three cellos, and the Duo (1971) for flute and piano. The Sextet (1937) for clarinet, string quartet, and piano is an alternate version of his *Short Symphony* (1933), which Copland considered unreasonably difficult.

It has been remarked that "Copland's music is essentially of the Twentieth Century and stamps its composer as an unquestioned 'modernist.' But he has been much less a theorist and much more a practical man of music than some of his most distinguished confreres abroad."[47] With Copland's death on 2 December 1990, America lost its most popular classical composer.

Notes

1. Ralph Waldo Emerson, *Essays by Ralph Waldo Emerson* (New York: T. Y. Crowell, 1951), p. 247.
2. In the collection of *114 Songs*, song 93, "Berceuse," has only the English text "O'er the mountain towards the west," but it was apparently written first to the words of Brahms's lullaby, "Guten Abend, gute Nacht." Similarly, song 71, "There Is a Lane," can be sung to the text "Widmung," famous in its setting by Robert Franz, and song 97, "The South Wind," can be sung to the text "Die Lotusblume."
3. Cited in Otto Deri, *Exploring Twentieth-Century Music*, p. 487.
4. Charles Ives, Postface to the *114 Songs*, (New York: Peer International, n.d.)
5. Song 26, "Like a Sick Eagle," for chamber orchestra; no. 44, "Watchman," and no. 46, "His Exaltation," in the Second Violin Sonata; No. 45, "At the River," in the Fourth Violin Sonata; No. 47, "The Camp Meeting," appears in the Third Symphony, and no. 48, "Thoreau," in the *Concord Sonata*, etc.
6. Ives withdrew the first movement of the Quartet, thereby reducing it to three movements. John Kirkpatrick discovered the missing opening movement among Ives's personal effects, which Mrs. Ives donated to the Jackson Music Library, Yale University. See John Kirkpatrick, *A Temporary Mimeographed Catalogue of the Music Manuscripts of Charles Edward Ives (1874–1954) Given by Mrs. Ives to the Library of the Yale School of Music, September 1955.*
7. Lowell Mason (1792–1872) of Medfield, Massachusetts, was active as a church musician, composer, and music educator. From 1812 to 1827, he was in Savannah. From 1827 until 1832, he conducted the Boston's Handel and Haydn Society. In 1833, he founded the Boston Academy of Music. He contended that music should be part of the public-school curriculum, and he did much to establish programs in the Massachusetts schools. His children, Daniel Gregory, Lowell, Jr., William, and Henry, were all musicians. Henry was father of another musician, Daniel Gregory Mason (1873–1953), who wrote three symphonies (1914, '29, '36), vocal, and chamber works. His String Quartet on Negro Themes (1919) is the best known of his chamber pieces. Ives was especially attracted to the many hymn tunes of Lowell Mason, perhaps owing to their similar views about the role of music in the life of the common person.
8. John Kirkpatrick and Gregg Smith have edited Psalm 90 for Merion Music, Inc., of Bryn Mawr, Pennsylvania (1970). In their Editors' Notes, they indicate that "the composition of Ives's 90th Psalm covered a span of over thirty years." Apparently, the first version of the Psalm dated from 1894; another version was left in the library of the Central Presbyterian Church when Ives resigned in 1902. Kirkpatrick and Smith suppose that "[Ives] learned that, when the church moved in 1915, these manuscripts were thrown out. So he evidently started to reconstruct the 90th Psalm in 1923, but actually, he recomposed it."
9. At the time Ives composed the Second String Quartet, the Kneisel Quartet consisted of Franz Kneisel, first violin; J. Theodorowicz, second violin; Louis Svecenski, viola; and Willem Willeke, 'cello.

10. Charles Ives, *Essays before a Sonata and Other Writings*, ed. Howard Boatwright (New York: Norton, 1964).

11. The second edition was issued by Arrow Music Press. The Arrow edition was subsequently acquired by Associated Music Publishers from whom it is currently available in an unaltered reprint.

12. Moses Smith, *Koussevitzky* (New York: Allen, Towne and Heath, 1947), p. 12.

13. Arthur Lourié, *Sergei Koussevitzky and His Epoch: A Biographical Chronicle*, Trans. from Russian by S. W. Pring (1931; reprint, Freeport, New York: Books for Libraries Press, 1969), p. 21.

14. Alexandria Vofstdky-Shiraeff, *Russian Composers and Musicians* (New York: H. W. Wilson, 1940), p. 122.

15. Koussevitzky's double-bass compositions were published in Moscow by Jurgenson in 1907.

16. Hugo Leichtentritt, *Serge Koussevitzky: The Boston Symphony Orchestra and the New American Music* (Cambridge, Massachusetts: Harvard, 1947), p. 6.

17. Lourié, *Sergei Koussevitzky*, p. 49.

18. Lourié, *Sergei Koussevitzky*, p. 50.

19. Lourié, *Sergei Koussevitzky*, pp. 50–51.

20. Smith, *Koussevitzky*, p. 36.

21. Olin Downes, "A Conductor's Musicianship: Baseless Rumors Concerning Koussevitzky's Lack of Technical Knowledge Shown Absurd by Quality of His Performance," *New York Times* (25 November 1928), section 10, p. 8, cols. 1–2.

22. Smith, *Koussevitzky*, p. 71.

23. Smith, *Koussevitzky*, p. 49.

24. Lourié, *Sergei Koussevitzky*, p. 96.

25. Concerning the Volga tours, see Oskar Bie and Robert Sterl, *Musik auf der Wolga, 1914* (Leipzig: Meissner & Buch, 1920).

26. 15 June 1924. Cited in Smith, *Koussevitzky*, p. 126.

27. Smith, *Koussevitzky*, p. 153.

28. Smith, *Koussevitzky*, pp. 175–176. But see Lourié, *Sergei Koussevitzky*, p. 211, who contends that for the 1925–26 season, "thirty-six excellent musicians were added to the personnel."

29. Smith, *Koussevitzky*, pp. 286–287.

30. Nicolas Slonimsky, "Kussewitzky, Sergej Alexandrowitsch" *Die Musik in Geschichte und Gegenwart*, Vol. 7. (Kassel: Bärenreiter, 1958), cols. 1919. Trans. M. A. R.

31. Aaron Copland and Vivian Perlis, (1989). *Copland: Since 1943* (New York: St. Martin's Press, 1989), p. 68.

32. The present-day Juilliard School of Music, established in 1946, is actually a combination of the New York Institute for Musical Art (founded in 1905) and the Juilliard Graduate School (which was organized in 1924).

33. The League of Composers had been founded in New York City in 1923, by members of the International Composers' Guild. The League commissioned works by Copland, Bartók, and Barber, and made possible the American premieres of many modern European scores. The League issued *Modern Music*, a quarterly, between 1924 and 1947. Copland was chairperson of the League from 1948 to 1950. In 1954, the League merged with the International Society for Contemporary Music. Claire Raphael Reis, one of the founders of the League, compiled a fascinating history of the League's activities and influence entitled *Composers, Conductors, and Critics* (New York: Oxford, 1955.)

34. Reis, *Composers, Conductors, and Critics*, pp. 64–65.

35. Robert Marsh, "Aaron Copland," *International Cyclopedia of Music and Musicians*, 11th ed. (New York: Dodd, Mead, 1985), p. 463.

36. Copland fussed about the title of the Variations. In his autobiography, Copland states: "When I wrote to John Kirkpatrick about the piece, calling it "Thematic Variations," he responded, advising me to find a better title. I wrote back, "I should like to call them like Bach did the 'Goldberg Variations'—but thus far haven't been able to think up a good one." Jottings on pencil sketches indicate that I was considering several titles: "Melodic Variations, Twenty Melodic Variations, Thematic Variations, Fantasie on an Original Theme, Variations for Piano, Variations on a Theme, Chaconne, Declamations on a Serious Theme, Theme and Variations." See Aaron Copland and Vivian Perlis, *Copland: 1900 through 1942* (New York: St. Martin's/Marek, 1984), p. 178.

37. Copland and Vivian Perlis, *Copland*, pp. 330–332.

38. Copland and Perlis, *Copland*, pp. 201–204.

39. Neil Butterworth, *The Music of Aaron Copland* (New York: Toccata Press, 1985), p. 69. For a precise listing of the tunes and their sources, see Howard Pollack, *Aaron Copland: The Life and Work of an Uncommon Man* (New York: Henry Holt, 1999), p. 299.

40. *Abraham Lincoln* (London, 1916).

41. Ford's name was Sean O'Feeny. He directed hundreds of movies and worked often with John Wayne (*recte* Marion Michael Morrison). In addition to *Stagecoach*, their most successful ventures together include the films *Fort Apache* (1948) and *Rio Grande* (1950).

42. Cited in Milton Cross, *Encyclopedia of the Great Composers and Their Music* (Garden City, New York: Doubleday, 1953), vol. 1, pp. 184–185.

43. Cited in Butterworth, *The Music of Aaron Copland*, p. 108. Eighteen proposals for fanfares were submitted to the Cincinnati Symphony, but the ten that were chosen to open concerts of the 1942–43 season were as follows: "Fanfare for the Paratroopers," Paul Creston; "Fanfare for the Forces of Our Latin American Allies," Henry Cowell; "Fanfare for the Medical Corps," Anis Fuleihon; "Fanfare for the Merchant Marine," Eugene Goosens; "Fanfare for the Signal Corps," Howard Hanson; "Fanfare for the Fighting French," Walter Piston; "Fanfare for Russia," Deems Taylor; "Fanfare for France," Virgil Thomson; and the "Fanfare for the Airmen," Bernard Wagenaar.

44. Butterworth, *The Music of Aaron Copland*, p. 149.

45. Cited in Joan Peyser, *Bernstein: A Biography* (New York: Beech Tree Books, 1987), p. 334.

46. Michael Steinberg, notes for *Inscape* in *New York Philharmonic Stagebill* (November 1999), pp. 48–48A. This and other commentaries were prepared as part of the New York Philharmonic's celebration concert series Completely Copland: 24 November–12 December 1999.

47. Oscar Thompson, "Aaron Copland," *International Cyclopedia of Music and Musicians*, ed. Robert Sabin, 9th ed. (New York: Dodd, Mead, 1964), p. 441.

Chapter 16

The Move to America: Stravinsky, Part IV

For most of his career, Stravinsky played the role of the king on a chess board, always trying to stay one move ahead of circumstances. He had tried the Swiss route during World War I and did not care to repeat that episode. His decision to relocate in the United States had much to do with personal acquaintances, such as Boulanger and Koussevitzky, who were there, ready to help.

The piece that he was composing during this transitional period was the Symphony in C. The first movement was completed in France, in 1938. When he finished the third movement, in 1940, Stravinsky was in Cambridge, Massachusetts. He put the final touches to the fourth movement as a resident of Beverly Hills, California, in the summer of 1940.

The symphony was written for and dedicated to the Chicago Symphony Orchestra, which was celebrating its fiftieth anniversary. His musical preoccupations at the time were symphonic works by Haydn, Beethoven, and Tschaikovsky. From these composers, Stravinsky got his model for the four movements, which observe symphonic traditions. The first is a sonata-allegro form with contrasting keys and themes, a conventional development section, and a well-ordered recapitulation. This is followed by a Larghetto in song-form with reduced scoring; this movement progresses without pause into the Allegretto, which is a scherzo with changing meters, syncopations, misplaced accents, and other rhythmic twists. A slow introduction (Largo) leads to the Finale. Here, Stravinsky takes his lead from Tschaikovsky, and he recalls, in cyclic fashion, the opening theme of the first movement, now as a bass line, at the climax. The Finale is highly contrapuntal, a feature Stravinsky might have noted in Haydn's symphonies.

Stravinsky's next large work was another symphony, the so-called *Symphony in Three Movements* (1945), which is dedicated to the New York Philharmonic. It was written during World War II, and certain elements of the score—especially in the first and third movements—were inspired by newsreels that Stravinsky saw.[1]

The second movement also has extra-musical associations, in particular, Franz Werfel's novel *The Song of Bernadette*. At Werfel's urging, Stravinsky tried his hand at a film score, but soon gave up. What he had written became part of the second movement of the Symphony.

The origin of the second movement accounts for its distinctive instrumentation, which includes a concertante part for harp. To achieve a proper balance between the solo harp and orchestral tutti, Stravinsky sometimes limits the brass to three horns. At other times, he uses the harp in a concertino, first with a handful of solo strings, later replacing the strings with pairs of flutes, clarinets, and bassoons.

The Finale is centered on C; however, the mode fluctuates between major and minor. The piano returns as the concertante soloist, thereby enabling the composer to resume his use of full orchestral brass in the tutti passages. The movement ends in an energetic passage that is impressive for, among other things, its sheer volume.

In the couple of years following the completion of the Symphony in C, Stravinsky composed smaller works for particular performers and ensembles, such as the *Ebony Concerto* for Woody Herman and his band, and the Concerto in D for Paul Sacher and the Basle Chamber Orchestra. The former work is a striking blend of classical and jazz techniques: The first movement, for example, is a sonata-allegro form in B-flat with a contrasting tonal plateau of E-flat followed by a reconciliation of elements in B-flat; its scoring for solo clarinet, five saxophones, bass clarinet, French horn, five trumpets, three trombones, piano, harp, guitar, double bass, tom-toms, cymbals, and drums, however, is strangely at odds with the movement's classical form. Similarly, the second movement has the traditional slow tempo and plaintive mood of a classical concerto, but the music is Texas Blues in the key of F. The last movement is a theme with variations in which Stravinsky displays his newly acquired virtuosity in writing Jazz. Perhaps the piece was a celebration of Americana in music: The occasion would have been appropriate, since Stravinsky became an American citizen on 28 December 1945, and this was his first score as an "American" composer.

Language was an issue for Stravinsky, but he made every effort to join in the life and culture of his new home. What better way to study English than to write an opera in the language?

The story line was suggested by a series of paintings by William Hogarth that Stravinsky saw in 1947. The set, known collectively as *The Rake's Progress* (1735), is a satire of decadent English society. Stravinsky immediately envisioned the paintings as a series of operatic scenes with stylized musical gestures. He joined forces with Wystan Hugh Auden and Chester Kallman to formulate details of the libretto.

Auden anticipated Stravinsky's difficulties with English; accordingly, he introduced the composer to Robert Craft, a musicologist, conductor, and performer, who went to live with Stravinsky in Hollywood and helped him with pronunciation. Work began in 1948, and by 1951, the three-act score for tenor, baritone, soprano, bass, mezzo, double winds, pairs of horns, trumpets, keyboard, tympani, and strings in five parts was completed.

The music of *The Rake's Progress* was inspired by the operas of Mozart, especially *Don Giovanni*, which has a similar plot, and *Così fan tutte*. In its formal design, too, Stravinsky's opera mirrors eighteenth-century number opera with recitatives, arias, and ensembles. The Epilogue, a quintet for Anne Truelove, Baba the Turk, Tom Rakewell, Mr. Truelove, and Nick Shadow, is a spoof on the moralizing ensembles that closed many mid-eighteenth-century vaudevilles, such as Rousseau's *Le devin du village* (village soothsayer; 1752).

The première at the Teatro la Fenice in Venice on 11 September 1951 was under Stravinsky's direction. That theater, modest in size, accorded ideally with the composer's conception of the work as an intimate chamber opera; nevertheless, the big houses quickly took the piece into their repertoire.

The Rake's Progress may well be considered the apogee of Stravinsky's neoclassical style. From this point onward, his works took a new direction, largely as a consequence of his friendship with Craft, who stimulated Stravinsky's interest in Serialism.

Ever the pragmatist, Stravinsky realized that listeners generally could not follow all twelve tones of the chromatic scale and their various permutations; accordingly, he constructed his rows using just a handful of pitches and intervals. In the first of the *Three Songs from William Shakespeare* (1953), for instance, Stravinsky sets the sonnet "Musick to heare" using a basic set of only four tones. He is nevertheless careful to employ all twelve tones in the various permutations of his smaller collections. Stravinsky's Serialism is different, too, because it often includes functional harmonic gestures.

Soon after the prèmiere of *The Rake's Progress*, Stravinsky had an idea for another theatrical work. It was to have been an opera with a libretto by Dylan Thomas. The composer and the poet met in May of 1953 at the Copley Plaza Hotel, Boston. Stravinsky eagerly anticipated working with Thomas, but his hopes were dashed when he received news on 9 November that Thomas had died at St. Vincent's Hospital, New York City, from an overdose of alcohol.

As a memorial to the poet, Stravinsky set one of his poems, the villanelle "Do not go gentle into that good night," which Thomas had written in memory of his own father.[2] Stravinsky used a row of five tones: The basic set consists of E, E-flat, C, C-sharp, D. This set is also used in the "Dirge Canons," antiphonal canons for quartets of trombones and strings. The inclusion of the four trombones was an afterthought, inspired by the fact that on the program of Monday Evening Concerts for 20 September 1954, Craft had scheduled "Fili mi, Absalom" from the first volume of *Symphoniæ sacræ* (1629) by Heinrich Schütz (1585–1672). Since the instruments were already at hand, and since the trombone has historically been used as a musical symbol for death, it seemed natural to use them in the memorial piece for Thomas.

Symbolism plays an important role in the construction of *In memoriam Dylan Thomas*. The poem contains six verses: The first five are tercets, the sixth a quatrain. The individual lines are in pentameter (i.e., five poetic feet). The texture of the song is five-part, string quartet plus the solo voice. Stravinsky's row consists of five tones. The "Dirge Canons" consist of five sections that may be represented: A, B, A, B, A. The word "dirge" contains five letters, and "canons" six. The performance timing given for the piece in the preface is six minutes, even though the total of the precise timings that follow each of the three movements exceeds six minutes. Stravinsky's preoccupation with the numbers five and six indicates that he was attempting to create a highly regulated formal design that would be musically analogous to the rigors of the villanelle as a poetic form. Stravinsky chose the numbers five and six because they represent the number of letters in the poet's name: Dylan (five letters) + Thomas (six letters).

Pervasive symbolism was a characteristic of classic serial repertoire, especially in the works of Berg, who embedded secret messages in his Chamber Concerto for violin, piano, and thirteen winds, in his *Lyric Suite*, and in the Violin Concerto. Stravinsky's use of encoded messages suggests that his neoclassical serialism was founded on a thorough knowledge of both the techniques and æsthetics of the original Viennese serialists.

Symbolism plays an equally important role in the *Canticum sacrum ad honorem Sancti Marci nominis* (sacred cantata in honor of the name of St. Mark; 1955), which was composed for St. Mark's Cathedral in Venice. Many of the cantata's formal features relate to the architecture of the building.

The cantata marked a turning point in Stravinsky's use of Serialism. Whereas previously he had built rows using fewer than twelve tones or more than twelve (as in the Passacaglia of the Septet; 1952), he now turned to the classic dodecaphonic manner. Twelve-tone sets form the basis of all of his subsequent works, of which *Threni* (1957), the *Flood*, an operatic mystery play written for the Columbia Broadcasting System and premiered on television in June of 1962, and the orchestral *Variations Aldous Huxley in memoriam* (1964) are noteworthy.

Notes

1. For details, see Eric Walter White, *Stravinsky: The Composer and His Works*, 2d ed. (Berkeley and Los Angeles: University of California, 1979), pp. 430–431.
2. A *villanelle* is an ancient fixed form built of three-line stanzas (i.e., tercets) that culminate in a final stanza of four lines (i.e., a quatrain). The first and third lines of the first stanza form alternating concluding lines of all subsequent tercets. The concluding quatrain contains the first and third lines as a final couplet. The rhyme scheme is │ABA│ . . . │ABAA│.

Chapter 17

Floods of Outcasts

Throughout the twentieth century, vast segments of the world's populace have been forced to migrate. Demographic upheavals took place during the second quarter of the century because of the Fascist and Nazi regimes in Italy, then Germany, and later Austria and other countries. Even after the conclusion of the war, forced migrations continued, owing to political suppression in the Soviet block. For many, the United States became a haven.

Among the formidable roster of personalities, certain names immediately grasp our attention: the dramatist and poet Berthold Brecht; the conductor and pianist Fritz Busch, who led the Stuttgart Opera from 1918 to 1922, and the Dresden Staatsoper from 1922 to 1933; the eclectic composer Ingolf Dahl (1912–1970); the renowned 'cellists Emanuel Feuermann and Gregor Piatigorsky; the notorious composer of both Expressionistic horror operas and appealing *Zeitwerke* and *Gebrauchsmusik*, Paul Hindemith (1895–1963); the conductor Otto Klemperer, a protégé of Gustav Mahler's who went on to conducting posts at Prague, Cologne, Berlin, Los Angeles, New York, and Pittsburgh; Erich Korngold (1897–1957), whose early success with dramatic works provided an ideal background for his work in Hollywood after 1934; another well-known composer of film scores, Miklós Rózsa (b. 1907); the legendary pianists Artur Schnabel and Rudolf Serkin; the self-taught Ernst Toch (1887–1964), whose output includes a vast amount of chamber music; the notoriously temperamental conductor Arturo Toscanini; Kurt Weill (1900–1950), the first composer to achieve a rapprochement between the popular cabaret style and opera; the novelist and librettist Franz Werfel; as well as the previously discussed cases of Bartók, Boulanger, Schoenberg, and Stravinsky. Later, Soviet policies forced others, including Karel Husa (b. 1921) and György Ligeti (b. 1923), into exile.

Mussolini became the Fascist prime minister of Italy in 1922, more than a decade before Hitler came to power; however, the Italian dictator was less concerned with the possible influences of art music than his German counterpart. Hitler declared that "95 percent of the national treasure of a people consists of its cultural achievements and only 5 percent of the so-called material assets."[1] This view, noble in itself, became a threat to any composer whose music did not advance the ideologies of the Reich. Many composers, by virtue of their ethnic or religious backgrounds, were deemed incapable of producing music suitable for Hitler's Aryan race (a race that has no more basis in fact than Wagner's Nibelungen).[2]

Astonishingly, the Nazi policy of safeguarding the Aryan race from contamination was exercised retrospectively too.

> The standard policy of [Hitler's] regime in regard to "racially putrid" composers was to destroy them. Even for those long dead, there would be ceremonial denunciations followed by burning of scores, melting of printing plates, tearing up of library index cards, and smashing of records to eradicate every trace of their creative existence.[3]

This fanaticism was serious; for many, it was a matter of life and death.

The migration of European intellectuals to the United States came in two principal waves: the first, shortly after Hitler's rise to power in Germany in 1933, the second, after the Nazi annexation of Austria in 1938; however, the exodus continued even after World War II had ended. As the Soviet Union annexed one satellite nation after another, many Central and Eastern European progressives were also forced into exile.

The exodus of old-world intelligentsia was a boon for Americans. Many of the nation's orchestras were able, despite limited budgets, to acquire the services of Europe's finest conductors: Maurice Abravanel, Antal Dorati, Husa, Erich Leinsdorf, Mitropoulos, Monteux, Rostropovich, William Steinberg, George Szell, and Bruno Walter for example. In these positions, they introduced recent European music to the United States, and by conscientious programming, they helped to form public opinions about music.

Important contributions were also made by exiled scholars and critics. Willi Apel, Manfred Bukofzer, Alfred Einstein, Hans T. David, Karl Geiringer, Hugo Leichtentritt, Paul Nettl, Hans Tischler, Leo Schrade, Felix Salzer, and Emanuel Winternitz became pillars of American academia, and their books are still widely available.

In the United States, opportunities for the exchange of ideas were readily at hand. Humanitarian ethics played an important part in this process; nevertheless, there was also a genuine interest among Americans that arose purely from intellectual curiosity. It is telling, for example, that within "three days after the Nazi book burning on 10 May 1933, the *New York Times* announced that the New School for Social Research was expanding to become a 'University in Exile.'"[4] New York University responded similarly. Walter Cook, chairperson of NYU's Institute of Fine Arts at the time, remarked that "Hitler is my best friend: he shakes the tree and I collect the apples."[5]

To examine the cultural impact on America of each personality mentioned would require a vast volume; nevertheless, we may look at the activities of a few representative figures to gain a sense of the social dynamics of this cross-cultural hybridization.

Kurt Weill, 1900–1950

By the advent of the Third Reich, Kurt Weill had achieved fame and success—including a ten-year contract with Universal Editions that was signed during Emil Hertzka's tenure as acquisitions editor.

Weill's musical experiences began in the theater. His earliest studies in composition and theory were with Albert Bing, director of the Dessau Opera. After three years' work with Bing, Weill studied with Englebert Humperdinck (1854–1921), Wagner's assistant during the composition and first production of *Parsifal*, and the composer of *Hansel and Gretel* (1893). Weill's work with Humperdinck during the 1918–19 academic year at the Hochschule für Musik in Berlin was cut short by Weill's desire for practical experience. After a brief stint on the production staff of the Dessau Opera with Hans Knappertsbusch and Bing, he left in December of 1919, to conduct a small opera company in Lüdenscheid.

When Ferrucio Busoni (1866–1924) became the professor of composition at the Berlin Academy of Arts, Weill applied to his class and was accepted as one of six students.[6] Busoni had a profound knowledge of Western musical traditions, and he revered the music of Bach and Mozart. In his own music, Busoni mapped their formal and stylistic clarity onto contemporary styles, using elements from Debussy, Strauss, Schönberg, and Reger. Busoni's virtuosity at the keyboard impressed Weill, too. Their relationship was fruitful, and when Busoni died in July of 1924, the young man lost a stimulating mentor and a valuable friend. Weill's esteem for his musical heritage is apparent in his two symphonies (1921, '34), two string quartets (the unpublished Quartet in B minor, 1920; and Op. 8, 1923), and the Concerto (1924) for violin and winds for Joseph Szigeti.

Weill's compositional work was complemented by activities in the world of theater. Beginning in 1925, he had a weekly column in *Der deutsche Rundfunk*, where he reviewed Brecht's works and identified him as one of the most innovative dramatists of the day.[7]

Weill's collaborations involved leading figures in German cultural life, especially dramatists: Georg Kaiser provided the librettos for *Der Protagonist* (the protagonist; 1926) and *Der Zar läßt sich photographieren* (the tsar is photographed; 1928); Weill composed incidental music for plays by August Strindberg and worked with Hindemith on the original score of *Der Lindberghflug* (the Lindbergh flight; 1929); Erwin Piscator's theories of political theater influenced Brecht's text for the librettos of *Die Dreigroschenoper* (threepenny opera; 1928), *Aufstieg und Fall der Stadt Mahagonny* (the rise and fall of the city Mahagonny; 1929), *Happy End* (1929), and *Die sieben Todsünden* (seven deadly sins; 1933).

In the works cited, Expressionism and Epic Theater are potent ideological and aesthetic elements, but Expressionism was on the decline in the decade following World War I.

To many post-war artists, expressionist art seemed to be so centred on the artist's examination of his own subjective response that it had no relevance to the real world and nothing to say about the political and social conditions under which many people lived.[8]

Piscator and Brecht envisioned what they called Epic Theater: a revolutionary approach to drama whereby the conventional appeal to win the listener's sympathy

Kurt Weill

was avoided. Instead, productions used montage—a mixture of self-contained scenes, characters' stepping outside their personæ to assess and criticize the events in progress, motion picture clips, and musical episodes—for the purpose of stimulating the viewer's skepticism. The dissolution of the stage into its component parts forced the audience into the role of critic.

Weill's keen sense of style predisposed him to the æsthetics of the Epic Theater: He could write music that was sincere, natural, and optimistic; he could also write music that was ironic, satirical, and banal. Similarly, Epic Theater allowed for music that was manifestly sectional. Because Weill's lyric theater pieces resemble the old number operas of the eighteenth century, much of the music invites performance as excerpts on recitals. Weill's preference for conventional forms is striking, too. Strophic and modified strophic designs, recitatives paired with lyrical passages, verses with refrains, and familiar metrical and phraseological designs make his music accessible. Piscator and Brecht found in Weill the musician who was absolutely right for Epic Theater.

One of the lesser-known theatrical names connected with Weill is that of Karoline Blamauer, who became his wife on 28 January 1926. She is commonly known by her stage name, Lotte Lenya.[9] Lenya created many of the lead roles in Weill's works. She had no formal vocal instruction, and her voice was high, light, and thin—a *Fach* associated primarily with popular music.

Weill scored a success with *Dreigroschenoper*, a modern-day remake of the *Beggar's Opera* (London, 1728) by John Gay and Johann Pepusch. Brecht and Weill retained the original *dramatis personæ*, consisting largely of whores, criminals, and other depraved, yet intriguing characters. Weill's music, however, was entirely new.[10] The idea of remaking the *Beggar's Opera* began with Elizabeth Hauptmann, Brecht's secretary and assistant. In fact, she made the earliest sketches of what became *Dreigroschenoper*. Other hands made contributions too: Harald Paulsen, who created the role of Macheath, complained that his part seemed innocuous. The result was the hurdy-gurdy man's "Moritat" ("Mack the Knife"), the most frequently performed number from the score. Other highlights include "Die Ballade der Sexuellen Hörigkeit" (ballad of sexual addiction) and "Seeräuber Jenny" (Pirate Jenny), moments that are equally astonishing for their nuance and their brutal exposure of human foibles.

Throughout his career, Weill was fascinated by the types of dissolutes that populated the stage of *Dreigroschenoper*. Anna, in *Die sieben Todsünden*, is an ambivalent figure, who tears herself apart in her alternating dedications to the straight-and-narrow way and the way of sin and corruption. Johann Mattes and David Orth, the principals in the three-act opera *Die Bürgerschaft* (the community; 1932), sacrifice their ethics, obligations, and their friendship, as they embezzle from the community. The sorry story ends with Mattes's handing Orth over to an angry mob for execution. In *Mahagonny*, this fascination with perversion provides the premise for the entire work.

The term "Mahagonny" probably referred originally to the brownshirts of the Nazi party, who had made their presence felt throughout Germany beginning with Hitler's Beer Hall Putsch of 9 November 1923. As Nazi power became centralized in Berlin, the allusion to the city of Mahagonny increasingly came to specify the German capital. Brecht's libretto transfers the action of the opera to the nineteenth-century Wild West of the United States. Within this fanciful context, we are to imagine that a band of wayward, destitute rogues found a city that, by virtue of its indolence and corruption, becomes a thriving metropolis. Jim, one of the inhabitants, complains that there are too many laws, proscriptions, and obstacles to hedonism. After an approaching hurricane bypasses the city, the inhabitants rejoice and announce the new, lawless way of life. Jim loses his money and, with it, his popularity. He is tried, convicted, and executed as Mahagonny is engulfed in flames and destroyed.

This scenario parallels the story of Sodom and Gomorrah in Genesis 19:1–26. For Weill, a Jew and the son of a cantor, the downfall of Mahagonny must have been a frighteningly powerful metaphor for the ethical poverty of Berlin. A related work, the biblical drama *Der Weg der Verheissung* (the way of the promise; 1934), was one of Weill's first projects after Hitler's rise to power.[11]

The score of *Mahagonny* is rife with Americanisms, like names of *dramatis personæ* such as Fatty, Jenny Hill, Jim Mahoney, Jack O'Brien, Bill, Joe, and Tobby Higgins; mention in the libretto of the Gold Rush and Alaska; instrumentation including saxophones, zither, and banjo; even American vulgarities thrown into German texts: "Dort in der Hütte am Fluß, in sieben Wintern, schnitt unser Messer in den Tisch unsre Goddams." (There in the hut, during seven winters, our knife etched our Goddams into the table.)[12] In Weill's general directions to the score, he warns that "Any approximation of the Wild West- and Cowboy-Romance, and any suggestion of a typical American milieu is to be avoided."[13] The explanation for this irony stems from the tenets of Epic Theater: The locale is changed from Germany to America so that Weill, Brecht, and the participants in the production could maintain their patriotic, nationalistic, proper German facade; nevertheless, the allegory is so transparent that the critique of German society only gains force.

Weill's acrid social commentaries did not go unnoticed by German officials. Knowing this, he fled first to France, then to England, and ultimately, in September of 1935, to the United States. Weill never looked back: He never spoke German again, and when the war was over, he neither returned to nor expressed interest in the land of his birth. He was quick to assimilate elements of American popular culture, since he felt that "art music had ceased to speak to a broader community in any vital way, that ossified 'aristocratic' cultural institutions should be abandoned as hopelessly irrelevant . . . , [and] that the concert hall had become obsolete."[14]

In America, Weill quickly became known to important theater people: Maxwell Anderson, Ogden Nash, Ira Gershwin, Elmer Rice, Langston Hughes, and Alan J. Lerner were among his collaborators. In 1940, he showed how well he had assimilated the Broadway style in his score of *Lady in the Dark*. Moss Hart and Ira Gershwin created the text, and Weill's music was so successful that Paramount Pictures bought the rights in 1944, for the fantastic price of $300,000. In the score, Weill pays subtle tribute to two composers when the leading female character, Miss Elliot, learns that she is to be the dedicatee of "Stravinsky's latest sonata and a new Shostakovich cantata."

In 1943, Weill set lyrics by Ogden Nash in a light romantic comedy entitled *One Touch of Venus*. The production was a smash hit that ran for 567 performances. Mary Martin, who had never yet appeared in a starring role, won critical acclaim that led to a career that is now theatrical history. Some contend that in these works, Weill simply picked up various Americanisms and made a quick buck. Others— including Elliott Carter—have given more thoughtful assessments. In his review of *One Touch of Venus*, Carter noted that

> Weill, who orchestrates and arranges his own work . . . has made himself at home in America. . . . In the atmosphere of Broadway, where so much music is unconvincing and dead, Weill's workmanlike care and his refined sense of style make up for whatever spontaneity and freshness his music lacks.[15]

Weill's American scores contain quasi-patriotic tunes, barber-shop harmonies, and imitations of popular composers of the day. His American works show both attention to detail and a thorough knowledge of American vernacular music.

Black culture was a novelty for Weill. He knew George Gershwin's work well and admired *Porgy and Bess* in particular, but he wanted a closer look at Afro-American music and its sociological context. The result was *Street Scene* (1946), an opera based on a 1929 Pulitzer Prize-winning play by that title written by Elmer Rice. Langston Hughes, who wrote the lyrics of *Street Scene*, recalls that Weill went with him to Harlem to see Black culture, hear Black music, and experience Blues in its natural environment.[16] Weill and Hughes must have found a common ground in their alienation from white, Christian bigots. Hughes cuts to the heart of the issue where he says

> The word *nigger* . . . sums up for us who are colored all the bitter years of insult and struggle in America: the slave-beatings of yesterday, the lynchings of today, the Jim Crow cars, the only movie show in town with its sign up FOR WHITES ONLY, the restaurants where you may not eat, the jobs you may not have, the unions you cannot join. . . . *Nigger! Nigger!* Like the word *Jew* in Hitler's Germany.[17]

With *Street Scene*, Weill returned to the socially responsible scores of *Die sieben Todsünden* and *Mahagonny*. The American public, however, seems not to have been ready for a lyric theater piece about the difficulties of life in a tenement. The previews in Philadelphia were a flop, and the New York production, which ran for only 148 performances, would not have taken place if not for Dwight D. Wiman, who put up the cash to cover the expenses.

Weill's next two scores, *Love Life* (1948) and *Lost in the Stars* (1949), exhibit similarly serious intent. The former, based on a text by Alan J. Lerner, traces the decline of the institution of marriage. The latter uses a libretto by Maxwell Anderson based on Alan Paton's *Cry the Beloved Country*.

In many ways, *Lost in the Stars* is a sequel to *Street Scene*: Both works focus on the sufferings of the disenfranchised. Both invite interpretation *vis-à-vis* Weill's personal history. In all three of these late works, Weill was striving for a rapprochement between Broadway and opera. None fared particularly well in the eyes of the critics or public, but American theatrical tastes have changed since 1950, and perhaps revivals may find a more enthusiastic reception.

In his American theater pieces, Weill did more than set lyrics in English. He devised a style that is genuinely different from the idiom he had used in Germany. In working with American writers, he examined American issues, taking into account the state of American lyric theater at the time, and he made use of distinctively American musical elements. In this eclectic approach, he anticipated the efforts of one of America's most talented and fascinating musical personalities, Leonard Bernstein.

Paul Hindemith, 1895–1963

Hindemith was in no immediate danger in 1933, when the Nazis came to power. He was a Christian man of repute. He thought that the Nazi regime was a momentary craze among political malcontents—a glitch that would pass out of power as quickly as it had come into it. His optimism was dispelled by an article entitled

"Ästhetik oder Volkskampf" (æsthetic or assault on the people) by Arnold Rosenberg, in the Sunday edition of the *Deutsche Allgemeine Zeitung* for 25 November 1934. There Rosenberg railed against Hindemith, saying

> If a man like Hindemith . . . has, for fourteen years, lived, and worked, and made himself comfortable in Jewish society . . . and, with their praise, cooperated with them; if he . . . perpetrates the sickest degradations of German music, that is his personal affair; however, each individual retains his right to reject him along with his entire circle of cohorts.[18]

By this point in his career, Hindemith had been conductor of the Frankfurt Opera Orchestra from 1915 until 1923. He had also played viola in Adolf Rebner's string quartet beginning in 1919, and from 1921 until 1929, in Licco Amar's quartet.[19] Hindemith's formidable experience as a performer was paralleled by his already considerable compositional output. In 1918, he published his first string quartet; the next year, he composed his first opera, *Mörder, Hoffnung der Frauen* (murder, hope of women; 1919). The librettist was Oskar Kokoschka, an Expressionist painter later banned by the Reich as a degenerate. The scenario is a shocker that explores the travails of marriage, gender conflicts, and the relationship between violence and sex.

More astonishing still is the scenario of the one-act *Sancta Susanna* (1921), based on a libretto of August Stramm. In it, Hindemith continued to explore Freudian notions of sexual repression, in the person of a nun who tears the loincloth from the corpus of a crucifix in order to have a sexual relationship with Christ.

In both of these operas, Hindemith pursued Expressionistic ideas aggressively, and his name became associated with the avant-garde. Fritz Busch, fearing a scandal, refused to conduct the premier of *Sancta Susanna*. When the premiere took place in Frankfurt on 26 March 1922, Busch's fears were confirmed: The League of Catholic Women drew up a formal protest. The work remains controversial, and when a production of it was given in Rome in 1977, legal charges were brought against the mayor and the general director of the theater.

Not all of Hindemith's music is radically modern. In fact, the scores from the late 1920s and early '30s reveal his concern with the gap between composer and audience. Hindemith addressed this situation by composing *Gebrauchsmusik* (utility music)—pieces directed to the intelligent music lover who may not be a professional musician, but who nevertheless is interested in sensible listening and performance. Hindemith's *Gebrauchsmusik* includes pieces for children, movies, radio, and sonatas for nearly every instrument.

On a higher plane than these scores is his song cycle *Das Marienleben* (The life of Mary; 1923, rev. 1948). The texts of "Das Marienleben" were put into their final form by Rainer Maria von Rilke in 1912, and published with illustrations by Heinrich Vogeler in the following year. The thirteen poems are arranged in a carefully planned dramatic sequence. The first four are lyrical and deal with Mary's youth: (1) "Mary's Birth," (2) "The Presentation of Mary in the Temple," (3) "The Annunciation to Mary," and (4) "Mary's Longing for Home." The fifth through ninth songs deal with Mary as the mother of Jesus: (5) "Joseph's Anxiety," (6) "The Announcement to the Shepherds," (7) "The Birth of Christ," (8) "Rest during the Flight into Egypt," and (9) "Concerning the Wedding at Cana." The final four are contemplations of Mary as the suffering mother of Christ crucified: (10) "Concerning the Passion," (11) "Pietà," (12) "The Quietude of Mary upon the Resurrection," and (13) "Concerning the Death of Mary." In setting the poems, Hindemith associated Christ with the key of E, Mary with the dominant (i.e., B), and heavenly grace with A, the subdominant. Throughout the cycle, the writing for both the voice and the piano is highly idiomatic; nevertheless, the tessitura of the vocal part is high, and requires great endurance.

The eight instrumental ensemble pieces that Hindemith wrote in the 1920s were given the straightforward title *Kammermusik* (chamber music). They were actually written in three batches: the two of Op. 24 (the first for twelve solo instruments and the second for wind quintet) date from 1921; the four pieces of Op. 36 (piano, 'cello, violin, and viola concertos respectively) and the two of Op. 46 (for viola *d'amore* and organ) were composed between 1924 and 1927. The number of movements is variable. Some have three, others four, and others five movements. Though the sleekness of Baroque style influenced Hindemith's textures and harmonies, he did not hesitate to make use of contemporary elements, including a siren and a tin can filled with sand in the percussion section of the first, and, in that same piece, a foxtrot in the Finale. These modern elements were appropriate, since the piece was written for the first Donaueschingen Festival, an annual event promoting contemporary music, with which Hindemith was associated from its inception in 1921 until 1930.

Of the eight scores of *Kammermusik*, the Violin Concerto, Op. 36 no. 3 (1925) is the most ambitious and serious piece. It was written for Licco Amar.[20] Its five movements are richly scored for a variety of colorful instruments, including two piccolos, E-flat and bass clarinets, brass with cornet and bass tuba, strings without violins, and percussion including small drums. Its musical gestures call to mind contemporaneous works of importance: The "signal," as Hindemith calls the opening, suggests Mahler's Fifth Symphony (an association confirmed by the ensuing march rhythms); the prominent passages for violin and small drum are echoes of Stravinsky's *Histoire du soldat*. The slow central movement is some of Hindemith's most lyrical writing. The fifth and final movement—"So schnell wie möglich" (as fast as possible)—gives some indication of Amar's prodigious technique.

In 1927, Hindemith was invited to become professor of composition at Berlin's Staatliche Hochschule für Musik; however, Rosenberg and his collaborators created an impossible situation for Hindemith. The regime established several powerful regulatory agencies whose purpose was articulated by Hans Friedrich Blunck, president of the Reichsliteraturkammer, who declared that "it is the duty of the state to cultivate harmony between the political and private life of the people . . . and to discover those who are capable of speaking for the people."[21]

Firmly in control by 1935, the Nazis took decisive steps against Hindemith. Broadcasts of his music were prohibited. Walter Gieseking was forced to drop Hindemith's music from his piano recitals. The violinist Georg Kulenkampff was reprimanded for performing the Sonata in E in Berlin. The string trio in which Hindemith played with Kulenkampff on violin and Enrico Mainardi on 'cello was banned. Frustrated at every turn, Hindemith had no choice but to resign from the Hochschule. He left Germany on 25 March 1937.

During this tumultuous period, Hindemith periodically visited Turkey, where he had been invited, in 1935, to reorganize the Conservatory of Music and Drama in Ankara.[22] There was also a visit to the United States in the spring of 1937. When Hindemith returned to Europe in 1938, it was to the neutral state of Switzerland.

Willy Strecker, Hindemith's friend and publisher, chatted with him as early as 1932, about the possibility of an opera about Matthias Grünewald (ca. 1475–1528), the painter best known for his Isenheim Altarpiece.[23] The proposal took a while to gestate in Hindemith's mind, but by 11 June 1933, he was writing to Strecker and his brother, Ludwig, that he was "busily occupied with Grünewald and am gradually beginning to have hopes of producing something."[24] While working on the opera, which considers Grünewald's career within the context of the Peasants' Revolt of 1524–1525, Hindemith was evaluating his own position as an artist. His feelings were ambivalent: He was an artist and a German who respected his German musical heritage, but he was a man of principles, who wanted to write in a contemporary style; he could not betray his artistic standards.

In the hopes of strengthening Hindemith's tenuous status in the eyes of the Nazi party, the conductor Wilhelm Furtwängler wrote an article entitled "Der Fall Hindemith" (the case of Hindemith), where he argued against Nazi censorship of Hindemith's work. Furtwängler's article did nothing more than to "unite the entire Nazi regime and its supporters against Hindemith and himself. Goebbels joined in the attack in person. Furtwängler was obliged to resign from his positions as musical director of the Berlin State Opera and Philharmonic Orchestra, and any idea of staging Mathis der Maler in Berlin had to be shelved."[25] Although Mathis der Maler was not heard in its operatic form in Germany until after World War II, there was, nonetheless, a performance of a symphonic suite of three movements extracted from the opera: "Engelkonzert" (angelic concert), "Grablegung" (entombment), and "Versuchung des heiligen Antonius" (temptation of St. Anthony). The premiere of the Mathis der Maler Symphony under the direction of Furtwängler in Berlin on 12 March 1934, was a great success. It is in this form that the opera's music is most often heard.

The first movement, "Engelkonzert," is in sonata form. It opens with a sixteenth-century tune, "Es sungen drei Engel einen süsses Gesang" (three angels sang a sweet song).[26] Next, the flutes and violins state the principal theme. Hindemith dispenses with the transition section and launches straightaway into the subsidiary theme in the violins and low strings. A solo flute provides the brilliant closing theme. A brief development section leads to a condensed recapitulation, where "Es sungen drei Engel" is combined in brilliant counterpoint with the principal, subsidiary, and closing themes.

The plaintive second movement features solo oboe against an orchestral background predominantly of strings. The concluding movement provides the rhythmic energy typically associated with third-movement scherzos, along with the triumphant and valedictory ambience of a symphonic Finale. In it, Hindemith uses the tune of the sequence for the feast of Corpus Christi, "Lauda Sion Salvatorem" (Praise thy Savior, o Zion).

In 1937, when Hindemith was in Florence for the Maggio Fiorentino (May Festival), he was amazed by Giotto's depiction of the life of St. Francis of Assisi, in the Church of Santa Croce. He got the idea of a ballet on the life of this Saint for the Ballets Russes, then directed by Léonide Massine. Like *Mathis der Maler*, the ballet contemplates the conflict between what is expeditious and what is required by personal integrity. The work that resulted is known under two authentic, but different, titles: *Nobilissima visione* (most noble vision) and *St. Francis*. The ballet had its American premiere under the later title. In this score, Hindemith quotes "Ce fut en Mai" (it was in May) by the thirteenth-century trouvère Moniot d'Arras.

Hindemith emigrated to the United States in 1940, taught that summer at Tanglewood, and then at Yale until 1953. His American works include the *Ludus tonalis* (the game of tonality; 1942), a set of twenty-five piano pieces embodying theories advanced in his treatise *Unterweisung in Tonsatz* (published in English as the *Craft of Musical Composition*; 1939). Here, Hindemith explains keys in relation-

EXAMPLE 8

Paul Hindemith, *Mathis der Maler Symphony*, "Versuchung des Heiligen Antonius"

ship to a single tone; the distinction of major and minor modes has no bearing on the tonal focus on a single note. As a consequence, his collection contains twelve fugues. The remaining thirteen pieces in *Ludus tonalis* consist of a prelude, a postlude, and eleven interludes. He uses the prelude in retrograde inversion as the postlude. Hindemith's other works for piano include the three sonatas of 1936 (in A, G, and B-flat).

The most ambitious of Hindemith's late works is his opera *Die Harmonie der Welt*, based on the life of Johannes Kepler. He began it in the late 1930s, but did not finish until 1957. Hindemith presents Kepler as a man of flesh and blood, capable of good and evil, motivated by hopes and aspirations as well as fears and self-doubts, who is caught in a web of circumstances. As with *Mathis* and *St. Francis*, he arranged *Die Harmonie der Welt* as an orchestral score, the symphony of 1951 known by the same title.

The derivation of the symphonic poem from the opera is an interesting story: Paul Sacher, director of the Basle Chamber Orchestra, had gone to New Haven to see Hindemith, inquire about the progress of his opera, and request a new work. He commissioned what became the *Sinfonia serena* (serene symphony; 1951). When Hindemith conducted its premiere, he was so excited by Sacher's orchestra that he made the symphony from his Kepler opera in just a few weeks. Sacher led the first performance on 25 January 1952.

The three movements of *Die Harmonie der Welt* are essays on the traditional divisions of music according to Mediæval and Renaissance theorists: *musica instrumentalis, musica humana,* and *musica mundana*. All are scored with utter brilliance. The ensemble is rich and varied, and the musical materials that Hindemith devised are consistently interesting, idiomatic, and colorful.

The first movement is an introduction and sonata, in which violas and clarinets have the first theme, oboes, horns, and trombones the second, and violins the third. After a fascinating development section, the three themes of the exposition return, amid counterpoints drawn from the introduction.

The second movement, a discourse on the duality of the human being, combines two melodies, the first featuring clarinet and strings, the second focusing on the plaintive tone of the oboe. Perhaps Hindemith's intention here was to explore the polarities of body and soul, mind and emotion, finite and infinite. At times, especially in the concluding violin solo, the Romantic nobility of Strauss's tone poems is recalled.

The form of the final movement was probably inspired by J. S. Bach's Passacaglia and Fugue in C minor. In Hindemith's score, however, the order is reversed: The fugue is the source from which the nine-measure passacaglia theme is derived. Introduced meekly by solo flute, the twenty-three repetitions of the ostinato culminate in a blaze of glory that testifies to Hindemith's optimism. In a letter of 6 December 1939, he expressed his vision of hope eloquently to his friends Emma and Fried Lübbecke:

EXAMPLE 9
Paul Hindemith, *Harmonie der Welt*, "Musica Mundana," mm. 48–57.

> If one can busy oneself lovingly with the things of the past and in addition create things that will one day . . . [be] worthy of admiration and continued attention, then the present disturbances . . . can assume gigantic proportions [and] smash mountains to pieces, but they cannot damage the tiny seeds.[27]

Although he became an American citizen in 1946, he returned to Europe to teach at the University of Zürich. He died in Frankfurt on 28 December 1963.

Karel Husa, b. 1921[28]

The Munich Agreement of 30 September 1938 set the stage for the Nazi takeover of Czechoslovakia in March of 1939, the year in which Husa completed his basic academic training and prepared to enter technical school to study engineering. He had just begun his work when the Nazis closed the technical school—that was on 18 November 1939.

Putting his hopes for a career as an engineer behind him, the resilient Husa thought about entering the Prague Academy of Art. He had already done quite a bit of painting, mostly commercial art for his father's shoe business. Here too, a glitch: Husa was asked to sign a statement swearing that he had never attended the technical school. Because he was unwilling to falsify his application, Husa sacrificed a second career; thus, he came to advanced studies in music.

He had played the violin since the age of eight, and had a natural fascination with putting things together. Husa was an ideal candidate for the profession of composer. Ultimately, he entered the composition class of Jaroslav Řídký at the Conservatory in Prague, where he worked from 1941 until 1945.

Husa's Sonatina, Op. 1, for piano got a hearing on 22 January 1945 and again in April of that year at the Czech ISCM conference. Despite the opus number, it was actually Husa's second work. The real Op. 1 was a youthful String Quartet (1942), but the publisher requested to issue the Sonatina as "Opus 1."

Karel Husa

Husa's Overture for Orchestra, Op. 3, was the occasion of his debut as a conductor: Karel Ančerl was slated to lead the Czech Radio Symphony Orchestra in the premiere, but Husa asked if he might direct the ensemble. Ančerl agreed, and, in the course of the next two years, Husa conducted the radio orchestras many times; thus began his career as a conductor and advocate of contemporary music.[29]

Chamber works, such as the Suite, Op. 5, for viola and piano and the Sonatina, Op. 6, for violin and piano flowed quickly from his pen. Advanced studies under Řídký continued at the Academy of Music from 1945 until 1947. He won a French Government Fellowship to study at the École Normale de Musique in Paris from 1946 until 1948. There he studied composition with Honegger and conducting with Jean Fournet. Additional studies in conducting with Eugene Bigot took place during 1948–49 at the Paris Conservatoire. From 1946 until 1949, Husa also studied composition and conducting privately, the former with Boulanger, the latter with André Cluytens.[30]

Honegger insisted on a solid background as the best path to freedom; he also required his students to write continually and prolifically—regardless of whether they liked the finished products or not. (This exercise was intended to produce fluency rather than masterpieces.) Honegger served more as an advisor than a dictator. In general, he did not interfere with the student's work, but simply offered his reactions. Boulanger was more philosophical in dealing with compositional matters. It was her intention to enable students "to use simple means to communicate complex ideas."

The training Husa completed under Honegger and Boulanger soon bore fruits, including the three *Frescos* (1947) for orchestra and the First String Quartet (1948). During a short visit to Prague in the summer of 1947, Husa enjoyed a twofold triumph: the completion of his diploma at the Academy of Musical Arts, and the premiere of his Sinfonietta (1945) by the Czech Radio Symphony Orchestra. The Sinfonietta scored a success, and in 1948, the Czech Academy of Arts and Sciences selected it as the winner of its annual prize.

1948 was an ironic year for Husa: It was a year of accolades and the year in which the marriage of his sister brought him back to Czechoslovakia, but it was also the year when he was exiled from his native land. He and his music were banned from that moment until the dissolution of the Soviet Union in 1989. When Husa's *Frescos* were performed in Prague in 1949, the press condemned him, declaring that "Husa got worse in Paris but now must return to our new political system," and that "he has committed artistic suicide by embracing Western formalistic ideas." Sadly, ideological conflicts with the regime prevented the composer from attending the funeral of his mother, Božena Dongresová-Husová, in Prague in 1955.

Despite censure in his homeland, Husa and his music were rapidly gaining followers in the West. His Divertimento (1948) for string orchestra was given by the Paris Radio Orchestra as part of the 1949 ISCM program of the Paris chapter. His First String Quartet was featured at the ISCM conference in June of 1950 in Brussels. The Quartet was given again in that same year at the Darmstadt Festival, where Husa met the publisher Schott, and at the Donaueschingen Festival of 1951. The success of the Quartet at Donaueschingen led to a second invitation in 1953. At that festival, Hans Rosbaud conducted the Südwestfunk Orchestra in Husa's *Portrait* (1953) for string orchestra, written in honor of Honegger.

Husa's reputation as a composer was quickly consolidating. Two works of 1953 critical in this process were the First Symphony and the Second String Quartet.[31]

In concert, the First Symphony gives the impression of a single continuous movement. A persistent pounding of the percussion, like the opening of the Brahms C-minor Symphony, accompanies a rhapsodic monologue in the low strings. This expansive recitative is then paraphrased in the bass clarinet, and then becomes the topic of discussion for all of the instruments of the orchestra. Elegant filagree—perhaps inspired by Messiaen's bird calls or Bartók's night musics—is apparent, especially in the passages for winds. As the score progresses, expansions on the opening recitative alternate with virtuosic escapades for the percussion and brass. Viewed as a whole, this work of about a half-hour's duration gives the impression as much of a concerto for orchestra as a symphony. Clear in either case are Husa's imaginative exploration of instrumental color and his sure sense of pacing: The subdued, mysterious passages are never prolonged into the realm of tedium, and cataclysmic torrents of percussion are cut short soon enough to ensure that each renewal of the tirade will be startling. Progressive features notwithstanding, the score is tonal throughout, and it is unified by the cyclic recollection of variously transformed themes.

In his second String Quartet, written for the Parrenin Quartet, Husa strove to write in a style uninhibited by formal considerations that—at least in his own opinion—dominated his thinking in the String Quartet of 1948. The outer movements of the three (in the order fast, slow, fast) are prefaced by slow introductions.

In Western Europe, Husa had a busy conducting schedule. He led the Grand Orchestre Symphonique of the Belgian Radio-Television Corporation in the 1951–52 season; the Chamber Orchestra of Lausane, the Orchestre des Cento Soli, and the Orchestre des Solistes de Paris in the 1952–53 season. His achievements by this time were attracting international attention, including that of Donald J. Grout, Music Department Chair at Cornell University.

On 24 September 1954, Husa left France for New York City. He arrived there on the 28th. His wife and children—two at the time—followed several weeks later. At Cornell University, Husa began teaching theory and composition. The next year, he served as interim director of Cornell's orchestras during the sabbatical leave of the principal conductor. A year later, the departure of the conductor created a vacancy that Husa filled, beginning in 1957. In this capacity, he worked with many of the world's leading composers and performers. As his reputation in the United States grew, Husa came to the attention of the country's foremost orchestras. In short order, his ongoing work in Europe was augmented by invitations to conduct the Rochester Philharmonic, Buffalo Philharmonic, Baltimore Symphony, Cincinnati Symphony Orchestra, Boston Philharmonia, and the New York Philharmonic. Conservatories and universities extended similar invitations, and by 1962, he had performed with ensembles at Harvard, Eastman, Peabody, and the New England Conservatory.

Husa's compositional style progressed at an equal pace with his conducting. In 1959, he wrote his *Poem* for viola and chamber orchestra, his first exploration of Serialism. "In this work, pitches, dynamics, row organization, and different string sonorities are submitted to serialization. From this it can be seen that it is not the traditional Schoenbergian technique that interests Husa, but the various serial procedures that have come into being since World War II and the methodology that they imply."[32] In 1967, Husa accepted an invitation to teach composition at Ithaca College. He taught there until his retirement in 1986.

International news focused on Husa in 1969, when he won the Pulitzer Prize for his Third String Quartet, commissioned by the Fine Arts Quartet in 1967. Given an ensemble of virtuosi, Husa made demands that he had not previously considered. He used microtones (shown in the notation with an upward or downward arrow preceding the affected note) only to find later that most performers—including high-school wind players—were perfectly comfortable in executing such passages. That the Quartet earned the Pulitzer Prize was a gratifying musical accomplishment for Husa, but it was equally rewarding from a personal perspective, coming as it did exactly ten years after he and his family became citizens of the United States.

Success in his new homeland notwithstanding, Husa still felt disappointed by his total rejection in the land of his birth. In 1968, he was gravely concerned by the Russian invasion of Prague to end the liberal regime of Alexander Dubček. Coincidentally, Husa had been commissioned in that year by Ithaca College to write a work for concert band. He seized the opportunity to compose one of his most powerful and original scores, the *Music for Prague 1968*, which had its first hearing under the direction of Kenneth Snapp at Ithaca College on 14 December 1968 and its official premiere, also under Snapp's baton, in Washington, D.C., on 31 January 1969 during the Music Educators' National Conference.[33]

Music for Prague 1968 is Husa's most frequently performed score. Perhaps the disheartening political circumstances in Czechoslovakia elicited a strikingly dramatic reaction from the composer; or, perhaps at that moment, his compositional technique had reached an unprecedented level; perhaps technique and circumstances peaked simultaneously to produce this singularly picturesque piece. These distinctions seem pointless in face of the overwhelming power of this symphony for concert band. Its four movements are Introduction and Fanfare, Aria, Interlude, and Toccata and Chorale. In the Introduction, a solo piccolo meanders carelessly until the menacing sounds of trumpets and percussion signal danger. Here, and elsewhere in the piece, the sound of ringing bells is conspicuous: This is because Prague is known as the City of a Hundred Towers; hence, the bells symbolize Prague, as well as alarms of warning and of victory. Equally important is Husa's quotation of the fifteenth-century Hussite song of combat "Kdoz jste bozí bojovníci" (ye warriors of God and his law), which, as he points out in his Foreword to the score, "has been a symbol of resistance and hope . . . whenever fate lay heavy upon the Czech nation." He notes further that the tune was used by Smetana in *Má vlast*.[34]

The serial structures of *Music for Prague 1968* move beyond pitch selection, and, in the Interlude for percussion instruments only, they extend to serial rotation of twelve different sonorities allocated in groups of four, to three percussionists. To complement vibraphone and snare drums, four basic sounds—antique cymbal, triangle, suspended cymbal, and tam-tam—are used in three different sizes: small for the first percussion group, medium for second, and large for the third; hence, unpitched sonorities are serialized. In the Finale, the powerful homophonic motif of the opening movement returns, as does the Hussite song. Here, however, the now-familiar theme is stated in confident defiance by full orchestra in unison, to bring the work to its dramatic close.

In 1970, Husa conducted his orchestral version of *Music for Prague 1968* in Munich with the Munich Philharmonic. It was quickly taken up by leading conductors like Erich Leinsdorf, Sergiu Comissiona, and Daniel Barenboim. The score uses various modern techniques, including irregular tremolo (indicated by the basic duration with conventional beams through the stem, but including a reversed bend sinister), quarter tones, pitch fields (shown by beamed stems without noteheads), and indeterminacy. For Husa, the most gratifying performance of the piece was his own rendering of it in the orchestral version with the Czech Philharmonic in Dvořák Hall in Prague in September of 1993, to mark the twenty-fifth anniversary of the Russian invasion of Prague.

Of his works, Husa is especially fond of his Concerto for Orchestra and the *Apotheosis of this Earth* (1970).[35] Husa originally scored *Apotheosis* for band and subsequently made an orchestral version.[36] As with *Music for Prague 1968*, Husa used the music of *Apotheosis* as a commentary on pressing issues of the time. He explains in the prefatory Note:

> The composition of *Apotheosis of this Earth* was motivated by the present desperate stage of mankind and its immense problems with everyday killings, war, hunger, extermination of fauna, huge forest fires, and critical contamination of the whole environment.
>
> Man's brutal possession and misuse of nature's beauty . . . can only lead to catastrophe. The composer hopes that the destruction of this beautiful Earth can be stopped, so that the tragedy of destruction—musically projected here in the second movement—and the desolation of its aftermath (the "postscript" of the third movement) can exist only as fantasy, never to become reality.[37]

In the course of its three movements, *Apotheosis* shows the Earth first as a speck in the cosmos that becomes the focus of the listener's imagination. This image is cleverly transformed into a musical structure by a concerto-like disposition of instruments: From the opening until at least measure 70, the instruments are to play *soli* (i.e., one per part); at measure 71 and following, woodwinds, then saxophones and contrabass clarinet, then trombones, then horns, then trumpets, then all remaining instruments gradually join to blossom into a rich, *tutti* ensemble.

In *Apotheosis*, the concept of pitch fields is further developed, and Husa uses what looks like shaped-note notation, with stemmed pyramids pointing up or down to indicate the lowest or highest notes that performers on particular instruments are capable of playing. (He notes that these "must be strong and powerful.")

The second movement, "Tragedy of Destruction," is a fantasy of the Earth's destruction. The music suggests the planet dying "as a savagely, mortally wounded creature."

The last movement, "Postscript," presents the image of Earth "pulverized into the universe, the voices scattered into space. Toward the end, these voices—at first computer-like and mechanical—unite into the words *this beautiful Earth*, simply said, warm and filled with regret . . . and one of so many questions comes to our minds: '*Why have we let it happen?*'"

The "Postscript" uses instrumentalists as chorus; hence, they need not be practitioners of *bel canto*. On the contrary, Husa wants a sound of simplicity. He has suggested that the closing lament for this "Beautiful Earth," assigned to a woman's voice, should ideally be spoken by a child.

Husa's fascination with picturesque manipulations of sound is manifested with equal intensity in his most recent works, many of which are concertos.[38] Among these, his concertos for Wind Ensemble (1982), Orchestra (1986), Organ and Orchestra (1987), Trumpet and Orchestra (1987), Violoncello and Orchestra (1988), and Violin and Orchestra (1993) are noteworthy. In most cases, Husa was writing these pieces for virtuosi. Zubin Mehta and the New York Philharmonic commissioned and premiered the Concerto for Orchestra; the Organ Concerto was written for Karel Paukert; the Concerto for Trumpet and Orchestra was intended for and premiered by Adolph Herseth, Sir Georg Solti, and the Chicago Symphony; the Cello Concerto was written with the technique of Lynn Harrell in mind, and he gave the first performance with the University of Southern California Orchestra in March of 1989, Daniel Lewis conducting. Glenn Dicterow, Kurt Masur, and the New York Philharmonic premiered the Concerto for Violin and Orchestra.

Husa's story is one of success. His musical technique and imagination are limitless; however, his experiences have taught him the frailty of his own life, of all life, and of life as we know it on this island home we call Earth. His works reflect both the musician and the person: a happy person who perhaps, of all the exiled musicians surveyed here, found the happiest life of all. In speaking about *An American Te Deum*, a large work for chorus and orchestra using texts that he assembled himself, Husa commented that it "is the way I look at the U.S. from an immigrant's point of view. Everybody wanted to work in this country."[39]

György Ligeti, b. 1923

When the Ligeti family resided in Germany, their surname was Auer. The renowned violinist Leopold Auer was Ligeti's great-uncle, but Ligeti never met him, because he had emigrated to the United States before Ligeti was born. When Auer died in 1930, Ligeti was a boy of seven, who had never left his native land.

Ligeti's family settled in Transylvania at the end of the nineteenth century and became residents of Hungary. (Since then, the town of his birth has become part of Romania.) Following the trends among Hungarian nationalists at the time, they changed their German family name to an approximation of it in Hungarian: Ligeti.[40]

As a boy, György attended school in the village of Cluj, which also had a conservatory of music. Ligeti studied there from 1941 to 1943, with Ferenc Farkas (b. 1905), who was professor of composition at Cluj Conservatory from 1941 until 1944. From 1946 to 1948, Farkas held an administrative post, but he left it to resume teaching composition at the Budapest Academy of Music from 1949 until 1975.[41]

The years of World War II were difficult for Ligeti. He was conscripted in 1944 and, since he was a Jew, he was assigned to perilous labor, transporting explosives. When the war ended, he returned to his music studies; however, he had lost both his father and his brother to the death camp at Auschwitz.

In 1945, Ligeti resumed his music studies, now at the Budapest Academy of Music with Sándor Veress (b. 1907). Veress left the Academy in 1948 and was succeeded by Ligeti's former teacher, Farkas. Ligeti completed his program in 1949 and joined the faculty as a teacher of harmony and counterpoint in the following year.

Government censors closely monitored the musical output of innovative young composers like Ligeti. Works in the quasi-Bartók style were permitted, but adventures like Ligeti's *Musica ricercata* for solo piano were prohibited. During the 1950s, Ligeti experimented with Serialism and other modern techniques.

These experiments coincided with the Hungarian revolution of October 1956. Imre Nagy appealed to the United Nations for aid against Soviet domination. With popular support, he become premier of Hungary and organized a neutral government. The Soviet response was decisive: Nagy was abducted and executed. Fearing for their own lives, approximately 190,000 refugees fled the country in the following months. Ligeti explains that his escape was possible in December of 1956, because the frontiers remained open. Soviet forces had surrounded Budapest;

> But the railway people organized trains for people who wanted to go [to] . . . . the Austrian frontier; of course, they never arrived at the frontier. The train stopped at every station, and they telephoned ahead to the next station to find out if there were Russian soldiers there.
>
> I and my wife took the train one day. . . . There had been some mistake and the warning had failed: the train was surrounded by Russian military. But they didn't have enough people to cover the whole train. . . . We in our end very quickly got out and into the town. Somebody told us to go to the post office. . . . The next day, the postman took us . . . with ten or twelve people hidden under mailbags.
>
> Then we were dropped quite close to the frontier . . . within the prohibited zone, with Russians patrolling. . . . We knew we had reached the border when we fell into the mud where the mines had been: the mines had been cleared during the revolution, because Austria refused to have trade with Hungary while the border was mined.[42]

After he arrived in western Europe, Ligeti worked during 1957 and 1958, at the West German Radio in Cologne, where he became acquainted with Karlheinz Stockhausen and the music of the avant-garde, especially Boulez. Ligeti's study "Pierre Boulez: Entscheidung und Automatik in der Structure Ia" reveals as much about Ligeti's approach to musical detail as it does about Boulez's score.[43] He immediately became involved with the Darmstadt Festivals, participating as an attendant in 1957 and 1958, and then as a lecturer annually from 1959 until 1972. He taught there again in 1976, and his works were featured in 1980 and 1984.

Ligeti is a man with a sense of humor, who is fascinated by the extraordinary, the unexpected, and the unorthodox. That attitude informs his musical style. Traditional harmonies with functional associations may suddenly surface from a sonorous web, or repetitive motifs may appear, or a series of notes may even suggest a melody.

The sonorous webs of Ligeti's music are one of the most distinctive aspects of his style. The composer himself associates these webs with a childhood dream, in which he imagined himself trying to get to his bed, but being hindered by a "fine-threaded but dense and extremely complicated web. . . . Beside me there were other beings and objects hanging up in the vast network. . . . Each movement of the stranded creatures caused a trembling carried throughout the entire system."[44]

The sonorous webs can be related to other, purely musical paradigms too: Ligeti worked briefly with electronic music, but gave it up completely in 1959.[45] He was disappointed by electronic music, but its techniques nevertheless suggested ideas for acoustic instruments. He was especially interested in building massive sonic complexes from minuscule elements that could be closely monitored. The subtle alteration of these particles within the larger structure was a process rather than an event; hence, the music tends not to move in discernible beats, phrases, or periods, but rather, it transpires in phases. Ligeti had already used ametric notation in his orchestral score of *Víziók* (visions; 1956), and his various methods of indicating time with spatial notation are indicative of his conception of musical time and form.

The polyphony of early Renaissance masters provided Ligeti with another important musical paradigm. Ockeghem, in particular, used "stagnating structures [in which] the individual voices are constantly overlapping, just like waves washing one over another."[46] When contrapuntal lines are piled up in this fashion, the individual strands eventually become obscure; hence, one perceives a mass of sound rather than its individual particles. Ligeti originally called this technique "micropolyphony," but he later rejected the term in preference for "supersaturated polyphony."[47]

Ligeti is remarkably lucid in explaining his compositional style.[48] His instruction presumes familiarity with traditional as well as contemporary music. (By "contemporary," he means Webern, Messiaen, Boulez, Kagel, Cage, among others.) Concerning traditional music instruction, Ligeti notes that the Western European focus has been limited almost entirely to harmony and counterpoint. He urges more attention to rhythm, dynamics, timbre, register, and other parameters, as well as to their cumulative impact on form.

In creating new works, Ligeti insists on the importance of a plan. He suggests that tone rows might be useful in constructing the pitch design, but he urges experimentation with multiple plans dealing with each aspect, so that the dynamics, for instance, would be subject to a different plan from the original row, register to another plan, and so forth. He notes, however, that should the plans at some point prove more restrictive than helpful, they should be modified or altogether abandoned.[49]

For Ligeti, possibilities are the main excitement of composition. He is open minded and willing to listen to anything, look at anything, read anything, and then decide whether or not it suits him. One distinction that he makes emphatically, is that between elite and pop culture: He has nothing to do with Pop at all, and he is skeptical of attempts to synthesize the two. The strict division between music for the masses and high culture, he says, is not unique to European society, but is apparent in the cultures of China and Japan as well.[50]

Ligeti has experimented with a wide variety of techniques, and encourages his composition students to do the same. Taking a tone cluster, for example, and changing its instrumentation constantly in order to modify the effect of the sound mass, is one experiment that he recommends. Noting that instrumentation will necessarily be related to the spacing of the original sound mass, he suggests trying this experiment with strings, so that quarter tones can be used in the sonic *Gestalt*. This experiment can use complexes of just three or four notes, or it can use all twelve chromatic tones or more. In order to keep dynamics and pitch totally independent, he suggests that the number of instruments be at least equal to the number of sonorities in the complex.

In explaining his sonic webs, Ligeti proposes a simple compositional model using a chromatic scale restricted to a single octave. One instrument begins playing from C to C^1; another plays from D-flat to C^1, and so on. In this process, legato is used for the ascending lines, but staccato for the downward leaps. At any given moment, at least one instrument moves downward to remain within the octave; consequently, the distinctive articulation stands out from the surrounding fabric.

In these and other exercises, Ligeti shows how some of the decisions are made automatically, since they are governed by the initial plan. At various points, however, the creative will of the composer enters into the mix.

An important factor of composition rests in the act of writing the music down. Ligeti recommends experiments here too, especially spatial notation (in which the score reflects duration so that, for instance, a quarter of an inch represents three seconds) and graphic notation (in which images represent gestures rather than precise musical events).

Ligeti's music vibrantly reflects this adventurous spirit and innovative method. Even as a young man restricted by political doctrines, his "acceptable" music was complemented by the wild pieces that went into envelopes on the shelf. Among those pieces was his *Musica ricercata* (1953) for piano solo. Beginning with a rigid premise, he composed a series of eleven pieces, the first using only two pitch classes, the second three, and so on.[51]

In his fascinating harpsichord piece *Continuum* (1968), Ligeti repeats motifs with slight variations at high speed, to suggest sonorous clusters undergoing transformation. The sound of the piece is very modern; in fact, one might almost mistake the harpsichord for an electronic instrument. The piece owes much to Ligeti's experiences in Stockhausen's studio, especially his discovery that tones heard in rapid succession merge into a continuum.

1968 was an important year for the recognition of Ligeti's music: In that year, Stanley Kubrick's film *2001: A Space Odyssey* was released. "Ligeti went to see the film. . . . He was amazed that over thirty minutes of his music had been used without consent or even his knowledge."[52] The film was a hit, and countless Americans became enthusiastic about this music by a composer whose works had been considered too bizarre, even by Europe's most progressive publishers: *Apparitions* (1959) for orchestra was published by Universal shortly after its premiere in June 1960, at the Cologne ISCM Festival, but his organ solo *Volumina* (1962), was issued by Peters. Ligeti's relationship with Peters proved more enduring, but by 1967, he had moved on to Schott. Kubrick's combination of Ligeti's music and sci-fi proved a winning match, however, and the composer was soon invited to Stanford University as visiting professor of composition (1972), then to the Berkshire Music Center at Tanglewood (1973), and to similarly prestigious institutions since then. During these visits, Ligeti won a commission from the San Francisco Symphony for what became his *San Francisco Polyphony* (1974). There he met Terry Riley and Steve Reich. Ligeti's admiration for their innovative ideas is expressed in his *Monument, Selbstportrait, Bewegung* (monument, self-portrait, movement; 1976) for two pianos. The "Selbstportrait" specifies "mit Reich und Riley (und Chopin ist auch dabei)"—"with Reich and Riley (and Chopin is there too)."

The use in a dramatic context of music originally composed without dramatic intentions was, for Ligeti, nothing new; he had already done it himself with his *Aventures* (adventures; 1963) for three singers and seven instrumentalists. The piece consists of distinct episodes, varying in expressive character from humorous to hysterical, hypnotic to horrific. Ligeti devised his own zany scenario for *Aventures et Nouvelles aventures* (adventures and new adventures; 1966) and expanded the duration of the work from about a dozen minutes to roughly a half-hour.

A more deliberate encounter with the lyric theater took place in *Le grand macabre* (the great dance of death; 1977), an opera based on Michael Meschke's version of Michel de Ghelderode's play *La balade du grand macabre*. The opera is populated by grotesque figures: a pubescent couple who copulate in a tomb and sing orgasmic duets, using the Monteverdian trillo at the precise moment of bliss; a male and female couple, the male member of whom is a cross-dresser; and Nekrotzar (i.e., tsar of the dead), who announces early in the opera, that the end will fall at midnight. The frenzy occasioned by impending death reaches its zenith at the conclusion of the third scene. Ligeti uses distinctive musical gestures to comment on the situation: cha-cha rhythms and ominous fanfares resound against the backdrop of a parody of the Finale of Beethoven's *Eroica Symphony*. When midnight does come, the only one to die is Nekrotzar; the other characters continue their bizarre and erotic amusements more or less as normal. In the fourth scene, which is the concluding Epilogue, all of the characters—including Nekrotzar—sing a moralizing verse in the form of a passacaglia.

During the early 1980s, Ligeti composed relatively little, but in 1982, he completed two important chamber works: a duo for violin and 'cello entitled *Hommage à Hilding Rosenberg* and the Trio for violin, horn, and piano. The trio shares the same instrumentation as Brahms's Op. 40, a piece that Ligeti admires. The rhythmic complexities of the first movement show the influence of American Minimalism. It is ironic that Ligeti designed the first movement in sonata form, considering the fact that of Brahms's twenty-four chamber music scores, the first movement of his Horn Trio is the only one that is *not* a sonata—because he was writing for a natural horn incapable of the tonal peregrinations required in a development section. The second movement uses Bulgarian rhythms *à la* Bartók. Traditional forms resurface in the third movement, which is a scherzo and trio, and the Finale is a Lamento, again recalling Bartók. Recently, he has written his Concerto (1988) for piano and orchestra and his Concerto (1993) for violin and orchestra.

The Violin Concerto was written for Saschko Gawriloff, whom Ligeti knew for many years and who played the premiere of the Horn Trio. The Concerto had its premiere in November of 1990, but Ligeti was not satisfied with its original, three-movements plan, so he wrote two additional movements, a new first movement, and an elaborated solo part throughout the piece. Gawriloff asked to write the cadenza, and Ligeti agreed. Gawriloff's contribution, based on music from the rejected first movement, comes as the fantastic conclusion to the entire Concerto.

His two books of six and eight Études (1985, '93) for piano will soon be joined by a third, which is in progress. The most recent of these pieces shows the influence of the American-Mexican composer Conlon Nancarrow (b. 1912), a student from 1929 to 1932 at the Cincinnati Conservatory, who later studied privately with Nicholas Slonimsky, Roger Sessions, and Walter Piston. Nancarrow's works are almost exclusively for player piano. They include complex rhythms, superimposed accelerandos and ritardandos, and other effects that would be difficult, if not impossible, for a single pianist to perform. Nancarrow has written over forty such pieces, all punched by hand on piano rolls. In 1982 and again in 1987, Nancarrow joined Ligeti in Europe for programs featuring this player-piano music, whose simultaneous ebbs and flows have penetrated into Ligeti's own idiom. Ligeti is not concerned about mechanically assisted music making: He anticipates that performance techniques will eventually rise to the level imposed by these demanding pieces.

Notes

1. Hellmut Lehmann-Haupt, *Art under a Dictatorship* (New York: Oxford, 1954), p. 70. Hitler made the statement at a Nazi Party rally in Nuremberg in 1937.
2. The word "aryan" is Sanskrit for "noble." Originally, the people described with the word were nomadic tribes who spread throughout present-day Russia during the second millennium B.C.E. They later moved on to the northwestern region of India, and their conquests were extolled in various Vedic hymns. The racist propaganda of the Nazis was a ludicrous attempt to trace the ancestry of "true Germans" back to these Aryan warriors.
3. Hans Fantel, *Johann Strauss: Father and Son, and Their Era* (Newton Abbot, England: David and Charles, 1971), p. 219.

4. Diane Peacock Jezic, *The Musical Migration and Ernst Toch* (Ames, Iowa: University of Iowa, 1989), p. 9.
5. See Peter Gay, "We Miss Our Jews: The Musical Migration from Nazi Germany," in *Driven into Paradise*, ed. Reinhold Brinkman and Christoph Wolff (Berkeley and Los Angeles: University of California, 1999), p. 21.
6. Douglas Jarman, *Kurt Weill: An Illustrated Biography* (Bloomington: Indiana University, 1982), p. 14.
7. See Kim H. Kowalke, *Kurt Weill in Europe* (Ann Arbor, Michigan: UMI Research Press, 1979), p. [55].
8. Jarman, *Kurt Weill*, p. 32.
9. Their extensive correspondence appears in Lys Symonette and Kim H. Kowalke, eds. and trans., *Speak Low When You Speak of Love: The Letters of Kurt Weill and Lotte Lenya* (Berkeley and Los Angeles: University of California, 1996).
10. The eighteenth-century music has had revivals from time to time. Noteworthy are those by Britten and Milhaud.
11. Weill's consciousness of his Jewish heritage is also manifested in the oratorio *Shulamith* (1920), the liturgically functional *Kiddush* for cantor, chorus, and organ (1946), and various pieces that, according to Jarman, *Kurt Weill*, p. 140, he wrote to celebrate the establishment of Israel in 1948.
12. Weill, *Aufstieg und Fall der Stadt Mahagonny: Oper in drei Akten*; ed. David Drew (Vienna: Universal Edition, 1969), Nr. 9. rehearsal number 119. Vulgarity was an important element in Epic Theater. Drew notes that "while the vocal score [of *Mahagonny*] was in preparation, [Weill] and Brecht were persuaded to modify certain passages whose frankness (particularly in the sexual sphere) was thought likely to be unacceptable at that time."
13. "Jede Annäherung an Wildwest- und Cowboy-Romantik und jede Betonung eines typisch amerikanischen Milieus ist zu vermeiden." Kurt Weill, *Aufstieg und Fall*, p. [iii].
14. Kim H. Kowalke and Horst Edler, eds., *A Stranger Here Myself: Kurt Weill-Studien* (New York: Georg Olms Verlag, 1993), p. 8.
15. Elliott Carter, *The Writings of Elliott Carter* (Bloomington: Indiana University, 1977), p. 95.
16. Arnold Rampersad, *The Life of Langston Hughes, Vol. II: 1941–1967, I Dream a World* (New York: Oxford University Press, 1988), p. 114. Hughes's autobiography, *The Big Sea* (New York: Alfred A. Knopf, 1940; reprint New York: Hill and Wang, 1993), was written before he met Weill.
17. Hughes, *The Big Sea*, p. 269.
18. "Wenn nun ein Mann wie Hindemith . . . 14 Jahre lang in jüdischer Gesellschaft gelebt und gewirkt und sich wohlgefühlt hat . . . und, von ihnen gelobt, dahinwirkte; wenn er . . . übelste Verkitschungen deutscher Musik vornimmt, so ist das seine persönliche Angelegenheit, die jedem jedoch das Recht gibt, ihn mit seinem ganzen Wirkungskreis abzulehnen."
19. The other members were Walter Caspar, 2d violin, and Maurits Frank, 'cello.
20. See Hindemith's letter to Willy Strecker (editorial director of B. Schott und Söhne) dated 25 August 1925, in Geoffrey Skelton, ed., *Selected Letters of Paul Hindemith* (New Haven: Yale, 1995), p. 41.
21. Robert A. Brady, *The Spirit and Structure of German Fascism.* (New York: Viking, 1937), p. 72.
22. See Hindemith's letter of 13 February 1935 to Willy Strecker, in Skelton, ed., *Selected Letters of Paul Hindemith*, p. 87.
23. The altarpiece, a commission completed ca. 1515 for St. Anthony's Monastery in Isenheim, is now in the Musé d'Unterlinden, Colmar, France. It contains nine panels on two sets of folding wings. The panels depict the Crucifixion with the Entombment below,

St. Anthony and St. Sebastian flanking, the Annunciation and the Concert of Angels, the Nativity and the Resurrection, and Sts. Anthony and Paul, and the Temptation of St. Anthony.

24. See his letter of that date in Skelton, ed., *Selected Letters of Paul Hindemith*, p. 70.

25. Skelton, *Selected Letters of Paul Hindemith*, p. 86.

26. The text, contained in Clemens Brentano and Aachim von Arnim's collection, *Des Knaben Wunderhorn*, was used by Mahler in the fifth movement of his Third Symphony.

27. Skelton, *Selected Letters of Paul Hindemith*, p. 143.

28. On 7 August, not 17 as incorrectly stated by Donald M. McLaurin, "The Life and Works of Karel Husa with Emphasis on the Significance of His Contribution to the Wind Band" (Ph.D. dissertation, Florida State University, 1985), p. 7. The error is reproduced in the generally reliable study by Susan Hayes Hitchens, *Karel Husa: A Bio-Bibliography* (New York: Greenwood Press, 1991), p. [3].

29. There were four orchestras in the Prague Radio at that time: two symphonic, one chamber orchestra, and one wind ensemble consisting of pairs of flutes, oboes, clarinets, bassoons, horns, and trumpets, with tympani. Communication from Karel Husa to the author, 17 January 2001.

30. Husa's work in Paris was reckoned as part of his degree requirements for the Academy of Music in Prague.

31. Husa's recording of his First Symphony with the Prague Symphony Orchestra is available on the CRI label. (New York: Composers Recordings, Inc., 1991, CRI CD 592). The Second String Quartet has been recorded by the Fine Arts Quartet (Phoenix Records, 1990, PHCD 113).

32. Lawrence W. Hartzell, "Karel Husa: The Man and the Music" *Musical Quarterly* 62 (January 1976), 97, n. 12.

33. The definitive recording of the work is Husa's performance with Temple University Wind Symphony (Albany Records Troy 271 CD, 1997).

34. Karel Husa, *Music for Prague 1968* for Orchestra (New York: Associated Music Publishers, [1969]), p. [ii].

35. Communication from Karel Husa to the author, 17 January 2001.

36. The commission came from the Michigan School Band and Orchestra Association, and it is dedicated to William D. Revelli, then conductor of bands at the University of Michigan.

37. Karel Husa, Note [1970] to *Apotheosis of this Earth* (New York: Associated Music Publishers, 1971).

38. Although Husa was a young, unknown composer, Copland immediately grasped his sense of instrumental color. In his 16 December 1957 letter to Husa anent *Fantasies* for orchestra (1956), Copland notes they are "strikingly picturesque."

39. Hitchens, *Karel Husa: A Bio-Bibliography*, p. 13.

40. Ligeti notes that the Hungarian is not quite right: In German, *Aue* is a meadow, but the Hungarian *liget* actually means thicket. See Paul Griffiths, *György Ligeti* (London: Robson Books, 1983), p. 16.

41. Farkas composed operas, musicals, ballets, piano music, orchestral suites and tone poems, choral music, chamber works, and film scores. He won the Kossuth Prize (1950), the Erkel Prize (1960), was named Honored Artist of the Hungarian People's Republic (1970), and has received similar awards in Germany, Italy, and elsewhere. A study of his life and works remains to be accomplished.

42. Griffiths, *Ligeti*, p. 24.

43. Originally published in *Die Reihe* (1958), 38–63; an English translation appeared in *Die Reihe* (1960), 36–62.

44. Quoted in Griffiths, *Ligeti*, p. 33.

45. He explains: "I quickly came up against the limits of possibilities in the electronic studio, and I really don't like the sound of loudspeakers anyway. I have this traditional proclivity, a preference for acoustical instruments. That is not a prejudice; I will accept electronic instruments as soon as they achieve the nobility of a Stradivarius or a Steinway, but technically they haven't yet achieved that nobility." (Ich bin sehr schnell an die Grenzen dieser Möglichkeiten im elektronischen Studio gestoßen, und ich mag eigentlich den Lautsprecherklang nicht. Ich habe diese traditionelle Neigung, die akustische Instrumente zu bevorzugen. Das ist kein Vorurteil, ich werde elektronische Instrumente akzeptieren, sobald sie die Noblesse einer Stradivari oder eines Steinway haben, aber dies Noblesse ist technisch noch nicht erreicht.") See Lerke von Saalfeld, "Im Gespräch mit György Ligeti," *Neue Zeitschrift für Musik* (January 1993), 33.

46. György Ligeti, "Rhapsodische, unausgewogene Gedanken über Music, besonders über meine eigenen Kompositionen," *Neue Zeitschrift für Musik* (January 1993), 24. ". . . bei ihm gibt es stagnierende Strukturen, da sich die Einzelstimmen stets überlappen, ähnlich den sich überschlagenden Wellen."

47. Ligeti, "Rhapsodische, unausgewogene Gedanken," 24. "Diese Technik . . . habe ich damals 'Mikropolyphonie' genannt, 'übersättigte Polyphonie' wäre noch adäquater."

48. The following observations are gleaned from György Ligeti, "Über neue Wege im Kompositionsunterricht," *Three Aspects of New Music* (Stockholm: AB Nordiska Musikförlaget, 1968), pp. 11–44. Ligeti's essay resulted from his teaching at the Stockholm Musikhögskolan, where he was visiting professor of composition from 1961 until 1971.

49. Ligeti, "Über neue Wege," p. 21.

50. Lerke von Saalfeld, "Im Gespräch mit György Ligeti," 33.

51. "Pitch class" indicates a specific tone of the scale, but without reference to its placement within a particular octave or its enharmonic spelling.

52. Ligeti later wrote to Kubrick complaining that he "took my music and . . . did not pay me." Ligeti did not sue MGM, but lawyers arranged for him to be paid $3,500. See Robert W. Richart, *György Ligeti: A Bio-Bibliography* (New York: Greenwood Press, 1990), p. 6.

Chapter 18

Central and Eastern Europe since the Mid Twentieth Century

Witold Lutosławski (1913–1994), like his father, had a penchant for being in the wrong place at the wrong time. In the town of his birth, a Russian province at the time, his father, Józef, was an ardent Polish nationalist. This put Józef in a difficult position. German forces invaded his homeland in the spring of 1915, and siding with them would have done nothing to achieve an independent Poland. Instead, he supported the Russians (then under the tsar), and later moved with his family to Moscow. After the overthrow of the tsar in October, 1917, the new Soviet regime formulated a concord with Germany in December, thereby making Józef's support of the Polish nationalist forces an act of treason. He was executed in September 1918.

Witold was a boy at the time, and he was probably too frightened and confused to make much sense out of these events. Witold, his brothers, and his mother, Maria, left Moscow and moved to Warsaw in the fall of 1918, after the German troops had withdrawn. There, Maria arranged for piano lessons for Witold. In 1926, he began playing the violin as well. In the next year, composition lessons with Witold Maliszewski were added to his curriculum. It was from Maliszewski that Lutosławski learned the approach to musical form that he would use for his entire career. According to Maliszewski's theory, music could serve any of four functions: introduction, narration, transition, or conclusion. The functions of introduction, transition, and conclusion are primarily formal. Narration, on the other hand, depends mainly upon content.

Lutosławski continued working with Maliszewski at the Warsaw Conservatory, where he enrolled in 1932. He graduated as a pianist in 1936, and with a degree in composition the next year. At this point, Lutosławski's luck—from his paternal side—took hold. Music was put aside in 1937 for service in the Polish army. In 1939, he was captured by Nazis. Fortunately, he escaped, returned to Warsaw, and earned a living by playing piano duos with Andrzej Panufnik

(1914–1991) at night clubs and cafes. Miraculously, he managed to complete his *Symphonic Variations* in 1938, and these had their premiere in Krakow in 1939. Few of his works from this era survive. Nazi forces smashed an uprising of Polish nationalists in the summer of 1944. Anticipating these events, Lutosławski fled Warsaw, leaving most of his scores behind. Among those rescued were his twelve *Variations on a Theme of Paganini* (1941).[1] In the *Paganini Variations*, the virtuosity of Rachmaninoff is combined with elements of Bartók and Debussy.

Other youthful works include the *Fifty Contrapuntal Studies* (1944), which are an important presage of the composer's predilection for this texture.[2] Their immediate consequence is apparent in the Trio for oboe, clarinet, and bassoon, Lutosławski's first post-war composition. Its premiere at the Festival of Contemporary Polish Music in September of 1945 seemed a good omen for the young composer, and he was elected an officer in the Union of Polish Composers. The sign was a deceiving one, however, and when Soviet ideals of Social Realism spread to Poland in 1948, Lutosławski found himself in a difficult situation; thus, he turned his talents to instructional music in the folk style. He was highly successful at this, and his piano arrangements of *Twelve Folk Melodies* (1945) became required repertoire in the public school system in 1958.

Lutosławski's First Symphony (1947) won him the label of "formalist" after its premiere in 1948, and he was expelled from the Union of Polish Composers. Its four movements contain characteristic elements of his later style, such as the dense chordal textures in the first movement; emphasis on a limited collection of intervals, in this case, thirds; chords that function as motifs; canons; and a unique type of composition with twelve tones (in the third movement) that is not serial in the traditional sense.

The *Three Postludiums* (1963) for triple winds, four horns, percussion, two harps, and strings were Lutosławski's last fully determined scores; hence their designation as "postludiums." He used choice operations in all subsequent works beginning with the *Jeux vénitiens* (Venetian games; 1961). His new concept of form is apparent in the first movement, which is built of eight distinct segments cued by *fortissimo* percussion signals. This same signaling technique is used in the First String Quartet (1964), where the reiterated Cs trigger either the end of one section or the beginning of another.

In *Jeux vénitiens*, the sections are alternately energetic and restful, thus approximating a rondo with episodes. In the Quartet, too, it is misleading to speak of aleatory music or chance operations. The musical segments are notated (although in the Quartet, he wrote parts rather than a full score). Lutosławski compared form in his music to a mobile in which the spaces occupied by the elements at any moment cannot be predicted; yet, the relationships among the parts change according to a logical pattern. Even with these mobile forms, many of Lutosławski's works are reminiscent of pattern forms. This is not a coincidence: Lutosławski makes it clear that this will occur "when the range within which chance operates is sufficiently limited by the author, when chance does not play a controlling part in the work and is subordinated to the aim indicated by the composer, and when, finally, it enriches the resources of means of expressions consciously used by the composer and is not used to organize sound occurrences which are to be a surprise not only for the listeners but also for the composer himself."[3]

Lutosławski's rhythms are also fluid. Sometimes he maintains a steady beat (*a battuta*), but at other times, he suspends that feeling (*ad libitum*). These rhythmic contrasts present a parallel to modulation and tonal stability in traditional repertoire. In Lutosławski's music, other parallels with traditional musical processes are apparent too: "the idea of making musical sections shorter and shorter the closer they come to the climax";[4] the close correspondence between tempo and form;[5] the importance of athematic linking segments based on motifs as a vehicle for transition to a new statement;[6] and pacing that either allows listeners to relax, or requires their complete attention.[7]

This last consideration had profound implications for Lutosławski's handling of multimovement works. In his large works, he preferred two movements, of which the first is prefatory and the second constitutes the body of the piece. He employed this plan in his First String Quartet, which was commissioned by the Swedish Radio Corporation and premiered by the La Salle Quartet in 1965. He used it again in his Third Symphony. The prefatory movement and the principal movement can assume any form; hence, it would be wrong to think of this design as a latter-day manifestation of the pavane and galliard, or the *lassú* and *friss* plan familiar from Bartók's music.

Lutosławski applied these structural principles in his Third Symphony, an exciting work that he composed for the Chicago Symphony, and which was premiered by them under Sir Georg Solti in 1983. Here again, the first movement is preliminary, and the second constitutes the body. Signaling devices delineate beginnings and endings of sections. In this symphony, the signal device is the main motif of the work; hence, a motto of four rapidly stated Es at *fortissimo* opens the work. The motto is followed by a transitional segment leading to a restatement of the motto. Here follow three more extensive segments—episodes separated by the motto—at the same tempo but with steadily decreasing surface activity. An extended statement of the signal motto alerts the listener that a shift to a more intense musical process is taking place. A series of elided fugal segments constitutes the core of the main movement, but here too, one can discern a slacking of tension, beginning with the descending brass glissandos that lead to the brooding Epilogue. This concluding portion is largely assigned to unison string tutti; however, subsections are created by two moments of heightened tension during the course of the Epilogue. The somber atmosphere of the Epilogue is mitigated in the closing moments by a sparkling cadenza for piano and percussion leading to the final statement of the motto, which now serves a framing function. At this point, the Es might even be heard as a tonal focus pitch.

The two knots in the Epilogue are characteristic of Lutosławski's music, and similar knots appear in all his works. He explains these moments as "fugitive" elements. In his discussion of the *Livre pour orchestre* (book for orchestra; 1968), he explained that "Every form is the product of the conflict between forces. We could call them centrifugal and centripetal. Centrifugal forces result from the variety of the musical material; they must somehow be balanced by a centripetal force which will bind these fugitive elements into a whole."[8]

The intensely dramatic nature of the Third Symphony has often been attributed to Lutosławski's difficult situation in Poland at the time of its composition: Martial law had been imposed beginning on 13 December 1981. At that point, he withdrew from official activities in his homeland until free elections were held in 1989. In the following year, the newly elected president of the Polish Republic, Lech Walesa, invited Lutosławski both to join the Polish Cultural Council and to serve on a new committee for the Reconciliation of Poles and Jews.

Among the younger generation of Central- and Eastern-European composers, Krzysztof Penderecki (b. 1933), Alfred Schnittke (1934–1998), Sofia Gubaidulina (b. 1931), Arvo Pärt (b. 1935), and Einojuhani Rautavaara (b. 1928) deserve particular attention.[9]

Penderecki's instrument is the violin. He studied composition with Artur Malawski (also a violinist) at the State Higher School of Music from 1955 until 1958. He served on the faculty there until 1966. Later, when the school became the Academy of Music, Penderecki served as rector from 1972 until 1987.

He became notorious with his *Threnody for the Victims of Hiroshima* (1960; originally called *8' 37"*). Scored for twenty-four violins, ten violas, ten 'celli, and eight basses, the piece has no meter (nor any bar lines), no melody, and—since the concept of consonance and dissonance is irrelevant—no harmony. The piece is constructed from blocks of sound, for example, extremes of register. For the highest, he uses a triangle pointing up; for the lowest, one pointing down. Sound masses are sometimes composed of strings that are plucked, or treated percussively, or used in tone clusters. Since *Threnody* is for strings only, microtones appear within these contexts.

Penderecki's scores use a mixture of graphic and conventional notation. He includes tables that explain the signs he uses to indicate particular sounds, such as bowing between the bridge and the tailpiece, tapping on the body of the instrument with the bow, or with the finger, and so on.

Penderecki uses extended techniques for conventional instruments as well as voices. What is surprising is the great success he has had in applying these ultra-modern techniques to classical texts of the Christian church, an irony apparent in his *St. Luke Passion* (1966), the *Dies Iræ* (1967), written in memory of the victims of Auschwitz, *Utrenia I* and *II* (1969–1971), treating the burial and resurrection of Christ, the *Canticum canticorum Salomonis* (1973), the *Magnificat* (1974), and the *Te Deum* and *Lacrimosa* (both 1980).

The *St. Luke Passion* was the result of a commission by the West German Radio to celebrate the 700th anniversary of Münster Cathedral.[10] The combination of "Germany" and "church music" brought to Penderecki's mind the music of

Bach, who wrote five settings of the Passion. Only two, those according to St. John and the St. Matthew, have survived; consequently, there seemed to Penderecki little point in setting these. Of the remaining Gospel accounts, that of St. Luke offered beautiful language and ample opportunities for expressive music. His choice, therefore, was influenced by the shadow of Bach, a fact reflected in Penderecki's use of the B-flat, A, C, H motif. As in the Bach Passions, newly composed music is complemented by borrowed tunes: in Bach's case, Lutheran chorale melodies, in Penderecki's case, the Polish church song "'Swiety Boze" (Holy God), from which he took the first four notes as a motto. Penderecki added four more notes to form a tone row that serves as an important structural element throughout the piece. Another imitation of Bach occurs in Penderecki's use of non-Biblical interpolations, specifically the Latin hymn "Vexilla regis prodeunt," portions of the *Improperia*, the hymn "Pange lingua gloriosi," and the "Stabat Mater," a traditional Roman Catholic sequence. In his setting of the *St. Luke Passion* for solo voices, chorus, and large orchestra, Penderecki draws on church traditions, music history, contemporary music, and his own deeply spiritual conception of music.

A similar spiritual seriousness is apparent in the works of Alfred Schnittke. He was equally German and Russian, both in ancestry and training. The lower-Volga area, where he was born, had been opened to German settlers by Katherine the Great after the eighteenth-century insurrection led by Yemelian Pugachev. (This is the region where Stefan Razin led peasant uprisings in the seventeenth century.) Since then, the population has been bicultural, and when Alfred was born in the port town of Engels, he assumed the Janus-faced customs of his Russo-German countrymen, though he always considered himself a Russian.[11] His father was an atheist of Jewish parentage, his mother a Roman Catholic, and Schnittke himself was baptized Catholic in 1982.[12] He studied piano in Vienna from 1946 to 1948. (His father was employed there by a German-language Soviet paper.) From 1953 until 1958, he studied at the Moscow Conservatory, and was a faculty member there from 1962 until 1972, when he resigned to concentrate on composition.

Schnittke composed prolifically in diverse genres and styles. His composition studies from 1953 until 1958 with Yevgeni Golubev (1910–1988) at the Moscow Conservatory were complemented by informal work with Filip Gershkovich. A native of Vienna and an admirer of its musical heritage, Gershkovich was equally interested in the city's contemporary music. He studied there with Anton Webern. After moving to Moscow, Gershkovich began sharing his knowledge of serialists with younger, Russian musicians. His influence extended to Schnittke's associates Sofia Gubaidolina and Edison Denisov.[13]

During his ten years teaching orchestration at the Moscow Conservatory, Schnittke also composed sixty-four film scores. He especially enjoyed working with the director Larissa Shepitko, who died in a car crash when she was forty-one. Cinema left its mark on Schnittke's style, and his music, "inspired by his cosmopolitan background combined with cinematic techniques, involved juxtaposing a variety of styles, . . . the concept [that came to be] known as poly-stylism."[14]

Polystylism differs from Neoclassicism in that it tends toward greater diversity in a collagelike context. Schnittke's interests in stylistic diversity and cinematic techniques predisposed him to orchestral works. This preference was strengthened by his friendship with the conductor Gennadi Rozhdestvensky, who, despite Soviet opposition, led the premiere of Schnittke's First Symphony (1972). Perhaps the lack of official recognition in his homeland influenced his decision in 1989, to accept a position as Professor of Composition at the Hamburg Musikhochschule.

Schnittke's skill at instrumentation and his imaginative approach to timbre are reflected in his unusual scorings, especially in his chamber pieces, which often employ unprecedented ensembles. His five-movement *Suite in Olden Style* (1972) was originally for violin and piano, but the largely conventional forms of Pastorale (in Siciliano meter), Ballet, Minuet, Fugue, and Pantomime, and their use of traditional tonalities (C, D, A, A, and C) left Schnittke wanting some novel element. He therefore rescored the piece for viola *d'amore*, harpsichord, vibraphone, marimba, glockenspiel, and bells. This ensemble, at once antique and modern, is ideally suited to the music, which sounds, at times, like authentic eighteenth-century stuff, but at other times, curiously modern.

Equally unusual is the instrumentation of Schnittke's *Hymnus* cycle, whose four pieces are scored respectively for 'cello, harp, and tympani (1974); 'cello and double bass (1974); 'cello, bassoon, harpsichord, and bells (1975); and 'cello, double bass, bassoon, harpsichord, harp, tympani, and bells (1976). The premiere of the complete cycle was given in Moscow in May of 1979. For conventional ensembles, Schnittke wrote four string quartets (1966, '80, '83, '89), a String Trio (1985), a Piano Quartet (1988), and a Piano Quintet (1976).

Schnittke's Piano Quintet was written in memory of his mother, Maria Vogel. (The later orchestral version is entitled *In memoriam*.) The Quintet is a five-movement work that opens with a piano solo reminiscent of Shostakovich. The body of the first movement suggests sonata principles: The first musical topic is primarily melodic and decidedly chromatic. The second idea is harmonic and largely triadic. The polarity of musical materials, therefore, is between the linear and the vertical, the chromatic and the triadic, the atonal and the tonal. Within this context, tone clusters play an important role. The second movement is a waltz, but it sounds deranged and disoriented. In the waltz, Schnittke uses the nineteenth-century technique of thematic transformation by recalling a theme from the first movement. A concluding cluster—like a cinematographic fade-out—leads to the third movement, which uses previous musical images in altered states. At this point, Schnittke modified the classical four-movement plan by placing after the third movement Andante, a still slower Lento for the fourth. The association with fade-out techniques in films seems especially appropriate here, and Schnittke uses clusters like painkillers for a dying victim. At the end of the ordeal, we reach the

Moderato pastorale. This fifth movement is not a Finale. It has nothing to do with traditional concluding movements; instead, it is like the ending (happy) to a film.

The string quartet occupied a special place in Schnittke's *œuvre*. The First, an essay in Serialism, was condemned by the Union of Soviet Composers as "formalist" and "anti-Soviet." Schnittke dedicated his Second Quartet to the memory of Larissa Shepitko, with whom he had worked on films including *You and Me*, *The Ascent*, and *Farewell*. Its themes often draw on Russian sacred music; the last movement quotes the *Kheruvimskaya piesn* (Cherubic hymn) from the orthodox liturgy of St. John Chrysostom. Schnittke's subdued dynamics, harmonics, and languid rhythms emphasize the elegiac character of the piece. The Third Quartet is the best example of Polystylism. The Fourth Quartet already shows the austere manner of Schnittke's Eighth and Ninth Symphonies. The sparsity of the style may reflect difficulties in writing caused by damage to his motor skills resulting from strokes— he suffered six before his death.

Schnittke's orchestral scores almost invariably include some *concertante* element. Among such works are four violin concertos, two 'cello concertos, a concerto for oboe, harp, and strings, and various pieces simply called *concerto grosso*. In some cases, the *concertino* is handled in the manner of a Baroque concerto grosso. In others, the relationship between soloists and orchestra is closer to that of the late-eighteenth-century *sinfonia concertante*. In his *St. Florian Symphony* (No. 2; 1980), the concertino is a chamber choir.

The origin of the *St. Florian Symphony* is quite remarkable. In 1977, Schnittke visited the monastery of St. Florian, where Bruckner had been organist, and where he was entombed in 1896. At dusk, when Schnittke arrived at the church, "Bruckner's grave was already closed. The cold, dark baroque church had something mysterious about it. Somewhere . . . a small choir was singing the evening Mass: a 'Missa invisibilis.'"[15] When Schnittke was asked for a new work for the BBC Symphony Orchestra, which Rozhdestvensky conducted from 1978 until 1981, he thought of the "invisible Mass" of St. Florian; moreover, he recalled the traditional cruciform of the church and incorporated the image of the cross in both the harmonic and melodic designs of the music. The six movements of the Symphony follow the traditional Ordinary of the Mass. The Latin texts, along with their traditional plainchant melodies in some cases, appear as the openings of the movements. These extracts from the Mass act as epigrams for the symphonic movements.

The "invisible" choir of the *St. Florian Symphony* is closely related to features of Schnittke's *Requiem* (1975), which draws from his Piano Quintet. Noting the vocal character of his themes in the chamber piece, he transferred them to the Requiem Mass. The Requiem originated as incidental music performed by an off-stage ensemble as background to Schiller's *Don Carlos*. Even then, Schnittke anticipated the possibility of concert performance of the Requiem. The entire Roman Catholic liturgical text, save for the "Lux æterna," is set. Another aberration is the insertion of the "Credo."

Death was a topic that concerned Schnittke, since he began having severe strokes in his early fifties. The first of these, in 1985, resulted in a near-death experience. Thrown into a coma on 22 July, he was unconscious for twenty days and was declared clinically dead. In August, he returned to a semiconscious state and drifted between consciousness and unconsciousness, imagining fantastic visions that he expressed in his Concerto for 'cello and orchestra.

By October, he had regained his ability to speak and write. He composed three movements of the concerto, but later added the fourth movement, a Largo that begins as though emerging from a comatose state—hardly even noticeable at first. The movement slowly grows in power: a progress not of horror, but of triumph. Bells announce the ultimate victory. In this work, Schnittke has given us a glimpse of his vision of the life of the world to come; but that joyful glimpse was, at the time, one of anticipation. The movement closes with a recollection of the opening depiction of failing strength and disorientation; but here its meaning is different: Having had the vision of triumph, the awareness of mortality seems far less frightening.

Schnittke's Eighth Symphony (1994) was written for and dedicated to Rozhdestvensky, who led the premiere on 10 November. The first of its five movements is based on an angular subject that acts like a migrant cantus firmus reiterated twenty-two times. Sometimes it functions like an ostinato; at other times, like a fugue subject; occasionally, its harmonic implications are paramount; Schnittke puts it into service as a monophonic melody line, too. At the end of the movement, the piccolo plays the subject against muffled thuds of the tam-tam. The terse second movement is built with motifs of only several notes each, and it seems like a transition to the vast central Lento. For most of its duration, the Lento is for thinly harmonized strings playing halting, angular melodies that are simultaneously somber and intense. Chamber-music episodes for woodwinds punctuate the continuing string monologue. The fourth movement is a counterpart to the second, not only in its recollection of themes, but also in its comparable duration. The Finale, the shortest of the movements, is an apotheosis; however, the transformation is a serene one, featuring two harps, celesta, harpsichord, and piano. The music ascends steadily with new instruments entering on each note to build a cluster. This movement approximates Wagner's Prelude to *Parsifal*; however, Schnittke's compression of gesture and affect into a movement of less than two minutes produces remarkable intensity. Despite its sparsity, the Eighth Symphony is an incredibly poignant work. Its astonishing combination of economy and expression may well mark it as the masterpiece of Schnittke's austere period.

Schnittke's use of music as a means for contemplation is shared by his deeply spiritual colleague, Gubaidulina. They met as students in Moscow, where they enjoyed the unofficial teaching of Gershkovich. Like Schnittke, Gubaidulina comes from a diverse background: Her father was a Tatar and Muslim, her mother was a mix of Russian, Polish, and Jewish heritage. Like most Soviets of that era, they were not particularly religious. Gubaidulina, on the other hand, is deeply religious and intends her music to be so.

Gubaidulina studied at the Kazan Conservatory (diploma 1954) and continued later that year with Nikolai Peiko (b. 1916) and Vissarion Shebalin (1902–1963) at the Moscow Conservatory. Both were students of Nikolai Miaskovsky (1881–1950), but Peiko was a conservative who wrote Social Realism, whereas the progressive Shebalin was repeatedly reprimanded for his decadent Formalism.

When Gubaidulina completed her graduate studies in 1959, Nikita Khrushchev was the head of the Communist Party and the premier of the Soviet Union. He denounced Stalin in 1956, and broke up Stalin's political machines in 1957; however, these reforms fell short of opening a forum for Gubaidulina. When Khrushchev fell from power in 1964, he was succeeded by Leonid Brezhnev, who tightened the reins on dissidents. (It was he who formulated the policy of justifiable intervention in the affairs of Communist states when their actions were considered detrimental to the Union. This policy was the justification for the invasion of Czechoslovakia in 1968.) "Gubaidulina's predilection for mysticism and metaphysics, her spirituality and musical fantasy, . . . her preoccupation with musical symbols of crucifixion, resurrection, and transfiguration, did not meet the requirements of Socialist Realism; hence, her works were condemned to be unrecognized, unperformed, and unpublished in the Brezhnev and post-Brezhnev Soviet Union."[16]

Since concert halls were closed to her, Gubaidulina sought alternatives. She spent 1969–1970 working in an electronic music studio in Moscow. From 1975 until 1981, she was a member of Astrea, an improvisation ensemble that she founded with Vyacheslav Artyomov and Victor Suslin. Sometimes they used ethnic instruments from Russia, the Caucasus, central Asia, and Siberia.[17] In her score of *In the Shadow of the Tree* (1999), for example, she uses koto, bass koto, and zheng. It was commissioned by Japan's NHK Orchestra.

Gubaidulina's works reflect her many interests—the spiritual, the scientific—and a global perspective. She is not an avant-gardist, and she insists that she has

> hated the word "avant-garde" for a very long time. When we were young in Moscow, the authorities called us "avant-garde artists" to curse us. . . . But now it sounds . . . like encouragement: "Oh, the avant-garde composer! How wonderful!" I do not like such praise. My desire is always to rebel, to swim against the stream! For me [that] means to introduce seriousness in art. . . . The contemporary artist is faced with an extremely important task: finding a correlation between intuition and intellectual work. . . . It absolutely does not matter whether it looks new or old. News is good for newspapers . . . but art strives for depth, not for the news![18]

She knows that novelty can distract from the point of the music. At the same time, she appreciates innovative techniques used sincerely. She explains that

Sofia Gubaidulina

"composers make efforts . . . not because they wish to show people that they are . . . 'newer' than the others, but because music itself demands it, and our efforts naturally start to turn in this direction . . . [as] an 'objective necessity.'"[19]

Gubaidulina's music contains many of these necessary innovations, such as quarter tones and gestural music. Her interest in quarter tones stems from her mysticism. She sees quarter tones as a metaphor for shadows, whereas the chromatic scale represents light.

In the twelve-tone compositions of the twentieth century, everything is as in the daytime; everything is enlightened and rationalized; there is no place of "night." "Night" existed as a supplement of the diatonic system: the diatonic sphere was "day," whereas the chromatic sphere was "night": one could go there and return. . . . In the twelve-tone compositions we lost "night": everything became "day." But within the twenty-four tone scale, we may have not only "a day," but also "a night."[20]

In her *Music for Flute and Strings* (1995), she divides the strings into two choirs tuned a quarter tone apart. The sonorities for each consist of major chords, thus imparting an unambiguous tonal integrity to each group. The string choirs function independently and do not take musical "notice" of one another; here the flute enters the picture. Because it can play quarter tones and glissandos, it can participate in either group; hence, the flute becomes the interlocutor in this extended single-movement composition. Gubaidulina notes that the piece is intended for a "big string orchestra [that] gives . . . the possibility of using a powerful sonority in each space."[21]

This work reflects her view of art as ritual. She contends that the public needs the composer's spirituality, and that it relies on the composer to present something that "allows people to experience a state of concentration, to bring themselves into a state of wholeness, to cure themselves from the state of dispersal and disconnection that they suffer in everyday life. . . . Listening to a musical composition . . . helps people restore themselves."[22]

Gestural music is essentially ritualistic. The classic example of it in Gubaidulina's works appears in her twelve-movement symphony, *Stimmen . . . verstummen . . .* (1986; voices . . . growing silent . . .). The title comes from the last words of the baritone in *Perception* (1983), a song cycle for soprano, baritone, seven strings, and tape. The texts are taken from letters exchanged between Gubaidulina and the

West German poet Francesco Tanzer. These letters were written as a free association ruminating on the differences between "male and female perception, particularly of suffering and pain."[23]

In Gubaidulina's symphony, gestural music depicts "verstummen" in the ninth movement, which is a solo for conductor. "The conductor here beats out the silence in gestures."[24] Upon seeing the score for the first time, Rozhdestvensky objected that the piece "would only be comprehensible to those who could actually see the performance. It could not therefore be recorded or played on the radio."[25] Gubaidulina countered that the earlier eight movements, when played exactly as intended, render the rhythms of the silent movement audible even in the absence of sound. The movement demonstrates the pervasiveness in her music of metaphysics, symbolism, ritual, and philosophically conceived forms.

The titles of many of her works reflect these characteristics. *Introitus* (1979), for example, refers to the opening of the Mass. In Gubaidulina's realization, it is a concerto for piano and chamber orchestra. *Offertorium* (1980) denotes the portion of the Mass when alms, bread, and wine are given to be consecrated. In Gubaidulina's piece, these offerings become a concerto for violin and orchestra.

In both works, the mystic premise is integral rather than superficial. *Offertorium*, for example, uses the concept of sacrifice as its core. That concept dictates both localized musical events and broadly based formal structures. Gubaidulina selected as her theme, the subject used by Bach in his *Musikalisches Opfer* (musical offering; 1747). The theme was not invented by Bach; it was given to him as a topic for improvisation by King Frederick the Great of Prussia. In stating the theme, Gubaidulina drops the final, tonic note, thereby shortening it to twenty notes. In so doing, she not only avoids harmonic closure of the melody, but also introduces the mechanism of her musical sacrifice: In each statement, the theme is shortened by one note at the beginning and one note at the end. Each of the variations on the theme is based melodically and harmonically upon the last interval remaining after the truncation of the melody. Once set in motion, this process continues until only a single pitch remains. This is the moment of apotheosis: Now the transformed life begins, as the theme is gradually reconstituted from the unison in retrograde.

Gubaidulina's musical process parallels the spiritual transformation of the Christian believer, whereby, according to scripture (John 3: 3–8), the person is "born again." *Offertorium* is, therefore, more than a musical score: It is a theological essay.

In presenting the theme of her sacrificial violin concerto, Gubaidulina changes the instrumentation on almost every note; consequently, sudden shifts in register give the line a disjointed, pointillistic character. Could such disparate elements of modern music and old-fashioned theology possibly be intended as a serious, religious statement? Gubaidulina is equally eloquent, it seems, in words and in notes. Her own statement about her art is unequivocal:

> All my works are religious. . . . I've never written non-religious pieces. . . . I feel a great desire to realize my religious needs within

EXAMPLE 10

Sofia Gubaidulina, Instrumentation of the *Musical Offering* Theme in *Offertorium*

art. . . . For us, the artists, it is absolutely necessary to experience this religious reunion with the highest essence of our souls. Without it we would be unable to work with such an inspiration. I understand the word "religion" in its direct meaning: as *re-ligio* (*re-legato*), that is, a restoration of *legato* between me (my soul) and God. By means of my religious activity I restore this interrupted connexion. Life interrupts this connexion: it leads me away, into different troubles, and God leaves me at these times. This is unbearable pain: by creating, through our art, we strive to restore this legato.[26]

The importance of spirituality in works by erstwhile Soviet bloc composers seems to have been spurred by the official proscription of religion. In an endeavor to compensate for this loss, artists created new foods for the soul. This hunger for spiritual nourishment also lies at the root of many of Arvo Pärt's most important works.

In 1935, the year of Pärt's birth, Estonia had been an independent republic since 1920. In 1940, it came under Soviet rule. Following the demise of the Soviet Juni, the country was occupied by Russian troops until 1994. During its history, the region had been under the rules variously of Denmark, Poland, Lithuania, and Sweden. The country consequently acquired an international character.[27]

As a boy, Pärt attended a children's music school in Rakvere, which is east of Estonia's capital, Tallinn. He played piano and oboe, and was always eager to hear the symphony broadcasts of the Finnish Radio. In 1954, he entered the college music program in Tallinn, a beautiful mediæval city on the Gulf of Finland, opposite Helsinki. His studies were interrupted by two years' military service, but he returned to complete his degree in 1957. He was accepted into the Tallinn Conservatory and began advanced studies in the fall of 1957.

Pärt's composition teacher, Heino Eller (1887–1970) studied violin with Leopold Auer and composition with Vasili Kalafati (1869–1942) at the St. Petersburg Conservatory. Eller's studio produced many successful composers including

Eduard Tubin (1905–1982), Jaan Rääts (b. 1932), and Lepo Sumera (b. 1950). Eller's chief works, which include three symphonies, symphonic poems, concertos, five string quartets, and four piano sonatas, use folk elements within a moderately progressive harmonic style; however, he was not opposed to avant-garde musics.

Pärt explored contemporary styles, including Serialism. His investigation of its techniques began with two widely circulated texts, one by Herbert Eimert, another by Ernst Krenek.[28] Pärt complemented his academic work with practical experience as a recording engineer with Estonian Radio, as musical director for the Pioneer Theatre in Tallinn, and by writing approximately fifty film scores.

Pärt used serial techniques in his early works. *Nekrolog* (1961) was deplored by authorities as Formalism. His First Symphony (1963), which is also serial, is dedicated to Eller. The score is rich in melodies, and its harmonic idiom retains a certain Romantic flavor. For the next several years, Pärt became increasingly interested in the music of Bach, an interest reflected in his scores like *Collage sur B-A-C-H* (1964), which uses the motif within its row, quotes works by Bach, and consists of three movements based on Baroque models: Toccata, Sarabande, and Ricercar. Two other works of that year, *Musica sillabica* and the *Quintettino* for winds also use the Bach motif.

The Second Symphony (1966) is also serial, but here austerity is conspicuous. Even the designation of movements seems strangely impersonal: First, Second, Third. The tone row F-sharp, A, G, G-sharp, B-flat, C-sharp, B, C, D, F, E-flat, E, is sequential in its repeating configuration of minor third, whole step, half step. Portions of the score are indeterminate, and extended instrumental techniques contribute to a generally harsh character.

Pärt juxtaposed tonal and atonal materials in *Pro and Contra* (for and against; 1966), written for Rostropovich, and again in *Credo* (1968), for chorus and orchestra. *Credo* does not use the conventional text of the Mass; instead, Pärt draws several words from the "Credo" and combines these with passages from St. Matthew's Gospel (5:38–9). Despite its warm reception by the public, *Credo* was condemned by the authorities and banned.

After *Credo*, Pärt focused on the Third Symphony (1971), a fitting capstone for his series of three polystylistic symphonies. The First, which he entitled *Polyphonic*, shows many different influences: The opening dyads are reminiscent of the fanfare opening of Tschaikovsky's Fourth Symphony; the "Canons" of the first movement seem indebted to Renaissance music; and in the second movement, "Prelude and Fugue," the allusion to Baroque forms is clear. Pärt concludes each of the movements with deliberately extravagant cadences in the Baroque manner. The Second Symphony's more pointillistic approach suggests the influence of Webern. Pärt seems to have been frightened by his own severity, and in the third movement, which begins in the atmosphere of torment and doom established by the previous two, he suddenly introduces an extended quotation from Tschaikovsky's "Sweet Dreams," Op. 39, no. 21. The unexpected appearance of this tender, overtly Romantic music negates everything that has preceded it. The

Third Symphony takes Pärt into the most ancient musical resources: *Ars antiqua* and *Ars nova*. Chant-like melodies pervade all three movements, and Pärt quotes the "Veni, veni Emmanuel" tune. Simple textures, often in two parts, are ubiquitous. The techniques of parallel organum frequently appear. Many passages terminate in cadences without thirds, and Landini cadences are used to the point of becoming a cliché. This neo-Mediæval score was a natural consequence of Pärt's interest in early music during the late 1960s.

The simple, yet effective idiom that Pärt discovered in ancient music inspired him to invent a comparable, but decidedly contemporary way of composing. In 1976, he wrote a two-page piano piece called "Für Alina." In it, he achieved his first characteristic application of Tintinnabuli style. He began with a line reminiscent of chant in its diatonic/modal simplicity. This functions in the manner of a *cantus firmus* against which Pärt adds a second line, the Tintinnabuli voice. The two voices move, like parallel organum, in the same rhythm at all times. The added voice (in this case, the lower of the two) consists exclusively of notes from the tonic triad, B minor. The notes of the added voice are the note in the B-minor triad closest to the melodic note.

"Für Alina" gave Pärt the prototype of his Tintinnabuli style, although the specific procedures governing each piece vary: The Tintinnabuli voice (T-voice) may be one note removed rather than the closest chord tone. This distribution of voices is analogous to open and closed positions in harmony. The T-voice, like the *vox organalis* in early polyphony, may be above or below the main voice. It is possible as well for the T-voice to jump—hocket style—above and below the main voice. Various voices may also be transposed to different octaves or doubled.

The Tintinnabuli style has served Pärt well, and his most recent works have been primarily choral pieces of a deeply spiritual nature. His setting of the *St. John Passion* (1982) for soli, mixed chorus, organ, oboe, bassoon, violin, and viola is an extended score in Tintinnabuli style. Other large works include his *Stabat Mater* (1985), *Miserere, Magnificat* (both 1989), *Berlin Mass* (1990), and the *Litany Prayers of St. John Chrysostom* (1994). These are complemented by smaller choral works, many of them accessible to practical church choirs. He has used the style in instrumental music as well, and his scores for *Fratres* (brothers; 1977, subsequently arranged for various chamber ensembles), *Cantus in memoriam Benjamin Britten* (1977), and *Tabula rasa* (blank slate; 1977) are noteworthy examples.

During the 1970s, Soviet Jews were permitted to leave the country. Pärt's wife, Nora, whom he married in 1972, is Jewish. Because his music was condemned by authorities, Pärt also had reason to leave Estonia; accordingly, Pärt, his wife, and their two sons left in 1980 for Vienna. He quickly obtained a contract there with Universal Edition. In the following year, the family emigrated to Berlin, where they presently reside.

Rautavaara is the only Finnish composer since Jean Sibelius (1865–1957) who has achieved an international reputation.[29] The seven symphonies that Sibelius composed between 1899 and 1924 and his symphonic poems, such as the four in the *Lemminkäinen Suite*, Op. 22 (1896), served as models for Rautavaara's own work. To date he has written eight symphonies and important tone poems including *Anadyomene* (1968) and the immensely popular *Cantus arcticus* (Arctic song; 1972). In addition, he has written many operas, concertos for 'cello, piano, flute, violin, organ, and double bass, chamber works, including four string quartets, cantatas, songs, piano pieces, and works that traverse generic boundaries.

Rautavaara studied composition with Aarre Merikanto (1893–1958) at the Sibelius Academy in Helsinki from 1950 until 1957. He came to the United States in 1955–1956, working first at Juilliard with Vincent Persichetti, then, with a Koussevitzky Foundation scholarship that he obtained on the recommendation of Sibelius, at Tanglewood with Aaron Copland and Roger Sessions. He studied serial techniques with Wladimir Vogel in Ascona, Switzerland, in 1957, and concluded his training at the Cologne Musikhochschule with Rudolf Petzold in 1958. From 1966 until 1976, he was a Lecturer at the Sibelius Academy, where he served as Professor of Composition from 1976 until 1990.

His works from the '40s and '50s show neoclassical and folk influences as well as experiments with serialism and other abstract techniques, including symmetrical contructions. The three *Symmetric Preludes* (1949) treat subjects in mirror images, but retain tonal elements. In fact, Rautavaara has always maintained strong links with traditional tonal music, and his serial music stems mainly from the manner of Alban Berg. Like Berg, Rautavaara incorporates tonal sonorities into his rows in order to create non-atonal dodecaphony, as in the case of his Second String Quartet (1958). His stylistic plurality extends from Mediæval chant-based works to pieces incorporating elements of Jazz.

Rautavaara's turning point seems to have taken place during the composition of *Anadyomene* (adoration of Aphrodite, 1968), which was originally to have been entitled *Riverrun*, the opening word of James Joyce's *Finnegan's Wake*. Rautavaara attempted to compose the first two paragraphs of Joyce's novel as purely instrumental music derived from structuralist principles inherent in the texts; however, the proliferation of musical materials forced the composer to abandon his original plan and break free from serial and other systematic restraints. This fact is reflected in the title's reference to Aphrodite, the goddess of love born from the foam of the sea. This exquisitely lyrical piece for large orchestra exhibits Rautavaara's current thinking: "The idea of a work constructed wholly on cognitive principles," he says, "according to a method, belongs to a causal-deterministic view of the world that is a thing of the past."[30] In this tone poem, Rautavaara has produced a brilliant synthesis of diverse modern structural principles with traditional techniques, to yield an expressive and appealing score. As he states, "that I should only use the techniques of today, those invented after 1940—I think that's senseless, that's idiotic nowadays."[31]

Rautavaara is keenly interested in literature—along with painting, writing is one of his hobbies. He has written the librettos for most of his texted works and all but one of his operas. *Vincent* (1987) offered the ideal venue for Rautavaara to combine his work in music, literature, and art, since it is an exploration of the life and mind of Vincent van Gogh. In 1992, he based his Sixth Symphony (*Vincentiana*) on materials drawn from the opera and the sketches for it.

Recent works of note include the tone poem *Isle of Bliss* (1995), which alludes to the island paradise Lintukoto (isle of birds) that appears in the poetry of the Finnish writer Alexsis Kivi. Rautavaara also associates it with a fabled island where time stops, and death is defeated by eternal youth. Equally compelling is his Third Piano Concerto (1998), which was written specifically for Vladimir Ashkenazy. Since Rautavaara is himself a concert pianist, he was able to achieve a style at once virtuosic and idiomatic in this work. Rautavaara's Eighth Symphony was commissioned for the 1999–2000 centennial of the Philadelphia Orchestra. Continuing in the manner of Sibelius, Rautavaara derives the musical materials of his Eighth Symphony from a limited number of motifs. These structural cells reappear in cyclic manner during the course of the four-movement work. Though most of his scores conclude with music that retreats gently into nothingness, the Eighth culminates in a blaze of glory—*con grandezza*.

Notes

1. Revised in 1978 for piano and orchestra. The theme, as in Rachmaninoff's *Rhapsody*, is that of the twenty-fourth caprice.
2. All fifty and their instrumentations are given in the List of Works in Charles Bodman Rae, *The Music of Lutosławski*, enlarged ed. (London: Faber, 1999).
3. B. M. Maciejewski, *Twelve Polish Composers* (London: Allegro Press, 1976), pp. 39–40.
4. Witold Lutosławski, *Conversations with Witold Lutosławski*, ed. Tadeusz Kaczýnskyi, trans. Yolanta May (London: J. and W. Chester, 1984), p. 46.
5. *Conversations with Witold Lutosławski*, p. 53.
6. *Conversations with Witold Lutosławski*, p. 139.
7. *Conversations with Witold Lutosławski*, p. 51.
8. *Conversations with Witold Lutosławski*, p. 57.
9. Concerning Penderecki, the best source—in journalistic style and heavily illustrated—is Wolfram Schwinger, *Kryzsztof Penderecki: His Life and Work*, enlarged English ed. (New York: Schott, 1989). For Schnittke, Aleksandr Ivashkin, *Alfred Schnittke* (London: Phaidon, 1996); also John Warnaby's obituary "Alfred Schnittke," *Musical Opinion* 122 (fall 1998), 4–5; Ivan Moody, "The Music of Alfred Schnittke," *Tempo* 168 (March 1989), 4–11; Solomon Volkov, "The A-Z of Alfred Schnittke," *Tempo* 206 (September 1998), "The ABCs of Alfred Schnittke," *Tempo* 206 (October 1998), 36–38. Concerning Gubaidulina, *Sofia Gubaidulina Catalogue* (Hamburg: Sikorski, 1994), which includes a Preface in English; also Gerard McBurney, "Encountering Gubaydulina," *Musical Times* 129 (March 1988), 120–125; Vera Lukomsky, "'The Eucharist in My Fantasy': Interview with Sofia Gubaidulina," *Tempo* 206 (October 1998), 29–35; Lukomsky, "Sofia Gubaidulina: 'My Desire Is Always To Rebel, To Swim against the Stream,'" *Perspectives of New Music* 36 (winter 1998), [5]–35; Lukomsky, Hearing the Subconscious': An Interview with Sofia Gubaidulina," *Tempo* 209 (July 1999). Regarding Pärt, see Paul Hillier, *Arvo Pärt* (New York: Oxford University Press, 1997); also Geoff Smith, "Sources of Invention [interview with Arvo Pärt]," *Musical Times* 140 (fall 1999), 19–25.

10. See Ray Robinson and Allen Winold, *A Study of the Penderecki* St. Luke Passion (Celle: Moeck Verlag, 1983), 124 p.
11. Volkov, "The ABCs of Alfred Schnittke," 36–37.
12. Volkov, "The ABCs of Alfred Schnittke," 37.
13. Warnaby, "Alfred Schnittke," 4.
14. Warnaby, "Alfred Schnittke," 4.
15. Alfred Schnittke, cited in the brochure for Symphony No. 2: *St. Florian*, cond. Leif Segerstam (BIS CD-667 © 1994), p. 3.
16. Lukomsky, "Sofia Gubaidulina: 'My Desire Is Always To Rebel,' " 6.
17. Lukomsky, "Sofia Gubaidulina: 'My Desire Is Always To Rebel,' " 6.
18. Lukomsky, "Sofia Gubaidulina: 'My Desire Is Always To Rebel,' " 8–9.
19. Lukomsky, "Sofia Gubaidulina: 'My Desire Is Always To Rebel,' " 12.
20. Lukomsky, "Sofia Gubaidulina: 'My Desire Is Always To Rebel,' " 11.
21. Lukomsky, "Sofia Gubaidulina: 'My Desire Is Always To Rebel,' " 11.
22. Lukomsky, "Sofia Gubaidulina: 'My Desire Is Always To Rebel,' " 9–10.
23. McBurney, "Encountering Gubaydulina," 123.
24. McBurney, "Encountering Gubaydulina," 125.
25. McBurney, "Encountering Gubaydulina," 125.
26. Lukomsky, The Eucharist in My Fantasy': Interview with Sofia Gubaidulina," 31, 33.
27. More extensive background is provided in Hillier, *Arvo Pärt*, pp. 24–29.
28. Eimert, *Lehrbuch der Zwölftontechnik* (Wiesbaden: Breitkopf und Härtel, 1950), 61 p.; Krenek, *Zwölfton Kontrapunkt-Studien* (Mainz: Schott, 1952), 51 p.
29. Concerning Rautavaara, see Mikko Heiniö, "A Portrait of the Artist at a Certain Moment," *Finnish Musical Quarterly* 4 (1988), 3–14; Martin Anderson, "Einojuhani Rautavaara, Symphonist: The Finnish Composer Talks to Martin Anderson," *Fanfare* 19, no. 6 (July/August 1996), 63–71; Neil Evans, ed., "Angels and Beyond," *Classic CD* (October 1998), 8–11, which includes a CD sampler of his music.
30. Cited in Christopher H. Gibbs, "Rautavaara: Symphony No. 8, *The Journey*," Philadelphia Orchestra program book, 27 April–2 May, 2000, p. 29.
31. Anderson, "Einojuhani Rautavaara, Symphonist," 64.

Chapter 19

American Composers since the Mid Century

Leonard Bernstein, 1918–1990

When Bernstein was born in Lawrence, Massachusetts, his father gave him the name "Louis"; he changed it legally to "Leonard" when he was sixteen years old. Samuel opposed his son's designs for a career in music, largely because of his unpleasant notions of *klezmorim*—low-brow Jewish music makers. Again, the elder Bernstein was no match for Leonard's indomitable will. Piano lessons with Helen Coates began in 1932, and by 1938, he was playing his own compositions in concert. At Harvard, he studied with Edward Burlingame Hill, A. Tillman Merritt, and Walter Piston. He graduated in 1939.

During the '30s, Bernstein's interest in contemporary music focused mainly on Copland and Marc Blitzstein. As a pianist, Bernstein was intrigued by Copland's Piano Variations, which he could play from memory by the fall of 1937, the year in which they first met.[1] Thus began their lifelong friendship. Bernstein's conducting career was the result of Copland's recognition of his talent for it. Copland's encouragement was repaid time and again over the years.

Blitzstein came to Bernstein's attention through "an up-to-the-moment Brechtian opera called *The Cradle Will Rock,* about an assembly-line foreman who challenges the rule of a . . . steel mill owner and brings about a successful strike for higher wages."[2] Bernstein liked the music and the scenario, so in 1939, he decided to mount a production of it. The end result—in which Bernstein's fifteen-year-old sister, Shirley, played the part of a prostitute—was a fabulous success. The experience clarified two issues for Bernstein: He was drawn to lyric theater, and he would need to refine his conducting skills in order to accomplish his goals.

In his capacity as conductor of the Boston Symphony Orchestra and director of Tanglewood, Serge Koussevitzky provided opportunities for Copland, Roy Harris, Walter Piston, Roger Sessions, Randall Thompson, and many other Americans. He was equally eager to develop a new generation of conductors, and the Berkshire Music Center provided an ideal venue for Koussevitzky to turn his vision into reality. The combination of the maestro eager to teach and the student craving instruction was magical, and Bernstein, in the summer of 1940, began a gloriously fruitful relationship with the eminent conductor. At Tanglewood, Bernstein met other musicians who played important roles in his life, among them, the clarinetist David Jerome Oppenheim, for whom he wrote his Sonata for clarinet and piano. The sonata had its premiere in Boston in 1942, but in 1943, it was included on a program given by the League of Composers at the Museum of Modern Art in New York City. (Copland

Leonard Bernstein

may have had a hand in arranging the program.) This was the first glimpse of the complete Bernstein: pianist, conductor, and composer.

In the summer of 1939, Bernstein began his First Symphony. A competition for new music, sponsored by the New England Conservatory, accelerated Bernstein's work, and he completed the score of the *Jeremiah Symphony* in December of 1942 in order to meet the submission deadline.[3] Fritz Reiner invited Bernstein to conduct the Pittsburgh Symphony in the premiere in 1944.

Bernstein's conducting career had gotten off to an auspicious start in 1943, when Bruno Walter, who was scheduled to lead the New York Philharmonic on Sunday, 14 November, in a performance of Robert Schumann's *Manfred Overture,* Miklós Rózsa's Theme, Variations, and Finale, Richard Strauss's *Don Quixote,* and Wagner's Overture to *Die Meistersinger,* became ill and turned the program over to a substitute. Bernstein stepped in, and the roster of the world's great conductors was forever changed. By 1945, he had conducted the New York Philharmonic as well as the symphony orchestras of Pittsburgh, Chicago, Boston, Cincinnati, and San Francisco.

Leopold Stokowski formed the New York City Symphony in 1944, and served as its conductor for its first season. When he resigned, they turned to Bernstein, who agreed to lead them in a twelve-concert season. His programs combined traditional fare and new works by Britten, Copland, Hindemith, Milhaud, Shostakovich, and Stravinsky.

From the late '40s on, Bernstein became increasingly prominent as a political voice. He spoke out in support of controversial figures like Hanns Eisler; he openly associated with Communists like Shostakovich; and he opposed the fanatical persecutions of creative artists, spearheaded by Senator Joseph McCarthy.

Bernstein's facility with both classical and pop music, his realistic approach to life in the twentieth century, and his liberal political views endeared him not only to musicians, but to an astonishingly wide cross section of the American public as well. These characteristics led naturally to his educational work with young audiences and to his associations with the Kennedy family during John Kennedy's presidency. Bernstein's *Mass*, composed for the opening of the Kennedy Center in 1971, at the request of Jacqueline Kennedy is, perhaps, the most significant musical consequence of the composer's political convictions.

During the 1940s, one of Bernstein's primary artistic goals seems to have been the integration of jazz and classical traditions. He wrote the *Prelude, Fugue, and Riffs* (1949) for Woody Herman and his band—perhaps to keep abreast of Stravinsky, who wrote the *Ebony Concerto* for clarinet and orchestra for that ensemble in 1945.

Bernstein was intrigued by Hollywood and the potentials of film scoring. His opportunity came in 1953 with Budd Schulberg's script for *On the Waterfront*, a film featuring Marlon Brando, Lee J. Cobb, Karl Malden, Rod Steiger, and Eva Marie Saint. Though the music was not singled out for an award, the film nevertheless won eight Oscars. Bernstein knew he was on the right track.

Through Blitzstein, Bernstein met Lillian Hellman, who was already well-known for plays including *The Children's Hour* (1934), *Days To Come* (1936), *Little Foxes* (1939), and *Another Part of the Forest* (1946). In 1954, she and Bernstein began work on a piece based on Voltaire. The end result—far from Hellman's original notion of a play with incidental music—was a virtual opera, *Candide*.[4] The score used for the opening (on 29 October 1956 in Boston, then on 1 December in New York City) went through many revivals and alterations. In 1973, Harold Prince mounted a one-act production with the Chelsea Theatre Center at the Brooklyn Academy of Music. For this second version, Stephen Sondheim wrote the text of "Life Is Happiness Indeed," which was set to Bernstein's music for the "Venice Gavotte." The orchestra was reduced to thirteen players positioned on four platforms. From the main acting platform, various walkways radiated through the audience; hence, there was an immediacy to the production that ensured its success. For these performances, which ran for seven weeks, Patricia Birch created the choreography. Bernstein made a third version for the New York City Opera production, again under Prince, in 1982. This operatic version, which was given on a conventional proscenium stage, restored the two-act plan and larger orchestra of fifty-five players. The final version, which Bernstein recorded with the London Symphony Orchestra and Chorus on the Deutsche Grammophon label, came into being for the 1989 performances by the Scottish Opera in Glasgow.

In *Candide*, Bernstein and Hellman walked a political tightrope: She had visited the Soviet Union in the 1930s, and she participated in Communist politics during the '40s after returning to the United States. Bernstein was an outspoken supporter of Blitzstein, Copland, Eisler, and other composers who were under investigation by McCarthy's congressional committee. In turning to Voltaire's novella *Candide, or Optimism* (1759), they were inviting contentiousness. Voltaire used the book to trash the philosophical movement known as Optimism and advanced by eighteenth-century writers such as Wilhelm von Leibnitz and Alexander Pope. The proposition is that existence validates; hence, that which is invalid cannot exist. Voltaire, confronted by natural disasters, corruption, and inequity could only laugh at the idea; however, laughter with a purpose is satire, and *Candide* is a bitter one indeed. (Just three years after Voltaire published the story, the Roman Catholic Church placed it on the list of forbidden books.)

Bernstein and Hellman's satire in *Candide* is of American society, and it is just as acrid and defiant as Voltaire's. That it opened at all was something of a miracle, especially since Bernstein was clear about the score's meaning: It is, he claimed, an attack against America's "puritanical snobbery, phony moralism, inquisitory attacks on the individual, brave-new-world optimism, [and] essential superiority."[5] His remarks during the concert performances in London during December of 1989 were still more pointed:

> The particular evil which impelled Lillian Hellman to choose *Candide* and present it to me as the basis for a musical stage work was . . . McCarthyism. . . . This was a period in the early '50s of our own century, exactly 200 years after the Lisbon affair, when everything that America stood for seemed to be on the verge of being ground under the heel of that Junior Senator from Wisconsin, Joseph McCarthy. . . . That was the time of the Hollywood Blacklist—television censorship, lost jobs, suicides, expatriation and the denial of passports to anyone even *suspected* of having once known a *suspected* Communist.
>
> I can vouch for this. I was denied a passport by my own government. By the way, so was Voltaire denied a passport by his. His answer was satire, ridicule, and through laughter to provoke in his reader self-recognition and, of course, self-justification—Who me? Not me!—which produces discussion, makes debate, and debate is, after all the cornerstone of democracy.[6]

The energetic and witty Overture, which gives a preview of the opera's principle themes, was an immediate success, and it has become a staple of twentieth-century American orchestral music. The choral writing is always idiomatic, but at every turn, Bernstein finds unexpected harmonies that enrich the meaning of the text and enhance the developing drama. Of especial note is the singularly effective chorus "Universal Good" (which begins with the strophe "Life is neither good nor bad./Life is life, and all we know./Good and bad and joy and woe/Are woven fine, are woven fine."). The music is of such richness, nobility, and eloquence that it might well find a place in a church service of any denomination.

The "brave-new-world optimism" that Bernstein notes is apparent in the rather stupid reasoning behind Dr. Pangloss's circumlocution with his pupils, "Best of All Possible Worlds." This simple-minded naïveté continues in the lyrical duet of Candide and Cunegonde, "Oh Happy We." Candide's plans soon take a sour turn. Cunegonde, who has been abducted during Mass and taken to perform sexual services for a wealthy Jew and a Roman Catholic clergyman, sings the remarkable "Glitter and Be Gay." She begins with a lamentation over her lost virtue, but quickly focuses on the material advantages of her liaisons: champagne, an expensive wardrobe, pearls and ruby rings, bracelets, diamonds, sapphires, gold earrings, and diamond necklaces. The aria, a coloratura showpiece modeled after the "Bell Song" in Leo Delibes's opera *Lakmé,* concludes with the sardonic couplet: "Observe how bravely I conceal the dreadful, dreadful shame I feel."

In many ways, *Candide* is Bernstein's theatrical masterpiece: The scenario is strong, the music effective, and the dramatic message convincing. With these elements securely in place, the score lends itself to adaptations for smaller or larger ensembles, longer or shorter performances, as well as intimate or grandiose productions. In *Candide,* Bernstein was ethically motivated, and he delivered a hard-hitting commentary on American society to match the best efforts of Brecht and Weill during their Berlin years.

Even before the premiere of *Candide,* Bernstein had begun thinking about another lyric theater piece, one based on *Romeo and Juliet,* but updated with characters and situations that would appeal to an American audience. The concept began with Jerome Robbins, who created the choreography. Bernstein had worked with him earlier on the 1944 score of *Fancy Free,* which was later expanded as *On the Town.* When Robbins first contacted Bernstein about the idea in January of 1949, the scenario of *West Side Story* centered on conflicts between Jews and Christians on New York's East Side. Eventually, the religious conflict was replaced by gang wars—which actually parallels Shakespeare's clan feuds more closely. A newspaper headline about strife between Mexicans and home-town boys in inner-city Los Angeles prompted the change of focus. As a New Yorker, Bernstein quickly made the association with life in the city he loved best of any in the world, and about which he had written so much music.

> In New York there were Puerto Rican gangs, and at the time papers were filled with stories about juvenile delinquents and their violent crimes. "Suddenly it all springs to life," Bernstein recalls in his diary. . . . "I hear rhythms and pulses, and—most of all—I can sort of feel the form."[7]

As Arthur Laurents solidified the scenario, other details fell into place. Stephen Sondheim was recruited to write the lyrics. Harold Prince took charge of the production. Oliver Smith, well versed in Broadway techniques after having made the decorations for *Brigadoon* (1947), *Paint Your Wagon* (1951), and *My Fair Lady* (1956), and equally skillful in operatic scenery from his work with the Metropolitan Opera, took charge of the stage design. Irene Sharaff invented costumes that enhanced characterization. Jean Rosenthal commented on the dramatic action through her subtle use of lighting, either to clarify or erase color and form. The music was by Lenny, but Oscar Hammerstein II gave the crucial advice to move "One Hand, One Heart" to a later point in the show. Originally, it came too early and did not achieve its full impact. This modification had the happy consequence of an extra number, "Tonight," which took its place.

In *West Side Story,* the feuding families of Montague and Capulet became rival New-York-City gangs, the Jets and the Sharks—the later being the Puerto-Rican gang. Carol Lawrence created the role of Maria (= Juliet), and Larry Kert was Tony (= Romeo). The success of *West Side Story* on Broadway was modest but certain: Opening in New York's Winter Garden Theatre on 26 September 1957, it closed on 27 June 1959 after 734 performances.[8] A greater triumph for Bernstein was its movie version, which won the Oscar for Best Picture and ten additional Academy Awards in 1961. These accolades must have been particularly sweet for Bernstein, since his experience of 1954 with the score of *On the Waterfront* was a bitter one indeed.[9]

The score is eclectic. Elements of *verismo* are there, to be sure; nevertheless, the mixture and balance of dramatic elements is more in keeping with the Wagnerian conception of the *Gesamtkunstwerk* than the bare-bones, one-act, low-budget, Italian operas of the 1890s. Contemporary Jazz is there too, especially in the number "Cool," which represents a style that was becoming increasingly popular among performers like Stan Getz, Miles Davis, and Dave Brubeck. Bernstein's title is telling, since this was, in fact, "cool jazz." Most cool jazz is at a medium tempo, is tuneful—almost relaxing—with nothing really fast or nervous. Languid counterpoints of two or three instruments, sometimes within small chamber ensembles like quartets, but often as large as octets, were typical.[10] The sound was acceptable to white listeners who would have been interested in hearing *West Side Story* on Broadway. There is, too, a good dose of old-fashioned New York vaudeville in the number "Gee, Officer Krupke," but Bernstein ultimately returns to his homeland in Maria's "I Have a Love," which recalls Brünnhilde's closing soliloquy in Wagner's *Die Götterdämmerung.*

Bernstein's subsequent dramatic works were disappointments: The plan, in 1964, to work on *The Skin of Our Teeth* with Betty Comden and Adolph Green came to nothing, and the same happened with the travesty of Brecht's *Exception to the Rule,* which, in its incarnation as a musical, was to have opened in September of 1965, with the title *A Pray by Blecht.* The theatrical works that did reach completion, *Mass* (1971), *1600 Pennsylvania Avenue* (1976), and *A Quiet Place* (1983; sequel to *Trouble in Tahiti*) were deplored by critics and public. In most cases, the music is ingenious and skillfully written, but dramatic content is vapid and—in the instance of *A Quiet Place*—downright revolting. Neurotic characters overburdened with sexual preoccupations and guilt provide little for amusement or edification.

Though *Candide* and *West Side Story* will likely prove to be Bernstein's only enduring scores for the lyric theater, he nevertheless produced a considerable number of very attractive and important works in other media. Among these, special note should be made of the *Serenade after Plato's "Symposium"* for solo violin, string orchestra, harp, and percussion. Commissioned by the Koussevitzky Music Foundation, *Serenade* had its premiere on 12 September 1954 at the Teatro la Fenice in Venice with Isaac Stern as soloist.[11]

Bernstein indicated that the five movements represent various speakers presenting their thoughts on the topic of love at a banquet; consequently, each speaker's argument—and, correspondingly, each movement—evolves in response to ideas advanced previously. The speakers are as follows: (1) Phædrus and Pausanias (Lento, Allegro); (2) Aristophanes (Allegretto); (3) Eryximachus (Presto); (4) Agathon (Adagio); (5) Socrates and Alcibiades (Molto tenuto, Allegro molto vivace). The most clearly connected movements are the last two, the second of which contains a varied reprise of the middle section of Agathon's deeply moving Adagio. The percussion section, which includes snare drum, tenor and bass drums, triangle, suspended cymbal, xylophone, Glockenspiel, chimes, Chinese blocks, and tambourine, requires five players. Its most effective use is in the final movement, where Alcibiades arrives with a drunken bunch of party goers, thereby provoking the concluding Allegro.

The 1965 score of the *Chichester Psalms* is frequently performed. At the request of the Very Reverend Walter Hussey, then Dean of Chichester Cathedral, Bernstein set the Hebrew texts of six different Psalms—some in part, others in full—for the annual combined choir festivals involving the cathedrals of Chichester, Winchester, and Salisbury.[12] In its general outlines, the score of the *Chichester Psalms* is symphonic, and Bernstein must have had Stravinsky's *Symphony of Psalms* in mind when he mapped out the plan for the piece. Bernstein calls for strings, three trumpets, three trombones, two harps, and a sizable battery of percussion. The introduction states majestically what will become a *cantus firmus* at later points. This is followed by an energetic setting of the complete text of Psalm 100. In keeping with symphonic traditions, there follows a relaxed second movement—here based on Psalm 23 and using boy soprano who is later imitated in canon by the choir. Verses 1 through 4 of Psalm 2 provide the text for the highly rhythmic scherzo: "Why do the nations so furiously rage together?" The "fourth" symphonic movement, the complete text of Psalm 131, is more relaxed than the typical finale, and it is rounded off with a varied restatement of the introductory *cantus firmus*, which leads to a unison "Amen" with a solo trumpet playing the *cantus firmus*.

Bernstein's fondness for vocal music is reflected in his song cycles. The songs of *I Hate Music* (1943) were originally intended for children's voices, but Jenny Tourel made them fair game for adults by performing the set on 25 August 1943. *La bonne cuisine* (1947) was written specifically for the French-speaking Tourel, and Bernstein took the texts from a French cookbook. (The idea is similar to certain works of *Les Six*—Milhaud's *Catalogue de fleurs*, for example.) There is, as well, a nod in the direction of Gabriel Fauré's song cycle *La bonne chanson* (1894).

Bernstein's last song cycle, *Arias and Barcarolles*, was composed in 1988. The curious title has a story: At the invitation of Dwight D. Eisenhower, supreme commander of the Allied forces during World War II and president of the United States from 1953 until 1961, Bernstein performed a piano recital at the White House in 1960. The repertoire included Mozart and Gershwin. After the program, the president commented to Bernstein that he liked the Gershwin—music with a good tune, "not all of them arias and barcarolles."

The *Arias and Barcarolles* are scored for mezzo-soprano and baritone with the accompaniment of four-hand piano (an orchestral version by Bright Sheng was approved by Bernstein). The texts of the seven songs are by various authors: five by the composer; one by his mother, Jennie Bernstein; and one, in Yiddish, by Yankev Yitskhok Segal. The songs reflect upon marriage. The music is sometimes ironic, sometimes serious, sometimes sincere and moving. Strongly traditional and tonal, the cycle is nevertheless flavored with dashes of Serialism, allusions to *klezmer* fiddle playing, scat singing, rhythmic elements derived from Jazz, passages written with unspecified rhythms, and quotations from Wagner's *Tristan und Isolde* (in the fourth song, "The Love of My Life"). The multifaceted musical idiom reflects accurately the composer's ambivalence toward marriage generally and his own specifically. The final movement, "Nachspiel: In memoriam," is a slow waltz with the two vocalists humming obbligato lines. The wordless lines of this two-and-a-half-minute piece are some of Bernstein's most touching music.

Bernstein's eclectic musical idiom is admired by some and scorned by as many others. Writing during the heyday of musical experimentation, Bernstein's insistence on tonality was interpreted by some as a lack of imagination, but Paul Myers, who, as a representative of Columbia Records, worked personally with the composer between 1962 and 1980, saw it as a prophetic sign of post-Modernism.[13]

The New Patronage: Campus Composers

We noted in Chapter 15 that music departments began springing up in American colleges and universities during the last quarter of the nineteenth century. These fledgling programs had come to maturity by the mid twentieth century, and many composers since about the 1930s have spent the majority of their careers in an academic context. The most influential and prolific among these were Howard Hanson (1896–1981), Peter Mennin (1923–1983), Vincent Persichetti (1915–1987), Walter Piston (1894–1976), Gunther Schuller (b. 1925), William Schuman (1910–1992), and Roger Sessions (1896–1985). Students from their studios went on to become leaders on the American musical scene for the second half of the century and beyond.

Hanson's family emigrated from Sweden, and Hanson's childhood home, Wahoo, Nebraska, had a large population of Scandinavians. Throughout his life, he maintained a nostalgic pride in his ancestry. His First Symphony (1922), entitled *Nordic*, was a great success, and when he conducted it in Rochester, New York, in 1924, George Eastman was so impressed that he invited Hanson to become director of the Eastman School of Music. Only twenty-eight at the time, Hanson proceeded to turn the school into an internationally renowned institution. The prolific Hanson wrote in all genres, including opera and ballet, and for all media, including band.

Generally conservative and clearly tonal, Hanson's scores are skillfully written and beautifully orchestrated. Occasionally, they contain experimental passages. Of his seven symphonies, which are probably his most important works, the Second Symphony, entitled the *Romantic* (1930), is the most frequently performed. His text, *Harmonic Materials of Modern Music*, shows his knowledge of modern techniques, even though he rarely used them in his own works.[14]

Mennin was one of Hanson's most gifted and prolific students. He completed his doctorate at Eastman in 1947. With three symphonies and performances by the New York Philharmonic under Bernstein's direction already to his credit, he joined the composition faculty of the Juilliard School, where he taught until 1958.[15] He then resigned to become the director of the Peabody Conservatory, only to return to Juilliard in 1962 as president. He served in that capacity until his death, all the while composing in abundance. His output is almost entirely orchestral, and his nine symphonies and various concertos are his major works. He also composed two string quartets. Mennin's music tends toward dissonant counterpoint predicated on motivic development within clearly articulated forms.

From his childhood, Persichetti had a voracious musical appetite.[16] He played piano, organ, double bass, and tuba, and he studied theory and composition while still a boy. After completing his Bachelor's degree in 1936, he joined the faculty of Combs Conservatory. At Curtis Institute, Persichetti studied conducting with Fritz Reiner, and completed the diploma requirements in 1938. A brief period of study with Roy Harris preceded Persichetti's appointment to the Philadelphia Conservatory in 1941. He resigned in 1947, to join the faculty of the Juilliard School, where he became chair of the composition department in 1963. He wrote a theory text entitled *Twentieth-Century Harmony: Creative Aspects and Practice*.[17]

Persichetti's teaching and administration did not prevent him from composing, and his vast output includes nine symphonies; twelve piano sonatas; a series of fourteen serenades for various instrumentations; twenty-four pieces entitled Parable, also for various solo instruments or ensembles; a huge amount of chamber music, including four string quartets; choral music including settings of the Mass (1961), *Stabat Mater,* and *Te Deum* (both 1963). His collection of *Hymns and Responses for the Church Year* (1955) is an anthology of aphoristic service music that is immensely useful, and written in an attractive contemporary style. These pieces are typical of Persichetti's elegant linear construction, restrained but powerful expression, and extended tonal idiom. His music contains considerable dissonance, polytonality, and polymeters, but these are invariably used in reference to a single tonic key and rhythmic fabric.

Walter Piston could easily have been a mechanical engineer or an architect.[18] After graduation from Boston's Mechanic Arts High School in 1912, he chose to study painting and architectural drawing at the Massachusetts Normal Art School rather than attend New England Conservatory. (This was a financial consideration.) His skill at drafting was not wasted, though, and throughout his career, he produced his own fair copy scores as well as line drawings for use in the textbooks he wrote. Upon completion of his degree program in 1916, he won a spot in the Navy Band playing saxophone. Piston played violin and piano, but he picked up a sax and learned to play it in a short time. While in the band, he mastered other instruments in his spare time. In 1920, he was accepted to Harvard, where he studied with Archibald T. Davison. A stellar student, he won the John K. Paine Fellowship, which funded his studies in France (1924–1926) with Dukas, Boulanger, and Georges Enesco.

Piston made his debut as a published composer with the Three Pieces (1925) for flute, clarinet, and bassoon. They reveal his distinctive style, featuring counterpoint and careful attention to the peculiar requirements of each instrument.

Piston's connections with Boulanger paid dividends upon his return to the United States in 1927. By then, Koussevitzky had been the director of the Boston Symphony for three years. He helped Piston to establish his reputation by commissioning the *Symphonic Piece* (1927). Koussevitzky turned the BSO over to the young composer for the premiere in 1928. For the remainder of his tenure with the BSO, Koussevitzky championed Piston's works, and Piston received Koussevitzky Foundation grants even after the maestro's death.

Many consider Piston's first great work to be his three-movement Sonata (1930) for flute and piano, a score revealing careful attention to formal details in its sonata, song, and sonata-rondo movements respectively.

Koussevitzky asked Piston for another work for the 1933 season of the BSO. This was the Concerto for Orchestra. Again, Koussevitzky turned the BSO over to Piston; however, Koussevitzky himself conducted the piece on many occasions. In its formal plan, Baroque elements are apparent, especially in the ritornello structure of the first movement. Piston's interest in Baroque forms and textures is also apparent in his Prelude and Fugue (1934) for orchestra, composed for the League of Composers. The piece proved to be problematic. Bruno Walter, who was scheduled to conduct the premiere, refused to perform it. The first performance had to wait for another two years, when it was finally given by the Cleveland Orchestra.

Piston wrote a tremendous amount of chamber music. Important early works include the First and Second String Quartets (1933, '35) and his Piano Trio (1935).

Piston's use of conventional genres and media should not be interpreted as a sign of an unadventurous mind; on the contrary, he was one of the first composers to write specifically for radio, and his Concertino for Piano and Chamber Orchestra (prem. 20 June 1937) was heard for the first time, not in a concert hall, but on the airwaves. Equally progressive is his Prelude and Allegro (1943) for organ and strings, which was not only intended for radio broadcast (by E. Power Biggs), but also designed with two segments, each four and one-half minutes long, so as to comply with 78 RPM format. Unfortunately, the Allegro was a bit too long; hence, the Prelude and several variations are on one side, and the break (bad) comes halfway through the Allegro. Piston was fascinated by the works of Stravinsky, Hindemith, and Schoenberg, and he first used serial techniques in his *Chromatic Study on the Name of Bach* (1940) for organ.

In the years after World War II, Piston reached his stride. His finest works include the *Divertimento for Nine Instruments* (1946), an interesting synthesis of Baroque ritornello forms, changing meters, Romantic lyricism, and extended tonality, scored for woodwinds and strings. Piston's Sixth Symphony (1955), commissioned by the BSO to celebrate their seventy-fifth season, is dedicated to the memory of Serge and Natalie Koussevitzky. In this piece, we can already detect a certain nostalgia. These elegiac sentiments are most prominent in the third movement, Adagio sereno.

In his late works, Piston's preferred medium was the concerto. His Variations (1966) for 'cello and orchestra , dedicated to Rostropovich and premiered by him with Rozhdestvensky, is a highly effective work. The Concerto (1971) for flute and orchestra was written for Doriot Anthony Dwyer and the BSO. This work required revision. Dwyer herself prevailed upon Piston to make improvements, especially in the Finale. She advised Piston on various details, especially in the cadenza of the third movement. Piston's last concerto was more of a sinfonia concertante: a Concerto for string quartet and orchestra, which occupied him from 1968 until 1976. At the time of its composition, his wife, Kathryn, was dying. Piston himself was elderly and infirm. The work reveals Romantic elements, to be sure, but it is not valedictory in any sense. It is, as he might have said, "the same old Piston."

During Piston's long teaching career at Harvard, he wrote texts on harmony, counterpoint, and orchestration that are still widely used.[19] His impact on contemporary American music will continue as long as these texts are in use. In addition, several of Piston's students have gone on to become leading figures in the present day. Among these, Elliott Carter (b. 1908), Daniel Pinkham (b. 1923), and John Harbison (b. 1938) merit attention.

At the age of sixteen, Carter befriended Ives, whose influence is apparent in the younger man's life and works.[20] As a student at Harvard, Carter majored in literature—not music. He did not devote his attention to music until 1930, when he began studying harmony and counterpoint with Piston and orchestration with Edward Burlingame Hill. Carter, following in Piston's footsteps, went to Paris to work with Boulanger from 1932 to 1935, while simultaneously studying Latin, Greek, and mathematics.

Carter's characteristic scores take their point of departure from Ives's Second String Quartet, insofar as he consciously associates the musical strands of an ensemble with the individuals—rather than the instruments—performing those strands. This conception is clear in Carter's First String Quartet (1951) as well as the Second (1959), which is scored "for four individuals." Sometimes, as in his Third String Quartet (1971), he arranges his players into teams: in this case, two duos. This conversational approach has predisposed Carter to chamber music. His

Wind Quintet (1948) and Brass Quintet (1974) are outstanding examples of the genres, and the latter, in particular, is widely played.

The notion of ensembles constituted from subcommittees, so to speak, is apparent in Carter's larger scores, such as his Triple Duo (1983) for flute, clarinet, piano, percussion, violin, and 'cello; the Double Concerto (1961) for piano, harpsichord, and two chamber orchestras; and his Symphony (1977) for three orchestras.

Carter's manner of delineating strands results in densely complex textures, often involving metric modulation. This technique involves strict control of durations; however, in progressing from one measure to the next, the elements chosen for definition of pulse are not simple proportions, such as 1=1, 2=1, 1=2, or the like. Instead, Carter establishes some new pulse by adding fractional and integral values: The last third of an eight-note triplet added to a quarter note in one measure, for example, may be equated with the duration of the half note in the following measure.

For most of his career, Carter has devoted his time to composition; however, he has periodically held academic posts. These were at St. John's College, Maryland, Peabody Conservatory, Columbia University, Queens College, Yale University, and the Juilliard School.

Pinkham attended Phillips Academy, where the music program was largely the work of Carl Pfatteicher, a musicologist and organist who was enthusiastic about early music.[21] Pfatteicher transmitted his zeal for this repertoire to the young Pinkham, who became increasingly committed to early music after hearing the Trapp family perform on viola da gamba, harpsichord, and recorders. Purchase of *The Interpretation of Seventeenth- and Eighteenth-Century Music* by Arnold Dolmetsch gave further impetus.[22]

In 1940, Pinkham matriculated as a music major at Harvard, where he studied with A. Tillman Merritt, Archibald T. Davison, Copland, and Piston. With Bachelor's and Master's degrees in hand in 1944, he decided to study with Boulanger at the Longy School. In 1947, he worked with Honegger and Samuel Barber at Tanglewood.

Pinkham's academic training was balanced with practical musicianship, and he studied harpsichord with Wanda Landowska and her pupil Putnam Aldrich, and organ with E. Power Biggs. 1948 marked the beginning of Pinkham's ten-year career in a duo with Robert Brink as violinist. Together they toured the United States, Canada, and Europe, playing both early and contemporary works. Practical experience also came with his work from 1958 until 2000 at King's Chapel, Boston, and beginning in 1959, at New England Conservatory (NEC).

When Gunther Schuller became director of NEC in 1967, Pinkham approached him with the idea of a Department of Early Music Performance. The program was so successful that it became the model for others across the nation.

In 1970, Pinkham prepared a performance of Richard Felciano's (b. 1930) *Pentecost Sunday* for organ, tape, and men's voices. Intrigued by the potential of electronic sounds, Pinkham began writing for intermedia ensembles. His anthem

Daniel Pinkham

"In the Beginning of Creation" (1970), for mixed chorus and tape is now standard repertoire, even among volunteer church choirs. Some of his instrumental works, like the organ pieces "Toccatas for the Vault of Heaven" (1971) and "When the Morning Stars Sang Together" (1972), as well as *Nebulæ* (1975) for organ and band, also use intermedia; nevertheless, the fascination with electronic sounds was short-lived, and by the end of the decade, Pinkham had returned to acoustic instruments, albeit with a new concept of sonority.

Pinkham's experiences with intermedia run roughly parallel with his thoughts about serial techniques. Having looked into Serialism, he arrived at a "very controlled kind of dissonant counterpoint—controlled from a harmonic standpoint." He suggests that he "would never have quite arrived at my present style had I not gone through twelve-tone techniques. It opened up many new possibilities for tonal and intervallic relationships."

Throughout Pinkham's œuvre, novel sonorities, adventurous harmonies, and counterpoint all seem to be regarded in a generally suave and subtle manner, inspired by the late works of Fauré, whose music he clearly admires.

Generally speaking, Pinkham has been partial to vocal music and wind instruments—perhaps owing to his being an organist. In his vocal works, scriptural texts are predominant, but secular literature, generally of a reflective character, is well represented too. Whether scriptural or secular, all of his texted pieces are basically dramatic, and he affirms the importance of communicating to the listener a basic "message." Pinkham thinks of every vocal piece as a drama, and, accepting the fact that even the best singers cannot make every word intelligible, he chooses texts that have an immediate impact. He avoids poetry heavily laden with allusions and complex metaphors.

Discussions of his works up to the mid 1980s are already available, but some of the recent compositions merit consideration here.[23]

Pinkham's Fourth Symphony (1990) for double winds (with three trumpets), tympani, percussion, celesta, harp, and strings was commissioned by the National Gallery of Art's fiftieth anniversary. Each of its three movements is a miniature tone poem on a word: "purling," "pining," and "prancing." Purling describes energetic motions taking place during a short duration and in a limited space—like leaves eddying in a swirl, or whitewater rapids. The movement is predicated upon closely related motifs of four or five notes subjected to permutations and transformations in rhythm and instrumentation. The second movement is a lyrical essay, full of pathos, but with rhythmic and intervallic elements closely related to the jerky motifs of the preceding movement. The Finale is the most aggressive movement of the three, but it too is linked with the previous two by common thematic and rhythmic elements. Dances, especially the *furiant* (alternating 3/4 and 3/8 time) and the waltz, form the substance of the movement.

The four-movement String Quartet (1990) shares many techniques with the Fourth Symphony. The Quartet's first movement relies on motifs in permutations and diverse combinations. The scherzo is a traditional A-B-A form, but the reprise is newly composed and much condensed. The third movement commences with biting dissonances and convulsive rhythms that quickly give way to an elegiac cantilena that is, at first, accompanied in homophonic texture.[24] Soon, the cantilena becomes the basis of a dialogue between first violin and 'cello with the remaining voices looking on and commenting in despair. The Finale, Allegro vivace (like the Finale of the Fourth Symphony) takes a look at triple meter alternately from relaxed and energetic points of view. Here, the complexity is enhanced by special effects: *glissando, sul ponticello,* and *pizzicato.*

The *Advent Cantata* (1991) sets the seven Great Antiphons for the Magnificat for the seven days from December 17 through December 23. The writing for chorus, which is largely homophonic, and for the accompanying wind quintet and harp, reflects late-century trends toward simplification and austerity as well as the composer's lifelong interest in early music. The *Cantata* forms an ideal companion piece to his most frequently performed composition, the *Christmas Cantata* (1957) for mixed chorus, brass quartet, and organ.

During the past decade, Pinkham has written many pieces for a single instrument with organ accompaniment, including English horn, clarinet, bassoon, 'cello, horn, trombone, and tuba. This same economy of resources is apparent in his *Missa domestica* (1993) for solo treble voice, flute, and guitar. The setting includes the Kyrie, Sanctus and Benedictus, and Agnus Dei of the traditional Catholic Mass. His String Trio (1998) for violin, viola, and 'cello is a welcome addition to the relatively sparse repertoire for that ensemble.

Though himself a keyboardist, Pinkham wrote surprisingly little music for solo piano until recent years. The turning point came when the Longy School of Music, Cambridge, Massachusetts, commissioned Pinkham to write a work in celebration of Victor Rosenbaum's ten years as Director. Accordingly, Pinkham wrote six Preludes (1995) for piano, which were premiered by Sally Pinkas on 8 September of that year. In 1997, Pinkham wrote six more preludes that he dedicated to her. Though written in two phases, the twelve pieces are clearly intended as a continuous set, and Pinkas gave the first performance of them as such on 30 January 1997. The pieces are remarkably diverse in character, ranging from brief but virtuosic showpieces like the opening Agitato, through dancelike movements such as the Scherzo (No. 4) and the Allegretto ballando (No. 11). In ordering the pieces, Pinkham not only moves effectively from one mood to another, but he also changes-up textures in successive pieces. The Cantabile e legato ma non troppo flessibile (No. 5) and the concluding Con moto are impressive contrapuntal studies using imitative counterpoint replete with augmentations and other manipulations of their subjects.

By good fortune, Pinkas's husband, Evan Hirsch, is also a pianist. In rapid succession, Pinkham composed for them *Quarries* and *Weather Reports* (both 1999) for piano four-hands. *Shards* (2000), a set of six pieces for solo piano, is dedicated to Hirsch, who gave its first performance. In this last set, we find the same judicious variations of affection and texture in its successive pieces. Con moto (No. 2) is a fugue based on the B-A-C-H motif (unintentionally, according to the composer). Pinkham's career-long admiration for the delicate harmonies and elegant melodic lines of Fauré's music is especially clear in the Allegretto (No. 5). Pinkham himself made the arrangement of *Shards* for wind ensemble (2000).

All of Pinkham's texted works—whether solo songs or choral pieces—are dramatic, but his most recent project has been a *de facto* opera: *The Cask of Amontillado* (2001). The libretto, written by the composer, is based on Edgar Allan Poe's classic tale by the same title. This lyric theater piece is tremendously accessible, not only on account of its powerful scenario, but equally for its modest scoring for two vocalists, small chorus, and an instrumental ensemble of six.

Pinkham, like Piston, has impeccable calligraphy, and many of his works are published duplicates of his manuscripts. Pinkham is a practical composer who has never written "concept music." His scores are all viable in performance, and he does not allow a single work to go into print until he has tested it in actual performance—what he calls the "Betty Crocker testing kitchen."

A native of New Jersey, John Harbison played piano and performed in a jazz band as a boy. He completed his undergraduate degree at Harvard in 1960. There, he studied with Piston. Like his mentor, he received the Paine Award, which enabled him to study in Berlin with Boris Blacher. Upon returning to the United States, he studied privately with Roger Sessions and completed a Master's degree at Princeton in 1963. He taught at Massachusetts Institute of Technology from 1969 until 1982, and has held composer-in-residence posts with the Pittsburgh Symphony (1982–1984) and the Los Angeles Philharmonic (1985–1988), as well as appointments at Tanglewood, Marlboro, and Santa Fe. As a conductor, he has worked with instrumental and vocal ensembles in both contemporary and historical repertoire. To date, he has written three string quartets, an equal number of symphonies, several operas and ballets, chamber music, and song cycles. His opera *The Great Gatsby* (1999), commissioned by the Metropolitan Opera, was greeted with enthusiasm.

Harbison's music is neoclassical in its formal orientation and texture. In his Concerto for oboe, clarinet, and orchestra, for example, he puts an anachronistic *concertino* within the context of a concerto grosso while using contemporary harmonies and rhythms.

The Juilliard School of Music has played a crucial role in the formation of American musical culture. Its reorganization during the mid century was largely the vision of William Schuman, a native of New York, who performed in a group called "Billy Schuman and His Alamo Society Orchestra" during the '20s. He was also its administrator, responsible for bookings, fees, and other practical matters. When he entered New York University in 1928, it was as a business major; however, he changed majors in 1930 after hearing Toscanini conduct the New York Philharmonic at Carnegie Hall.[25]

Schuman quickly acquired the necessary musical skills through studies with Max Persin, Charles Haubiel, and Bernard Wagenaar. By 1935, he earned his B. Mus. Ed. from Columbia University; two years later, he had completed his M. Mus. there as well. Studies from 1936 until 1938 with Roy Harris (1898–1979) completed his schooling.

He wrote prolifically while teaching at Sarah Lawrence College from 1935 to 1945, but most of his early works were withdrawn or heavily revised. With his Second Symphony (1937), he found his characteristic voice, and became a key player in the contemporary-music scene. Copland admired the piece and called it to the attention of Koussevitzky, who performed it with the Boston Symphony in February 1939. Leonard Bernstein—who would graduate from Harvard that spring— was also impressed; thus the foundation was set for what later became a vibrant professional relationship between Schuman and Bernstein.

Koussevitzky continued to foster Schuman's career, and in 1939, he led the BSO in Schuman's just-completed *American Festival Overture*. Two years later, he gave a critically acclaimed performance of Schuman's Third Symphony (1941). In another two years, he conducted the premiere of Schuman's Symphony for Strings—his Fifth Symphony—which was a Koussevitzky Foundation commission.

In 1945, Schuman was invited to become president of what is now the Juilliard School: It was Schuman who negotiated the merger of the Juilliard Graduate School and the Institute of Musical Art. Schuman revised the curriculum, hired new faculty, and expanded the opportunities for performance.

Despite his administrative obligations, Schuman's composing continued unabated. The Concerto (1959) for violin and orchestra, written for Samuel Dushkin, caused unprecedented problems. In this unique case, Schuman took a dozen years to produce the definitive score. In the meantime, he had written the Sixth Symphony (1948), a band piece entitled *George Washington Bridge*, the Fourth String Quartet (both 1950), the *New England Triptych* (1956), and more.

Schuman benefited from Koussevitzky's favor even after the conductor's death: In 1960, he completed his Seventh Symphony as a Koussevitzky Foundation commission, celebrating the seventy-fifth anniversary of the BSO. In the following year, Schuman was elected president of the Lincoln Center for the Performing Arts, and he assumed the position in January of 1962.

At this point, Bernstein stepped into Koussevitzky's shoes: The first instance was in the commissioning of the Eighth Symphony to celebrate the opening of the new center. Bernstein led the premiere of this three-movement work in the fall of 1962. The piece won a warm reception. Bernstein helped Schuman win another triumph eight years later with his rendition of *In Praise of Shahn: Canticle for Orchestra*, which was written in memory of the artist Ben Shahn. The relationship between the two men remained fruitful throughout their careers, and Schuman expressed his esteem for Bernstein when, for the conductor's seventieth birthday, he composed *Let's Hear It for Lenny*, a set of orchestral variations on "New York, New York."

Schuman's late works include the three-movement Ninth Symphony (1968), written in memory of 335 Italians massacred in the vicinity of the Ardeatine Caves near Rome in 1944, by German soldiers. In 1968, incidentally, Schuman relinquished his position as president of Lincoln Center. In 1973, he completed his five-movement *Concerto on Old English Rounds*, which includes women's chorus. His last major work was that of the Tenth Symphony (1975), commissioned by the National Symphony Orchestra to celebrate the Bicentennial.

Gunther Schuller's academic career is a wonderful irony: He quit high school, never got a diploma, and never went to college. His background was more like an apprenticeship, and it began when he became first hornist in the Cincinnati Symphony in 1943. At the end of his second year there, he performed his own Concerto for horn and orchestra with Eugene Goosens conducting.[26]

The lack of academic pedigrees notwithstanding, Schuller's education was vast. His father was a professional violinist with the New York Philharmonic; hence, music was always a part of Gunther's life. From 1932 until 1937, he was sent to school in Germany. (Language was not an issue since German was spoken in his home.) While he was in Europe, Schuller also learned French.

Schuller's musical tastes are as diverse as his linguistic skills, and his enthusiasm for Jazz is well known. In the summer of 1945, Schuller met Eduard Steuermann and Rudolf Kolisch, colleagues of Schoenberg, and that began Schuller's interest in twelve-tone music. He tried the techniques himself in his *Symphonic Study* (1948).

Schuller left Cincinnati to join the Metropolitan Opera Orchestra in the fall of 1945, and he held his post as a hornist in that orchestra until 1959. During the summers, he played horn in pit orchestras for Broadway productions. In his own compositions, Schuller began synthesizing diverse musical materials to devise what he eventually dubbed Third Stream: a style that was somewhere between Jazz and classical music. In 1954, his *Dramatic Overture* (1951) was premiered at the Darmstadt Festival. The late '50s were productive years, and his Concertino (1959) for jazz quartet and orchestra was the major essay in Third Stream up to that point.

In 1961, Schuller completed his *Music for Brass Quintet*, one of the most important pieces for that medium to date. In that year, he was also featured—along with Ligeti and Berio—at the Donaueschingen Festival.

Schuller took music education seriously, and during his career he wrote books on Jazz, conducting, and other topics.[27] He also composed educational scores, such as his *Journey into Jazz* (1962), for narrator, alto and tenor sax, trumpet, drums, and bass with orchestra. It works in much the same way as Britten's *Young Person's Guide to the Orchestra.*

Education was an important concern during Schuller's tenure at Tanglewood, from 1963 until 1983. A brief stint at Yale University was the prelude to his major academic post as president of New England Conservatory from 1967 until 1977. At Tanglewood and NEC, Schuller conducted a wide variety of repertoire. By this time, his interests had expanded to include American Ragtime, and he eventually made his own performing version of Scott Joplin's opera *Treemonisha.*

During his final year at NEC, Schuller composed three concertos: one for violin, one for horn, and a concerto for orchestra. This medium became his focus during the next decade, during which he completed the concertos for contrabassoon (1978), trumpet (1979), piano (1981), saxophone (1983), bassoon, and viola (both 1985).

Roger Sessions spent fifty-seven years of his life teaching composition: "at Princeton University (for 33 years), at The Juilliard School (for 16 years), and at the University of California at Berkeley (for 8 years)."[28] In the years before his teaching career, he was no stranger to the halls of learning: In 1911, he matriculated at Harvard at the age of fourteen. He completed his Bachelor's degree in 1915. Studies with Horatio Parker at Yale followed, and in 1917, Sessions had a second Bachelor's degree. His training was capped with private lessons with Ernest Bloch, which began in 1920 and ran through about 1925. In 1921, Bloch went to Ohio to become the director of the Cleveland Institute, and Sessions followed him. Sessions taught theory, *solfège,* and music history, and he accompanied the chorus.

In 1925, Bloch and Sessions both left Cleveland; Bloch had been fired, and Sessions had gone in musical directions that Bloch found disappointing. From then until 1933, Sessions lived mainly in Europe, a situation that created difficulties for him professionally, since Europeans considered him an American, and Americans considered him a European.

The first difficulty arose with Copland, with whom Sessions was supposed to present the Copland-Sessions Concerts. In fact, a few programs were given during the years from 1928 to 1931, but Sessions was *in absentia* most of the time. Disturbing, too, was the fact that his Piano Sonata No. 1 (1930) was to have been given on the first program; it was not ready in time. Difficulties were worse in the case of his Concerto (1935) for violin and orchestra, which was written for Albert Spalding, Serge Koussevitzky, and the Boston Symphony Orchestra. Spalding disliked the piece; Sessions refused to make any modifications; and Koussevitzky refused from that moment to conduct any of Sessions's music. Perhaps this catastrophe was an omen: Slonimsky points out that though Sessions "is recognized as one of the most important composers of the century, . . . performances of his works are exasperatingly infrequent."[29]

We can be glad for Sessions's obdurate attitude: In fact, the Concerto is one of his finest works. Its four movements are in an intricate, dense, yet crisp contrapuntal style. Constructive principles such as rhythmic modulation, polytonality, and coordination of articulation *vis-à-vis* tempo impart a progressive, if not prophetic, quality to the score. Noteworthy too, is the distinctive orchestration without first or second violins, in order to give greater brilliance to the solo line. Like most of his music, it is fantastically difficult.

By the time he completed the Second Symphony in 1946, Sessions had already developed his own sort of twelve-tone style. This manner was not fully achieved until the Second String Quartet (1951), which may be considered his first fully twelve-tone score.

Sessions wrote seven more symphonies, an opera entitled *Montezuma* (1963), a Double Concerto (1971) for violin, 'cello, and orchestra, and a Concerto (1981) for orchestra, as well as many smaller pieces; however, his most enduring influence stems not from his music, but from his many gifted students, especially Milton Babbitt, Peter Maxwell Davies, David Diamond, Leon Kirchner, and Ellen Taaffe Zwilich.

Kirchner (b. 1919) grew up in Los Angeles and enjoyed the guidance of Ernst Toch and Schoenberg. When he completed his degree at the University of California at Berkeley, he went briefly to Europe. Returning to the United States, he worked briefly with Sessions in New York and then returned to Berkeley for further work with Toch and Sessions. Positions at San Francisco Conservatory, Yale, Juilliard, and Mills were a prelude to his appointment in 1961 as successor to Piston at Harvard. Holding the post until 1989, he taught many important young composers, including John Adams. Kirchner's three string quartets, especially the Third, are important works. In the Third String Quartet (1967), he included a part for electronic tape, which has since been transferred to CD format. The work was acclaimed a masterpiece and won the Pulitzer Prize; however, Kirchner, like Pinkham, soon became disenchanted with the restrictions of recorded sounds. Among his recent works, Kirchner's *Music for 'Cello and Orchestra* (1992) is exceptional. It was written for Yo-Yo Ma, who had been a student of Kirchner's at Harvard in the early '70s. The piece consists of four segments played without break and unified by recurring motifs. As in most of his works, he does not compose according to a theory. Modernist techniques appear as needed and disappear as soon as they have served their purpose. Certain passages are highly dissonant, but there is an equal portion of consonant writing; in fact, the Romantic elegance of certain passages of *Music for 'Cello and Orchestra* calls to mind the styles of Wagner and Strauss.

George Crumb's parents were both musicians, and he was born, on 24 October 1929, into a household where music was an essential commodity. (The day of his birth was Black Thursday, the day of the stock market crash that began the Great Depression.) The symphony orchestra of Charleston, West Virginia—Crumb's hometown—performed some of his earliest compositions while he was still in high school. These were *Poem* (1946) and *Gethsemane* (1947). He completed his undergraduate degree in 1950, then went on for a Master's at the University of

Illinois at Champaign-Urbana. A few lessons with Boris Blacher in Berlin on a Fulbright grant during the 1954–55 academic year were followed by completion of his doctoral studies at the University of Michigan at Ann Arbor, where his mentor was Ross Lee Finney (1906–1997). Finney studied with Boulanger, Berg, and Sessions, and Crumb recalls that Finney "stressed technique: he insisted on the need for constant rewriting, he emphasized the necessity for logical form and for the 'right' notes, and he expected a meticulous notation."[30] Crumb completed the degree in 1959 with his "unplayable" score of orchestral *Variazioni*, a theme with six variations and epilogue. The theme is a twelve-tone row, though the work as a whole is not serial. Crumb confesses to traces of Schoenberg, Berg, and Dallapiccola, but he neglects to mention Britten, whose Finale to the *Young Person's Guide to the Orchestra* works in similar fashion to Crumb's epilogue, insofar as it combines all of the entries while building to a *tutti* conclusion. George Crumb assumed his first significant academic post in 1959, at the University of Colorado at Boulder, where he taught class piano and composition until leaving for the University of Pennsylvania in 1965.[31]

Crumb arrived at his distinctive voice through the midwifery of David Burge, for whom he wrote the Five Pieces (1962) for piano when they were colleagues at the University of Colorado. Burge recalls that he thought Crumb's passages to be played *inside* the piano were "terrible," and that he found "the very idea . . . rather insulting." Tactfully, Burge kept these thoughts to himself. When he played the premiere soon afterwards, he was delighted that one of the listeners, Karlheinz Stockhausen, found them immensely interesting, "listened to them repeatedly," and noted "all of the things in the score that *he* wished *he* had done."[32]

In the formation of his style, Crumb has embraced historical influences. Bartók, Webern, Ives, Messiaen, and Berio are important, but he attributes the most profound influence to Debussy. Crumb's fantastic use of color and timbre certainly support his claim. Pop, Rock, and Jazz are part of his world, and he does not consider them pollutants of contemporary music. He acknowledges, as well, his cultural relativism, and is delighted to hear unfamiliar sounds in Asian, African, South American, and other non-Western repertoires. Electronic music fascinates him, and he considers Mario Davidovsky "the most elegant of all the electronic composers whose music I know."[33] In his own music, Crumb's forays into the electronic world are limited to amplification—of flute, 'cello, piano, or just about anything; nevertheless, his invented techniques for playing traditional acoustical instruments often produce what sounds like electronic music, but without the technological and logistical impediments of electronics. In this respect, his approach is like Ligeti's.

Crumb's extended techniques are not limited to instruments. He commonly asks vocalists to hiss, howl, shout, scream, whisper, vocalize on some phoneme, sing into a piano with dampers lifted, and so on. Similarly, he is not content to let instrumentalists be instrumentalists; he has his flutist sing while playing in the opening of *Vox balænæ* (voice of the whale; 1971), and throughout his

George Crumb

four-movement, Pulitzer Prize-winning *Echoes of Time and the River* (1967), instrumentalists sing or chant various texts.

In both of these pieces, music is complemented by drama. In *Vox balænæ*, the three players (fl, vc, pf) wear masks, and should be bathed in aquamarine lighting. *Echoes of Time and the River* is subtitled "Four Processionals for orchestra," and during the four movements of this suite, the players move onto, around, or off the stage in steps that are synchronized with the music. The sequence of movements is also significant, and the progress from "Frozen Time," through "Remembrance of Time," "Collapse of Time," and "Last Echoes of Time" exhibits musical processes that are suggested by their titles. The "remembrance" of time, for example, asks the listener to project back two thousand years, by quoting from the hymn tune "Were you there when they crucified my Lord?"

Symbolism pervades all of Crumb's music, but is especially apparent in *Black Angels* (1970), which is subtitled "Thirteen Images from the Dark Land." The piece, written during the frenzied years of the Vietnam War, is a parable exploring the fall from grace in the first movement, "Departure," spiritual emptiness in the second, "Absence," and redemption in the third, "Return." Numerology (often imperceptible without the score) informs the structure of the piece, and 7 and 13 affect the choice of intervals, durations, motivic patterns, and other details. Counting in German, French, Russian, Hungarian, Japanese, and Swahili constitutes part of the music.

The sonic resources of *Black Angels* are acoustical instruments—a conventional string quartet—amplified; however, extended techniques, such as stopping the strings with thimble-covered fingers, bowing on the wrong side of the strings, etc., produce quasi-electronic sounds. In addition to their violins, the quartet are required to play maracas, tam-tams, and goblets filled with varying amounts of water. References to tonal music include paraphrases of the *Dies iræ*, Schubert's "Death and the Maiden," and an original sarabande in a neotonal style. The trill is used as a motif to represent the fallen angel—this via Tartini's famous "Devil's Trill Sonata."

The score is dated "Friday 13 March 1970 (in tempore belli)." Is this inscription symbolic or actual? Does "in tempore belli" refer to Haydn's *Missa in tempore belli* (Mass in time of war)? The composer assures me that the "black" Angel refers only to the symbol in Mediæval iconography depicting Lucifer, and that his birth on "black" Thursday did not enter his mind at the time he formulated the title.

In general, Crumb's works tend to be for small, distinctively constituted ensembles. An exceptional work is his 1977 score entitled *Star-Child*, which uses Latin texts from the *Dies iræ*, a thirteenth-century contemplation of the massacre of the Innocents, and the vulgate version of John 23:36. The work is not intended to reflect any denominational theology; instead, Crumb intends it as an expression of hope and joy after struggle, a reflection of the transcendental nature of the spirit.

The colossal ensemble of *Star-Child* is managed in performance by four conductors. (Pierre Boulez was the principal conductor of the premiere.) Soprano, two children's choirs, speaking choir of male voices, and bell ringers are combined in this work with quadruple winds, six horns, seven trumpets, three trombones, tuba, eight percussionists, organ, and strings. In many portions of the piece, Crumb avoids coordination of the various subensembles, and in measured passages, irregular meters of five or eleven are generally preferred. Crumb has identified the "Music of the Spheres," a tranquil essay for strings only, as the germinal idea for the piece. This music reappears throughout the score as the backdrop for foreground events of a more dramatic nature, in a manner similar to Ives's "Unanswered Question."

As in so many of Crumb's scores, *Star-Child* is pervaded by symbolism: the seven trumpets of the apocalypse are rendered literally; the four horsemen of the apocalypse correspond to the four drummers playing sixteen tom-toms; death and destruction appear as a thematic transformation (based on the whole-tone scale) of the *Dies iræ* melody. At the end, however, there is hope.

Notes

1. Joan Peyser, *Bernstein: A Biography* (New York: Beech Tree Books, 1987), p. 54.
2. Meryle Secrest, *Leonard Bernstein: A Life* (New York: Alfred A. Knopf, 1994), p. 53.
3. His own performance of the symphony with Jennie Tourel and the New York Philharmonic is available on Sony Classic CD 60697. Bernstein later recorded the work with Christa Ludwig and the Israel Philharmonic on Deutsche Grammophon CD 45245. Both recordings include Bernstein's second symphony, *The Age of Anxiety.*
4. Bernstein's official designation for the score was "operetta."
5. Leonard Bernstein, cited in Peyser, *Bernstein*, p. 249.
6. The "Lisbon affair" that Bernstein mentions was an earthquake that occurred in 1755, leaving the city in a shambles and many inhabitants dead. This was one of the provocations for Voltaire's rejection of Optimism. Bernstein's remarks are in the brochure for *Bernstein Conducts Candide* (Deutsche Grammophon CD recording 449 656-2 [1989 revision], 1991), p. 7.
7. Keith Garebian, *The Making of West Side Story* (Toronto: ECW Press, 1995), p. 35.
8. Mort Goode, Notes for *West Side Story* (New York: Columbia Records S32603, © 1973).
9. Elia Kazan assembled a cast including Marlon Brando, Lee J. Cobb, Karl Malden, Rod Steiger, and Eva Marie Saint, but when the score went through the dubbing room at Columbia, dynamics were altered to accommodate spoken dialogue; at other times, the music was turned off completely. Musical forms were totally disregarded if, for example, a scene happened to end before the music. In such cases, the music would just

fade out or be cut altogether. See Peyser, *Bernstein,* pp. 225–226 for details including Bernstein's own account.

10. The Gerry Mulligan Quartet and the Dave Pell Octet cultivated this style, as did the Modern Jazz Quartet. The MJQ recording *A Cold Wind Is Blowing* (United Artists UAL 4063) has been cited by Frank Tiro (*Jazz: A History;* 2d ed. [New York: Norton, 1977], p. 334) for its "slowing down of the pulsations . . . cool and quiet performance . . . and the rise of cool jazz in the 1950s."

11. Bernstein also published his arrangement of the piece for violin and piano. (New York: Amberson Enterprises, 1956). The fingerings and editing of the solo violin part are by Stern.

12. N.B., Not to be confused with the Three Choirs Festival, which dates from the early eighteenth century and involves those of the cathedrals of Gloucester, Hereford, and Worcester.

13. Paul Myers, *Leonard Bernstein* (London: Phaidon Press, 1998), p. 133. Note the "Classified List of Works" at the conclusion of the monograph.

14. Hanson, *Harmonic Materials of Modern Music: Resources of the Tempered Scale* (New York: Appleton, Century, Crofts, 1960).

15. Regarding Juilliard composers, see Andrea Olmstead, *Juilliard: A History* (Urbana: University of Illinois Press, 1999).

16. A monograph on Persichetti by his wife has never been published. A useful source is Donald L. Patterson and Janet L. Patterson, *Vincent Persichetti: A Bio-Bibliography* (Westport, Connecticut: Greenwood Press, 1988).

17. (New York: Norton, 1961).

18. Concerning his life and works, see Howard Pollack, *Walter Piston* (Ann Arbor, Michigan: UMI Research Press, 1981); regarding Piston's professional acquaintances and influence, see Pollack, *Harvard Composers: Walter Piston and His Students from Elliott Carter to Frederic Rzewski* (Metuchen, New Jersey: Scarecrow Press, 1992).

19. *Principles of Harmonic Analysis* (Boston: E. C. Schirmer, 1933); *Harmony* (New York: Norton, 1941; rev. 4th ed. with Mark De Voto, 1978); *Counterpoint* (New York: Norton, 1947); *Orchestration* (New York: Norton, 1955).

20. David Schiff, *The Music of Elliott Carter,* 2d ed. (Ithaca, New York: Cornell University Press, 1998), examines Carter's works up to 1997. The glossary explains theoretical terms commonly associated with Carter's music.

21. Concerning Pinkham, see Kee De Boer and John B. Ahouse, *Daniel Pinkham: A Bio-Bibliography* (Westport, Connecticut: Greenwood, 1988); Pollack, *Harvard Composers,* Chapter 9, "A Tradition Upheld: Daniel Pinkham," pp. 189–207; Leonard Raver, "Daniel Pinkham: A. G. O. Composer of the Year," *American Organist* 24 (December 1990), 28–44; Mark A. Radice, "An Interview with Daniel Pinkham," *American Organist* 31 (August 1997), 56–61.

22. (London: Novello, 1946).

23. See Pollack, *Harvard Composers;* and Kee De Boer and John Ahouse, *Daniel Pinkham.*

24. The Quartet is a memorial for Donald Outerbridge. Robert Light had asked Pinkham for a song cycle, but the members of the Boston Composers' String Quartet suggested a string quartet instead.

25. K. Gary Adams, *William Schuman: A Bio-Bibliography* (Westport, Connecticut: Greenwood, 1998).

26. A survey of Schuller's life and works as well as secondary writings about them up to about 1986 are in Norbert Carnovale, *Gunther Schuller: A Bio-Bibliography* (Westport, Connecticut: Greenwood, 1987).

27. *History of Jazz* (New York: Oxford, 1968); *Musings: The Musical Worlds of Gunther Schuller* (New York: Oxford , 1985); *Compleat Conductor* (New York: Oxford, 1968).

28. Andrea Olmstead, *Roger Sessions and His Music* (Ann Arbor, Michigan: UMI Research Press, 1985), p. 93. For more on Sessions, see her ed. of the *Correspondence of Roger Sessions* (Boston: Northeastern University, 1992); and her *Conversations with Roger Sessions* (Northeastern University, 1987).

29. Nicholas Slonimsky, ed., *Baker's Biographical Dictionary*, 8th ed. (New York: Schirmer Books, 1992), p. 1688.

30. Don Gillespie, *George Crumb: Profile of a Composer* (New York: C. F. Peters, 1986), p. 34.

31. Concerning Crumb, see Don Gillespie, ed., *George Crumb: Profile of a Composer* (New York: C. F. Peters, 1986); Kyle Gann, *American Music in the Twentieth Century* (New York: Schirmer Books, 1997); Edward Strickland, *American Composers: Dialogues on Contemporary Music* (Bloomington: Indiana University, 1991).

32. Cited in Gillespie, *George Crumb*, p. 6.

33. Cited in Gillespie, *George Crumb*, p. 17.

Chapter 20

The American Avant-garde: Henry Cowell and John Cage

"Go West, young man, go west" became a nineteenth-century American slogan signifying opportunity, open-mindedness, and potential. The history of the American avant-garde suggests that the slogan had some basis in reality. Two figures, both West Coasters, played critical roles in expanding our understanding of just what "music" is: Henry Cowell (1897–1965) and John Cage (1912–1992).

Cowell began composing before he had any formal training; he was thus unaware of being unconventional. After violin lessons from age five until eight, he bought a piano in 1910. By the time he made his debut as a pianist and composer, he had written over one hundred pieces. Cowell remained prolific, and by the time of his death, he had written more than 140 orchestral works, including twenty-one symphonies. His chamber scores exceeded that number by about thirty, and his works for piano ran to over two hundred titles.

Cowell's first published work, *Tides of Manaunaun* (1912), used tone clusters as a backdrop for a modal melody in the right hand. In subsequent piano works, Cowell took a more whimsical approach, requiring the performer to pluck, strum, and bang on the strings. In his 1923 score entitled *Aeolian Harp,* he instructs that the keys for indicated sonorities be depressed silently (thereby lifting the dampers) while the player reaches inside to strum the strings. A similar concept can be seen in the 1925 score of *Banshee,* but in this piece, Cowell requires two performers, one who operates the keys and pedals while seated at the bench, another who leans into the instrument to strum and pluck the strings.

Indeterminacy, a process whereby either the composer or the performer (or both) may exercise choices, is the most important innovation of Cowell's music. The *Quartet Romantic* (1917) and *Quartet Euphometric* (1919) are early examples, but this process becomes more prominent in his Third String Quartet, the *Mosaic Quartet* (1935), where performers arrange its five segments—with or without repeats—

in an order of their choosing.[1] The resulting piece, an example of *elastic form*, is different in every performance.

Cowell was an innovator, and he explained many of his novel concepts, especially the role of the overtone series, in his journal entitled *New Music Resources*.[2] Shortly before his death, he edited a collection of essays entitled *American Composers on American Music*.[3] Important, too, is his insightful monograph on Charles Ives that he coauthored with his wife.[4] In 1925, Cowell founded the New Music Society to complement his prose writings with performances. The society issued a newsletter providing information on repertoire to be performed as well as commentary on the contemporaneous musical scene. Copland, Ives, Schönberg, Stravinsky, and Varèse were among the modernists whose works the society promoted.

Cowell's musical inquiries extended beyond the Western tradition. He appropriated World musics in his work, a feature commonly described as "transethnicity."[5] He found many sympathetic ears, both among professionals and amateurs, and his flexible approach to music and the arts had profound consequences. His most famous and influential student was John Cage.

John Cage

Cage advocated a thorough revaluation of "music." For Cage, who had studied in New York with Cowell from the spring of 1933 until the fall of 1934, and then in his native California with Schoenberg until 1936, music was a creative means for confronting and participating in time.[6] Cage rejected the binary relationship of consonance and dissonance, preferring to contrast music and noise. Within such a broad context, novel sounds play a crucial role. Cage's *Construction in Metal* (1939), for instance, uses bells, sheet metal, gongs, brake drums, anvils, cymbals, tam-tam, and piano.

In order to put a percussion ensemble at the disposal of a single performer, Cage devised the *prepared piano*. Music for prepared piano uses conventional notation, but it assumes new significance on a prepared instrument. (For Cage, notation was also graphic art, a fact evidenced by the fascinating compilation of contemporary scores that he assembled to be displayed as an art show. The collection was published under the title *Notations*.[7]) A grand piano may be "prepared" by the insertion between its strings of screws, nuts, bolts, washers, strips of plastic and rubber, and the like, according to the composer's schedule. With such preparation, the conventional notation serves only to tell the player where the fingers ought to be, but the customary pitches and timbres are superseded by novel sounds. Between 1946 and 1948, Cage wrote his *Sonatas and Interludes* for prepared piano. In January of 1949, Maro Ajemian gave the premiere at Carnegie Hall.[8]

Cage sometimes used the prepared piano in ensembles. In the "Duet" for voice and prepared piano from his unfinished score *She Is Asleep* (1943), the pianist

John Cage

accompanies a singer who invents unconventional methods of voice production. In the more ambitious Concerto (1951) for prepared piano and orchestra, Cage preserves the conventional three-movement design; however, the movements are continuous, so that the silences may be more keenly felt. In the first movement, the pianist is invited to explore the affections possible in music, whereas the orchestra is to play only according to instructions—without the expression of personal sentiment. During the second movement, the pianist relinquishes by degrees the subjective element. In the third, which is constructed in the manner of Indian rhythmic cycles called *talas*, both soloist and orchestra follow the same chart, but silence becomes increasingly important. The cycles of twenty-three beats are arranged in the pattern of 3+2+4+4+2+3+5, but these groupings are not audible. As in Hindu music, performance is coordinated with physical gestures showing the progress through the designated durations; hence, the music must be *seen*.

Throughout his career, Cage worked with dancers. The invention of the prepared piano, in fact, came about in 1938, when Cage was working with Syvilla Fort on *Bacchanale*. Owing to restrictions of finances and space, Cage devised this compact percussion ensemble. In 1938–39, Cage was the accompanist for Bonnie Bird's dance classes at the Cornish School in Seattle. There he met Merce Cunningham, a young man for whom he eventually divorced his wife Xenia (*nee* Andreevna Kashevaroff), and for whose dance productions he wrote much music. Cage's dance music was unconventional, as was Cunningham's choreography. Music and movement transpired concurrently, but whatever correspondences or divergences might occur were fortuitous—like random boom-boxes sounding in an airport during the movements of pedestrians en route from one point to another.

Perhaps this combination of sound and movement provided Cage with the idea for the genre that he called the *Musicircus*. The objective is to assemble "as much music as can be played by all those who are willing to perform without being paid. No entrance ticket or payments. Loud and soft. Serious and popular. Young and old. Student recitals. Church choirs. Athletics or dance."[9] The first Musicircus took place on 17 November 1967 in a stock pavilion. The concept, which can actually be traced back to Charles Ives's *Universe Symphony*, embodies many of Cage's most important æsthetic tenets: It is a democratic art; it reflects the reality of contemporary urban life; it introduces chance elements along with predetermined parameters, and it provides, through art, a model for creative confrontation.[10]

Within the Musicircus, the "composer" is often transformed from a position of supreme authority to one of bystander. For Cage, this new role offered exciting possibilities. He had become fascinated by Zen during the 1940s, and he began making musical "decisions" based on chance operations, such as flipping a coin or tossing dice, as indicated in the ancient Chinese Confucian oracle book known as *I Ching* (ca. twelfth century B.C.E.) This approach led Cage to compose music of nonintention, like *Music of Changes* (1951) and the Concert (1958) for piano and orchestra.[11]

Cage discovered that in many non-Western musics (and in early Western repertoires) the purpose of music was to induce a state of spiritual receptivity by suppression of the ego. The notion of music predicated on developmental procedures, having a beginning, middle, and ending, and exhibiting a discernible form, was irrelevant.

Though he never considered himself part of the mainstream of concert music, Cage made a lasting impression on musical culture throughout the world. At least some of his success was the result of support from Wolfgang Steinecke, the founding director of the Darmstadt Internationale Ferienkurse für neue Musik (international summer courses for new music). Heavily subsidized by the United States in the years immediately after World War II, the Darmstadt Festivals provided two important opportunities: The first was for a general updating of German musical culture, which had been forced into ultra-conservativism during the war years; the second was for the United States to present an image of benevolence, culture, and wisdom. Beginning in the mid 1950s, Cage was in regular contact with Steinecke, visited Darmstadt, influenced the young German avant-garde, and was well represented by the pianist David Tudor; hence, the promulgation of Cage's music and theories at the festivals "did much to boost Cage's position in Germany."[12] He was elected as a member of the American Academy and Institute of Arts and Letters in 1968. Ten years later, he was similarly honored by the American Academy of Arts and Sciences. In 1982, the French Minister of Culture named him Commander of the Order of Arts and Letters, and in 1989, he was awarded the Kyoto Prize by Japan. Cage achieved sainthood in the American avant-garde when he was invited by Harvard University to give the Charles Eliot Norton Lectures during the 1988–89 academic year.

These awards were gratifying for Cage, but they also precipitated a critical revaluation of his œuvres, which had not always been taken seriously. Exploration of Cage's early works has been a relatively recent phenomenon, but here, too, musicians are making fascinating discoveries. His early piano solo entitled "A Room" (1943), for instance, is an excellent example of the style now called *Minimalism*. A few notes are repeated over and over within the context of changing metrical patterns within a larger rhythmic plan.[13] Though the term Minimalism was unknown in 1943, the essentials of the style were nevertheless planted in this short and apparently simple piece.

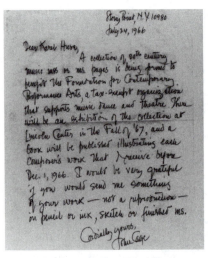

John Cage Letter to Karel Husa

When he died at the age of seventy-nine, *Time Magazine* called him "an indifferent musician, but one of the century's seminal theoreticians." The article notes further that his æsthetic theories were to have dramatic impact on "three generations of American composers, including Morton Feldman, Frederic Rzewski and Philip Glass."[14] To the names cited, we could add those of La Monte Young (b. 1935), John Adams (b. 1947), and Louis Andriessen (b. 1939), all well-known composers associated with the Minimalist movement. Doubtless, the number will grow as the new millennium progresses. Significant, too, is the fact that Cage was the first American composer who attempted to address Asian musical culture in a serious way and to utilize its musical riches for new expressive ends.

Notes

1. The term "aleatory" refers to random results of throwing dice, but it is also widely used to indicate music involving *choice* rather than *chance*.
2. Though largely written in 1919, the book was not published until 1930. (New York: Alfred A. Knopf), 143 p.
3. (New York: F. Ungar, 1962), 226 p.
4. Henry and Sidney Cowell, *Charles Ives and His Music* (New York: Oxford University Press, 1955), 245 p.
5. The term was coined by Lou Harrison. The most extensive discussion of transethnicity in music is Alex J. Lubet, "Indeterminate Origins: A Cultural Theory of American Experimental Music," James R. Heintze, ed., *Perspectives on American Music since 1950* (New York: Garland, 1999), pp. [95]–140.
6. For Cage's observations concerning his work with Schoenberg, see Thomas S. Hines, "Then Not Yet 'Cage,'" in Marjorie Perloff and Charles Junkerman, eds., *John Cage: Composed in America* (University of Chicago Press, 1994), pp. 92–93.
7. John Cage, with Alison Knowles, *Notations* (New York: Something Else Press, 1969).
8. Her recording, which Cage considered definitive, has been reissued by Composers Recordings, Inc. in the American Masters series. (New York, 1995).
9. John Cage, cited in Charles Junkerman, "New Forms of Living Together: The Model of the Musicircus," *John Cage: Composed in America*, p. 40. See also Richard Kostelantez, ed., *John Cage* (New York: Praeger, 1970), pp. 171–177.
10. As Junkerman notes, "Cage argues that encounters along contested social borders [entail] . . . conflict, but there is no reason why conflict can't be creative and charged with the exchange of information, in other words 'communicative.'" "New Forms of Living Together," p. 47.
11. Critics including Alan Watts and the composer Chou Wen-chung are skeptical of the connection of Zen and Cage's music. Concerning Asian influences generally, Lubet notes that: "Since trans-Asianism represents the ultimate manifestation of transethnicism . . . it is inevitably the most attractive metaphorical foreign destination for composers working in experimentalism, a tradition of extremism. Asia provides useful

imagery for a composer interested in, or seeking a reputation based upon, risk-taking and exploration." Lubets, "Indeterminate Origins," p. 110.

12. Amy C. Beal, "Negotiating Cultural Allies: American Music in Darmstadt, 1946–1956," *Journal of the American Musicological Society* 53 (spring 2000), 125.

13. The piece is recorded by Joshua Pierce in *John Cage: Works for Piano and Prepared Piano* (Mainz: Wergo Schallplatten, 1986), vol. 1.

14. *Time Magazine*, "Milestones," (24 August 1992), 17.

Chapter 21

Electronic Music

Electroacoustic music is intertwined with both popular culture and technology. Electroacoustic music can be divided into the general categories of Acousmatic music, Computer music, *musique concrète,* Electronic music, and Multimedia (also called Intermedia).

Electronic music is generated by oscillators and electronic modules. Computer music implies that computers generate either the sound itself or the composition and structure of the music. *Musique concrète,* while originally designating electronically altered acoustic sounds, now includes sampled sounds that undergo some transformation. Acousmatic music differs from live electronics in that it is designed to be performed from a fixed source, usually a computer tape or disk played through an amplification system.

Thaddeus Cahill's Telharmonium was the first electronic musical instrument. A 200-ton monstrosity, invented and assembled in Holyoke, Massachusetts, in 1906, it was transported to New York City and reassembled. Music performed by the keyboardist was transmitted through leased telephone lines to subscribers, thus creating the first cable entertainment medium; however, the Telharmonium caused interference with nearby voice lines, so the company folded, and the Telharmonium was disassembled.

In Moscow in 1920, Leon Theremin introduced the first electronic instrument for live performance, the Theremin, whose most celebrated performer was Clara Rockmore.[1] An explosion of electronic instruments followed, with Friedrich Trautwein inventing the Trautonium in 1928. Trautwein worked with Hindemith, who used the instrument in several pieces. A later version, the Mixturtrautonium, was used in Alfred Hitchcock's film *The Birds.*

That same year in Paris, Maurice Martenot invented the Ondes Martenot, which found applications in the works of Messiaen, Milhaud, Honegger, Ibert, Jolivet, Varèse, and Boulez. None of these instruments became popular enough to be more than a curiosity; but in 1935, John Hammond invented the Hammond organ, the first commercially successful electronic instrument. It quickly found a home in churches and early rhythm-and-blues groups.

The live performance of electronic sounds became the focus of John Cage's experiments in "found sound." Cage contended that any sound can be music if treated as such. Experiments with the alteration of sound continued through the 1930s and '40s. In 1939, Cage brought found sound to the forefront with his *Imaginary Landscape No. 1*, which employed variable speed phonographs, tin cans, and oscillators in a live situation. Intermedia performances by the Merce Cunningham Dance Company featured live improvisations on synthesizer accompanying dancers.

In 1948, Pierre Schaeffer, working at the Radiodiffusion-Télévision Française studios in Paris, created a piece entitled *Étude aux chemins de fer* (study with iron tracks) from recordings of locomotives. He coined the term *musique concrète* to describe this and other pieces presented at the first electroacoustic music radio concert, aptly titled Concert des Bruits. Subsequent early pieces by Schaeffer in collaboration with Pierre Henry were *Étude aux tourniquets* (study with a revolving door), *Étude pathetique* (study of pathos), and *Symphony pour un homme seul* (symphony for a single person). These formed the basis of *musique concrète* as a genre. Schaeffer used sounds for their unique qualities, much as the Expressionist painters were concerned with light and color devoid of representation; hence, the sounds of *Étude aux chemins de fer* provide acoustic materials that invite alterations. This approach presaged Karlheinz Stockhausen's and Luciano Berio's uses of the voice for its purely sonic qualities. This concept of composition—assembling and manipulating recorded acoustic sounds—became the focus of the Milan studio.

In 1952, Schaeffer reestablished the RTF studios as the Groupe de Recherche de Musique Concrète (GRM), which attracted Boulez, Messiaen, Stockhausen, Milhaud, and Varèse. Varèse's *Déserts* for orchestra and tape (1954) is the first genuine concert work in the field of electroacoustics.

Bruno Maderna and Stockhausen established a studio in Cologne devoted to the exploration of electronic music produced by oscillators rather than acoustic sounds. The studio was formed partially as a response to the acoustic leanings of the RTF studios in Paris, and partly to explore applications of serial principles within the context of electronics. Here Stockhausen created his *Studie I* (1953), *Studie II* (1954), and—albeit in contradiction to the intent of the studio—his *Gesang der Jünglinge* (1956). In this last work, he utilized recordings of a boy reading from the Book of Daniel. Stockhausen eventually moved from Serialism to his self-defined statistical form and to his concept of *moment form*, in which each moment in time (and the sounds that occupy that moment) is a miniature structure, independent of the larger form. His *Kontakte* (1960) is the definitive work utilizing this procedure. Later moment-form works include *Telemusik* (1966), which incorporates Asian sounds, and *Hymnen* (1967), which uses the characteristics of one sound to transform others—a process called *intermodulation* that became popular in the early 1990s.

In the United States, Vladimir Ussachevsky presented five tape pieces at a concert at Columbia University. Henry Cowell, who regularly contributed reports on New York City's musical life in the "Current Chronicle" section of the *Musical Quarterly* reviewed these enthusiastically in 1952.[2] Otto Luening invited Ussachevsky to Bennington College to present his works: Thus began a long and fruitful association between the two. That summer, Luening and Ussachevsky gave a concert at the Museum of Modern Art in New York, produced by Leopold Stokowski. Usshachevsky's *Sonic Contours* and three of Luening's pieces, (1) *Low Speed,* (2) *Invention,* and (3) *Fantasy in Space,* were featured. The concert was broadcast in both New York and Boston.

Ussachevsky and Luening were joined by Milton Babbitt, and they succeeded in winning grant money to begin the Columbia-Princeton Electronic Music Center with the newly developed RCA Mark II synthesizer. Among the first works created there were Babbitt's *Composition for Synthesizer,* Mario Davidovsky's *Electronic Study No.1,* and his *Synchronisms 1–6,* which explored interactions between acoustic instruments and tape accompaniment.

Luciano Berio heard the Museum of Modern Art concert and was impressed. When he returned to Milan in 1955, he joined Maderna and formed the Studio di Fonologia Musicale. The Milan studio had no specific compositional philosophy. Berio composed many of the seminal works from the early period of electroacoustic music, among them, his *Thema, Omaggio à Joyce* (1958) and *Visage* (1961).

Studios soon sprang up in universities and colleges in the United States. In Ann Arbor, Robert Ashley and Gordon Mumma formed the Once Group in 1961. Later, the live, electronic, performance ensemble called the Sonic Arts Union included David Behrman, Mumma, Ashley, and Alvin Lucier. Many of these early pieces were experiments, rather than definitive compositions. Electroacoustic music was still in its infancy and needed investigation and development.

In 1957, Max Mathews, working at the Bell Telephone Laboratories in New Jersey, created the first computer-generated sounds, with the program Music I. The Bell Labs attracted composers such as Jean-Claude Risset, James Tenney, Charles Dodge, and Barry Vercoe. Later versions of Music I (Music IVB and Music V) set the foundation for computer music of the 1970s and '80s.

In 1957, Lejaren Hiller and Leonard Isaacson, working at the University of Illinois at Urbana, created a program that generated a score for performance on acoustic instruments. The result was the *Iliac Suite* for string quartet, the first automated composition.

In 1964, Bob Moog, who had been building Theremins for several years, teamed up with Herb Deutsch to develop an analog modular synthesizer based on voltage control. In 1965, the first Moog synthesizer was sold to the Alwin Nikolais Dance Company.

Donald Buchla, working on the West Coast, developed the Buchla synthesizer at about the same time. In 1968, Walter Carlos (later transsexually named

Wendy Carlos) released an album of classical works performed on the Moog synthesizer: *Switched on Bach*. Not only did Carlos's release expose the traditional classical audience to the synthesizer, but it proved that electronics could match or even enhance traditional performances.

Synthesizers at the time were monophonic; hence, each line had to be recorded separately and with absolute precision. Despite the fact that the synthesizer was not yet capable of realtime control of dynamics, the record was a hit. Electroacoustic music had found acceptance in both the pop and classical worlds. Keith Emerson popularized the synthesizer in the commercial music world with the song "Lucky Man," recorded on the classically influenced rock album *Emerson, Lake, and Palmer*.

These first commercial synthesizers were limited: They were monophonic, took a long time to reset for each new timbre, lacked dynamic control from the keyboard, and drifted out of tune. Still, in 1966, Nonesuch records commissioned Morton Subotnick to write *Silver Apples of the Moon*, the first electroacoustic work to be recorded for release on record.

The first portable synthesizers appeared in 1969 with the arrival of the Minimoog. In 1978, Dave Smith, working at Sequential Circuits, solved the problems of quick programmability and polyphonic performance with the Prophet-5 synthesizer. By the late 1980s, the synthesizer was a regular component of pop bands and often substituted for orchestral instruments.

Until the advent of *musical instrument digital interface* (MIDI), most electroacoustic music was too costly, save for institutionally supported studios. With the introduction of MIDI in the early 1980s, the cost of synthesizers dropped, and studios began to sprout in smaller institutions and homes.

The marriage of electronic sound-producing techniques and the computer fueled an expansion of processes and techniques. As an example of algorithmic composition, Gary Lee Nelson's *Fractal Mountains* (1988) embodies the close relationship between mathematics and music. In this work, Nelson derived his pitch material by mapping the mathematical iterations of a fractal generating equation to pitches, and allowing the formula to generate the music, albeit with his guidance. Xenakis coined the term *stochastic music* for compositions based on the mathematical laws of probability, such as his *Achorripsis* (1957).

Granular synthesis is a method of sound generation in which timbres are created from extremely short "snapshots" of sound (thousandths of a second) that are linked together in clusters. The result is a vibrant, dynamic timbre with a sense of an inner vibration. Jon Christopher Nelson uses the program called Csound to generate granulated timbres.

Joel Chadabe has explored new composer/computer and performer/computer interfaces. His short-lived but influential Intelligent Music Corporation developed or licensed several innovative pieces of software that allowed creative artists to control the sonic textures and shapes of sounds in live, interactive situations. His *After the Songs* CD demonstrates the flexibility of his programs.

Working at the Institut de Recherche et Coordination Acoustique/Musique (IRCAM) in Paris, Miller Puckette began the development of MAX, a program that allowed composers to devise automated processes. David Zicarelli perfected the program which, along with Csound, became one of the defining pieces of music software for the classical electroacoustic-music composer during the 1990s. In combination with MIDI, MAX and similar softwares allow composers to write electronic music that is truly interactive. Performers can trigger synthesizers, computers, lights, and any other media sources. Dancers, and even robots, can directly control sound and develop their own compositions and improvisations.[3]

Notes

1. The most detailed study is Albert Glinsky, *Theremin: Ether Music and Espionage* (Urbana and Chicago: University of Illinois Press, 2000), 403 p. Rockmore's performances are reissued on Delos CD 1014. See also Steven M. Martin, *Theremin: An Electronic Odyssey.* Videorecording (1993).
2. Henry Cowell, "Current Chronicle: New York," *Musical Quarterly* 38 (1952), 599–600.
3. For more information on Electronic Music, see Lloyd Ultan, "Electronic Music: An American Voice," James R. Heintze, ed., *Perspectives on American Music since 1950* (New York: Garland, 1999), pp. [3]–39; Joel Chadabe, *Electric Sound: The Past and Promise of Electronic Music* (Englewood Cliffs, New Jersey: Prentice Hall, 1997); Peter Manning, *Electronic and Computer Music*, 2d ed. (New York: Oxford University Press, 1993); and Paul Griffiths, *Guide to Electronic Music* (New York: Thames and Hudson, 1979).

Chapter 22

Concert Music in Asia: Japan

The musical heritage of Asia is ancient, rich, and diverse. A systematic survey of the traditional musics of these countries is beyond the scope of this text; however, the confluence of European and Asian musics has yielded some of the most interesting and impressive scores of recent times.

This hybridization can be traced to the late nineteenth century, when Luther Whiting Mason (1818–1896) introduced Western musical practices into Japanese schools during the early Meiji period. In collaboration with the Japanese government, Mason published his *Shôgaku shôkashu* (elementary school songs) in 1881.[1] Similar musical interactions took place in China during the final decades of the Ching dynasty (1644–1911), when Western orchestras, music festivals, concert programs, and music criticism mingled with indigenous institutions.[2]

In the late nineteenth century, Japan witnessed a wholesale importation of Western culture, including Christian hymn tunes, military bands, orchestral instruments, and the piano.[3] Mason, who was appointed by the Japanese Ministry of Education to devise a music curriculum, formulated the "Plan for Promoting the Teaching of Singing in the Public Schools."[4] His curriculum included Protestant hymns, sometimes with new texts dealing with the beauty of nature and other topics appealing to Japanese sensibilities. The popularity of these tunes led to a modification of traditional Buddhist rituals, and congregational hymnody in the Western manner appeared.

Congregational participation in Buddhist liturgical music represented a break with tradition. In earlier practice, male priests had sung the chants (*shomyo*), generally without accompaniment, but sometimes with percussion instruments. In the early history of this tradition in Japan, priests commonly traveled to China for training; consequently, the Chinese tradition, which died out in that country, was transplanted to Japan and survives there even today.

As in the plainchants of the West (which may be Old Roman, Gregorian, Ambrosian, Gallican, Mozarbic, etc.), Buddhist *shomyo* varies according to region. The Tendai style, centered around the ancient city of Kyôto, is among the more influential performance practices.[5] Variations in Buddhist chant also resulted from the degree to which they interacted with the traditional music of the Japanese imperial court. This repertoire, known as *Gagaku* (literally "elegant music"), included both instrumental (*togaku*) and vocal pieces, which were often musical recitations of poems. The Buddhist chant repertoire is preserved in written neumes (*hakasa*), which represent the structural pitches of the chants. In actual performance of the chants, ornaments may be added.

The musical heritage of *Gagaku* and Buddhist chant has been a valuable resource for recent Asian composers. In contemporary composition, ancient scales, traditional instruments, and formal organization of music into small, medium, or multiple-movement works (*shokyoku, chukyoku,* and *taikyoku* respectively) are important and distinctive elements that, when combined with Western musical materials, offer fascinating possibilities.

The earliest Japanese ensembles were the *togaku* orchestras, which used winds, strings, and percussion.[6] Western instruments entered the Japanese musical scene as a result of the military bands that Commodore Perry brought during his visit to Japan in 1853. In aristocratic Japanese homes at the time, Western fife and drum bands (*koteki-tai*) became status symbols; however, with the downfall of Japan's feudal system during the Meiji Restoration (1868), these bands were amalgamated into national bands attached to both the army and the navy. "The military bands introduced to Japan not only standard band repertory and instruments, but also orchestral instruments and piano, martial songs, Western singing style, and the public concert."[7] Western notation was used, but in the vocal music, new lyrics of high literary quality reflected traditional Japanese respect and admiration for the beauty of nature.[8]

The advent of Western musical practices did not lead to a rejection of local traditions; instead, a distinction was drawn between traditional music (*dento ongaku*) and music of Western provenance (*seiyo ongaku*). This dialectic has been responsible for many of the most innovative scores produced in the last half century.

Asian aesthetics differ from those in the West. Japanese musicians, for example, avoid "individual invention; . . . Performers cultivate the art of music within its bequeathed restrictions."[9] The intention here is for such "refined and highly mannered" performance to "prevent the performer's self-expression," thereby exalting the dignity and power of the music.[10] The concept of *ma* is also crucial.

> Sound . . . separates itself from a silent space . . . equally diverse and significant. This space, called "ma," is understood by Japanese as having a life of its own, containing an infinite number of sounds. . . . Actual sounds do not rank as superior to silence. Furthermore, since each sound terminates itself by being complete, a logical linkage of sounds is

unattainable. Instead, "ma" constitutes the acceptable relationships between sounds. A Japanese performer "listens" to the vibrant "ma" in which fortuitous and unintentional . . . sounds are created.[11]

Silence—the antithesis of sound—gives sound its significance. This active role of silence lends emphasis to the importance of individual sonorities. Both sound and silence are natural events; hence, music is an expression of and participation in the world of nature, a world to which human beings belong. Finally, the interactions of sound and silence, of musical events, and of performer and listener are examples of antithetical, yet complementary, phenomena that occur naturally as part of the experience of music. These dichotomies correspond to the concept of *yin* and *yang*.

Akira Ifukube, b. 1914

The beauty of nature brought Akira Ifukube to his career in music. Born into a family that boasted several generations of Shinto priests, Ifukube played guitar and violin as a teenager. When he began his higher education, it was as a forestry student at Hokkaido Imperial University. The program required his traveling to remote areas of Japan, where, surrounded by nature and immersed in tranquility, he composed his first important orchestral work, the *Japanese Rhapsody* (1935), which won the Tcherepnin prize. Alexander Tcherepnin was touring Asia as a concert pianist between 1934 and 1937. He taught many Asian composers and married a Chinese pianist, Lee Hsien-ming. It was during this time that Ifukube studied with Tcherepnin, who, in his own compositions, explored the potential of symmetrical scales and folk musics.

Ifukube's studies with Tcherepnin were complemented by his interest in the instruments of his native land. Like his teacher, he explored folk repertoires. Japanese instruments appear in many of his works, including the *Eclogue symphonique* (1982) and his *Five Poems after Inaba Manro*. The poems are scored for soprano soloist, alto flute, and twenty-five-stringed koto.

Japanese temple music often uses percussion instruments as the sole instrumental accompaniment to *shomyo*. In such a context, it was natural for Ifukube to explore the rich potential of percussion as he does in his *Lauda concertata* for marimba and orchestra (1976; rev. 1979) and his *Three Eclogues after Epos among Aino Races* (1956) for solo voice and four tympani.

Eclogues are the pastoral poems of ancient Greece. Typically, they are in dialect, and they are often dialogues between rustic characters. The notion of a dialogue is apparent in the first of these songs, which is an example of *shinotcha*: music of tranquility or diversion. In this genre, the singer begins an improvisation, inventing not only the music, but also the syllables, which may be meaningless. In the course of such a fantasia (often precipitated by the singer's confrontation with a natural phenomenon, such as reflections in a pond, wind rustling through pine boughs, and so forth), the singer discovers a subject expressing his state of mind. This spiritual attitude is then explored in improvisational song. Similar to the *shinotcha* is the *yaishama ne na,* in which the singer repeats this phrase in the manner of a litany. The second of Ifukube's *Eclogues* is such a piece.

In keeping with the eclogue tradition, Ifukube has used Ainu texts in their original dialects. These people apparently are descendants of Caucasoids who originated in northern Asia. Invading tribes from the mainland eventually forced the Ainu peoples into the northern islands of Japan, especially Hokkaido, where many of them earn their living by making handcrafted reproductions of ethnic artifacts. The Sakhalin and Kuril Islands, both heavily forested and technically a part of Russia, are also inhabited by Ainu.

Ifukube's interest in regional dialects and folk idioms is apparent in many of his works, especially the set of songs entitled *Ancient Minstrelsies of Gilyak Tribes* (1946) and the *Three Lullabies among the Native Tribes on the Island of Sakhalin* (1949).

As a child, Ifukube's teacher, Tcherepnin, moved with his family to Paris in 1921. He remained there during World War II. Even after becoming a U. S. citizen in 1958, he maintained his principal residence in Paris. He passed on to Ifukube his interest in early twentieth-century French styles. Ifukube's *Lake of Kimtaankamuito* (1992), for soprano, viola, and harp, contains many reminiscences of Debussy's Sonata for flute, viola, and harp. This expansive, lyric outpouring uses a text by Genzo Sarashina.

After the Second World War, Ifukube taught orchestration at the Tokyo National University of Music and Fine Arts until 1953. From 1974, he taught at the Tokyo College of Music, where he was dean from 1975 until 1987, when he became the director of the College's Institute of Ethnomusicology.

Teizo Matsumura, b. 1929

Ifukube's success as a composer has been duplicated in his teaching, and his studio has produced many of Japan's leading talents; among them, Teizo Matsumura figures prominently. His studies in piano were complemented by work in counterpoint and harmony with Tomojiro Ikenouchi (1906–1991) and in composition with Ifukube, whom Matsumura honored in his orchestral score of 1988, entitled *Hommage à Akira Ifukube.*[12]

Matsumura's career took root in the 1950s, when Japanese concert music was heavily influenced by Serialism. Matsumura found little of interest in Serialism, but his dislike for it intensified his interest in his native Asian heritage. Early works, like his *Introduction and Allegro Concertante* (1955) and his *Music for String Quartet and Piano* (1962), utilize Japanese melodic formulations within conventional European instrumentations. Textures tend to be transparent, and sonorities are reminiscent of Impressionism.

In his recent works, Matsumura seems to employ two distinct styles: one for chamber music, another for larger, more formal pieces. In the chamber works, he has explored the potential of traditional Japanese instruments such as the *biwa, koto, shakuhachi,* and *shinobue* (two plucked, stringed instruments and two flute-like winds, respectively). In his *Poem I* (1969) for shakuhachi and koto, the different inflections of individual notes assume an important role; consequently, the notes in Matsumura's scores require interpretation. Depending on the context, a tone may be approached through a slide, or require a sort of *messa di voce,* or chromatic "twist," or may conclude with a fall-off.[13] In general, these elements of *Te* (motivic figures of Japanese classical music, usually associated with particular instruments) are not authentic; nevertheless, Matsumura approximates traditional gestures.

Teizo Matsumura

In his orchestral works, such as his Symphony (1964) and his Prelude (1968) for orchestra, the influence of Japanese classical music is less apparent—save, of course, for careful attention to details of instrumental timbre. Matsumura's Symphony, which was commissioned by the Nippon Philharmonic Orchestra, was begun in 1960. It consists of three movements, of which the second and third are played without break. In the first movement, an introduction leads to superimposed layers of sound, eventually involving the entire orchestra in a thunderous climax. Four such cataclysmic sound masses occur during the movement, but each is counterposed with subdued interludes featuring solo violin and reeds. The second movement, an Adagio featuring solo flute accompanied by harp and piano, gives the impression of chamber music. (Here, incidentally, fall-offs in the flute line recall the Japanese classical style.) The Finale is a combination of *perpetuum mobile* and *ostinato.* The clarinet begins the movement with a long, winding motif, mostly in conjunct motion, but reiterations of the motif add or subtract a note so that the pattern is never exactly the same; nevertheless, the persistent beat imparts a tremendous momentum to the music. In this movement, Matsumura builds several powerful orchestral climaxes, but ultimately the force is spent and the work concludes in solemn tranquility.

Toshiro Mayuzumi, 1929–1997

Mayuzumi studied at the Tokyo National University of Fine Arts and Music with Ikenouchi and Ifukube from 1945 until 1951. At that time, he went to France to

Todaiji Temple

study for a year at the Paris Conservatoire. Returning to Japan, he organized a new-music ensemble called Ars Nova Japonica to introduce the most recent European developments. *X, Y, Z* (1953) was the first example of *musique concrète* in Japan; *Study I* (1955) was the first Japanese example of synthesized sounds; and his Pieces (1957) for piano and string quartet were the first application in Japan of Cage's innovative modifications of piano sonorities. Mayuzumi explores the possibilities of traditional Japanese music, Serialism, film scoring, Buddhist chant, electronic music, and other idioms. His style is an elegant distillation of a vast array of contemporary and traditional techniques. Early scores include many chamber pieces, but after graduating from Tokyo University, he has generally written for orchestra and wind ensemble.

In his studies of Buddhist chant, Mayuzumi constantly came in contact with the sounds of temple bells. He explored these sonorities in a piece called *Campanology* (1957). At the labs of Nippon Hoso Kaisha (NHK, Japanese Broadcasting Company)—the equivalent of PBS, CBC, or BBC—Mayuzumi analyzed the temple bells of Todaiji Temple in Nara. The complex overtone configurations triggered his imagination, and he replicated these sounds in his scoring for conventional orchestral instruments. Soon, he wrote two more campanologies, which became the third and fifth movements of the *Nirvana-Symphony*. The second, fourth, and sixth movements of the piece are entitled "Suramgamah," "Mahaprajna paramita," and "Isshin Kyorai," respectively. The second movement's title refers to a type of meditation practiced in Zen Buddhism. In this movement, Mayuzumi uses men's voices traditionally disposed as *kyogashira* (i.e., precentor) and *daishu* (i.e., respondents). In actual *shomyo,* these chants consist mainly of repetitions of a single pitch; however, Mayuzumi gives the chant an orchestral backdrop. He also calls for twelve-part chorus and six soloists (totaling anywhere from 60 to 120 singers). The fourth movement is based on a ritual text, "hail to the Diamond of Wisdom," that concludes the Suramgamah. Vocally, it employs vibrato and portamento. The text of the Finale, "Praise be to the single thought," uses a *shomyo* from the Tendai school of Buddhist chant; hence, Mayuzumi's combination of stylistic elements inspired by both the Tendai and Nara schools of chant might be likened to a Western composer's appropriation of more elaborate Ambrosian chants along with simpler Gregorian versions.[14]

In his discussion of the *Nirvana-Symphony*, Toru Takemitsu argued against making too much of the role of temple bells. He says:

> I have no doubt that . . . the *Nirvana Symphony* is a masterpiece of symphonic literature, [but] in my opinion the gong effect . . . is not the most

crucial part of the work. . . . There is something in the music that goes beyond the sound of the gong. That something is what I would call true expression, that special element that cannot be explained.[15]

Toshiro Mayuzumi

In the *Nirvana-Symphony* Mayuzumi calls for three performing groups, two located at the rear of the auditorium on opposite sides, and the main ensemble on stage. The smaller groups are disposed as follows. Group I: 2 piccolos, 1 flute, 2 clarinets in B-flat, 1 clarinet in E-flat, glockenspiel, sleigh bells; Group III: 3 horns in F, 3 trombones, 1 tuba, 2 double basses, tam-tam; Group II (i.e., main ensemble): 2 piccolos (flute, bass flute), 1 flute, 2 oboes, 1 cor anglais, 2 clarinets in B-flat, 1 bass clarinet, 2 bassoons, 1 contrabassoon, 3 horns in F, 3 trumpets in B-flat, 3 trombones, celesta, harp, piano, strings, tympani, xylophone, tubular bells, vibraphone, crash cymbals, suspended cymbals, tam-tam, bass drum, and men's chorus.

Toru Takemitsu, 1930–1996

Takemitsu's formal instruction in music was limited to several months' work with Yasuji Kiyose (1900–1981), one of the founders of the Japan chapter of the ISCM, and its president from 1951 until 1956. Takemitsu's music reveals powerful influences of Debussy and Messiaen. Takemitsu especially admired Debussy's ability to draw diverse elements, such as timbre, dynamics, and rhythm, simultaneously into focus. In this, Takemitsu saw a refreshing alternative to the German proclivity toward concentration on a single musical element at any given moment.

Toshi Ichiyanagi was responsible for introducing the music of Messiaen to Takemitsu, and Messiaen's Préludes for piano solo were the stimulus for Takemitsu's decision to become a professional musician.[16] Messiaen's influence is conspicuous in Takemitsu's works like *Lento in due movimenti* (1950) for piano solo, which uses modes of limited transposition, and *Quatrain* (1975), which uses the same ensemble as Messiaen's *Quatuor pour le fin du temps,* and was written with Messiaen's guidance and encouragement.[17] Takemitsu's enthusiasm for the French master's music led him to organize Jikken-kobo (experimental workshop), which gave many Japanese premieres of Messiaen's works. This ensemble included some of Japan's most important young composers and performers, such as Kuniharu Akiyama (b. 1929) and Joji Yuasa (b. 1929).[18] Takemitsu's interest in performance of contemporary music was lifelong, and late in his career, he founded the chamber ensemble Sound Space Arc (flute, clarinet, piano, percussion, and harp).

In the years after World War II, the United States occupation forces in Japan organized a Center for Information and Education in Tokyo. There, Takemitsu had access to recent American works including those of Copland. Takemitsu got to know Copland personally in February 1967, when Copland conducted Takemitsu's *Dorian Horizon* (1966) for seventeen stringed instruments. The piece was influenced by Cage's *Quartet* for twenty-four strings (in which no more than four instruments play at any time). In *Dorian Horizon*, Takemitsu disperses his instrumentalists over a wide space in order to elucidate spatial and textural events.[19] Late works, such as his *Variations for Orchestra on a Theme of Leonard Bernstein* (1988), show Takemitsu's continued interest in American music. In this piece, he included references to works by Berio, John Williams, and Leon Kirchner.[20]

In the late '50s, Takemitsu began exploring *musique concrète*. The first product of this effort was *Water Music* (1960) for tape, but many of Takemitsu's more than one hundred film scores use either *musique concrète* or some type of electronic music.[21] Another important Western influence for Takemitsu was the music of Xenakis, whom Takemitsu knew personally.[22]

Western literature, especially the writings of James Joyce, also inspired Takemitsu. *Finnegan's Wake* fascinated Takemitsu by its cyclic structure, frequent lapses from one language into another, use of double entendre, playful exploration of puns, and novel uses of stream of consciousness. Takemitsu took the titles of *Far Calls, Coming Far!* (1980) for violin and orchestra, *A Way a Lone* (1981) for string quartet, and *Riverrun* (1984) for piano and orchestra from the text of *Finnegan's Wake*. Although this last novel by Joyce has been the subject of much scholarly discussion, it can hardly be claimed that the work is understood in any conventional way, since Joyce pushed his linguistic games beyond the realm of comprehensibility. Takemitsu's titles drawn from this inscrutable source are, consequently, ambiguous. In the program notes for *A Way a Lone,* which was written for the tenth anniversary of the Tokyo String Quartet and premiered by them at Carnegie Hall on 23 February 1981, Takemitsu points out that the full line in Joyce's novel is: "The keys to. Given! A way a lone a last a long the." The music is draped around three notes that spell the word "sea" (in German usage, "Es" for E-flat, then E, then A). Takemitsu made an arrangement of *A Way a Lone* for string orchestra that he designated as *A Way a Lone II*.

Takemitsu seems to have enjoyed the dialectic between East and West. The juxtaposition of æsthetics is obvious in *November Steps* (1967) for biwa, shakuhachi, orchestra.[23] *November Steps* was written for the 125th anniversary of the New York Philharmonic, and its premiere in November 1967 was conducted by Seiji Ozawa.

The combination of Japanese and Western instruments is not the critical ingredient of this work. The simplistic use of exotic sounds would not make a work any more "Japanese" than a performance of Vivaldi's *Four Seasons* by koto ensemble would make it Japanese. The ethnic elements in Takemitsu's scores are both subtle and organic. In the title, for instance, "November" is not only its first word, but also the month of the piece's premiere; further, the fact that this is the eleventh month finds its parallel in the eleven sections of the work. The title's second element, "steps," refers to *danmono,* a musical work divided into acts.[24] In its many aspects, the title refers to a month in the calendar, the month of the premiere of the piece, the number of sections in it, to the act scheme in Noh drama and other Japanese theatrical works involving music, and—although the homonym "steppes" is spelled differently—to a type of landscape. The title, then, is like a little *haiku* that reveals personal and analytical aspects of the music.[25]

Display of virtuosity was not a priority of Takemitsu's. Although he wrote for incredible virtuosi—such as Ani and Ida Kavafian, Heinz Hollinger, Yehudi Menuhin, Richard Killmer, and Peter Serkin—mere technical facility never rose to the forefront of his compositional style. This observation extends to his own role as composer. He composed to engage the listener in a spiritual way, not to display his knowledge of theories; yet, the compositional virtuosity is there, discreetly grounding each of his works. A fascinating application of theoretical principles appears in his orchestral masterpiece *A Flock Descends into the Pentagonal Garden* (1977).[26]

Much has been made of the dream that Takemitsu described as the inspiration for the piece—a blackbird leading a flock of white birds into the garden. His own criticism of Mayuzumi's bells in relation to the *Nirvana-Symphony* might be cited as an argument against becoming overly involved in such details. Suffice it to point out here that Takemitsu's title, with its "pentagonal" garden, gives us a clue that pentatonic scales are important. Similarly, the notion of "descending" indicates the motion of the pentatonic scales. The blackbird leading the flock would be the central bird in the formation, since the following birds glide in the wake of the lead bird.[27]

Relating these concepts to musical structures resulted in a piece predicated on a pentatonic scale consisting of C-sharp, E-flat, F-sharp, A-flat, B-flat. The intervals in this scale—major second, minor third, major second, major second, with a final minor third to reach the starting C-sharp an octave higher—produced the following: 2-3-2-2-3.[28] If we imagine these intervals in a circular context, like the face of a clock, we can reproduce the same intervals in a different succession by starting at successive numbers each time: (a) 2-3-2-2-3; (b) 3-2-2-3-2; (c) 2-2-3-2-3; (d) 2-3-2-3-2; (e) 3-2-3-2-2.

Now if we imagine the formation once again, we might picture the scales on C-sharp and E-flat—i.e., the intervals of (a) and (b)—as descending, and those on A-flat and B-flat—(d) and (e)—as ascending. By viewing these scales as vertical collections, Takemitsu obtained his harmonic resources as well.

In its overall structure, the segments of *A Flock Descends into the Pentagonal Garden* exhibit the same balanced formation as its tonal elements. The piece begins with a bird theme using winds, especially oboe. Strings are deployed for the

EXAMPLE 11

Petatonic configurations in Toru Takemitsu, *A Flock Descends into the Pentagonal Garden*

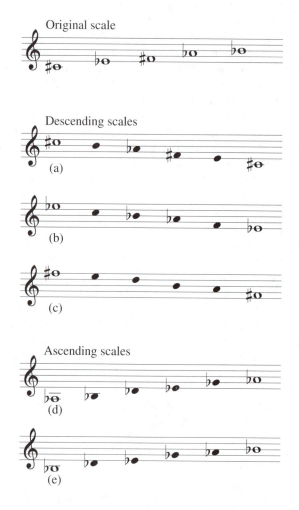

musical depiction of the garden that follows. The marriage of the birds with garden is represented in the following episode. At this point, the blackbird (cor
anglais) has a soliloquy. Now Takemitsu writes vignettes devoted to the union of
birds and garden, the string evocation of the garden, and a final solo utterance
(albeit a brief one) for the oboe.

In *A Flock Descending into the Pentagonal Garden*, Takemitsu has synthesized
Eastern and Western philosophies and musical techniques. The rotations of the

pentatonic pitch collection are structured in a manner similar to row permutations in Serialism. A tender sensitivity to the beauty of nature is suggested in a title that is, again, both picturesque and informative. In preparation for a first hearing, Takemitsu's own advice is helpful: "The listener need not understand the different operations. . . . I wish to avoid overemphasizing these. My music is composed as if fragments were thrown together unstructured, as in dreams. You go to a far place and suddenly find yourself back home without having noticed the return."[29]

Toshi Ichiyanagi, b. 1933

In Japan, Ichiyanagi studied piano with Chieko Hara and composition with Kishio Hirao (1907–1953), a prolific composer of chamber music, who had studied in Paris at the Schola Cantorum from 1931 until 1934.[30] Hirao's death contributed to Ichiyanagi's decision to study in the United States, at the Juilliard School of Music from 1954 until 1957, then with Cage until 1961, when he returned to Japan. During his years in the United States, Ichiyanagi won grants from the Elizabeth S. Coolidge Foundation, the Koussevitzky Foundation, and the Rockefeller Foundation.

Back in Japan, in 1963, Ichiyanagi organized the Tokyo International Music Ensemble, New Directions, a performance group that specialized in traditional Japanese instruments and Buddhist chant. In 1966, he worked with Takemitsu in organizing the Orchestral Space Festival. Later that year, he returned to the United States and gave concerts with Cage and the pianist David Tudor.

In his music, Ichiyanagi investigates many of the possibilities opened by Cage. Ichiyanagi's *Music for Electric Metronomes* (1960), for example, uses multiple electronic metronomes, whose speed and timbre can easily and quickly be modified, in conjunction with strings, flute, percussion instruments, textless voices, clapping, and other sounds, to produce a fifteen-minute theater piece.[31] Like Cage, he is especially interested in percussion instruments, and he has written important solo pieces such as *Portrait of the Forest* (1983) for solo marimba, and *Rhythm Gradation* (1993) for solo tympani. *Portrait,* which Ichiyanagi composed for a recital featuring works by Cage, is a musical reminiscence of the two composers' rambles through forests in New York looking for mushrooms. *Rhythm Gradation* explores polarities, such as highly active and relaxed rhythms, precise intervals and amorphous pitches, dry and reverberant sonorities, and so on. Both pieces were written for Atsushi Sugahara.[32]

In both his Third String Quartet, *Inner Landscape* (1994), and his Fifth Symphony (1995), Ichiyanagi deals with time as a philosophical concept and as a musical condition. The Symphony reflects this duality in its design as a two-movement piece with both movements structured according to parallel plans: an introduction followed by an ostinato. In the first, tympani and low brass begin, and quiet winds are added, ascending from bass to treble to stack up thick chordal textures. From

Toshi Ichiyanagi

these sound blocks emerges a cascade of piano arpeggios, leading to an interlude for English horn. The three-minute introduction concludes with a plaintive passage for solo violin. The ostinato section, in the character of a slow march, builds over six minutes to a gigantic climax that tapers off into the low strings. The second introduction uses entirely different sonorities: strings *sul ponticello* playing glissandos in contrary motion. At the extremes of these glissandos, isolated sounds—such as a single tone on a small triangle—appear. A nervous motif emerges as the ostinato of the second movement, but in this case, the pattern is altered by additive rhythms and changing instrumentation. The pair of preludes and ostinatos serve both to compare and contrast aspects of time; however, these features work as complementary rather than opposing forces. Ichiyanagi emphasizes this reciprocal relationship in the closing, where a varied reprise of the introductory piano and violin solos from the first movement brings the piece full cycle.

Teruyuki Noda, b. 1940

Noda's output covers a wide variety of genres and media. His Trio (1963) for violin, horn, and piano is one of the few chamber pieces with that unusual instrumentation since Brahms's Trio, Op. 40 and Ligeti's Trio that it inspired. Noda's other works have equally distinctive scorings. In his Quartet (1965), he uses the provocative combination of horn, 'cello, tympani, and celesta. Noda's imaginative instrumentations often use traditional Japanese sonorities: His Quartet (1969) is scored for shakuhachi, two kyotos, and jyushitigen; his second and third quartets (1973, '75) also use Japanese instruments. *Ten Rai* (1992), for twelve Japanese instruments, is his largest traditional ensemble.

Noda has also written quite a few impressive scores for Western instruments. Among these, one of the most attractive is his Sonata, *In the Garden* (1986), for violin and piano. The piece has a fascinating history. In 1985, Noda was invited by the International Harp Society to join them as a guest in Jerusalem. There he lodged in Mishkenat, a residence built for artists by the generosity of the violinist Isaac Stern. Mishkenat is on a hilltop and overlooks incredible sights.

> From the window of my room, I could see a gold dome, the church of Golgotha, and the guest hall where the last supper had been held. Being close to the origin of its great history, I found myself surrounded by mysterious quiet and calmness.

I got the inspiration for this piece when I visited the Garden of Gethsemane, which was twenty-minutes' walk from Mishkenat. . . . The
Garden of Gethsemane, where Jesus spent his last night, still exists as a
garden and gives us the image of the warmness of his humanity. That
was the image of Gethsemane that I had for many years.[33]

Guitarists will want to note Noda's *Rhapsodie Adriatique* (1988) for guitar and
string orchestra. The *Rhapsodie* is one continuous movement of more than twenty
minutes; however, its title obscures the fact that the piece is a three-movement concerto with a moderate opening, a slow, recitative-like central section, and a brilliant toccata as the finale. Toward the end of the slow movement, Noda even
includes a cadenza for the solo guitar. The brilliance of the piece, which stems in
part from its exploitation of the guitar's tuning, inspired the title: The glistening
sonorities, in Noda's thinking, became associated with sunlight dancing on the
surface of the Adriatic Sea. The *Rhapsodie* was composed for the guitarist Ichiro
Suzuki, who gave its premiere with the Radio-Television Orchestra of Belgium on
24 February 1989, in the Broadcast Concert Hall in Brussels. Noda subsequently
improved the balances of sonorities and registers by using only a single double
bass and modifying the guitar part.

Shin-Ichiro Ikebe, b. 1943

Studies in piano and composition began for Ikebe in childhood. Perhaps this
accounts for his impressive fluency and productivity. He has written in virtually
all genres for small and large instrumental ensembles, voices, lyric theater, and the
dance. In addition, he has written scores for four of Akira Kurosawa's films:
Shadow Warrior, Dreams, Rhapsody in August and *No, Not Yet*. Ikebe has written
more than 300 scores of incidental music. He uses Western instruments, Japanese
instruments, and early musical instruments such as the harpsichord.

Ikebe's formal training at the Tokyo University of Fine Arts, where he completed his undergraduate and graduate degrees in 1967 and 1971 respectively, was
with Tomojiro Ikenouchi and Akira Miyoshi.[34] Early works, like Ikebe's *Crepa in
sette capitoli* (fissure in seven chapters; 1966) for violin, three violas, 'cello, and bass,
show the influence of Messiaen. Other scores of that vintage reveal Ikebe's fascination with the music of Bartók.

Among Ikebe's works for solo instruments or small ensembles are the series
Monovalence I–III (1972–1977), *Trivalence* I and II (1971–1973), *Quinquevalence*
(1991), and *Quatrevalence* (1996) for solo, trio, quintet, and quartet respectively. In
all of these pieces, the term "valence" (borrowed from chemistry) refers to the
capacity of one element to combine with another.

In *Quatrevalence*, for violin, viola, 'cello, and piano, vestiges of Messiaen still
appear, but they are integrated into Ikebe's distinctive style. The piece, which is

Shin-Ichiro Ikebe

highly sectional yet fluid, makes extensive use of glissandos, and pitches often appear as outer limits of these sonic strands, rather than as demarcations of specific intervals. At no point is the writing virtuosic, but special effects and transitions among textures and sonorities are impressively carried off. Ikebe lavished particular care on this score, since it was written as a memorial for his colleague and friend Takemitsu.

Ikebe has composed many pieces for large orchestra, some more complex than others; however, he has generally avoided any approach that is theoretical first and musical later. Two striking examples of the importance Ikebe places on direct and powerful musical materials are his Third (1984) and Fifth (1990) Symphonies.

The Third Symphony, entitled *Ego phano*, is scored for triple winds, four horns, a huge battery of percussion requiring five players, piano, celesta, harp, and strings. Though written as a single movement, its four distinct metronome indications create the effect of a traditional Western four-movement symphony with scherzo and slow movement as an internal pair framed by fast movements. The tempo scheme (eighth note =160, quarter note =80, half note =40, eighth note =160) preserves a consistent underlying pulse. For the entire duration of this symphony of a bit more than twenty minutes, the tone G is heard or implied. This tonal mooring weakens only for a while in the slow section (i.e., half note =40). The return to the original metronomic status is accompanied by a varied restatement of the principal motifs of the opening.

Shortly after the premiere of his Fourth Symphony (1990) by the NHK Symphony Orchestra, the Tokyo Metropolitan Symphony commissioned Ikebe to write a symphony with the one condition that anything difficult should be avoided. According to Ikebe, he considered various models of simplicity, including the Ninth Symphony of Shostakovich, the *Simple Symphony* of Britten, the *Classical Symphony* of Prokofieff, and the Concertino for piano and orchestra of Honegger. He also studied various "fifth" symphonies, since many composers in the Western tradition seem to have made their fifth symphonies a *magnum opus*. Among the models mentioned by Ikebe are Beethoven, Bruckner, Mahler, and Shostakovich. Of these, Ikebe's Fifth Symphony seems most indebted to that of Shostakovich.

Each of the three movements—in the order fast, slow, fast—uses the same basic theme, but in transformation. His reworking of the energetic opening as a serene and ethereal central portion is remarkable. In the outer movements, the theme is bold and dynamic, but the most conspicuous feature of its treatment is the use of imitation. The imitations are transparent, streamlined, and largely in

two-part counterpoint. The composer gives his audience lively, interesting, energetic music conveying complex ideas with simple means. Ikebe's Fifth Symphony
has a nickname (assigned by the composer himself): *Simplex*.

Notes

1. (Tokyo: Monbusho, 1881–1884. 3 vols.; reprinted Tokyo: Holpshuppann, 1978).
2. See Francisco Feliciano, *Four Asian Contemporary Composers: The Influences of Tradition on Their Works* (Quezon City, Republic of the Philippines: New Day, 1993), p. 5.
3. Takako Matsuura, "Japanese and Western Confluence in the Development of Japanese Children's Music in the Meiji Period: 1868–1912," *Ars Musica Denver* 6 (spring 1994), 18.
4. Elizabeth May, *The Influence of the Meiji Period on Japanese Children's Music* (Berkeley and Los Angeles: University of California Press, 1963), p. 115.
5. Many of the Tendai chants are preserved in the *Gyosan-shomyo-rokkanjo,* which is still in use today.
6. Concerning Japan's many traditional instruments, see Hugh de Ferranti, *Japanese Musical Instruments* (New York: Oxford University Press, 2000). This book contains 29 full color plates as well as numerous black and white images.
7. Matsuura, "Japanese and Western Confluence," 18.
8. Matsuura, "Japanese and Western Confluence," 23.
9. Noriko Ohtake, "Creative Sources for the Music of Toru Takemitsu" (DMA dissertation, University of Maryland, College Park, 1990), p. 86. The dissertation was published as a book with the same title by Ashgate Publishing in 1993.
10. Ohtake, "Creative Sources," p. 87.
11. Ohtake, "Creative Sources," p. 88.
12. Ikenouchi was the first Japanese student at the Paris Conservatoire. He studied there from 1927 until his return to Japan in 1939. His best works are chamber pieces, such as his three string quartets (1937, '45, '46), and the sonatas for flute and violin (both 1946).
13. In performing sustained tones on the koto, the player sometimes pinches the string and "twists" it, resulting in a microtonal bend.
14. Mayuzumi notes that "Tendai Shomyo is characterized by its use of protracted melismata known as *inzei*," whereas the style of the Nara school "sounds unrefined . . . verging on the uncouth, although at the same time uninhibited and vital." See his remarks (pp. 7–8, trans. Robin Thompson) in the brochure accompanying the CD of *Nirvana-Symphony*, Hiroyuki Iwaki cond. Tokyo Metropolitan Symphony Orchestra (Denon Records/Nippon Columbia Co., 1996), CO-78839.
15. Toru Takemitsu, *Confronting Silence: Selected Writings* (Berkeley, California: Fallen Leaf Press, 1995), pp. 22–23.
16. Noriko Ohtake, "Creative Sources for the Music of Toru Takemitsu" (DMA dissertation, University of Maryland, College Park, 1990), p. 15.
17. *Litany* (1990) is a digest of *Lento in due movimenti* with the more obvious Messiaen paraphrases deleted.
18. Yuasa was a premed student at Keio University until his work with Takemitsu at Jikken-kobo induced him to a career in music. His works have been featured regularly at ISCM festivals (1971, 1974, 1978, 1979, 1981, 1983, 1984, 1991, 1993), and he writes for a wide variety of media such as chorus, orchestra, and intermedia. He often combines electronic sounds with acoustical sounds, and when using acoustic instruments he does so in such a way that they frequently give the impression of synthesized sound. Yuasa has accepted commissions from many leading arts organizations, including the Koussevitzky Music Foundation, the National Endowment for the Arts, the Suntory

Music Foundation, and the NHK Symphony. From 1981 until 1994, he was on the faculty of the University of California at San Diego. For a sampling of his music, see Joji Yuasa, *Nine Levels of Ze-Ami* (Acton, Massachusetts: Acton Records, 1997), CD NEUMA 450–96.

19. Takemitsu became familiar with Cage through his friend Toshi Ichiyanagi, who returned to Japan in 1961, after studies with Cage.

20. Though born in Italy in 1925, Berio studied at Tanglewood (with Luigi Dallapiccola!) and taught at Juilliard from 1965 until 1972. He has maintained his ties with the United States since then.

21. A systematic study of Takemitsu's film scores is needed, particularly in view of the fact that he worked with Japan's foremost directors, including Akira Kurosawa.

22. Ohtake, "Creative Sources," p. 26.

23. The *biwa* originated in China and was brought to Japan during the seventeenth century. It is a lute-like instrument with four or five strings that was originally associated with court music, though it subsequently became a common instrument used by persons of various societal ranks.

24. Ohtake, "Creative Sources," p. 95.

25. The *haiku* is a traditional Japanese poetic form with three lines and seventeen syllables. Subjects often deal with nature, but they often have broader philosophical implications.

26. (Paris: Salabert, 1977).

27. Takemitsu's drawing of the scene is reproduced in Toru Takemitsu *Confronting Silence*, p. 98.

28. In his discussion of the piece, Takemitsu reckons these intervals with theoretical exactness: diminished third, augmented second, diminished third, major second, augmented second. See Toru Takemitsu, *Confronting Silence*, p. 103. Note that I have corrected an error: The final interval (i.e., augmented second) is incorrectly given as an augmented third.

29. Takemitsu, *Confronting Silence*, p. 106.

30. Some of Hirao's representative chamber pieces include his String Quartet (1940), Octet (1944), Piano Quintet (1945), Sonata (1947) for violin and piano, Trio (1949) for flute, violin, and piano, Wind Quintet (1950), and Sonata (1951) for oboe and piano.

31. *Music for Electric Metronomes* precedes similar works by Ligeti (*Poème symphonique* for 100 metronomes, ten operators, and conductor, 1962) and Birtwistle (*Chronometer*, 1971). The technological device seems to have served as the model for Ligeti in the third movement (Movimento preciso e meccanico) of his Chamber Concerto (1970) for thirteen instruments.

32. Both works are available on *Thirteen Drums: Music for Percussion Solo* performed by Atsushi Sugahara (Tokyo: Camerata, 1996) CD30CM-414.

33. Teruyuki Noda, *Selected Works*, vol. 2, (Tokyo: Camerata, 1994. CD 30CM-344), brochure p. 10. The same performance is also issued in an anthology of pieces for violin and piano performed by Sonoko Mumata and Akemi Tadenuma. The anthology includes Ikenouchi's three-movement Sonata No. 2 (1956).

34. Miyoshi (b. 1933) studied with Ikenouchi as well as the French composers Raymond Gallois-Montbrun and Henri Challan. Although a composer of considerable reputation, his primary expertise is in French literature. An excellent recording of his Sonata (1955) for violin and piano has been made by Sonoko Numata and Akemi Tadenuma (Tokyo: Camerata, 1995) CD 30CM-409.

Chapter 23

Concert Music in Asia: China

The overthrow of the Ching dynasty by the Nationalist Revolution of 1911, was a major step toward modern China. Nationalists were also eager to expel imperialists, especially the Germans occupying portions of the Shantun province. In 1917, China declared war on Germany and Austria. After the war, the Versailles Conference's ruling of 28 April 1919, awarding portions of the Shantun province to Japan, fomented further rebellion, especially among students and workers in Shanghai, who staged a massive protest on 4 May, leading to a nationwide boycott of Japanese goods. The intellectual upheaval associated with these events, known as the May Fourth Movement, was an important stimulus for revaluation of Confucian ethics and traditional customs. At the same time, it provoked Chinese liberals to look to the West for new ideas and ideologies.

After the war, Chinese leaders were divided into pro- and anti-Communist forces, the former led by Sun Yat-sen, the latter by Chiang Kai-shek. Sun's Kuomintang party, centered in Canton, won the support of the southern provinces. The northern government of war lords resided in Beijing. Also active in the Kuomintang party was Mao Tse-tung, who in 1931, was elected Chairman of the newly organized Soviet Republic of China in Kiangsi. Chiang opposed Sun's and Mao's cooperation with the Communist forces of the USSR., and in 1928, he established a government in Nanking. Chiang's troops forced Mao and his Red Army on the Long March (1934), a trek of approximately six thousand miles from Kiangsu to Shensi.

The instability of China made the nation vulnerable to invasion, and during the late 1930s and early '40s, Japan seized much of the country. Japan's invasive policies led to the Resistance War against the Japanese, which lasted from 1937 until 1945. In the areas conquered by Japan, arts organizations were taken over and politicized. In the case of the Shanghai Conservatory, the resistance forces among faculty and students broke away from the Japanese-controlled school and formed the Shanghai Private Conservatory. When Soviet forces withdrew from Manchuria after World War II, they turned over the Japanese military bases to the Chinese Communists, thereby strengthening their power against Chiang and his supporters. Beijing capitulated to Communist forces in 1949. The United States had supported Chiang with money and weapons, but his power had eroded so severely that continued aid was pointless. In that same year, Mao became Chairman of the People's Republic of China.

During the 1950s, China struggled to energize its agriculture and industry. Mao advocated cooperative agriculture and communal work, rather than technology; thus, his program was both sociological and economic. The Great Leap Forward, initiated by Mao in 1958, placed half a billion people into more than twenty-four thousand communes, where they were promised food, shelter, and clothing; however, they relinquished their rights to private property. The program failed, but Mao narrowly managed to hold his post as Communist Party chairman.

The years from 1966 until 1969, witnessed Mao's Cultural Revolution. The recruiting of youth for the Red Army was a major aspect of the program, and they were encouraged to attack bourgeois elements that, supposedly, weakened cultural and bureaucratic organizations. This ultrazealous movement led to the disruption of traditional families, widespread violence, and social chaos.

Although he came from a peasant background, Mao was an educated man who had graduated from teachers' training college in 1918. Later, he worked in the library of Beijing University, had a career as a school teacher, and attempted to organize programs for general education. His frustration in this last endeavor precipitated his move into politics.

In his speeches during the Yenan Forum on Art and Literature in May of 1942, Mao advocated art in service of workers, peasants, and soldiers. The purpose of art, he claimed, was the "education of the masses through popular art forms while integrating an elevated style in order to raise cultural standards. The source of artistic inspiration would be the people themselves, and for the artist to know their needs and how to communicate with them, he must live and work with them."[1] To oversee the implementation of this policy, the Chinese Musicians' Union was organized.

At face value, Mao's ideas were liberal; however, art that would serve the populace had to meet certain requirements. "Art," he explained, should be "beneficial, not harmful, to socialist transformation and socialist construction; [it should] help to consolidate, not undermine or weaken, the people's democratic dictatorship; [it should] tend to strengthen, not cast off or weaken, the leadership of the Communist Party."[2] These ambiguous guidelines were often interpreted proscriptively, thereby restricting musical styles. Art in support of the state played an important role during Mao's regime, and he cultivated supporters among Chinese intellectuals, while chastising critics of Communist programs by denying them access to study and performance. The cultural agenda of the Party extended to China's musical institutions, especially those for music education.

At the time of Mao's Cultural Revolution, China's conservatory system and artistic organizations already had a significant history. Beginning in 1927, the Shanghai National Conservatory offered formal musical training.[3] Soon, comparable programs were instituted in Beijing, Tientsin, Chengtu, and Shengyang. Historical musicology played a role too, and the Chinese Folk Music Research Society[4] (founded in 1940), the Beijing Institute of Musical Instruments, and the research of Yang Ying-liu contributed to a revival of early music.[5] The Shanghai Municipal Orchestra, which was established in the late nineteenth century, mainly by Italian musicians, later became the Shanghai Symphony Orchestra. The influx of German Jewish instrumentalists during the Hitler era was a great boon to the orchestra, since they brought not only a highly developed manner of playing but *also* the most recent Western European repertoire.

Instruction in indigenous musical traditions was slow in gaining acceptance, because there was among the elite Chinese, a certain embarrassment about old-fashioned, local traditions. Popular instruments, such as the two-stringed fiddle (*erhu*), were viewed with condescension in some quarters, while others argued that any instrument might be capable of exciting the good or bad aspects of the seven emotions.[6] The publication of traditional music in Western notation, beginning in 1933, with Liu Tianhua's scores of pieces and études for *erhu* and *pipa*, ameliorated critics by endowing this music with a legitimacy that it did not have as illiterate, folk music.[7] Publication of Chinese music linked East and West in a modernization that preserved "Chinese 'essence' through Western 'means.' "[8]

The training of Chinese instrumentalists and conductors in Western music usually required a residency in the Soviet Union; however, the Central Conservatory of Music in Beijing implemented a conducting program that produced its first four graduates in 1962.[9]

The confluence of Eastern and Western musical practices was partially a result of practical considerations. During the 1930s, the composer Xian Xinghai became director of the Music Department of Lu Xun Arts Academy. He had studied at the Paris Conservatoire and was familiar with Western instruments, but his supply of these was limited; hence, he freely mixed Chinese and Western resources.[10] The scores that resulted came to determine the conventional style of mainland China's music during the mid twentieth century. Programmatic works composed by trained musicians used traditional Chinese elements in conjunction with Western techniques to create modern works that would address the populace in a nationalistic way.

Traditions may be either of two types: dead traditions, or living traditions. In the former, (for example, the Latin language), working materials are fixed and immutable. This does not mean that they are bereft of power; indeed, one advantage of such a tradition is its absolute stability. A living tradition, on the other hand, is subject to constant transformation. Thus, for example, the *pipa* was modified in the twentieth century to include additional frets; tunings and temperaments of Chinese instruments were brought into conformity with Western Europe's equal temperament; and so on. These living traditions were vital steps leading to today's modern Chinese music.

The coexistence of traditional and modern creative arts produces an interesting dialectic, however, and "one has to distinguish clearly between form and content. It is quite possible for a traditional form to be centered on modern content, and the converse is equally true. On the other hand, apart from the period 1963–1977, there has been a fairly strong tendency for form and content to go hand in hand."[11]

If it is true that "almost every mainland Chinese composition written between 1949 and about 1980 has a socialist programme or theme," then we may have the reason why Mao's wife, Chiang Ching, and her supporters opposed "any traditional form beside the Beijing Opera."[12] The national policy of art as a venue for forming and directing popular tastes, standards, and mores set Chinese musics apart from the repertoires of most Western nations; hence, a distinction must be made at the outset between music by Chinese composers working in mainland China and composers of Chinese heritage who emigrated to Western countries. Among the former category, important figures include Chiang Wen-yeh and Ma Sicong.[13]

Chiang (1910–1983) was born in Tamsui, Taiwan. He is also known by the Japanese version of his name, Bunya Koh, because he went to Japan in 1923, and entered the Musasi Technical College of Tokyo in 1929, as a major in engineering. Simultaneously, he pursued music through night courses at the Musasi Academy of Music. He continued music studies privately with Yamashida Kosaku (1886–1965) after his graduation in 1932. Returning to Taiwan in August of 1934, he became involved in the Home Town Music program, which sponsored concerts throughout the island. During these sojourns, he discovered many different folk traditions in Taiwan and began collecting folk materials.

Chiang's talents as a composer had already been noted in 1932, when he won the National Music Contest of Japan, but more important was the publication by Alexander Tcherepnin in 1936, of Chiang's "Little Sketch" and *Bagatelles* (piano solo) and his *Four Seiban Songs* (1935) for voice. These piano pieces won the prize in composition at the fourth International Music Festival in Venice in 1938. In April of that year, Chiang joined the Music Department of Peiping Normal University, but he soon relocated to Beijing in order to research ancient Chinese music.

Chiang was a Roman Catholic, and his works include psalm settings, hymns to the Virgin, and three Masses: the first for vocal solo with unison chorus (Op. 45, 1946), the second for voices in two parts (Op. 48, 1947), and the third for chorus and orchestra (1947).

From 1949 until 1957, Chiang taught composition at the Central Conservatory of Music in Beijing. His teaching career ended abruptly when he was accused of spying for Japan. Condemned, he was sent to a labor camp. The Cultural Revolution was still more hurtful to his career, and his name all but disappeared from musical circles until 1977, when he won a redress. He died in Beijing on 24 October 1983, from a cerebral thrombosis.

Chapter 23 Concert Music in Asia: China   273

Chiang's works include orchestral, piano, chamber, ballet, and vocal music. The orchestral pieces range from small tone poems to orchestral suites. He wrote three symphonies: the First Symphony, Op. 34 (1940), the *Beijing Symphony*, Op. 36 (1943), and the brief *Symphonia universalis*, Op. 42 (1943). The piano pieces include his First Piano Concerto (1950); among the chamber works we find sonatas for flute and piano (1936), violin and piano (1951), and 'cello and piano (1936), as well as a Chamber Symphony (1955) for seven soloists, and a Woodwind Trio (1960).

Chiang's three-act ballet score of the legend of *Princess Shian-fei* (1942) is representative of his style, which typically includes heterophonic textures and pentatonic melodies, but also shows strong influences of Bartók, Stravinsky, Debussy, and Malipiero. Occasional passages using pentatonic melodies in canonic textures reveal interesting hybridizations of Western and Asian elements.

The scenario of the ballet shows parallels to Puccini's *Turandot*; however, Chiang's work takes the tragic route for its resolution. Act I, set in Tay-An Palace, presents the victory dance of the Emperor's general. Shian-fei's arrival is announced, but she appears sorrowful at having been separated from her beloved. In Act II, she reveals her nostalgia in a solo dance. When her beloved appears, Shian-fei refuses his embrace and holds a dagger to her chest. A comic interlude for two eunuchs concludes the act. In Act III, set at the court of the Dowager Empress, Shian-fei explains her plight in a *pas de deux* leading to Shian-fei's solo dance, in which—with the Dowager's permission—she takes her life, rather than submit to the Emperor. The act concludes with three scenes showing respectively, the Emperor's attempts to save Shian-fei, his sorrow at her death, and his consolation by the Dowager.[14]

Ma (1912–1987) was a native of the Guangdong province. He came from a wealthy family, and his father was a governor. Ma was the fifth of ten children, of whom four others were musicians. As a boy, he was fascinated by the sound of the harmonium. His cousin owned one, and Ma began to play on it in 1918. Ma's father bought one, and soon the boy learned keyboard technique. Later musical studies were on the violin, and in 1925, he entered the Nan-Hsi music school, where he studied violin and piano. For advanced work, he went to France for training at the Paris Conservatoire (1927–1929). In 1931, he returned to China, began a career as a violinist, and set up the Private Kwangchow Conservatory. He founded the Chunghwa Symphony in 1940, and conducted extensively. In 1946, he moved to Canton to become dean of the Music Department of the Canton Provincial Academy of Arts.

When the People's Republic of China created the Chinese Musicians' Central Conservatory, Ma became its director. He also became the editor of *Yinyue chuangzuo* (music composition). During the 1960s, he spent time in the United States, where he composed the ballet *Sunset Clouds* and the opera *Rebia*. Other works include two symphonies, a Concerto (1944) for violin and orchestra, an orchestral suite, choral music, and chamber pieces.

Ma's works tend toward simplicity. Harmonies are mildly dissonant, but tonal orientation is never in doubt. His preference is usually for heterophonic textures, and individual lines make almost equal use of conjunct and disjunct motion. Melodic contours are sometimes modal—as in his Second Symphony (1959), which is written predominantly in the Phrygian mode. Instrumental techniques are often colorful, and *sul ponticello*, pizzicato, muted winds, harmonics, and other distinctive sonorities appear throughout his works. At the same time, these extended techniques are always held tightly in control, and moderation is a hallmark of his style.

The Second Symphony is a symphonic poem recounting the struggles of the Red Army, although Ma claims that the piece is not related to any specific incident.[15] He has written the three movements without break, and has introduced an interesting structural design, whereby the first movement presents the exposition and development of a sonata form, the slow movement (also a sonata form) follows, and the concluding fast section acts as a recapitulation. The second theme of the first movement is a folk song from Shensi (possibly an allusion to the Long March), and the Finale includes a *yangge*, a type of folk dance popular in rural areas.

Ma's larger works do not show as much sonorous invention as is apparent in his shorter works, like the five-movement suite entitled *Song of the Mountain Forest* (1953). These character pieces for large orchestra use tunes inspired by the folksongs of southwest China. Attractive passages for solo strings, chamberlike groupings of several instruments, and unusual modal and rhythmic inflections impart a delicacy that contrasts with the larger, formal works.

Ma's career progressed well until the Cultural Revolution, when he was compelled to flee with his wife, daughter, and son. On 15 January 1967, they stowed away on a boat in Hong Kong, eventually arriving in the United States. In 1985, he obtained a redress of the miscarriage of justice. He died in Philadelphia on 20 May 1987.

Works by Chinese composers that did not advance a Communist program usually adhered to a conventional late-Romantic manner, often with some programmatic element. A fascinating example of such a piece is the *Butterfly Lovers Violin Concerto* (1959), which was composed by two students at the Shanghai Conservatory, Chen Gang (b. 1935) and He Zhan-hao (b. 1933). The work seems to have been influenced by Rimsky-Korsakoff's *Scheherazade* (1888), which was definitely a favored piece among Chinese musicians at that time. Chen was a composition major and He a violinist; nevertheless, there can be little doubt that both studied *Scheherazade* at the conservatory. The solo violin in *Butterfly Lovers* recounts the story of Liang Shan-po and Chu Ying-tai. (In China, their names are the conventional title of the piece.)

Disguised as a boy, Ying-tai studied for many years with Shan-po, and they became deeply attached. When her marriage to a wealthy young man was arranged, Ying-tai had to leave Shan-po. In the hopes of seeing Ying-tai, Shan-po visited her home, only to learn the truth about her gender and her impending marriage. In despair, Shan-po died of a broken heart. Ying-tai, visiting Shan-po's grave, wept and implored the heavens to open his tomb. Her cries brought from heaven a clap of thunder that opened the grave. From it, Shan-po emerged as a butterfly, and Ying-tai, similarly transformed, fluttered away, united at last with her beloved.

The music, like its scenario, is sugary sweet. The violin part is elegant and idiomatically written for the virtuoso player. The melodies are memorable, based for the most part on pentatonic scales. "This piece was held (and still is) by Chinese critics as a successful model combining traditional Chinese musical elements with Western classical musical tradition. It was actually regarded as very 'modern' and 'daring' when it came out."[16]

After 1980, a softening of the Iron Curtain took place, and Western compositional procedures became more widely used. In the article "Letter from China: The Use of Twelve-Tone Technique in Chinese Musical Composition," Zheng Ying-lie called attention to many Chinese serialists.[17] In their works, they have "combined twelve-tone techniques with national style . . . producing twelve-tone works with Chinese characteristics."[18] In some instances, composers have constructed tone rows using complete pentatonic collections; in other instances, they have used folksong characteristics—such as the "three-note tunes" common in Hubeian melodies. These approaches unite tradition and innovation.

Among the Chinese composers who have emigrated to the United States, the most important is unquestionably Chou Wen-chung (b. 1923). Though he studied music throughout his childhood, he began his professional training in more practical areas, including architecture, then mechanical engineering at the National Chungking University. He came to the United States to study architecture at Yale; however, he had been interested in music since his childhood, and he realized that this would be his opportunity to embrace a career in music. He changed his major, and from 1946 through 1948, he worked at the New England Conservatory. During 1948–49, he studied with Nicolas Slonimsky.[19] From there, Chou went to Columbia University, and completed a Master's degree in composition with Luening in 1954. During the years from 1949 until 1954, his primary work was with Varèse. Academic positions at the University of Illinois (Champaign-Urbana), Brooklyn College, and Hunter College led to his appointment to the faculty of Columbia University in 1964, where he became full professor in 1972. From 1984 until his retirement in 1991, he was Columbia's Fritz Reiner Professor of Composition, a position that was established specifically for him.

Chou's early orchestral tone poems—*Landscapes* (1949), *All in the Spring Wind* (1953), as well as *And the Fallen Petals* (1954)—exhibit a Taoist respect for nature. In *Landscapes*, Chou uses three Chinese traditional melodies. Although their treatment is purely instrumental, Chou provided translations of their texts. The first describes an old fisherman on his boat at dusk. He looks beyond gulls flying overhead to see the moon ascending over the hilltops. The second paints a plaintive picture of a woman at bedtime on the day of parting with her beloved. In the sounds of temple bells, falling rain, wind, and her lute, she perceives only her own

Chou Wen-chung

broken heart. She is wary of sleep: "Dreams are coming; the candle is flickering; pillows awry." The final poem is pure landscape: green grass, low clouds, cries of geese, willow trees in the sunset, and ravens dotting the evening sky. Chou's evocative music is reminiscent of Debussy, and he creates a mood of tranquility with pentatonic melodies in heterophonic textures.

All in the Spring Wind continues Chou's investigation of synthesizing Western and Asian music theory. In this case, he has drawn from Peking Opera, China's principal form of lyric theater since the nineteenth century, which uses existing vocal and instrumental elements, adapted to texts and circumstances as necessary. The instrumental ensemble, located at stage left, consists mainly of strings and percussion. The *sona*, a double-reed instrument, is used for special effects. The instrumental ensemble plays stock rhythmic patterns appropriate for the dramatic action. As a young man, Chou heard such ensembles, and the interludes he knew from this repertoire provided the basis for *All in the Spring Wind*.

As a college student, Chou learned folksongs from all over China from his classmates. These minority folksongs (which Chou used freely without any concern for "authenticity") provided the foundation of *And the Fallen Petals*. In all three of these early works, the tunes are never the dominant or apparent element; rather, they are used freely, in the manner of *cantus firmi* in Renaissance Masses and motets. The pieces also form an autobiographical triptych, since *Landscapes* sprang from songs Chou learned in his childhood, *All in the Spring Wind* from the opera interludes he learned as an adolescent, while *And the Fallen Petals* incorporates traditional melodies from across the entire nation of China.

Chou's early works include his piano solo "The Willows Are New" (1957), which is based on *Yang Kuan*, an ancient piece for *chin* (Chinese zither). This instrument and its performance techniques are crucial in understanding Chou's compositional æsthetics. The *chin* piece and its poetic text by Wang Wei (Tang Dynasty) allude to a mountain pass that was the "point of no return" for travelers from China. Since arduous journeys were usually begun under propitious springtime conditions, sprigs of willow—the first tree to leaf out—were presented as symbols of parting. The plaintive character of the poem is assumed into the music by the exploitation of the profound register of the piano and subdued dynamics. The composer notes that there should be no stratification of the music into melody and harmony; instead, the two hands should "always merge to create a single sonority."[20]

In later works, such as *Pien* (1966), Chou applied Asian philosophy to Western concert music—in this case, *yin-yang*, the coexistence of antithetical phenomena. The ensemble of piano, flute, alto flute, English horn, clarinet, bassoon, French horn, two trumpets, two trombones, piano, and four percussionists includes pitched and unpitched groups. The pitched instruments alternately contribute segments to a longer musical line. The percussion instruments operate as a vertical sonority that is responsive to the horizontal flow. (Here, Chou takes a hint from traditional Chinese calligraphy, an important influence on his thinking.) Musical materials are organized into sixes by pitch, duration, dynamics, and types of attack and release.

Among Chou's recent works, *Echos from the Gorge* (1989), *Windswept Peaks* (1990), the Concerto (1992) for 'cello and orchestra, and his First String Quartet (1996) are noteworthy. *Windswept Peaks* is an attractive work for violin, clarinet, 'cello, and piano. The *yin-yang* notion of commodious coexistence of antipodes is reflected in the scoring, which employs the strings as the counterpart of the reed and piano team. The images of stasis (mountain peaks) and flux (wind) continue this idea, but also redirect the extramusical association of the title. The piece is dedicated to Chinese men of the arts—they use the term *wenren*. Chou comments that these powerful thinkers, often ostracized and persecuted, have towered like mountains in the history of civilization. Ironically, he began this piece shortly before the massacre in Tiananmen Square on 4 June 1989. This led him to weave contemplations of these tragic events into the image of the winds pounding against the mountains. Interestingly, these musical surges evaporate, rather than culminate—an indication of the power of the human spirit to withstand adversity. The instrumentation (determined *prior* to the Tiananmen Square incident) is the same as Messiaen's *Quatuor pour la fin du temps*.

The First String Quartet was commissioned by the Barlow Endowment for Music Composition of Brigham Young University. In the preface to the score, Chou notes that the subtitle, "'Clouds,' . . . refers to . . . the phenomenon of 'mingling and melting clouds'—in transformation, aggregation and dispersion—[this] is the æsthetic impetus for the musical events and progressions in the quartet."[21] The second movement uses *saltando* and other specialized bowings in addition to *pizzicato* (generally to be played with a soft guitar pick) to suggest the sounds of *yueh-chin* (i.e., the fretted "moon guitar" with four strings tuned in pairs a fifth apart), *pipa* (Chinese lute), and other Asian instruments. The pitch content of the Quartet is based on Chou's "variable modes," in which the octave is partitioned into minor thirds. These cells are further subdivided into various distinctive groupings of major and minor seconds. The manipulations of these cells produce thematic transformations, as well as distinctive affective characteristics, within each of the five contrasted movements. In accordance with Asian and European traditions, the opening measures set forth the modal foundations of the work. The composer is currently working on a second string quartet.

Chou's influence on contemporary music extends beyond his own composi-tions. He is an authority on the music of Varèse and became the executor of Varèse's musical estate in 1965. He completed the score of *Nocturnal* and *Tuning Up* from Varèse's drafts, and has edited *Amériques*, *Intégrales*, and *Octandre*.[22] From

1970 until 1975, he was the president of Composers Recordings, Incorporated (CRI), which has issued many important premiere recordings of new music.[23] Chou visited his homeland for the first time in 1972, shortly after Richard Nixon's historic trip. During Chou's second visit, in 1977, he laid the groundwork in Beijing for Columbia's Center for United States-China Arts Exchange. Since it began operation in October 1978, the Center has sponsored a wide variety of projects, such as the Oscar-winning documentary film *From Mao to Mozart* (1980), which traces Isaac Stern's 1979 concert tour of China; and the Pacific Music Festival and Composers' Conference, held in 1990 in Sapporo, Japan, with featured guests Leonard Bernstein and the London Symphony. Chou has also taught composers from around the globe: Americans, like Joan Tower (b. 1938), as well as many he brought from Asia. Among these are Tan Dun (b. 1957), Zhou Long (b. 1953), Chen Yi (b. 1953), and Bright Sheng (b. 1955).

Tan has shown great imagination in inventing sounds. Like Harry Partch (1901–1974), who invented instruments to suit his immediate needs, Tan is not satisfied with the conventional instruments of West or East. In fact, he has collaborated with Ragnar Naess (a potter) to develop his consort of ceramic instruments—similar to the ocarina—called EarthSounds. He uses these sounds in his *Nine Songs Ritual Opera* (1989). Tan's *Intermezzo for Orchestra and Three Tone Colors* (1985) is an excellent example of his playful approach to sonority as a discrete musical element. Bass clarinet, contrabassoon, and voices interact with the orchestra in this piece. The human voice provides microtonal inflections and glissandos that seem to be inspired by Asian opera and the horizontal plucked zithers of those lands. The bass clarinet and contrabassoon also use microtonal inflections.

Tan's interest in Chinese instruments is shared by many composers of his generation. The explanation of this phenomenon has much to do with the Communist government's promotion of modernization during the mid twentieth century. This trend extended to musical instruments, and specialists were encouraged

to redesign traditional instruments, enhancing the acoustic properties and range of these instruments, as well as filling in chromatic steps and adjusting tone quality. Privately owned workshops were combined into collective factories. New sizes of instruments were constructed to provide the national music composer complete SATB families of Chinese wind, bowed, and plucked instruments. For instance, further frets were added to the *pipa*, and their spacing reconsidered, such that the instrument yielded an increased and fully chromatic range of equal-tempered pitches. On the *erhu*, steel strings . . . replaced those of silk. Deeper-pitched fiddles were constructed, most notably the two-stringed *zhonghu*, or "mid-pitched fiddle," tuned a fifth below the *erhu*, and the four-stringed *gehu*, or "reformed fiddle," modeled on and tuned as the cello.[24]

Zhou Long comes from a background of Westernized artists: His father was a painter, and his mother was a vocalist. His boyhood musical surroundings included Verdi, Puccini, and Tschaikovsky. Zhou's involvement with traditional Chinese instruments began during the Cultural Revolution, when he was sent to work on a state farm in Northeastern China. A back injury freed him from farm duties in 1974, and he began playing the accordion and composing for a dance troupe in a town near Beijing. When Mao's Cultural Revolution ended in 1976, Zhou entered the Central Conservatory of Beijing, where he studied traditional Chinese music as part of his program in composition.

Zhou Long

In his 1983 score of *Valley Stream*, Zhou used bamboo flute, *guanzi, zheng,* and a mixture of Chinese and Western percussion. The judges of the Fourth Chinese National Composition Competition were impressed, and they awarded Zhou the prize. Zhou's *Su* (tracing back; 1984) is a duo for flute and *guqin* (a zither with seven strings).

Zhou moved to the United States in 1985, and studied composition at Columbia with Chou, Davidovsky, and George Edwards. He quickly became familiar with Serialism and aleatoric techniques, but his characteristic style is what he calls "pan-tonal." His works in this manner include tonal gestures, but they are not oriented around a central tonality.

Zhou has continued using Chinese instruments in his American works. His score of *Tian Ling* (nature and spirit; 1992), for instance, is a concerto for *pipa* and a chamber orchestra consisting of flute, oboe, clarinet, bassoon, horn, trumpet, trombone, violin, viola, 'cello, double bass, percussion (2 players), and piano. For some works—*Su*, for instance—he has made alternate versions using only Western instruments (flute and harp in this case; 1990).

One of Zhou's most interesting pieces is *Ding* (merger of meditation and its object). In its original version (1988), it was scored for clarinet, *zheng*, and double bass. In the alternate version (1990), Zhou rescored it for clarinet, percussion, and double bass. A twelve-tone row and a tonal melody join in a quasi-improvisatory fantasy for wind, string, and percussive sonorities, exploring extremities of registers and discrete sounds. Perhaps the merger that Zhou has in mind here is the absorption of Western serial techniques into Asian musical contexts.

In his recent *Out of Tang Court*, Zhou assembles his largest international orchestra to date. This one uses double winds, four horns, three trombones, and three percussionists performing on Western and Eastern instruments, in addition to *pipa, erhu, zheng,* and strings. Although music of the Tang era (618–907 C.E.) has disappeared in China, it was transplanted to Japan, where it became *gagaku,* and Korea, where it provided the basis of *tang-ak.* These various courtly musics provide the abstract inspiration for Zhou's score. He explains that

> For *Out of Tang Court* (1999), I am not attempting to replicate the Tang court music, but trying to give it a new lease on life. . . . The past does not freeze in time; its spiritual and philosophical essence flows continuously into the present as an unbroken, long river, transcending historical boundaries. Through artistic imagination, the past becomes not only the past, but also imagery reflecting and mirroring the present.[25]

Another musician upon whom the impact of Mao's Cultural Revolution fell heavily is Chen Yi. She was born in southern China in the city of Guangzhou. As a teenager, her interests in violin performance were handicapped by animosity toward Western European classical music. A willful young woman, she pursued her interests in secret. Her determination paid off, and she became a student at the Beijing Conservatory, where she studied composition with Wu Zu-qiang and Alexander Goehr. In 1980, she was one of six members of Goehr's advanced classes in composition, and she became familiar with the most recent developments in Western European music. She was the first woman in China to earn a Master's degree in composition. In 1986, she came to the United States and studied at Columbia with Chou and Davidovsky, completing her D.M.A. in 1993.

Her works display incredible inventiveness in combining timbres, registers, and dynamics. *Sparkle* (1992), which is dedicated to Davidovsky, uses rhythmic cycles of eight beats (a traditional Chinese pattern called *baban*). The ensemble for *Sparkle* includes flute/piccolo, E-flat clarinet, violin, 'cello, double bass, percussion (two players) and piano. The drama of the piece, in which the composer intends to "express . . . impressions of sparks—everlasting flashes of wit, so bright, nimble, and passionate," stems from the superimposition of rhythmic cycles on constantly changing strands of instrumental sonorities.[26] Although each element progresses with an inherent regularity, the points of change within the various layers do not correspond. The result is a convoluted and fascinating imbrication of beat divisions, timbres, dynamics, and articulations.

Chen's other important orchestral works include her Second Symphony (1993) and her tone poem *Ge Xu* (antiphony; 1994). Both of these were commissioned by the Women's Philharmonic. *Ge Xu* was inspired by the custom in Southern China of celebrating the lunar New Year by antiphonal singing, either by solo voices or in choruses. The texts are improvised, and performed as though in a competition. The orchestra suggests, at times, the cries of birds and other sounds of nature. Tone clusters pass like mists through which we see images in the distance. Certain passages lack definite meter, while others are strongly metrical and, at times, dancelike. The centerpiece of the work is a thrilling cadenza for percussion. The concluding half of the piece recalls themes from the first half, and the work ends with a varied reprise of the opening melody, fading quietly into the mists of the tone clusters.

Chen Yi

Chen Yi's *Chinese Myths Cantata* (1996) for large orchestra, men's choir, and four traditional Chinese instruments (*erhu, yangquin, pipa,* and *zheng*) is a three-movement cantata representing the creation of heaven and earth by Pan Gu, the creation of human beings by Nü Wa, and the sad story of the Weaving Maid and the Cowherd. The protagonists of the last tale correspond to the stars Vega and Altair, who are separated by the Silver River (Milky Way).

The story of the creation of the heavens and earth begins with a depiction of chaos. In Chen's cantata, the word "chaos" is chanted in English and Chinese as other voices repeat nonsense syllables accompanied by microtonal motifs in the strings. In the story of the creation of humans, a goddess fashions little people out of mud. Chen suggests the steady growth of the population by having the chorus involve the audience in the singing of nonsense syllables until the entire concert hall is abuzz with sound. The story of the separated lovers is the longest of the three. Roughly, the first two-thirds of the movement consists of an orchestral tone poem (in which wordless voices function in a quasi-instrumental capacity), and the final third is a choral setting of a poem from the Han Dynasty (206 B.C.E.–220 C.E.).

The *Chinese Myths Cantata* was a joint commission from the Women's Philharmonic and the men's chorus, Chanticleer. At its premiere on 14 June 1996, it was presented with full staging including choreography by the Lili Cai Chinese Dance Company. The vocal portions of the cantata make extensive use of falsetto. In this feature and others, the cantata seems to derive much of its musical and dramatic style from Beijing Opera.

Important recent compositions include the *Golden Flute* (1997) and the *Dunhuang Fantasy* (1999). The former piece was written for James Galway, who had been impressed by Chen's Concerto for viola and orchestra. The *Golden Flute* is actually a concerto in three movements for Asian and Western instruments. As with so many Asian titles, this one is an invitation to the listener's imagination. The flute is an important folk instrument in many cultures, and Chinese folk flutes include the *dizi* (a bamboo flute, often with a piece of stiff paper over one of its holes to make a buzzing sound) and the *xun* (made of clay). Clearly, the word "golden" is contradictory in describing either of these. In fact, the golden flute comes from the Western tradition, where the finest flutes are those of platinum, gold, or silver. At the same time, Chen's writing for the golden (i.e., Western) flute includes many elements that suggest traditional Chinese performance practices. Chen has made a reduction of it for flute and piano.[27]

The *Dunhuang Fantasy* for organ and wind ensemble (1999), which was commissioned by the American Guild of Organists, is another concerto. Despite the title, one can easily perceive the three-movement concerto plan. In this case, it begins with a brief, but technically demanding, toccata for organ that leads straightaway into the Allegro. A restful central movement follows without break and leads (again without break) into an energetic Finale. The title of the piece alludes to the Dunhuang area in western China, historically an important gateway to the West. In particular, Chen has been inspired by the Mogao Grottoes, which were constructed from the fourth to the fourteenth centuries. The paintings, sculptures, and art works of this area are a testament to the rich potential occasioned by the meetings of different cultures.

This survey of Asian concert music, admittedly brief, is nevertheless sufficient to demonstrate the rich and fascinating artistic accomplishments that have already taken place as a result of the confluence of Western and Eastern cultures. At this point, it may be worth recalling that Cage's pioneering work, first with Asian concepts and then with Asian students, represented a turning point in music history. Varèse's similarly unbiased approach, at approximately the same time, was of equal importance. Subsequent work, especially that of Chou, offers proof that this success story can be duplicated in other contexts in years to come.

Notes

1. Alan L. Kagan, "Music and the Hundred Flowers Movement," *Musical Quarterly*, 49 (October 1963), 420.
2. Cited in Kagen, "Music and the Hundred Flowers," 419, n7.
3. Jonathan P. Stock, *Musical Creativity in Twentieth-Century China* (Rochester, New York: University of Rochester Press, 1996), p. 143.
4. David Holm, *Art and Ideology in Revolutionary China* (Oxford: Clarendon Press, 1991), pp. 132–133.
5. Kagen, "Music and the Hundred Flowers," 426. Traditional instruments are discussed in Stock, *Musical Creativity in Twentieth-Century China*, chaps. 3–5.
6. In Chinese thought, these are: joy, sorrow, anger, fear, love, hate, and desire.
7. Stock, *Musical Creativity in Twentieth-Century China*, p. 145.
8. Stock, *Musical Creativity in Twentieth-Century China*, p. 145.
9. Kagen, "Music and the Hundred Flowers," 427.
10. Stock, *Musical Creativity in Twentieth-Century China*, p. 147.
11. Colin Mackerras, *Performing Arts in Contemporary China* (Boston: Routledge and Kegan Paul, 1981), p. 76.
12. Concerning socialist programmes, see Jonathan P. Stock, "China: History and Theory since 1911," *New Grove Dictionary of Music and Musicians* (London: Macmillan, 2001),

vol. 5, p. 650. Chiang Ching's suppression of traditional forms is discussed in Mackerras, *Performing Arts in Contemporary China*, p. 77.

13. Chinese family names appear first, with the given name in second position.

14. A recording by the Moscow Conservatory Orchestra is available on Sunrise Records (Taipei, Taiwan, 1993), CD 8531. This disk also contains the *Symphonia universalis* and other works.

15. Ma Sicong, Symphony No. 2, Chinese Composer Series, (Munich: Marco Polo CD 8-223950; MVD Music and Video Distribution, 1996).

16. Communication with the author from Su Zheng, Associate Professor of Music and Women's Studies, Music Department, Wesleyan University (5 April 2001).

17. In *Musical Quarterly* 74 (1990), 473–488. The composers are Luo Zhong-rong, Lu Shi-lin, Wang Jian-zhong, Li Bao-shu, Wang Xi-lin, Zhou Jin-min, and Yang Heng-zhan. Zheng Ying-lie is professor of composition at Wuhan Conservatory and has translated R. E. Middleton's *Harmony in Modern Counterpoint* (Shanghai Music Press, 1984). Zheng is the author of *Fundamentals of Serial Composition* (Shanghai Music Press, 1989).

18. Zheng Ying-lie, "Letter from China," 473.

19. In addition to his work as a lexicographer, Slonimsky was also a composer and champion of modern music. He gave many first performances of works by Ives, Cowell, and Varèse.

20. Chou Wen-chung, "Performance Notes," *The Willows Are New* (New York: C. F. Peters, 1960).

21. Chou Wen-chung, String Quartet: "Clouds" (New York: C. F. Peters, 1997).

22. Chou's editions of these are published by Ricordi. His completion of *Tuning Up* (1946) and his edition of *Dance for Burgess* (1949) will also be published by Ricordi.

23. CRI was founded in September 1954 by Luening and Douglas Moore of Columbia University working with Oliver Daniel, who had been an administrator for CBS Radio. CRI currently has three series of recordings, one devoted to emerging young composers (punishingly named Emergency Music), another to composers incorporating materials drawn from World musics, (eXchange/Music at the Crossroads), and one for American classics (American Masters).

24. Stock, *Musical Creativity in Twentieth-Century China*, pp. 148–149.

25. Zhou Long, communication to the author, 14 February 2001.

26. Chen Yi, *Sparkle* (New York: Composers Recordings, Inc., 1999), brochure, p. 4.

27. Chen Yi, *Golden Flute* (Bryn Mawr, Pennsylvania: Theodore Presser, [1997]).

Chapter 24

Minimalism

Minimalism is associated with developments in graphic arts, especially the paintings of Robert Rauschenberg (*recte*: Milton), a friend of Cage's who became notorious for his all-white and all-black paintings in the early 1950s. These canvases "have more to do with leaping the boundaries of art in the spirit of Dada than . . . with the Abstract Expressionist movement in America."[1] The term was first applied to music in Michael Nyman's 1968 review for the *Spectator* of Cornelius Cardew's *The Great Learning*. Later, Nyman attached the designation to La Monte Young, Terry Riley, Steve Reich, and Philip Glass.[2]

Minimalist music was reactionary: against the dense harmonic manner of Romanticism and its twentieth-century descendants; against Serialism; against prodigal orchestral resources; against Eurocentric views of culture; and against the condescension of classical musicians toward pop music. The liberalism of minimalists led them to embrace electronic music, and many minimalist techniques, such as phase shifting, are based on electronic models. Minimalism attempted to restore music to the general populace through an idiom incorporating familiar elements.[3] At its outset, Minimalism was based on simplicity and directness: clear tonality, persistent beat, driving rhythms, distinctive motifs, repetition, and simple instrumentation.

La Monte Young (b. 1935), one of the movement's vanguards, came from a small town in Idaho. When his father gave him a saxophone as a combined gift for his seventh birthday and Christmas, La Monte's musical career began. He played in dance bands and later became interested in Jazz, Bebop, Charlie Parker, and pop music.

Academic music followed: Leonard Stein, a Schoenberg pupil, taught Young at Los Angeles City College. At the University of California at Los Angeles, he heard World music, including *gagaku*, *gamelan*, and *ragas* for the first time. After graduation in 1958, he went on to the graduate program at the University of California at

Berkeley. He studied there for a year with Seymour Schifrin (b. 1926), an important composer who had worked with Schuman, Luening, and Milhaud; but Schifrin's music, which combines elements of Serialism with Neoclassical techniques, is highly chromatic, with rapidly changing harmonies. Young rebelled, went to New York City in 1960, and never returned to complete his degree program.

In New York, Young quickly ensconced himself among the Beatniks and Hippies. He explored electronic music with Richard Maxfield at the New School (1960–61). Yoko Ono and John Lennon (1940–1980) were among the more famous of Young's acquaintances.

Young became interested in just intonation. In this respect, he shares a common ground with composers such as Lou Harrison, Ben Johnston (b. 1926), György Ligeti, Edwin London (b. 1929), and Harry Partch, who have also experimented with different tunings.[4] Young's most extensive work using this temperament is his *Well-Tuned Piano,* begun in 1964, which explores "the idealized relationship between every pair of frequencies . . . represented as the numerator and denominator of some rational fraction."[5]

Young found enthusiastic supporters, many of whom went on to become well-known figures in contemporary music. Among these was Terry Riley. Following the premiere at Seymour Schifrin's home in 1958, of Young's Trio for Strings, a serial work whose tones unfold at such a glacial pace that melody and rhythm are effectively eliminated as compositional parameters, Young became the talk of the Berkeley Music Department. His unique lifestyle and his equally distinctive music attracted Riley, who was a newcomer to campus.

Terry Riley

As a native of Colfax, California, Riley (b. 1935) had limited contacts with concert music during his early childhood. Popular music, Jazz, and Bebop were more important to him at that time. He played the violin a bit, but eventually, he switched to the piano. During high school, he discovered composers like Debussy and Poulenc. When he met Young at Berkeley, he had already completed a bachelor's degree in composition at San Francisco State University under Robert Erickson.

A new element in Riley's music of the 1960s was his use of tape loops. The dancer Anne Halpern asked him to write music for her "Three-Legged Stool," and he responded with his piece M[escaline] *Mix* (1961), which used sound chips of piano music, spoken words, and concrete sounds. Here, with the superimposition of sounds and constant repetition, Riley found what has become his hallmark. In November 1964, at the San Francisco Tape Music Center, a program of new music included Riley's *In C.*

The score of *In C* consists of fifty-three motifs, which progress at different rates, since the performers are free to decide when to move on to the next motif. Accordingly, the duration of *In C* is variable, and no two performances are alike. In order to prevent rhythmic laxity, it was necessary to have an anchorman: a percussionist sounding a steady beat. At the premiere of the piece, that function was carried out by Steve Reich.

Riley's scores of the 1970s, such as *Persian Surgery Dervishes* (1971), show the influence of his study of the music of North India. Equally distinctive is the more lyrical and traditional approach apparent in his works of the 1980s—especially *Sunrise of the Planetary Dream Collector*, which he composed for the Kronos Quartet.

In these later works, Riley's original concept of variously reiterated motifs remains, despite the appearance of additional layers of musical materials—especially World musics and vernacular idioms. In *Sunrise of the Planetary Dream Collector*, fourteen-beat units in the Dorian mode provide the basic materials of the piece. Unlike *In C*, however, performers may elect to return to previously played units.

Riley's thirteen-movement *Cadenza on the Night Plain*, composed for the Kronos Quartet and premiered by them at the Darmstadt Festival in 1984, is his most "American" work. It commences with an Introduction that leads to the first Cadenza, this one for the first violin. Subsequent movements are interspersed (and, therefore, grouped) by cadenzas for viola, second violin, and 'cello respectively. The philosophical motivation of the work—the inhumane treatment of Native Americans during the era of expansion and colonization—is clearly stated in the title of the third movement, "Where Was Wisdom When We Went West?" This topic is confirmed in subsequent movements, especially "Tuning to Rolling Thunder" (who was a medicine man in Nevada) and "The Night Cry of Black Buffalo Woman." Riley's social consciousness is not unique among minimalists. Indeed, the use of music to advance a cause seems to be a consistent feature in the music of Reich, Philip Glass, and John Adams, too.

Steve Reich and Philip Glass

As the son of an upper-middle-class Jewish lawyer, Reich (b. 1936) enjoyed the culture of his hometown, New York City. His mother was a singer and lyricist. Reich's friends introduced him to the music of Bach and Stravinsky, and he was enthusiastic about Pop and Jazz, especially the music of Charlie Parker and Kenny Clarke.

Reich studied philosophy at Cornell University, then music at Juilliard and Mills College. His training in composition included private lessons with Hall Overton, William Bergsma, Persichetti, and Berio. When Reich entered Cornell in 1953, he was an amateur jazz musician. His thesis was a study of selected writings of Ludwig Wittgenstein. One of those works was *Culture and Value* (1946), which includes the little aphorism "How small a thought it takes to fill a whole life." This became the text of Reich's *Proverb* (1995) for three sopranos, two tenors, two vibraphones, and two organs. *Proverb* is a skillfully crafted work that seems more conventional than many of his earlier compositions; nevertheless, it draws on elements formulated in earlier works.

As a novice composer active during the 1950s and early '60s (he completed his Master's degree at Mills in 1963), Reich experimented with Serialism, which was all the rage then.[6] Berio, Reich's teacher at Mills, candidly advised him to forget about Serialism and to write the music that he wanted to write. This was the most liberating moment of Reich's career.[7]

During the 1960s, he experimented with tape-recorded sounds. Thinking along the lines of piano builders, who use triple stringing to produce richer sounds, Reich tried to enrich recorded sounds by playing identical tape loops simultaneously, but he was unable to keep the tapes synchronized. He was intrigued by the resulting canonic imitations, replete with elaborate rhythmic variations. Here, he found the basis for what he calls "phasing."

In his works of the 1960s, Reich applied the concept of phasing, first to vocal, and then to instrumental, lines. Among his most notorious works is *Come out* (1966), a phased elaboration of the voice of Daniel Hamm, a Harlem youth who, with five other young blacks, was tried for murder. *Come out* consists entirely of a taped statement by Hamm subjected to phasing. In his *Violin Phase* (1967), Reich applied the same concept in a mixed medium, combining acoustic and taped sounds. Here, a prerecorded violin part is juxtaposed with a live violin line; nevertheless, the same complex canonic design results from the gradually shifting lines. The final step in the process was to attempt to create phasing with two live, acoustical instruments. The result was *Piano Phase* (1967).

Reich's early works, such as *It's Gonna Rain* (1965) and *Come out*, tend to use either recorded sounds or very small ensembles like those of *Violin Phase* and *Piano Phase*. During the late 1970s, he became interested in the potentials of larger ensembles. The resulting works were *Music for Eighteen Musicians* (1976), *Variations for Winds, Strings, and Keyboards* (1979), and *Music for a Large Ensemble* (1978).

During the 1970s, Reich discovered World music. A trip to Africa (cut short by a case of malaria) led to his score of *Drumming*. Study of Balinese gamelan at the University of Seattle, and a trip to Israel to study the musical traditions associated with the Torah had important consequences, especially his Psalm settings entitled *Tehillim* (1982).

As Reich indicates in his notes to the recording of *Tehillim*, the title is the Hebrew word for "psalms."[8] The ones that he set are excerpts from Psalms 19, 34, 18, and 150. *Tehillim* is available in two versions, a chamber version, and a larger version for full orchestra. In its overall form, *Tehillim* falls into four sections. The first is a canonic treatment of a vocal line with percussion accompaniment. The second section is homophonic with instrumental enrichment. The melodic lines are gradually elongated by the insertion of melismatic passages. The third section abandons the hyperactive rhythms of Minimalism. It is, as Reich points out, "not only the first slow movement I have composed since my student days, but also the most chromatic."[9] The fourth and last section returns to the tempo and tonality of the opening movement. There is no attempt to recreate any Hebrew tradition of psalmody in Reich's score. In fact, his choice of the texts was motivated in part by the absence of a firm musical tradition that he would have had "to either imitate or ignore."[10] His settings of the texts enhance their intrinsic rhythms and meanings; hence, repetition tends to involve whole verses and to maintain the sense and continuity of the words.

Words sparked Reich's next major work, *Desert Music* (1984), which is based on texts by William Carlos Williams. Reich has treated these in the manner of an oratorio for mixed chorus and orchestra. The title comes from Williams's collection of poems by that name, but Reich also drew on verses contained in *Journey to Love*.

Desert Music consists of five movements, of which the third functions as an axis flanked by pairs of movements. Musical gestures relate the first to the fifth and the second to the fourth. In its form, musical style, and treatment of text, *Desert Music* tends toward an expressive, almost Romantic manner.

Reich composed a considerable amount of orchestral music during the 1980s, including Three Movements (1986), a reworking of his Sextet (1984) for percussion and keyboards, and the *Four Sections* (1987), written for the seventy-fifth anniversary of the San Francisco Symphony.

Words provided the impetus for *Different Trains* (1988), but in this score, the words are attacks, vowels, releases, and inflections. Though the words are sometimes comprehensible, they are treated as abstractions: a collection of sonorities that Reich arranges in an impressive mosaic to commemorate the Holocaust. These taped phonemes are combined with string quartet to recall his childhood train rides from New York (where his father lived) to Los Angeles (where his mother lived after divorcing). The train trips that Reich remembered from his boyhood would have been very different had he been in Germany during that same time. It is this irony that Reich dramatically depicts in his score, which uses sound samples of four basic types: (1) reminiscences of his governess, Virginia, recalling their train rides; (2) the voice of Lawrence Davis, a porter who rode from New York to Los Angeles; (3) reminiscences of three Holocaust survivors; and (4) European and American trains of that era.

The three movements of *Different Trains* are (1) "America—Before the War," (2) "Europe—During the War," and (3) "After the War." Reich notes that the piece presents a new direction that may "lead to a new kind of documentary music video theater in the not too distant future."[11] This vision was fulfilled when he collaborated with his wife, Beryl Korot, on *The Cave* (1993). Call the piece an opera, a cantata, an oratorio, or whatever you will: *The Cave* closes the gap between MTV and the oratorios of Handel.

For the orchestration of *The Cave*, Reich uses flutes, oboes, English horn, clarinet, bass clarinet, four percussionists—on vibraphones, bass drums, kick drums, and claves, pianos, sampler, computer keyboards, and string quartet. Amplification is freely used. The two sopranos, tenor, and baritone, "sing in a natural nonvibrato voice that you would find in [Reich's] earlier pieces and in earlier eras, Medieval and Renaissance."[12] The music derives from interviews with various people—Jews, Arabs, and Americans. The questions were simple: "Who for you is

Abraham?" "Who for you is Sarah?" "Who for you is Hagar?" and so on for all of the personalities associated with Abraham, his wife, his concubine, his three guests, and his two sons in the story recounted in "Genesis," Chapters 15, 16, and 19. (The story also appears in Islamic sources).

In his 1995 score for *City Life*, Reich applies minimalist techniques to car horns, the sounds of machinery, and the noises of metropolitan populace to create a five-movement soundscape; thus, he establishes a link with comparable scores, such as Janáček's Sinfonietta and Luigi Russolo's *Risveglia d'una citta*.

If Minimalism strikes some listeners as atavistic noise, those skeptics need to experience Reich's intriguing score of the *Proverb*. The piece came about at the suggestion of Paul Hillier, then conductor of the Hillier Ensemble. Reich turned "for guidance and inspiration" to the music of Perotin, the leading figure of the twelfth-century Notre Dame school.[13] He begins the piece with what approximates a *cantus firmus*, in this case, a newly composed melody that has not a thing in common with plainchant. Reich's tune is more like Baroque music—riddled with affective, angular intervals; but these gestures are part of the compositional strategy: In the first half of the piece, these jaunty leaps follow one after another in a generally downward motion. In the second half, the theme surges upward. Even the casual listener can discern that here, the theme has been inverted. In each half of the piece, the basic theme is gradually augmented in the three soprano voices; hence, the canonic imitations recall the phasing of Reich's earlier pieces, like *Come out*.

The parts for the two tenors are fascinating, since they contain the most metered music of the piece. They correspond to what would be called, in Notre Dame style, *discant clausulæ* (i.e., rhythmic voices in a fixed triple meter moving against slower voices).

Reich's neo-Gothic polyphony is not without irony: Certainly, the instrumentation with two vibraphones is anachronistic; but another, more subtle anachronism is present, too. The authentic repertoire of the Notre Dame school was dominated by rhythmic *perfection*: the reflection in musical meter of the number three, the symbolic representation of the Trinitarian unity of God the Father, Son, and Holy Ghost. Reich's *Proverb* introduces elements of the *Ars nova*. In fact, much of the piece's interest lies in the shifting accentuation of duple and triple groupings of note values. Reich accentuates these constantly shifting accents in the vibraphone parts.

Proverb is a neoclassical piece that unifies disparate musical materials to yield an esthetically and technically impressive result. It is an ironic work, too, since Reich, a Jew, has drawn upon Christian musical traditions. The juxtaposition of dichotomies extends to the text as well: Wittgenstein's secular aphorism assumes the significance of Talmudic or Christian scripture. In this fifteen-minute piece, Reich achieves an astonishingly effective synthesis.

Reich's music strikes a happy balance between simplicity and complexity, and between tradition and innovation. Like many great composers before him,

Reich writes for performance. Beginning in the mid 1960s, he performed with a regular group of colleagues. For a time, his ensemble was joined by supporters of Glass (b.1937); hence, Glass's music also arises from practical contexts. As the two composers grew in notoriety and performing demands were increased, they were compelled to form two independent ensembles: Steve Reich and Musicians, and the Philip Glass Ensemble.

Glass's works composed before 1965, which are both numerous and published, are so conventional that Glass does not count them among his works. For the most part, they were written in the styles cultivated by Bergsma and Persichetti, the leading composers at Juilliard when Glass completed his Master's degree there in 1961.

In the summer of 1960, Glass studied with Milhaud at the well-known music camp in Aspen, Colorado. The consequence was a renewed interest in French music and culture; hence, Glass set out in 1964 to study with Boulanger, with whom he worked until the fall of 1966. During his residence in France, Glass also came into contact with the "fanatical serialism" of Boulez and his circle.[14] Glass describes the scene as a "wasteland" inhabited by "maniacs" and "creeps."

When he began his career as a Minimalist composer, Glass's path ran roughly parallel with Reich's. His music became reductive, employing simple harmonies supporting diatonic melodies. As a mature composer, Glass has focused on lyric theater. In his case, the term must be used in the most liberal sense. He generally rejects the idea of a continuous scenario with narrative (i.e., recitative) connecting dramatic highlights (i.e., arias or ensemble numbers). He prefers a loose assembly of images, sounds, and sentiments.

Glass has written more than a dozen operas, and his name became internationally known as a consequence of *Einstein on the Beach* (1976). His reputation as a man of the theater grew with *Satyagraha* (truth force; 1980). That was followed by *Akhnaten* (1983). Glass showed that he was in sync with the times by his choice of topics. The nuclear arms race and the years of the Cold War were a direct consequence of Einstein's discoveries. "Satyagraha," a term coined by Mahatma Gandhi as part of his program for liberating India from British rule, reflected international dissatisfaction with imperialist policies, especially those of Europe and the United States. *Akhnaten,* a portrait of the first monarch in history to profess monotheism, reflects contemporaneous efforts to rediscover spirituality. In 1992, he completed *Voyage,* a commission from New York City's Metropolitan Opera, to commemorate Columbus's journey to America.

In these operas, Glass has demonstrated a remarkable ability to touch the psyche of his audience. He has identified issues and topics that are of the time, and he has addressed them through *art*—not just *music*. From this fact, two consequences follow: (1) A discussion of the music of Glass's operas cannot do justice to the composer or the works, since it excludes the experience of lights, staging, costumes, and the manifold components that are integral to lyric theater; and, (2) Glass speaks not only as a composer, but as a modern-day prophet as well. He criticizes and rebukes, chastises and encourages. In typical prophetic language, much is allegorical and ironic, perceived as much by intuition as by intellect, and open to a wide variety of (mis)interpretations.

Glass's idiom is Janus-faced and attempts to bridge the gap between pop culture and concert music. The cause is noble, but the works are so eclectic and loosely structured that it is unlikely that they can be perceived as a totality. They have been hailed as a turning point by many, but those voices of affirmation come largely from a disenfranchised population: persons with little or no musical training; individuals who spend most of their time and money in the realm of pop music; an audience intimidated by concert halls, opera houses, and tuxedos, and who feel most comfortable listening to Glass's *Olympian* as a TV sound clip from the opening and closing of the Summer Olympics in Los Angeles in 1984.

Thus far, Glass has written five symphonies, the last of which was written for the celebration of the new millennium.[15] Of the others, the Third (1995) merits consideration. Written for the nineteen string players of the Stuttgart Chamber Orchestra and their conductor, Dennis Russell Davies, the Third Symphony is a four-movement essay intended to treat each of the players as a soloist. According to Glass, the first movement is introductory to the second and third, which form the core.

In the second movement, unison writing predominates, but Glass deploys his ensemble in rendering an expansive line that drifts from one register and instrument to another while meters change freely. In its symphonic function, this movement may justly be called a scherzo. The third movement—a bit faster-paced than most symphonic slow movements—has the brooding character of that type. Modal conflicts, effective solo writing for the high strings, and stabbing, syncopated rhythms impart a pathos that seems more Romantic in inspiration than Minimalist. Structurally, it is an ostinato, a compositional process that Glass uses in other works, especially his "portrait opera" of Mahatma Gandhi, *Satyagraha*. The fourth movement is a terse Finale, recollecting the changing meters of the second movement and its closing theme as well. The Third Symphony is highly traditional in its overall design, as well as in its use of cyclic recollection of themes and straightforward tonality. Glass's Third Symphony suggests a composer who first made a reputation, but, having established one, prefers ultimately to write in a manner that is more relaxed—-and perhaps more genuine.

Glass has composed many film scores, especially for the director Godfrey Reggio. *Koyaanisqatsi* (1981) is a freewheeling environmentalist essay that, by its use of a Hopi Indian title meaning something like "life gone haywire," manages a nod toward Native Americans. *Powaqqatsi* (1987) idealizes rural life, but implies that urban life is debilitating. The score relies on various unusual and ethnic instruments. *Anima mundi* (1991) celebrates the world's wildlife. In all three, Glass shows both his responsiveness to issues and a certain accessibility that is suitable for immediate consumption.

John Adams, b. 1947

At thirteen, Adams was playing the clarinet, composing, and conducting. When the time for college came, he went to Harvard, where he studied composition with Kirchner. Adams quickly discovered that his interest in Pop and Rock was alien to the ivy halls, where Adams felt as though in a "mausoleum where [he] would sit and count tone-rows in Webern."[16]

When he completed his Master's degree in 1971, he turned to the work of Cage for new directions. He relocated to California, where he directed contemporary music performance studies at San Francisco Conservatory from 1972 until 1982. This period was full of experiments—chance music, electronic music, and just about anything that came across the airwaves. In the mid 1970s, Adams encountered the music of Reich and Glass. Their rejuvenated uses of tonality validated Adams's instincts, which directed him toward a style that avoided the complexities of Serialism and other hyperintellectual formulations. Still, he felt that Minimalism lacked something: That something was pathos—the force in music that enables the composer to engage the listener on a deeply personal and profoundly emotional level.

In this respect, Adams clearly parts company with the classic minimalists like Riley. (Does a listener really react "emotionally" to *In C*?) The emotional character of Adams's music is apparent even in his earliest works. The 1973 triptych entitled *American Standard* is an ironic title that uses the brand name of a company known for its lavatory fixtures. At the same time, it refers to standard American musical genres, in this case, march, hymn, and ballad. While the title may be funny, the music is not. The central movement, "Christian Zeal and Activity," is an elaboration of Sir Arthur Sullivan's hymn "St. Gertrude" (usually sung with the text "Onward Christian soldiers").

In redirecting the hymn's original homophonic texture to create a more elaborate voice leading, and by drastically decreasing the tempo, Adams has magically transformed it into a piece that is touching, even to the most jaded ears, a piece that very closely approximates the spirit of the Adagietto of Mahler's Fifth Symphony. In all three movements of *American Standard*, Adams invites the addition of "found" sounds. In his realization of the piece, Edo de Waart uses a taped sermon expounding on the healing of a man with a withered hand.[17] By inviting such juxtapositions, Adams allows multiple interpretations; hence, he restores the collaborative relationship between composer and performer.

A similar concern with modern musical techniques and traditional values is apparent in *Shaker Loops*. An initial attempt at this piece was the 1978 string quartet *Wavemaker*, which Adams withdrew. Later that year, a septet in modular notation was given the now-famous title. In 1983, Adams made a version for string orchestra, in which he converted the modular notation to a fully notated score. The title *Shaker Loops* is a pun: It alludes to "shakes" (i.e., trills and tremolos) as well as to

EXAMPLE 12

The *cantus firmus* of John Adams's *Christian Zeal*

St. Gertrude 6 . 5 . 6 . 5   12 l.   Sir Arthur Sullivan, 1871

1. On-ward, Chris-tian sol – diers, March-ing as to war,   With the cross of Je – sus

Go–ing on be – fore: Christ the Roy–al Mas – ter   Leads a-gainst the foe;

Refrain

For-ward in – to bat – tle,   See His ban-ners go.   On-ward Chris-tian sol – diers,

March-ing as to war,   With the cross of   Je – sus   Go-ing on be-fore.   A - men.

the religious group known as Shakers. Adams grew up in Concord, New Hampshire, and during his childhood he had access to nearby Shaker communities; hence, the piece is a picturesque reminiscence of his boyhood. "Loops" refers to the use of tape loops, a technique cultivated by many early minimalists. In *Shaker Loops*, though, the "loops" are repeated musical cells, rather than recorded sounds.

From the septet, Adams made a version for string orchestra in 1983. Its four movements, "Shaking and Trembling," "Hymning Slews," "Loops and Verses," and "Final Shaking," are so immediately appealing that the first movement became (after the fact) the sound track of *Barfly*, a film about the Los Angeles poet Charles Bukowski.

The evolution of *Shaker Loops* from string quartet to string orchestra parallels developments in Adams's career: He had become the contemporary music consultant to Edo de Waart, conductor of the San Francisco Symphony, in 1978. He continued in that capacity until 1980 when he was named "composer-in-residence," and he remained in that capacity until 1985, when de Waart left San Francisco to become the conductor of the Minneapolis Symphony.[18] "Adams was one of the first to present a new model of composerly activity—that of consultant. By evaluating new scores, organizing special series, and writing commissioned works for the orchestra, he helped launch a movement for composer residencies which is one of the few bright institutional developments in new American music."[19]

The San Francisco Symphony commissioned two works by Adams, *Harmonium* (1981) and *Harmonielehre* (1985). The former work is a setting of texts by John Donne and Emily Dickinson for chorus and orchestra. Repetitive modules and steady pulse remain in place, but Adams reveals a distinctly neo-Romantic penchant since "the rate of harmonic change sped up dramatically from the classic minimalist model."[20]

In his *Grand Pianola Music* (1982), the impact of Romanticism is equally clear. The title is ironic: A pianola was a small, player piano manufactured in East Rochester, New York, by the Aeolian company, and intended for the parlors of middle-class Americans during the early twentieth century. It is, in effect, the antithesis of the grand piano, a large instrument designed for the concert hall, the virtuoso performer, and an entirely different audience. The ensemble for the three-movement *Grand Pianola Music* consists of two pianos, three sopranos (who vocalize, but sing no texts), and wind ensemble. The piece combines elements of the grand, Romantic piano concerto, Pop, Americana, patriotic marches, and more under one roof. Some have drawn parallels with the music of Ives. Others see it entirely as a joke. "One interprets the music as either ridiculous or beautiful, depending on gross standards of taste."[21]

Harmonielehre is the title of Schönberg's theoretical treatise of 1911, which is dedicated to the memory of Mahler; thus, in appropriating the title for his three-movement symphony, Adams manages a twofold tribute. But Mahler and Schönberg both owed a tremendous debt for their musical materials to the works of Wagner. The central movement of *Harmonielehre*, "The Anfortas Wound," completes the triptych, which proclaims Adams's admiration for the music of late Romanticism in the Austro-German tradition.

Adams became a hero of American lyric theater with the 1987 premiere of *Nixon in China,* a triple commission by the Houston Grand Opera, the Brooklyn Academy of Music, and the Kennedy Center. He collaborated with Peter Sellars as producer and Alice Goodman as librettist in writing what they consider an epic tale about monumental characters of the twentieth century: Richard M. Nixon, Mao Tse Tung, and their interactions during Nixon's historic visit to China from 21 to 27 February 1972. The scenario includes their wives, Pat Nixon and Chiang Ching, as well as their advisors, Henry Kissinger and Chou En-lai.

Alice Goodman asserts that when Sellars approached her with the idea for the opera, she insisted "it had to be a heroic opera. I would not write it as a satire."[22] She wrote the libretto in couplets, but more impressive by far is her well-informed and even-handed treatment of each character. In her article "Towards *Nixon in China,*" Goodman identifies the sources that she consulted for historical information; she also states that she became "more and more certain that every character in the opera should be made as eloquent as possible."[23] She worked from February 1985 until December 1986 in crafting a libretto that demonstrates a deeply felt sympathy not only for political issues, but for the cultural heritage of China as well. Mao's soliloquy in Act I, scene ii, "We no longer need Confucius," is a striking example of the consistently high quality of Goodman's literary contribution to the opera.

Adams's score is equally powerful in its use of musical materials for characterization. Popular elements, like the fox trot, are skillfully woven into the dramatic action. Mao's dance with Chiang Ching, a brief episode in Act III of the opera, exists as an independent and considerably more elaborate tone poem under the title *The Chairman Dances.* This symphonic fox trot, completed in 1985, had its first performance by the Milwaukee Symphony under the baton of Lukas Foss in January 1986. The opera as a whole was such a success, that it was broadcast on television.

An international commission by the Brooklyn Academy of Music, the Théâtre Royal de la Monnaie, Brussels, the Opéra of Lyon, Glyndebourne Productions, the Los Angeles Festival, and the San Francisco Opera led to Adams's next lyric theater piece, the *Death of Klinghoffer* (1991). Goodman and Sellars again joined forces with Adams in producing this hybrid, combining opera and oratorio.

The cast features the Captain, Leon and Marilyn Klinghoffer, three women from Switzerland, Austria, and England respectively, and four young Palestinian terrorists. Both acts are prefaced by substantial, dramatically effective, and beautifully written choral movements, and both acts contain two internal choral movements of equal force; hence, the chorus plays a vital role in the work. Among the score's many effective numbers is the "Aria of the Falling Body," which we are to image being sung by Leon Klinghoffer as his earthly remains are thrown overboard in Act II, scene iic. Adams calls this movement a "Gymnopédie," presumably after the three piano pieces so called by Satie in 1888. (In fact, the name refers to an athletic event for young men in ancient Sparta.)

The deep concern for social issues that Adams demonstrates in these operas is also apparent in *The Wound Dresser* (1989) for baritone and orchestra, which is based on Walt Whitman's writings about his experiences as a Civil War nurse. Adams dedicated this piece to those who care for AIDS patients. It is among Adams's most moving and effective works.

Adams uses synthesized sounds in many of his scores as part of a larger ensemble consisting mainly of acoustic instruments. In May 1993, however, he completed a series of small pieces including "Coast," "Disappointment Lake," "Tourist Song," "Tundra," "Bump," "Cerulean," and "Hoodoo Zephyr," all for electronics. The pieces, which occupied Adams for a bit over a year, are accompanied by poems—apparently by Adams himself. Imagery in the texts (which are *not* set to music, but serve instead as a programmatic guide to the pieces) is both rich and novel. Conventional metaphors involving moonlight and love songs are ditched in preference for "selenium eyes" and the "inflatable midi-babe." In this amusing instrumental song cycle, Adams makes his most extensive reconciliation between Pop, Techno, and classical Minimalism.[24]

In 1993, Adams also completed his Concerto for violin and orchestra, a three-movement work of an essentially traditional nature, save for the fact that it was intended from the outset for choreographic treatment. The second movement is a chaconne with the title "Body through which the dream flows," a line taken from a poem by Robert Hass. Adams explains that this image may be applied to the whole concerto: The orchestra represents the human physiognomy, whereas the solo violin represents the spiritual force that animates its diverse elements.[25]

Adams's most recent score is the opera-oratorio *El Niño* (2000), a multicultural remake of Handel's *Messiah*. Confronted by the happy challenge of simultaneous commissions, one from the San Francisco Symphony for a piece for chorus and orchestra and another from the Châtelet Theater of Paris for an opera, Adams drew on elements of both genres—in addition to film and dance—in working out what became *El Niño*. (The title was originally "How could this happen," a line from a motet by Orlando di Lasso, but Adams maintained the element of surprise implied by his original title, while combining it with a decidedly Hispanic flavor, in naming his oratorio after the erratic maritime phenomenon responsible for a host of meteorological aberrations.)[26]

For the text, Adams and Sellars drew on a wide variety of sources, including the King James Bible, Gnostic scriptures, Luther's sermons, Mediæval mystery plays, mystical writings of Hildegard von Bingen, and Latina poets ranging from the seventeenth to the twentieth centuries.

The oratorio is divided into two parts, and is scored for soprano, mezzo, baritone, three countertenors, mixed chorus, children's chorus, orchestra with single winds, three horns, three trombones, percussion, synthesizer, two guitars, harp, and strings. As in much early music, voices are not assigned according to a dramatic concept of roles; hence, for example, the three countertenors simultaneously represent Gabriel, but they are used in other applications as well. Perhaps the most powerful aspect of the libretto is the use of poems by women reflecting over the centuries on the event of childbirth *per se* as well as other momentous events in the history of civilization.

El Niño has been recorded and released on CD by Nonesuch. The work is significant from many perspectives: as the most recent development in Adams's compositional style; as a multicultural, polylingual mixture of the best that the world community has to offer; as a reflection on the changing role of women in society; as a social statement about human dignity and the responsibility of each to another; as an expression of wonder at and appreciation of the ongoing generations of the human family. It also stands as a gateway between the old millennium and the new one, as a herald of greater sensitivity and awareness, and as a testimony to the importance of art and its potential to comfort, instruct, uplift, edify, and transform our world.

Notes

1. Nicola Hodge and Libby Anson, *The A–Z of Art: The World's Greatest and Most Popular Artists and Their Works* (San Diego, California: Thunder Bay Press, 1995), p. 311.
2. For details on terminology, see Timothy A. Johnson, "Minimalism: Aesthetic, Style, or Technique," *Musical Quarterly* 78 (1994), 742–773.
3. For detailed accounts of the movements, see K. Robert Schwarz, *Minimalists* (London: Phaidon Press, 1996) and Keith Potter, *Four Musical Minimalists* (Cambridge, England: Cambridge University Press, 1999).
4. Johnston uses a fifty-three tone scale in serial fashion in his Second and Third String Quartets. See William Duckworth, *Twenty/Twenty: Twenty New Sounds of the Twentieth Century* (New York: Schirmer Books, 1999), 125–133.
5. La Monte Young, "Notes on the *Well-Tuned Piano*," (New York: Gramavision. LP 18-8701-1), p. 5. The album cover for this five-hour recording of Young's performance shows Zazeela's *Magenta Lights* as they were created at the Harrison Street Dream House concert in New York City on 25 October 1981.
6. Joseph Straus has argued against the notion of the hegemony of Serialism during this era in his article "The Myth of Serial 'Tyranny' in the 1950s and 1960s," *Musical Quarterly* 83 (fall, 1999), 301–343. Though his statistics are cogent, those of us who studied composition during that era will be comforted by Leon Botstein's remark that the "composers and students that seem never to have trafficked in serialism sensed that [they were] . . . the moral equivalent of sinners. They either could not or would not integrate the 'right path' into their own lives and work. Yet they never forgot its daunting presence and claim to truth." See Botstein's "Notes from the Editor: Preserving Memory," in the frontmatter to the above-cited issue of *Musical Quarterly*, 298.
7. Detail on many biographical episodes is presented in Steve Reich, *Writings about Music* (New York: New York University Press, 1974).
8. Steve Reich, commentary for *Tehellim* (ECM New Series CD 1215, © 1982).
9. Reich, commentary for *Tehellim*.
10. Reich, commentary for *Tehellim*.
11. Steve Reich, commentary for *Different Trains* (Nonesuch CD 979176-2, © 1989).
12. Steve Reich, commentary for *The Cave* (New York: Nonesuch Records, © 1995), p. 13.

13. Steve Reich, commentary for *Proverb* (New York: Nonesuch Records, © 1996). CD 79430-2.

14. K. Robert Schwarz coined this term to denote the Serialism promulgated by Boulez and Stockhausen during Boulez's reign at Darmstadt from 1955 until 1967. See *Minimalists* (London: Phaidon, 1996), p. 114.

15. The U.S. premiere of the *Millennium Symphony* was given at the Brooklyn Academy of Music on Wednesday 4 October 2000 by the Brooklyn Philharmonic under Dennis Russell Davies. In his *New York Times* review (Monday 9 October, section E, p. 5) Paul Griffiths criticized the twelve-movement score for large orchestra, chorus, and vocal soloists for its "deadening uniformity" and "preposterous pretensions."

16. John Adams, cited in Schwarz, *Minimalists*, p. 175.

17. The account appears in Mark (3:1–6), Luke (6:6–11), and Matthew (12:9–14). The recording is *John Adams: The Chairman Dances*, Edo de Waart cond. San Francisco Symphony (New York: Nonesuch Records, © 1987).

18. Michael Steinberg, notes for John Adams, *Nixon in China* (New York: Elektra/Asylum/Nonesuch Records, © 1988), p. 16. According to Schwarz, the formalization of Adams's position as composer-in-residence did not occur until 1982. See his *Minimalists*, p. 182. The 1982 date is probably the official one, when the "Meet the Composer" residency program was initiated.

19. Robert Carl, "Six Case Studies in New American Music: A Postmodern Portrait Gallery," *College Music Symposium*, 30 (spring 1990), 51.

20. Carl, "Six Case Studies," 52.

21. Carl, "Six Case Studies," 52.

22. Alice Goodman, "Towards *Nixon in China*," brochure for John Adams, *Nixon in China*, p. 11.

23. Goodman, "Towards *Nixon in China*," pp. 12–13.

24. Most of Adams's recordings are accompanied by Michael Steinberg's commentaries, but *Hoodoo Zephyr* provides the texts for the (non) songs and color photos of far-west landscapes. See John Adams, *Hoodoo Zephyr* (New York: Elektra Entertainment, 1993), CD 79311-2.

25. See his commentary for Violin Concerto (New York: Nonesuch Records, 1996), CD 79360-2.

26. Michael Steinberg, Notes for *El Niño*, in *San Francisco Symphony Playbill* (January 2001), p. 26A.

Index